Frank Franke 1860–1930
m. Otillie Schwab Sutter 1859–1942
m. Marie Weichbrodt 1860–1914

Carl David Franke 1887–1972
m. Dorothy Sheplor 1887–1970
┌─**Marjorie Eileen Franke** 1914–2000
│ m. George Bolles 1913–
│ ┌─**Jeffery Bolles** 1949–
│ │ m. Sandra Woolsey 1950–
│ │ m. Linda Flowers 1949–
│ │ └─**Jennifer Bolles** 1973–
│ └─**Stephen Bolles** 1946–
│   m. Charlotte Ann Watkins 1949–
│   ├─**Wesley Terrell Bolles** 1977–
│   ├─**Jordan Ann Bolles** 1983–
│   ├─**Alexandra Meredith Bolles** 1986–
│   m. Mary Rebecca Roberts 1971–
│   └─**Sarah Katherine Bolles** 2002–
└─**Carl David Franke, Jr.** 1918–
  m. Bette Underwood Hughes 1923–
  ┌─**Glenda Kay Franke** 1948–
  │ m. Thomas Casey McNichols 1948–
  │ ├─**Eret Casey McNichols** 1978–
  │ ├─**Michael Thomas McNichols** 1983–1983
  │ └─**Ann Underwood McNichols** 1984–
  ├─**Carolyn Ann Franke** 1949–
  │ m. James Niedringhaus 1949–
  │ ├─**Brooke Selwyn Niedringhaus** 1977–
  │ └─**Brent Sheplor Niedringhaus** 1973–
  ├─**Carl David Franke III** 1952–
  │ m. Jennifer Winter Barker
  │ ├─**Melissa Winter Franke** 1982–
  │ └─**Elizabeth Ann Franke** 1985–
  └─**Franklin Sheplor Franke** 1955–
    m. Carole Sudduth 1955–

A B C D

Elizabeth Margaret Franke 1889–1972
m. Frank Wesley Long 1892–1950
┌─**Drusilla Jane Long** 1918–1979
│ m. Walter C. Carlson 1920–
│ └─**David Kinard Carlson** 1948–
│   m. Rose Mary Hooper
│   ├─**Jodi Marie Carlson** 1970–
│   │ m. Raymond Allen
│   │ m. Jeffrey Jass Rose
│   │ ├─**Meagan Nicole Rose** 1996–
│   │ └─**Andrew David Rose** 2002–
│   └─**Janice Aileen Carlson** 1972–
│   m. Jark Sullivan
├─**Helen Louise Long** 1920–1997
│ m. Glen Alden Mester 1913–1988
│ ┌─**Glen Alden Mester, Jr.** 1944–
│ │ m. Patsy Kay Smith 1946–
│ │ ├─**Michael Alden Mester** 1967–
│ │ │ m. Charlotte Elizabeth Conrad 1965–
│ │ │ ├─**Emma Rose Mester** 1996–
│ │ │ ├─**Daniel Alden Mester** 1998–
│ │ │ └─**Jason Michael Mester**
│ │ └─**Melissa Kay Mester** 1969–
│ │   m. Charles Fornoff 1967–
│ │   ├─**Kayla Nicole Fornoff** 1991–
│ │   ├─**Rachel Elizabeth Fornoff** 1992–
│ │   └─**Madilyn Noel Fornoff** 1999–
│ └─**Robert Randall Mester** 1946–
│   m. Linda Gilbert 1949–
│   m. Peggy Lou Higgins 1948–1993
│   ├─**Tracy Sue Mester** 1968–
│   │ m. Scott Edward Anderson 1968–
│   └─**Jason Randall Mester** 1973–
│   m. Heather Waldipian 1973–
└─**Frank Wesley Long Jr.** 1925–
  m. Thelma Elizabeth Keil 1927–
  ┌─**Stephen Wesley Long** 1953–
  │ m. Sandra Ishikawa 1955
  │ m. Elizabeth Ann Lipski 1952–
  │ ├─**Kyle Zeldon Long** 1985
  │ └─**Arthur Wesley Long** 1987–
  ├─**William Douglas Long** 1954–
  │ m. Paula Claire Kirby 1954–
  │ ├─**Kirby Cameron Long** 1979–
  │ ├─**Connor Christian Long** 1986–
  │ └─**Stewart MacPherson Long** 1987–
  └─**Valerie Elizabeth Long** 1957–
    m. Geoffrey Allen Feiss 1953–
    ├─**Katherine Elizabeth Feiss** 1984–
    ├─**Peter Wesley Feiss** 1986–
    ├─**James Austin Feiss** 1990–
    └─**Hunter William Paul Feiss** 1993–

A B C D E

WITHDRAWN

A = 2nd generation
B = 3rd generation
C = 4th generation
D = 5th generation
E = 6th generation

CUT FROM WITHDRAWN
WHOLE CLOTH

CUT FROM
WHOLE CLOTH

An Immigrant Experience

RICHARD J. FRANKE

DISTRIBUTED BY
THE UNIVERSITY OF CHICAGO PRESS

Printed in the United States of America by Edwards Brothers, Inc., Ann Arbor
13 12 11 10 09 08 07 06 05 04   5 4 3 2 1
ISBN 0-226-26030-5

Library of Congress Cataloging-in-Publication Data

Franke, Richard J., 1931–
    Cut from whole cloth : an immigrant experience / Richard J. Franke.
        p. cm.
    Includes bibliographical references.
    ISBN 0-226-26030-5 (cloth : alk paper)
    1. Frank family. 2. Franke, Frank, 1860–1930 — Family. 3. Immigrants — Illinois —
Springfield — Biography. 4. Germans — Illinois — Springfield — Biography. 5. Spring-
field (Ill.) — Biography I. Title.
CT274F (Frank family)+

                                                      2004018505

TO THE CHILDREN OF THE

Franke family,

PAST, PRESENT, AND FUTURE

TRUE *Love is founded in rocks of Remembrance*
In stones of Forbearance and mortar of pain.
The workman lays wearily granite on granite,
And bleeds for his castle, 'mid sunshine and rain.

Love is not velvet, not all of it velvet,
Not all of it banners, not gold-leaf alone.
'Tis stern as the ages and old as Religion.
With Patience its watchword and Law for its throne.

SPRINGFIELD POET VACHEL LINDSAY, *LOVE AND LAW*

Contents

Prologue

Every family has a story to tell. Some are spoken about openly, while others are communicated only through innuendo. Some are proud and some are shrouded in darkness. In truth, there are hundreds of stories in every family, but each of these, like threads in a cloth, is guided by a pattern, which in turn makes up the fabric of the family. And because no one is privileged with a full view of the pattern, it appears different to every member of the family. Tugged this way and that, the family fabric is an ever-shifting garment, but one that cloaks us everywhere we go.

In 1998, my wife and I helped celebrate my brother Allyn's eightieth birthday in Italy with his family. We were staying in an Umbrian villa on top of a hill overlooking a beautiful valley, and I found a perfect place to sit, read, and enjoy the view. I had brought *The Education of Henry Adams* with me as holiday reading. In the first chapter Adams recalls the memory of his grandfather and considers the importance of his family in his life. After reading for an hour or so, I paused to come in from an afternoon rain shower and thought about how long it had been since my brother and I had talked about our parents. Since I was thirteen years younger than Al, my days at home with our parents were surely different than his, but it had been so long since we talked about growing up in Springfield that I asked him if he would sit down each day for an hour to discuss our family and our childhood. By the end of the week I had several pages of notes on our conversations and a strong sense that I should do something more.

For years I have had re-occurring thoughts about my father, for whom I have great admiration. Bill Franke, or Will as many called him, was a friendly, generous, and honest man with simple needs and ideas. He attended school through the seventh grade, as did his brothers, and he was proud to send his children to college. He was a large, hardworking man who cared deeply for his family and was very expressive of his love for us. He was gentle and never even considered spanking us. Nevertheless, he commanded enormous respect and an almost unquestioning obedience from us. He was known as a friend to a very wide cross section of society in Springfield. He was friendly with the business leadership of the city as well as the policemen and firefighters there. He enjoyed the reputation of being well liked by almost everyone he came into contact with.

The one troubling story in our family, which my brother and I had always known about but could never fully explain, was the fact that my father and his oldest brother Carl, who both lived in Springfield, did not speak to each other for at least twenty years before they died. Both men owned dry-cleaning businesses and were competitors in this town of fifty thousand people. No one in either family spoke to or knew anything about the members of the other family. It was as if they did not exist. Only once, when I asked, did my father briefly say that his brother was not the kind of person he ever wanted to see again. As far as I know, he never did.

What then would cause a man as friendly as my father to be so angry with his oldest brother that their respective families never met each other over a period of seventy years? It has been one of those unanswered questions that, despite years of silence and obscurity surrounding it, never left me.

The week of discussions with my brother framed the puzzle for me. There seemed to be four great questions about my family history that I could not reconcile. First, the character of my father—benign, magnanimous, forceful but gentle—and the deep animosity between him and his brother that radiated out to their siblings and continued to the next generation. Second, why did we know so little about my father's other siblings? What caused the various parts of this family to be so alienated from one another? Was it a gradual drifting apart, or did the rift result from specific causes and events? The third piece of the puzzle was the suicide of Otto, the brother between Carl and my father. It was an act that haunted everyone in the extended family.

Shame, guilt, blame, denial, pity, and hate accompanied the event and calcified the divisions in the family over the succeeding five decades. And finally there was the issue of inheritance. Rumors abounded about what each child received after the death of my paternal grandfather, Frank Franke. Resentment followed, and the specter of primogeniture was often raised.

As I thought about the range of issues woven into the fabric of the family, I gradually came to the conclusion that the problem of the inheritance was common to every aspect of the puzzle and that a thorough understanding of my grandparents, Frank and Marie Franke, was critical to its solution. They died before I was born, and my father seldom talked about them. They were the ones who courageously came across the Atlantic from Germany to begin a new life in America. What cultural baggage did they carry off the ship in New York in 1884? And what elements of their German culture were passed on to the succeeding generations? Furthermore, what sacrifices did they have to make in order to manage the transition from being Germans to becoming Americans?

Between 1998 and 2002, I reviewed as many personal and public documents as I could find both here and in Germany. My cousin Frank Long possessed Frank Franke's 1880 military passport from his days in the German army. I had it translated into English, and it proved the single most important source of information about Frank before he immigrated, serving as guide to all subsequent research. In order to understand better the cultural background of Frank and Marie, I researched the social and political history of Germany, especially between 1860 and 1931, the years of Frank's life. Similarly, I studied the histories of Springfield, Chicago, and German immigration to the Midwest. In addition to locating facts in the public record, I interviewed every cousin I could find for family anecdotes and histories, which resulted in over two hundred hours of taped interviews.

I knew that to write this story I had to visit my grandfather's birthplace, Derz, in Germany. I wanted to walk the trails of his neighborhood and sit in the pews of his church. In June of 2000 I traveled to Derz. None of the nineteenth-century German graves there had been maintained, and it was impossible to read any tombstones. Derz had a recorded population of 520 in 1880, of whom 99 percent were listed as being Catholic, all German speaking. As the result of two world wars, the Derz I saw in June of 2001 consisted merely of six houses at the intersection of two roads, with maybe twenty residents. The houses were ringed with marginal pastureland. Because Poland acquired East Prussia as part of the peace treaty after World War II, the only remaining archives were church records, written in Latin, which by some quirk of fate had survived both world wars. A local historian took us to the Catholic church that the Franke family had attended in the neighboring village of Lemkendorf and helped us find numerous birth, marriage, and death listings, confirming that our family had lived there for a considerable time. I was advised that if I wanted to learn more about them, a visit to Berlin would offer the best chance of finding meaningful information about my grandfather and his siblings.

Returning to Chicago, I continued my interviews with cousins, and in 2001, as luck would have it, the Berlin nexus was confirmed during my final interview with my cousin Milton Franke Jr., the son of Frank Franke's youngest son, Milton Franke. Before we met, Milton had rummaged through the dusty boxes in his attic for family memorabilia he had packed up when his father died twenty years before, some of which he had never seen before. We talked about and looked over the material for two days. Hundreds of pictures and innumerable new stories were added to the burgeoning Franke family archives. Milton's kitchen table became our workspace: photos on the left, letters in the middle, and personal articles on the right. The real prize turned out to be two letters in their original envelopes that stared up at us as we systematically worked and talked our way across the table. They were brittle documents written in German on a delicate tissue, postmarked 1883 and 1884 respectively. Once translated, they functioned as the Rosetta Stone in solving the puzzle of Frank and Marie's courtship in Berlin. These letters were the key evidence that our grandparents had come directly from Berlin to the United States and had probably lived in the Prussian capital city for several years. The hunt was on. Passenger manifests of ships going from Germany to America yielded the critical dates of their arrival. Armed with this information, my wife Barbara and I made a trip to Berlin, and in a short time we were at the city archives, which provided us with specific addresses where Franz Frank and Marie Weichbrodt had lived before they were married.

Franz Frank traveled to New York from Bremen, Germany, aboard the ship *Fulda,* arriving on March 24, 1884 when he was twenty-four years old.[1] He arrived in Springfield about a week later, most likely by train via Chicago. Five months later, Marie arrived from Bremen aboard the *General Werder,* landing in New York City on August 29, 1884.[2] She was listed on the ship's manifest as Marie Franke. I suspect that they were married in a civil ceremony in Berlin before Frank left for America. After Marie's arrival in Springfield, the couple went directly to the courthouse and, on September 8, became man and wife according to Illinois law, using their new surname: Franke.

Although we have no documentary explanation of why Frank chose Springfield, Illinois, as his new home in America, there were probably many German families who had settled in Springfield and had written back to relatives in Germany about the favorable conditions they found in central Illinois. Networks of support were established for the new immigrants, and Frank must have corresponded with people in Springfield before leaving Germany. Sangamon County had the same type of agriculture as North Germany, making it a place of comfort for German immigrants.

My cousin Frank Long was convinced that our grandfather's name in Germany was *Franz Frank,* and that on arrival in Springfield he had changed his name to *Frank Franke.* My subsequent research supports this assumption. Several misspellings in documents of the family name at first threw me off the chase, but I concluded that copying errors were not uncommon in nineteenth-century record keeping. The military passport and the two letters written at that time confirm the name in Germany as Franz Frank. The Springfield city directory shows that Franz changed his name to Frank Franke. It was a new name to meet his new opportunities. "Frank" sounds more American than the obviously German "Franz." But Frank Frank as a full name was a little awkward. By adding the "e" to his surname he had a German-American name that resonated in both his old and his new country. Accordingly, I refer to my grandfather as Franz Frank during those years in which he was a German citizen and as Frank Franke thereafter, when he was an American citizen. Frank Long discovered through close inspection of the Military Passport that someone had added the final "e" to our grandfather's last name at a later time, probably in Springfield after he assumed the Franke name.

After I had gathered as much information and opinion about the Franke family history as I could, I realized that I had little more than a chronology of facts and anecdotes. While I was closer to understanding the split in the family fabric, a mere presentation of my research would not solve the puzzle that had propelled me down the corridors of the past in the first place. Because so much of the history depends on private motivation and character, I decided to stitch together a narrative in an effort to better understand the forces that, in my judgment, determined those events. My technique has been to anchor the book around key historical documents, photographs, letters, dates, and historical events, all of which have been annotated, chapter by chapter, at the end of this book. I have used real names for the characters that are introduced and developed in the history. The reader will note that in some places I have provided detail that could not have existed in specific family records. In these instances I conjured up as much storytelling skill as my imagination would accommodate and created a narrative which, to the best of my ability, is consistent with actual stories from the family. I have tried to remain true to the historical characters as I have understood them. And, indeed, I see these imaginative efforts less as a bridge between historical documents than as an exploration of character, which would have been difficult, if not impossible, had I restricted myself exclusively to the historical record.

Cut from Whole Cloth was chosen as the title for this book for several reasons. The idea came to me when my cousin Dorothy Strand told me a story. Her mother Mayme and the rest of Frank's children remembered the trauma of going to the tailor shop after school. Frank would lay them on the cutting table and flatten out their spine just as he would a piece of cloth before cutting a suit of clothes. Then, taking out his tape measure, he would measure them. If they hadn't grown since the last time he measured, he would accuse them of stooping over too much. After that, Frank would have them stand up and observe their posture, constantly reminding them that "they must stand tall."

There will, of course, be more to discover. Indeed, the researcher in me always hopes to find additional material. At a certain point, however, waiting for the historical record to yield more information precludes a dialogue and, indeed, a sense of community from developing. Thus, in anticipation of such conversations, the story begins.

Early Family Chronology

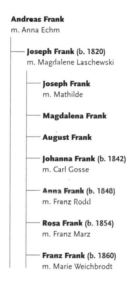

Andreas Frank
m. Anna Echm

— **Joseph Frank** (b. 1820)
   m. Magdalene Laschewski

   — **Joseph Frank**
      m. Mathilde

   — **Magdalena Frank**

   — **August Frank**

   — **Johanna Frank** (b. 1842)
      m. Carl Gosse

   — **Anna Frank** (b. 1848)
      m. Franz Rodd

   — **Rosa Frank** (b. 1854)
      m. Franz Marz

   — **Franz Frank** (b. 1860)
      m. Marie Weichbrodt

Scant information is available on the origins of Franz Frank and Marie Weichbrodt, but we know that Franz and his six siblings were the children of Joseph Frank and Magdalene Laschewski, who lived in the town of Derz in East Prussia. In turn, Joseph Frank was the child of Andreas Frank and Anna Echm, both of whom came from the adjacent community of Fleming.

Acknowledgments

Before embarking in earnest on this story, I contacted my friend and Lincoln scholar Cullom Davis for advice on how to make oral history a part of my project. He gave me a crash course on interviewing techniques, and with a tape recorder in hand I set off to visit my cousins. Over two hundred hours of taped interviews later, and with boxes full of old photos and papers documenting the past, I started to think about writing. A professional associate, Nancy Bailey, spent days transcribing these vital discoveries.

Without the help of several people, writing this book would have been impossible. Many hours were spent on the telephone and in the homes of key members of our family. Most importantly, Frank Long, Dorothy Strand, Otto Franke, Frances Marie Shelden, Bette Franke, Allyn Franke, Bill Kinney, and Milton Franke were instrumental in providing pictures, documents, and remembrances. They were generous with their time, and it was energizing for me to work with them.

In Springfield the public library was a treasure trove of information; and Ed Russo, the manager of the Sangamon Valley Collection, was a source of valuable background material. The cemetery offices at Oak Ridge and Calvary were also helpful. Susan Karena at the Springfield Catholic Diocese office provided useful information.

In search of information about Franz Frank in East Prussia, I traveled to Olsztyn, Poland (before 1945 this was a German city, Allenstein), where I was assisted by Gregory Grilonky, to research the nearby village of Derz, Germany.

I expanded my knowledge of German history and art, studying, among others, the works of the historian Gordon Craig, and the art of the eighteenth and nineteenth centuries. Medical issues were discussed with Dr. Leo Henikoff in order to provide as accurate a description of health problems as I could.

In Berlin, Michael Cullen, the historian for the Reichstag, searched city records for the residences and business locations for both of my grandparents, Frank Franke and Marie Weichbrodt. A visit to Berlin in April 2002 presented me with the opportunity to look at their residences while they lived and worked there in the 1870s and 1880s. A visit to Marie's childhood home in Swinemünde, however, was unproductive because of bombing in 1945.

Several family biographies and histories were very helpful in conceiving how such a story could be constructed. These are listed in the bibliography.

Special recognition is reserved for my colleague Michael O'Leary, without whom there would be no book. His long hours of searching for information, cataloging material, giving encouragement, drafting certain passages, and editing were vital to the completion of this book. Also, two invaluable critiques were given me at midstream by Professor James Chandler of the University of Chicago and Professor Katherine Franke of the Law School of Columbia University. Together, they caused me to rethink the organization of the material and introduce a broader context for this story. Tom Gawne gave me valued help in working with digital images.

THE TAILOR

Love is a powerful motivator. It has an intensity that is hard to describe, but it is one of the building blocks of a great life. When it is good, love can persist over a lifetime in the face of the devastating events in our imperfect world.

As I researched this story, I continually asked the question, Why did Frank and Marie emigrate to the United States? Gradually, it became clear that their decision was formed around their love. This love was the clinching factor to leave Prussia. It was there that I wanted to start the story, with the love letters left to us in the documents handed down over the generations. This is essentially an immigrant's tale of courage, difficult decisions, and motivations that we can only imagine a century later.

The first solid proof we have of our grandparent's courtship was contained in a modest love letter that was found by Milton Franke Jr. in his attic in Dayton, Ohio, in 2002. This letter had remained in its envelope for 119 years and was passed on in a cardboard box as part of Marie's valuable possessions through her youngest son's family. The letter established that Private Franz Frank was stationed in Berlin on May 21, 1883, and was seeing a young woman, our grandmother to be, Marie Weichbrodt. The stationery that Franz used for this letter places him in the seventh company, second guards infantry, in Berlin. His assignment is shown as tradesman.

BERLIN, MAY 21, 1883

Dear Fräulein! I am taking the liberty of dropping you a few lines since I am thinking of going to the theater Thursday evening, and if you would like to come with me, I would pick you up at 8:20, where we met the last time. If you should happen not to have the time, please drop me a line. It would give me great pleasure. Please respond.

Love and kisses.

Franz Frank

P.S. Please forgive my bad writing. It was written in a hurry.

Perhaps the most important exhibit of this history is Franz Frank's Militär-Paß, *literally a military passport, but which might more accurately be described as a record of military service, presented to German soldiers on assignment to reserve military duty. The first page of the* Paß *gives the name of the bearer, Franz Frank, the year in which he began his active military service, 1880, and his status within the military, namely that of* Oeconomie Handwerker. *This phrase is difficult to translate, but the term "practical tradesman" works the best. More specifically, as is stated in the later portion of the* Paß, *Franz Frank was a tailor. In the military he was assigned similar duties, as the army didn't contract out for such work at the time.*

After completing the three-year term of obligatory service, the German soldier was transferred to reserve duty, which is what happened to Franz Frank. He began his service in 1880 and was released in September 1883, at which time he was presented with this document and told to report within fourteen days to his reserve commander.

The length of service in the reserves was open-ended. Once a mobilization order was given, all reservists could be called back into active service, even thirty years after completing their active service. It is precisely for that reason that, in the first six pages of the Paß, *soldiers are reminded repeatedly and to the minutest detail of their responsibility to keep their superiors informed of their whereabouts at all times, under penalty of fines and imprisonment.*

Franz Frank was born in the village of Derz, in the "county" (literally, governmental district) of Allenstein, which belonged to the Kingdom of Prussia, the largest state in the German Empire. Dating back to the last half of the thirteenth century, Prussian land was granted to German knights and soldiers as compensation for their participation in the Crusades. East Prussia, one of the oldest parts of Prussia, was a land of large agricultural estates run by the Junkers, and its major city was the old university town of Königsberg (today the Russian City of Kaliningrad). Since the end of World War II in 1945, the county of Allenstein has been a part of Poland, and the Polish (and thus current) name for Allenstein is Olsztyn.

Berlin den 2t 5/ 83

Geehrtes Fräulein!

[...]

Franz Francke

After attending school until the age of twelve or thirteen, Franz would have acquired a fairly rudimentary knowledge of reading, writing, and arithmetic as well as religious instruction. He probably began a period of apprenticeship to a tailor once he moved to Berlin; since that is the occupation he claims on his military passport. Records show that in 1880 Franz was Catholic in the predominately Lutheran northern part of Germany, making him a member of a confessional minority. However, the county of Allenstein was 90 percent Catholic in the 1880s, because during the sixteenth and seventeenth centuries it was administrated by Polish (Catholic) authorities and never became Protestant during the Reformation. By the eighteenth century, however, it returned to Prussian control. In keeping with the nature of his service and the fact that he served in peacetime, it should come as no surprise that Franz Frank was neither transferred, promoted, honored, nor wounded (hence the blank entries on pages 8 and 9). Although he was born in East Prussia, it seems that before he entered military service, Franz had moved to Berlin, since it was to the Berlin District Reserve Unit that he was assigned on his release from active service in 1883. Normally, one was assigned to a unit close to one's place of residence. On October 4, 1883, five days after his release, he reported to his district authorities in Berlin.

Franz probably attended the military exercises for reserve troops held in November 1883, designed for only those soldiers who had been released between April 1 and September 30. For on March 6, 1884, he received permission to travel to America, receiving a two-year leave from his military obligations. Common sense dictates that we view this two-year leave as an unofficial release from military service. While Europeans of the upper-middle and upper classes were surprisingly mobile, even for them a trip to America would, in most cases, be considered a one-way trip. The German military authorities were fully aware of this. That the military authorities were willing to grant such a request shows that, while the status of a reservist was technically important in day-to-day terms, it actually meant very little. As it was, the military did not place much value on those who served in non-combat positions, like tailors; therefore, in peacetime, it could well afford to allow soldiers (especially one like Franz who had a support rather than a combat function) to emigrate.[1]

Military Pass Book

Military-Passport for the "Practical Craftsman" Franz Frank,
    Recruitment Class of 1880
Regulations for the soldiers in the reserves and in the militia and for those
    on temporary leave from active service {. . .}

GENERAL INFORMATION OF THE BEARER OF THE DOCUMENT

1. First and Last Names: Franz Frank
    Born on: 14 April 1860
    at: Derz
    Administrative District: Allenstein
    State: Kingdom of Prussia
2. Occupation or Trade: Tailor
3. Religion: Catholic
4. Whether married: No
    Children: {blank}

5. Date when service began, and assignment.
   October 1, 1880, as "Practical Tradesman"

6. In which unit? (name company, squadron, battalion)
   2nd Guard Infantry, 7th Company

   Transfers: None

   Promotions: None

7. Date and Conditions of Release:
   Released September 29, 1883, to reserve duty in Berlin on completion of mandatory term of service

8. From which unit?
   2nd Guard Infantry

   Number in Troop Register   16/80

9. Medals and commendations   None

10. Campaigns, injuries   None

11. Special military training: None

    Shooting skills: NA

12. Remarks:

    Received a certificate of qualification as: {blank}

    Prepared, Berlin, September 28, 1883

The aforementioned received the following pieces of clothing on his release:

   1 uniform

   1 pair of cloth pants

   1 pair of underwear

   1 cap

   1 neckband

   1 shirt

   1 pair of boots

In his march to his future place or residence, Berlin, the aforementioned is to use the train from—to—{here unnecessary, he's already stationed in Berlin and will stay in Berlin}. Additionally, he is to pay the train and other necessary costs in cash with the—Marks and—Pfennig provided to him.

Conscripted into the Army on

Conscripted into the local militia on

{Pages 14–17 reserved for additional comments, notices on the part of the military authorities relating to the bearer's military service/record, namely in the event of redeployment.}

Presentations and Leaves

{The first entry here is rather faint in the photocopy; however, all it is is a

certification that Franz presented himself to his Reserve commander on
October 4, 1983, as he was required to do.}

The bearer of this document receives hereby a two-year leave to go to
America, namely from March 6, 1884, until March 6, 1886. He is released
from participation in peacetime military exercises, but only under the
condition of immediate return in the case of mobilization.

On return to Europe or in the event of emigration to a non-European
country bordering on the Mediterranean or Black Sea, this leave will be
considered expired and the said Frank must report once again to one of
the nearest Regional Commands.

Berlin, March 6, 1884. Signed, Lieutenant Colonel at the Royal Prussian
Army Command at Berlin.

I

There are evenings in the spring when the twilight lingers past its appointed hour and the last threads of the day stretch from the shores
of the continent to the smoky mist hovering over the chimneys of
Berlin. Into evenings such as these, the officers march through the
brightly lit streets to the restaurants and dance halls along Friedrich
strasse and Unter den Linden, clicking their heels, flashing their
neatly polished buttons, and toasting the supremacy of the empire
with tall glasses of champagne. Into evenings such as these, the factory workers of Wedding stroll along the Spree and breathe a sigh of
relief at the end of their day's work, taking in the almost balmy air
coming up from the Spree Valley. Into evenings such as these, the
shopkeepers set their chairs by the doors of their establishments and
gossip in the streets, and the daughters of the shopkeepers stare up at
the hazy night sky in vain for evidence of the stars, dreaming of
woods and gardens and all the quiet retreats along the coast of the
Baltic Sea.

Franz Frank stood outside the barracks staring into the selfsame
sky over Berlin in 1883, wondering where in the world she was at that
moment and hoping that the clemency of the weather would continue through tomorrow evening, when he would stroll with her
along Unter den Linden, shoulder to shoulder with countless other

enlisted men and officers. Little rings of smoke curled around his mustache and hung briefly under the brim of his stiff private's cap as he let cigar smoke slowly escape from the corner of his mouth. Others entered the barracks on their way back from the dining hall, while across the road Franz could see officers walking rather stiffly in greatcoats bedecked with epaulets. He stubbed the end of his cigar on the bottom of his shoe and tossed it into a can at the barracks' entrance marked for just such a purpose. When he went inside there was the usual scene of enlisted men at their nightly ritual before lights out. Some of the men sat quietly at the end of their beds polishing their boots and brass buttons, while others spoke of their plans for the next evening. The regiment would be off duty for three days, starting the following afternoon. Some of the men were returning home for the long weekend and a home-cooked meal; the rest would find their diversions in the casinos and cafés along Friedrichstrasse. Amid the chatter in southern accents—as a Catholic, Franz was quartered with all the other Catholics in the regiment, most of whom were from southern Germany—Franz stole away to the end of his bunk and tried to ignore the tales of drinking and revelry erupting around him in anticipation of the long weekend leave.

It was hard not to feel a stranger among these men, despite the common bond of fidelity. They were, in fact, strangers to one another. Had it not been for Bismarck's decisive victory at Königgrätz in 1866, Franz would have regarded them as no more his brethren than the Italians or the Austrians. Catholic or not, Germans from Saxony, or from Bavaria or Swabia, were simply different, so different, in fact, that Franz, in many respects, was better able to understand the Protestants from Prussia and his native East Prussia. The comportment of Prussian Protestants, their sense of duty, and their ways of speaking were much more familiar than the curious customs and slow tongue of the Saxons and the Southern Germans. But the familiarity ended there. His Protestant cousins from the heart of Prussia wore a privilege, if not cast in actual brass then in title and name, which proved to be worth more than all the brass in his native Ermland, a Catholic enclave in the otherwise Protestant East Prussia.

The success of the German Empire lay in its military strength. The world had been stunned by the swift and decisive German victory over France in 1871, and Chancellor Bismarck well understood how to use the German military diplomatically. As a result, military culture flourished in the early days of the empire, so that by 1883 a young man could easily make a career in the military; this was particularly true of the second and third sons of Prussian descent. Tough, strong and resourceful, the Prussian recruit was regarded as physically and morally superior to all other soldiers. But for Bismarck and for the hierarchical German society to which he belonged, the term "Prussian" decidedly did not include Catholics who lived in Prussia. While Catholics might work well enough in the fields and the factories, their loyalties were always considered to be divided between their devotion to Rome, on the one hand, and their fealty to the Kaiser on the other. As a result, the German political establishment felt that Catholics could never make good Germans. That, at least, was how Sergeant Hutten explained it to Franz shortly after he entered the army in 1881. And that was why Sergeant Hutten assigned Franz the task of becoming one of the regiment's tailors. Tailoring was a necessary support task but an unworthy activity for a Prussian soldier. As Sergeant Hutten explained mockingly, Franz's fingers seemed delicate enough for the delicate art of tailoring.

Franz never minded. It was better than the other job Sergeant Hutten might have deemed worthy of a Catholic peasant: boot repair. All his time in the army was just that, time. Except for those fortunate sons who were allowed into the university, all German men past the age of eighteen were required to serve in the army for three years, after which they were put on active reserve. Without prospects for a military career, Franz was simply biding his time. If he could improve his skill in the meantime, all the better. And tailoring offered its own rewards. Despite the lowly rank accorded by the sergeant, Franz discovered a certain respectability in performing the service with timeliness and aplomb. Protestants or Catholics, Prussians or Swabians, they all wanted well-fitting uniforms and were grateful when Franz returned their uniforms and civilian clothes well tailored and neatly pressed. Thus, while he generally kept to his own, Franz commanded as much respectability as possible for a man of his low rank, a poor Catholic peasant from the eastern reaches of the empire.

With fifteen minutes before lights-out, Franz reached for pen and ink in the upper drawer of his dresser and began scratching out a note to the woman he had just been dreaming of. At first he gushed in anticipation of their meeting tomorrow evening at the theater and just as he was about to seal the letter for next morning's delivery, he reviewed his note. The penmanship was that of a hurried man, and the letter suggested a mood of desperation. It was true, he was desperate to see her, but he certainly did not want to let on how desperate. With very little time to spare, Franz was careful to keep his invitation reserved. The handwriting was still embarrassing, so he added an explanation and sealed the envelope without reviewing it again. Just as Sergeant Hutten was calling for the lights, Franz addressed the envelope to Marie Weichbrodt, care of Weichbrodt Imported Dry Goods, Schönhäuser Allee 1, Berlin.[2]

Marie was no ordinary shop girl. She was courage, kindness, modesty, and beauty. She was his summer breeze off the Baltic Sea. She was everything that quivered with anticipation and hope and resilience, from the first daffodil of spring to the last aster of fall. In her, life at last seemed possible rather than merely necessary. And yet, like explorers in the age of discovery who were overjoyed to feel the gentle breezes of those distant shores, not knowing that a continent grander than the imagination could conjure lay beyond the trembling palmetto leaves, Franz recognized that although he had been courting Marie for nearly a year, he was still lingering among the heliotropes and hibiscus of her gentle shores. Because of their circumstances—she was only able to see him on Friday evenings after she had completed the inventory at her father's import store, and that was when he was on military leave—they still hardly knew each other and had to settle for scraps of information with which to hazard an outline of the continent of their love. Thus Franz, weary with the day's toils, lay awake in bed mapping all possible passages to the interior.

The following morning brought the usual routine of training drills, inspection, and cleaning details. His regiment began their leave at noon. Free to go, Franz remained in the barracks in order to refit his uniform for his evening at the theater with Marie. While the soldiers were not required to wear their uniforms on leave, most of them did, particularly those privates returning to their home village. Many, in fact, preferred to wear their uniforms while performing the most routine civilian activities such as dining, dancing, or walking along Unter den Linden. Quite simply, the uniform commanded respect, and unless decorum required otherwise, most soldiers opted for such respect. Even on the most mundane occasions, the uniform lent an air of dignity and ceremony. Like the vestments of the village priest, the uniform set the soldier apart from the rest of society while providing him with an inherent sense of worth that no other experience in his life could.

There was a brief period in his adolescence when Franz had considered the priesthood. Hardly any Catholic boy doesn't, at least for a moment, especially when he comes from such a humble background as Franz's. The youngest son of a peasant farmer, Franz was without prospects in his native village of Derz. While his father owned a small plot of land in the fields behind their cottage, it was strictly understood to be the property of his oldest brother, Joseph. Primogeniture was the local custom and law in East Prussia, which meant that the firstborn son received substantially all the family inheritance. For Franz this meant one of three options: either he could continue to work in the fields at one of the nearby estates and earn enough to pay rent on a small cottage, or, like many younger sons, he could consider joining the military or the priesthood. These were the only practical options for young men who wanted to remain "at home" in East Prussia. Of the three choices, the priesthood was very attractive. Free of the backbreaking labor of the fields, all that was required was celebrating the Mass and visiting the sick and the dying, far easier tasks than harvesting beets all day long. The military didn't offer Catholics any opportunity for advancement, but compulsive military service for three years was required of all young men. As he grew older and his eye began to wander toward the opposite sex, the priesthood began to seem less and less possible. Nevertheless, another option had emerged. Throughout all of Germany, people were leaving their ancestral villages for work in the factories of Berlin. Franz had a few cousins who had done so and managed to find work shoveling coal at one of the steel mills in Wedding. At the age of eighteen, Franz left home for good. With almost no money and even fewer possessions, he made the long journey to Berlin, sometimes on foot, sometimes in the back of a wagon, stopping along the way for fieldwork when it was available. Having timed his journey during the fall harvest of 1878 with such work in mind, he arrived in Berlin by November, nearly a month after he had set out from Derz, with little money in his pocket.

Adolph Menzel, *Rolling Iron Mill* (1875), detail. Alte Nationalgalerie,
Staatliche Museen zu Berlin–Preussischer Kulturbesitz.

Franz first worked in one of the beer halls that lined the streets outside the factory gates. His job was mopping up after the nightly revelries. He next had a job shoveling coal at a steel mill. By the end of his first year in Berlin, his cousin heard about an opening as an apprentice in a tailor's shop. This was a real step up and Franz jumped at the opportunity to learn a trade, even though the pay was less than he made working at the mill. His uniform at that time—for he had come to regard it as his uniform, the only presentable clothing that he owned —consisted of a pair of gray wool trousers, a dark gray coat, and a white shirt underneath. Embarrassed not to own a waistcoat— indeed, he almost felt naked without one—he was further chagrined to have lost his pinstripes as his work shoveling coal continued. He did own one other suit of clothes, but that was strictly reserved for Sundays, when he washed his work clothes and went to Mass. It was only after entering the army that Franz owned more than two pairs of pants. Previously he had saved every last penny he earned in order to escape the crowded tenements of Wedding. In addition to being issued a new uniform upon entry into the army, however, he purchased his own cloth to try his hand at a suit complete with waistcoat. While counting it among his proudest accomplishments, Franz still preferred the stiffness of his military uniform when journeying out into the rather unfamiliar world of Berlin theaters and cafés. Indeed, he regarded his simple private's uniform almost as suit of armor to protect him from the haughty glare of oncoming class-conscious citizens. Who would know where he came from or just how menial most of his work in the army actually was? The uniform protected him from both scorn and inquiry. Who wonders about what a soldier does or thinks? As it is with a police officer, the citizens feel comforted by a soldier's presence and follow his orders agreeably. There is an instant respectability. But without the soldier's uniform, all that comfort and respect would be lost. The uniform is the man.

This was how Franz felt about his own uniform as he sat at the end of his bed, finishing his work on his pants the afternoon preceding his evening with Marie. He was taking them in a bit at the waist; he had noticed of late that they had been drooping slightly, and nothing annoyed him more than something that didn't fit. He hated to see it on the men in his regiment, and he hated it even worse on himself. While he regarded the uniform as a kind of protection, he also thought of it as support. Or, more to the point, he wanted there to be as little distinction as possible between himself and the uniform. Almost out of nervous habit, he found himself trying to tailor his way toward the respect and respectability his uniform offered.

Ultimately it was his experience living in Wedding that convinced Franz of the virtue of the German army. In the army, order was always a priority. It was no mystery why everything was clean and efficient. It took work and commitment to free the interiors of dust and cobwebs. And while Franz always regarded it with a shred of skepticism (he was, after all, surrounded by Protestants who despised his religion), the army provided him with a real education. Granted, his modest social standing barred him from the higher echelons of authority, but he did acquire a valuable trade in the army. He learned how to conduct himself socially, and ultimately he learned how to fend for himself in a world in which opportunities were scarce. He learned how to work quickly and efficiently, characteristics that would serve him well for a lifetime. And the army food, while it never measured up to his mother's cooking, was certainly better than the watered-down turnip soup served in the taverns outside of the steel mills.

As he stood before the mirror in preparation for the evening, he tugged at his sideburns and considered whether whiskers trimmed after the manner of the kaiser would suit him. Deciding against that idea, he smoothed his tapered light brown beard and placed his cap carefully on top of his head so as to avoid ruffling his close-cropped hair. In the bright light of the barracks, the peak of his cap shaded his deep-set eyes, and only his long nose pierced the shadow. The recently polished buttons marched up from his belt and disappeared into his beard, and the white cuffs of his undershirt remained covered by the expertly tailored sleeves of his coat. As was Franz's intention, only his uniform, boots, gloves, and beard were immediately visible to the world. As he stepped out of the barracks, Franz carefully lit a thin cigar and began puffing away calmly and with great satisfaction before he set out into the heart of Berlin. It was several hours before he had to meet Marie, and he decided to forgo eating dinner in case they might take a late meal at one of the cafés on Friedrichstrasse. So instead of calling a droshky, as a horse-drawn cab in Berlin was known, to take him to Brandenburg Gate, Franz walked through the southern neighborhoods of Berlin.

When he first moved to Berlin, Franz was burdened by the monotony of the buildings along Unter den Linden and Königstrasse. Roughly three to five stories in height, these buildings were unvaried except for the lettering and what was sold or housed inside. There were no gaps between them. Turning a corner brought no interruption in the limestone facade; the wall of buildings and shops and apartments continued as before. In those early days, when he still had enough energy and curiosity to explore the new city, Franz often wondered what lay behind the wall of buildings. Did the individual buildings continue straight back, so that together they formed not merely a wall but a continuous structure whose length and width was determined by the street? Or did they rather conceal an inner courtyard of civility? It didn't matter; he would never find out, except in the case of Wedding, where he lived in a tenement in a single room with his cousin and family. The further one penetrated a tenement in Wedding, the further one was removed from the protections of civility and had one of those awful buildings full of screaming children and exhausted men and women actually contained an interior courtyard it was undoubtedly filled with the foulest refuse.[3]

After he had walked for an hour, night was coming on. The smoke-stacks over Wedding were visible from where he stood taking in the haze of violet that hung above his old neighborhood. Spring was certainly in the air, but this evening lacked the gentleness of the night before. He looked northwest for evidence of rain. Concluding that the skies were clear beyond the haze, Franz continued past newly built homes and could smell the distant odor of kerosene lamps. These new homes stood squarely on their regular plots, generously proportioned with wide staircases and double doors, but their facades were nearly without ornament. Franz tried to determine who might live in these homes, but he could not see beyond the curtains that revealed only the warm glow of lamplight within. They struck him as appropriate, well appointed, and enviable homes, new and clean but free of the festoons and lettering that marred so many buildings in Berlin; their very anonymity stood as surety for their security and longevity. The plain facades struck him as another kind of uniform, neither betraying too much information nor deviating from acceptability. In short, they were exactly the types of homes Franz wanted to live in.

II

It was extraordinary to see fabrics so neatly stacked in tall columns: merino, cheviot, flannelette, and woolens from England descending in attractive blocks of grays and blues from the ceiling of Weichbrodt Imported Dry Goods. The linens and calicoes from Flanders were next, in columns of equally pleasing colors: the linens at the top were white; below were pale shades of yellow, pink, and purple, ending with the calicoes at the bottom. Next to these were stacks of Venetian rose-point lace, German Val lace, Brussels and Baby Irish appliqué, and flounces of every kind. There were strips of fur hanging from the shelves: ermine, sable, rabbit, Siberian squirrel, and American mink. And finally, next to the knitted goods, stood Marie Weichbrodt's favorite stacks of fabrics. Three separate columns of silks, satins, and velvets ranging from the most delicate flower tones to the deepest shade of black and the mellowest caramel graced the back shelves of the store. Some came from Venice, Vienna, Paris, or London, where they were embellished with floral patterns or embroidered with eyelet effect, while some pieces of Japanese crepe and

China silk remained unadorned and shimmering in their pure pale tones.

Marie stood at the back of the store in her favorite black skirt of worsted Chiffon Panama cloth, trimmed at the waist with Persian lamb. Her mother had made the skirt for her, but she had chosen the cloth. She knew she wanted it as soon as it had arrived in the store. Her mother had suggested that she add taffeta folds, but Marie had insisted that it only be the Panama cloth. There was nothing special about it; she had needed a new skirt for work. But the cloth itself was durable and exceptionally soft. And the more she wore the skirt, the more comfortable it had become. As she finished the inventory and contemplated the gorgeous stacks of satin so familiar to her, Marie wondered whether her mother had been right when she suggested taffeta folds or, better still, satin folds.

Before she could decide on taffeta or satin, her father called her from the office in the back of the store.

"Yes, Father, what is it?"

Johan Weichbrodt was less than average in height, a somewhat thick man with immaculate grooming and, given his height, an imposing presence. His short, stubby fingers frequently twirled the ends of his thick, dark mustache into perfect little points. His fingers always appeared to be active, whether he was smoking a cigar, counting change in the cash register, or writing in his ledger. And he was always writing. "It's the only way to keep track of what you have and what you've lost," he would tell his wife whenever he brought his business habits upstairs into their apartment. Herr Weichbrodt was fastidious almost to a fault, as was evident in the eternal crispness of his collars and the precision with which the sleeves of his morning coat covered his cuffs. "By no more than a hair," he would always say. Because of his need to know exactly what had entered the store on any given week and what had been sold, he was often under pressure. So many pieces of decorative lace came and went, and so many different styles passed through the store, that it was nearly impossible to know with certainty the full inventory. In an effort to reduce tension in the store, Marie volunteered to do a weekly inventory, for which her siblings and uncles were grateful. Although the task was tedious, Marie discovered a certain pleasure in cataloguing the store's stacks of fabrics. It wasn't so much arranging the fabrics that she liked, despite her pleasure in seeing her father rest assured, but rather the catalogue of textures recorded in her mind next to the name and origin of each fabric in the store's ledger.

"I want you to help me with the orders this evening," her father said, not looking up from the papers on his desk.

"Yes, Father, but I thought you wanted to do the orders on Monday."

"I know, Marie. But Uncle Hermann sent a telegram this afternoon informing me that the shipment from London had arrived early."

Marie looked confused.

Johan Weichbrodt sent out his orders on Monday. Like every other routine in his life, he had it down to an exact science. There was an appointed hour when he signed the order sheet and the courier came into the store to take the orders. This was followed by a telegram to one of his brothers in Swinemünde, inquiring about recent shipments there. The Weichbrodts originally came to Berlin from Swinemünde, a small port and resort town in Pomerania on the Baltic Sea.[4] After years of selling fabrics to Berlin dealers, Herr Weichbrodt decided greater opportunities existed if the family opened its own business in Berlin. So he and two of his brothers moved to Berlin with their families (Marie was only ten years old at the time) and opened Weichbrodt Imported Dry Goods in a modest store off Friedrichstrasse, just south of the Konzerthaus. They left a brother and two brothers-in-law up in Swinemünde to maintain the old business. That way Herr Weichbrodt could ensure that he was getting the best prices from Swinemünde and in turn offer the most competitive prices in Berlin. His plan worked beautifully, and within three years, Weichbrodt Imported Dry Goods moved to their current location on Schönhäuser Allee on the corner at one of the key intersections in Berlin. Shortly after, in the late 1870s, the German economy went into recession,[5] and the Weichbrodt textile sales dipped with the rest of the clothing industry. They were lean years, to be sure, with hardly a ham gracing the Sunday dinner table, except on holidays. Nevertheless, the family and the family business persevered, so that by 1883 the business was flourishing again, as it had been ten years earlier. Weichbrodt Imported Dry Goods officially consisted of Johan and his two younger brothers, Helmut and Theodor, but all of the children who were old enough worked in the store as well, so Marie worked alongside her uncles, aunts, cousins, and siblings. Her Uncle Helmut and his family lived in the apartment above Marie's family, who in turn lived above the store. Since Uncle Theodor lived in an apartment just down the street, it was nearly impossible to get away from the family.

After watching him write in his ledger with deliberateness that bordered on fury, Marie meekly reminded her father that she had already made plans for the evening.

"Where are you going?" Herr Weichbrodt looked up from his writing momentarily.

"To the theater."

"Oh well, this should only take us an hour."

"But it's already five o'clock and I still haven't finished the inventory. Why can't Anna help?" Marie asked, referring to her younger sister.

Herr Weichbrodt looked up from his ledger again and set down his pen. As he leaned back in his chair, he began twirling his mustache. Then he inquired, with some suspicion, "What time does the performance begin?"

Marie was obviously abashed. She put her hand in the pocket of her skirt and felt the letter from Franz that had been delivered to her surreptitiously that morning. Her sister Anna had intercepted the missive, and after several minutes of taunting and bribing had finally given it to Marie. It was nothing, of course, just a note confirming what they had written to one another the week before. But it was another note, which meant that he was thinking of her again. And any time she knew that he was thinking of her, it somehow relieved her sense of embarrassment and anguish at thinking of him so often. In fact, she often chided herself that she thought of him a disproportionate amount of time with respect to the time she actually spent with him. She had been seeing him on various evenings ever since he had wandered into Weichbrodt Imported Dry Goods on a Saturday afternoon in the spring nearly a year ago looking for "the finest English worsted."

It had been an eerie morning colored by a somber mood outside; the winter had been especially cold that year and the ice was only just beginning to melt, so the streets were filled with puddles of mud and ice, which caused Herr Weichbrodt endless consternation when his customers came in and refused to wipe their feet on the mat carefully marked, "For the customer." Then Franz entered the store in his greatcoat and uniform. Before the bell on the door finished ringing, Herr Weichbrodt regarded with satisfaction the young soldier meticulously wiping his feet on the appointed mat. Marie had been at the sales desk that afternoon when she asked Franz if he needed any assistance. Before he had finished speaking, Marie could barely contain her surprise. It was unmistakable. She knew this man from somewhere else. She had seen him on Unter den Linden during the march celebrating the tenth anniversary of the Franco-Prussian war. It had been nearly a year and a half since the celebration, but he had made such a strong impression on her that she could never forget his face. On that fateful September afternoon, so she told herself, Marie had clumsily dropped her hat on the lawn beneath the linden trees and this shy young man had rather gallantly picked it up. She remembered his face—his lean cheeks and knowing but innocent eyes. She remembered the modesty with which he had introduced himself. "I am Franz Frank," he said, and she stood dumbly before him, not saying a word. Here he was, a year and a half later, no longer a laborer but a handsome soldier in the kaiser's army with a brand-new uniform to prove it. After overcoming her initial surprise at running into this stranger again, Marie wondered if he recognized her. He had to have remembered. There had been some connection, hadn't there? Or was it that in her loneliness and desperation she would have taken any encounter as portentous? Looking at him on that soggy day in March, she couldn't see past the shadow of his cap, but she persisted in her interest and led him to the shelf containing bolts of the finest English wool. He stood there sheepishly, feeling the various textures and considering the different patterns, until she asked him what he planned to do with the wool. Explaining that he was a tailor in the army, he told her that he wished to make himself a suit of clothes along with a waistcoat, to which Marie confidently responded that she knew exactly the material he needed. She led him to a bolt of navy blue serge. When she realized that he clearly didn't know everything there was to know about tailoring, she walked him to the back of the store, to the stacks of rich satins. "Of course, you'll need a satin lining for your suit," she said, and suggested one of her favorite Belden satins: almost lavender, it was a pale gray that seemed to capture the subtlest changes of light. Without knowing it, she had Franz Frank spell-

The Reichstag, Berlin.

bound, and after paying for his material he asked her if she wouldn't mind joining him for dinner that evening on Friedrichstrasse so that he could discuss with her further the art of tailoring. "Yes, that would be nice," she said, her heart fluttering.

Since then things had been wonderful. He wrote her notes almost every week and brought her flowers and together they discovered a Berlin neither of them had dreamed of. It was not merely the dinners and cafés and theaters, but it was evenings in the park with mist rising from the Spree. It was strolling through the neighborhoods of Berlin on a rainy fall afternoon, talking to the shopkeepers and stopping at a corner café for coffee or wurst.

The filthy, noisy, dark Berlin she had formerly regarded with disgust and fear had blossomed in their season together into possibility itself. She loved to walk past the Reichstag to the Markt-Halle with Franz to sample the oranges and figs.[6] She loved to visit the Tiergarten, the zoological gardens, and watch the children mimic the animals. And there were so many conversations and so many destinations at which they had yet to arrive together. Because they were only able to see each other once a month, Marie often found herself scouting out locations in the city where they might spend an afternoon. She had planned day trips for them to Potsdam and Kopenick to walk among the forests and flowers, but when the appointed hour arrived they were invariably more content to find a quiet bench in the Tiergarten and talk the afternoon away. She had never met anyone with whom she felt more comfortable talking. She could have listened all afternoon to his descriptions of his childhood, fishing in the streams of East Prussia and gathering wheat for the fall harvest. She could have talked all evening of her memories of Swinemünde and the stormy days staring at the sea, walking the beach with her brother and sister. In truth, even in her most romantic imaginings of love she had never quite conceived of its being so natural, so effortless, and so much a mutual discovery of herself and him.

After Marie had admitted to her father that tonight's performance started at eight, she explained, "I always like to get there early."

Finally, her father asked the question. "And who will be accompanying you to the theater this evening."

Her face flushed and her eyes widened as if she was surprised by the question. "Franz Frank, the soldier," she said, and held her breath for her father's response.

Herr Weichbrodt stopped twirling his mustache and picked up his pen as if he were about to commence writing. His stubby fingers overwhelmed the delicate pen, and all at once a thought seemed to cross his mind; he slammed the pen down on the desk. "I'm sorry, Marie, but I can't let you go this evening. There is simply too much work to do."

She would have protested had she not detected her father's resolution on the matter as he returned to his work. She was furious, and she would not look at her father. Leaving the office without a word, she returned to the neatly folded stacks of satin at the back of the store.

There had been a time when her father would have yielded to such a request. Only six months before, in the fall of 1882, he had done just that. It was October, and Marie had planned to take the train with Franz to the Schlossgarten, the castle gardens. She wanted to wander the woods west of the Spree and look at the autumn leaves. The trip had been planned months in advance. Fall was her favorite season as the rains always reminded her of the melancholy afternoons of her childhood in Swinemünde. There weren't any forests where she lived, but her father often took the whole family by carriage to the southern portion of town where the woods began. Amid stately oaks, they would sit down for a delicious picnic prepared by her mother. Inevitably, the picnic would be interrupted by a game of hide-and-go-seek initiated by her father—he was so much more carefree in those days, before he brought the family business to Berlin. But it was the air of autumn that held the headiest fragrance of her youth. It was days spent wandering the beach with her sister after the last of the vacationers had returned to Berlin for the season. It was the color of the water and the pale tones of the rock and the almost almond color of the sand. It was the great chestnut leaves pressed into the path leading up to her house on rainy days. It was, above all, the last time she could recall being alone with her thoughts. And somehow, she would swear that she could smell the Baltic Sea in the rains scouring the October streets of Berlin. As a teenager she would go out into the rain, despite strong protests from her mother, just to remember what it felt like to live by the sea. Nonetheless, she wanted to share that experience; she wanted to revisit that longing with Franz, so she had scheduled a trip for the first weekend in October when he was on leave. It was the Friday night before their day trip. Marie was cleaning the dishes from that night's meal; Uncle Helmut and his family had eaten with them that night. Her father came into the kitchen and explained to her what he needed done the following day. She panicked. She told him that she had plans for the following afternoon and that she had already switched her duties with Anna so that she could go to the Schlossgarten the following day. When she explained that Private Franz Frank would be attending the gardens with her, her father's broad smile seemed momentarily to straighten the curls on his mustache.

Going through the flounces again at the back of the store, Marie remembered the warmth of her father's smile that day and only wished that those halcyon days would return. But that was impossible now. Ever since her parents had invited Franz over for dinner before Christmas, it hadn't been the same. It was one of the worst nights of her life, and yet it had begun so beautifully with a gentle snowfall filling the glow of the streetlamps, covering the dirty streets of Berlin. Franz was prompt as always and handsome in his uniform, his face still flushed from the cold. How badly she wanted to kiss him then! How badly she wanted that to be *their* life together, with the snow gathering in the gutters and crowning the chimneys, a pot of potatoes on the stove, and a roast in the oven. Franz was reserved at first and even a bit shy, speaking only when he was spoken to, and when he did speak it was as if he were replying to an officer in the kaiser's army. But Herr Weichbrodt insisted that Franz have a glass of wine, so that by the time dinner was served Franz had loosened up a bit. Herr Weichbrodt continued to ask Franz about Derz (none of the Weichbrodts had ever heard of Derz) and about his family.[7] It was all friendly and everything went beautifully, and there was laughter and no trace of intimidation in Herr Weichbrodt's tone until Franz mentioned that fatal word: "Mass." Herr Weichbrodt was exchanging fishing stories with Franz, who in the spirit of the evening decided to share his own passion for fishing. He described the beautiful rivers and lakes in East Prussia and all the fish that could be caught in the waters of his childhood. Franz went on to tell that it was his father's custom to take him fishing after Mass on Sunday. When he mentioned Mass, it was as if a pall had suddenly been cast over the dinner table. There was simply nothing further to talk about. Marie flushed, and her ears burned with shame and embarrassment. She could feel her father's eyes on her burning neck; she couldn't look at Franz at all. Nobody at the table said a word, and Franz sat with a puzzled, hurt expression, his brow furrowed, an awkward smile. Frau Weichbrodt asked Marie into the kitchen to help with the roast. For a moment Marie feared that her mother was going to berate her when she turned around. But it was only her mother's eyes that attacked. It would have been easier if her mother had chased after her; she had no defense against that disapproving glare. The rest of the evening went on like that—silent accusations and whispered intimations of the horrible things to come. When she finally sent Franz away that night, Marie realized she had not spoken a word to him since he had mentioned going to Mass. She watched him stumble down the street over little tufts of snow that had gathered during dinner, and realized she had no idea where he was going. Letting the door close behind her, she stepped out into the street and chased Franz to the corner, where she stopped him abruptly. "Will I see you tomorrow?" she asked. He looked confused and wary. "At the café?" she persisted, taking his gloved hands into hers. The tears in her eyes were all the balm Franz needed for the inexplicable wound he had received that night. "The café it is," he smiled, and gave her a kiss. She watched him disappear down the long corridors of Berlin, her heart leaping, and without a thought of what was in store for her at home.

At first it wasn't so bad. Her father waited for her on his favorite chair in the living room. He was calmly smoking a cigar and the room was almost totally darkened except for the lamp burning on the table next to his chair. Marie approached her father but did not dare look at him. Out of the corner of her downcast eyes she could discern him still twirling his mustache between puffs of cigar smoke. "Please sit down," her father said, indicating the chair opposite his. "Why didn't you tell me that Franz Frank was Catholic?" he asked coldly. The walls of the living room suddenly seemed miles away, and the room was filled with cold thin air that could barely carry her voice. Marie stuttered and before she could answer, her father kept up the questioning. "Are you telling me that you didn't know Franz was Catholic until this evening?" Marie was silent, waiting for her father to pass sentence. But he didn't do so, at least not that night. After an excruciating silence, Johan simply concluded that it was time to go to bed, as there was much work to do the following morning. As she left the room, Marie felt the rasp of her father's whisper rattle her very bones. "I am very disappointed in you, Marie."

Marie was not able to make her appointment with Franz at the café and was forced to write him, saying that her parents would have to meet him again. When she didn't hear back from Franz for over a month, she was sure it was over; either Franz had never received her note of regret, or having received it, he had decided never to see her again. Marie was devastated. She spent all of February in a gloom of silence and resignation. She would have to spend the rest of her life in her father's dry goods store, counting out the flounces and dreaming of all the places she would never see. Her sister, her brother, even her father began to notice her sadness and distracted manner and began to worry. Had they been too hard on Marie? But Herr Weichbrodt evaded any responsibility for his daughter's misery by taking the position with the family that neither he nor Frau Weichbrodt issued any punishment for Marie's deception. As far as he was concerned, she got off scot-free.

At the end of February, Anna furtively told Marie to meet her in the receiving room within fifteen minutes. When Anna saw that her sister barely registered her request, she insisted that it was extremely important. She had a note from Franz Frank. Marie opened it immediately. It was a simple request to see her at the café. There was no indication of bitterness or resignation: The note was in the same tone as in all his previous notes; it was neither overwrought nor hastily written. Regardless of her parents' consent, Marie had to see Franz that Saturday evening. At first she developed an elaborate scheme wherein she would tell her parents that she was going to meet several of her old friends from school for a reunion, until she considered the remote possibility of running into one of her cousins, aunts, or uncles strolling along Unter den Linden. She decided that such deception was not right and that it was best to simply speak her intentions. That night at dinner, after she had finished eating, she calmly pushed her plate forward and looked directly at her parents with her pale blue eyes. "I am going to meet Private Franz Frank for dinner at Café Kirkau on Saturday evening." Frau Weichbrodt turned nervously toward her husband waiting for his response. The linen tablecloth puckered beneath Herr Weichbrodt's fingers when he said, "That's fine."

It was as if a weight had been lifted off the entire family. No one had realized the degree to which Marie's mood had cloaked the whole household in a heavy resignation. She dressed smartly that evening. Her dark gray skirt was trimmed with buttons, and the coat was semi-fitted with a lap-over front. She wore a dark silk scarf plaited with tassels and a hat bedecked with taffeta roses that her mother had sewn together. Franz waited rather stiffly at the same table where they always met. He stood up awkwardly, his smile spilling over his beard. Marie seized him by the arms, and to maneuver around the canopy of her hat, he tilted his head and kissed her twice. They were positively giddy to see one another. It turned out that Franz had never arrived at the previous rendezvous either; he had to go east with his regiment near the Mazurian Lakes in East Prussia for a series of training maneuvers. He had sent a letter to that effect, but apparently it never arrived. After her misery for the past two months—and for nothing, or so it seemed that night—Marie basked in Franz's company. As they parted ways on the corner in front of Marie's house, they kissed again. Flushed with modesty and excitement, Marie demanded that they meet again the following week, regardless of Franz's duties to the regiment. "Next week, then." Franz tried to maintain a formal manner, but it was no use. She threw her arms around him again, and he laughed. He removed his hat in the street and kissed her once again before they finally parted. It was as if the dinner before Christmas had never taken place.

As March progressed, they saw each other almost every weekend, so by the time the linden trees had shed their first seed husks, Franz and Marie were quite accustomed to being with one another. They had even begun discussing plans for the future. There were no strict pledges of marriage, but they would spend hours in the café discussing the kind of house they wanted to live in and the type of life they wanted. If neither mentioned the other out of modesty or embarrassment when they spoke of their lives, then it was always assumed that they would be together.

Meanwhile, Herr Weichbrodt began to complain of the frequency of Franz and Marie's dates. "It's not good for her," he told his wife. "She's only going to get hurt." Finally, he decided to have a talk with his daughter. On a Tuesday afternoon in early April, he called her into the office. He stood up while he spoke to her and periodically jingled the keys in his pockets. "Remember when you invited Franz Frank over for dinner this past winter? He is fine young man, but . . ." Herr Weichbrodt struggled to find the words. "It was awkward, wasn't it?" Marie pretended not to understand. "Marie, it was an embarrassment. Franz Frank is a country boy disguising himself as a soldier. He has no idea how to take care of himself in the city. I just don't think it's wise for you to continue to spend so much time with him. Where could it possibly lead? Believe me, Marie, his coarse habits and unfamiliar country manners may charm you now, but how long can that last? You can't make a life out of coarse manners." It was the first time in her life that her father truly disappointed her, and, even worse, she was disgusted by his dishonesty. There was only one reason that her father was worried about her future with Franz Frank: he was Catholic, and Catholics were nothing but lazy, second-rate citizens in a first-rate German Empire.

As Marie was finishing the inventory, after her father had just refused to let her go to the theater with Franz on a beautiful spring evening, she grew angrier at the reckoning of each flounce. She had followed the thread of the story and had become disgusted with both of her parents. They had always been very observant Lutherans, her father especially. When she was a child, Marie sometimes wished she could have been playing on the beach instead of going to church on Sunday, but she had come to respect her parents' faith as she grew older. In Berlin, where money seemed to have become the official religion, Marie found her parents' adherence to the old values a refreshing relief from the materialism of the day. But just last week at church, her family had listened to the passage in the Gospel of Matthew in which Jesus exhorts his followers to love their neighbor as themselves. Wasn't Franz Frank a neighbor? Certainly he was Catholic, but there was nothing in the Gospel that said, "Love your Lutheran neighbor." In fact, she argued to herself, Jesus said that we must learn to love our enemies, for otherwise there would be nothing to distinguish ourselves from the Romans. With this thought, Marie set down her completed inventory and marched into her father's office.

"Do you remember last week's Gospel reading, Father?"

Herr Weichbrodt was surprised and let his pen fall onto the blotter next to his ledger.

"Last week?"

"Yes, the passage from the Gospel of Matthew?"

Herr Weichbrodt frowned for a moment, and when he had recalled the passage, he twirled the end of his mustache.

"Of course, it was the Golden Rule."

"The Golden Rule. Love your neighbor as yourself." Marie stared at her father, waiting for a response. She stood at the door to make clear that there was no avoiding this conversation. Herr Weichbrodt had never seen his daughter like this.

"Yes. Love your neighbor as yourself." And to change the tone of the conversation, Herr Weichbrodt smiled, adding, "It isn't called the Golden Rule for nothing."

"No, it isn't," Marie returned sharply. She spoke boldly: "Is Private Frank not your neighbor?"

Herr Weichbrodt flushed slightly, and in a moment a smile grew on his face he smiled as if he understood what was the matter with his daughter. "No, I don't think so," he concluded calmly.

"Why not?"

"He doesn't live anywhere near here. He lives in the barracks at the southern end of Berlin."

"Is Herr Broch your neighbor?" Marie retorted, referring to an old man who worked for Uncle Hermann in Swinemünde.

"No. Not anymore, but he's an old friend, which is why we still take care of him."

"Then you don't believe in the brotherhood of man?"

"Of course I do!" said Herr Weichbrodt, growing impatient with his daughter's inquisition.

"Well, if you believe in the brotherhood of man, then Private Franz Frank is your brother just as much as Herr Broch and Uncle Hermann and Uncle Theodor are. And if Private Franz Frank is your brother, then you should treat him as your brother."

"And what do you mean by that, Marie?" he asked, his voice louder.

"I am going to the theater tonight with Franz Frank with or without your permission."

Herr Weichbrodt pushed aside his ledger book and stood up. He was quivering with anger. "Have you ever heard of the fourth commandment, young lady? Honor thy father and mother? Honor thy father, Marie! Or have you forgotten that commandment in your search for brotherly love?" His hands were raised, his fingers fully extended. Pausing, Herr Weichbrodt stared at his daughter. Tears were rolling down her cheeks, and she struggled to keep her composure; his words had struck her to the heart. He quickly sensed that he had gone too far, and was ashamed. He approached his daughter as a gesture to re-open the conversation, but it was too late. Marie was shattered and didn't want her father near her. She walked away.

"Marie?"

"No, Father, I can't."

And she slowly disappeared up the stairs.

III

It was nearly an hour before her mother could calm Marie down. She persuaded her daughter to meet Franz Frank at the theater, despite her agreement with her husband on the issue of Private Frank's religion. There was no contempt for Catholics, Frau Weichbrodt had reasoned with her husband months before. It was simply a matter of practicality. "Even if he knew how to take care of Marie, would he be capable of taking care of her?" she had asked. And that was exactly how she felt. Private Frank was a fine young man, but certainly not fine enough to marry her daughter. How would he pay for the things to which Marie had become accustomed? With his worker's wages, he couldn't possibly afford the silks to adorn her daughter. It was as simple as that; their worlds were too far apart to join in holy matrimony.

But Frau Weichbrodt had never seen her daughter like this. When Marie came up the stairs, her spirit seemed broken. The light had gone from her eyes, the color from her face. She was crying, but not uncontrollably. It was as if she were determined not to acknowledge the spear in her side. So her mother urged her to keep her date with Franz.

Marie resisted at first, gazing out of the window and gazing down on the passersby. Men were more than their hats and their topcoats, more than the name of their faith; men were full of blood and the breath of life coursing through their veins. Resigning herself to a cloistered life of service then and there, Marie decided out of love and respect to listen to her mother's advice, without any intention of heeding it.

"You have to go. It wouldn't be proper to make plans with a young man and break them without warning. Your father knows that. He never taught you to miss an appointment. I don't understand where his head was this evening."

Marie's face had suddenly grown calm. It was obvious what she had to do.

"What you must do," her mother continued, "is to meet Private Frank and explain to him most tenderly that you will not be able to meet him again. Have a wonderful evening with him and explain that this will be the last time you can meet each other."

Marie nodded. "Yes, Mother. You're right. I can't just leave him standing outside the theater."

There was something strange and blank about Marie's expression now, but Frau Weichbrodt thought better than to try to guess its meaning. "Well, if you are going to go, go Marie. It's already 7:45."

"Yes," Marie responded, and began to walk toward her bedroom. Then she turned around. "There's no way I will be able to get dressed and make it to the theater in fifteen minutes. It's impossible."

"Fifteen minutes? I thought the play started at 8:30."

"It does, but I have to meet him there beforehand. I can't just show up at the last minute and walk into the theater." Quite suddenly, Marie appeared to be her old self again.

"Fine. I'll have your uncle call you a carriage."

A carriage! A carriage seemed so luxurious, especially this evening when it would be so difficult to enjoy. Of course, she had been in many carriages before with her parents, but she had never been in one alone. Marie slipped on a brown silk dress. She stood in front of the mirror. This would be the last night of her life with Franz Frank. Her face was gaunt with sobbing, and her hair looked like a large golden sugar loaf listing awkwardly to one side.

"Marie, the carriage is here!" her mother called from downstairs.

"I can't believe this!" Marie tried to fix her hair; she pushed it up and watched it return to the same position as before. Removing several hairpins, she reinserted them in different positions, only with the same effect. It would have been comical if she hadn't been in such a hurry.

"Hurry up, Marie. It's time."

"I'm coming!" She quickly powdered her face and shook her body so as to let her dress fall into place. Frau Weichbrodt assisted her with her boots and coat. As Marie was walking out the door of the apartment, her mother asked, "Aren't you forgetting something?" and looked to the top of her head.

Marie touched her hair. "Hat! Of course."

Her mother handed Marie her favorite hat; it was a brown, almost turban-shaped hat with chiffon piping on its short brim. The wing effect on the side was of fine netting, tied with a chiffon braid. Marie felt a burst of confidence as she headed out the door when she realized that she needn't remove the hat for the entire evening.

"Good bye, Marie."

"Good bye, Mother. Thank you."

Anna and her brother Stefan emerged from the kitchen to wish their sister good bye, but her father was nowhere to be seen.

Marie stepped into the tiny carriage with only five minutes to spare before her appointment with Franz. It had all been so confusing, and her seat was dirty and a little damp. As the driver pulled away, Marie looked out of the side window and saw her father. Their eyes met briefly, and Marie felt a mixture of guilt and anger. Had she made all this fuss, just to have her way and go to the theater tonight? But she wasn't getting her way at all. She was going to do exactly what her mother had told her to do. She was going to tell Franz that she could no longer see him. She was bitter about being forced to choose between Franz and her family. But she really didn't have a choice. It was all over.

The carriage seemed to fly through the streets, and when the traffic looked heavy, the driver quickly turned down an unfamiliar side street filled with shops and well-appointed businesses. Berlin was alive with the spring air. People sat on stairways and chairs, chatting; others strolled in the direction of Unter den Linden. A little girl peered out an apartment window above a small café, calling to a kitten down below. Three men sat near the corner puffing on pipes, while the smell of sauerbraten drifted out onto the street. A young mother could be seen through a pointed arch window soothing her child. There was so much of Berlin that she hadn't seen, even a side-street four blocks away from where she had lived for the last ten years. It was strange and sweet to think that somehow this was the last she would see of Berlin. She would never love again, and if she couldn't love again, what world was there for her to discover? The driver pulled out onto Friedrichstrasse. She could already see the crowds gathering on the benches beneath the linden trees. Before she knew it, they were stuck in traffic, waiting for pedestrians to cross Friedrichstrasse.

"Driver, you can let me out here."

When she offered payment, the driver informed her that her uncle had already paid the fare. It had to have been at least ten minutes since she left home so Marie hurried through the traffic of carriages and people. She couldn't believe how many people were out, and she wondered if a military parade was scheduled. By the time she reached the corner of Friedrichstrasse and Mittelstrasse, it was nearly 8:30. Through the crowd, Marie could see Franz checking his pocket watch and stroking his beard nervously. He looked crisper and more elegant than she remembered. She could feel her pulse in her eardrums.

"I'm sorry I'm late Franz, I had to do the inventory."

Without a word, he kissed her, and before she could say another word, he kissed her again.

"But we'll be late to the theater."

"Does it matter?" he smiled at her.

"I really wanted to go."

"What's playing?"

"I don't know," Marie admitted. They both laughed and began walking toward Unter den Linden, arm in arm.

"Shall we try the Viktoria Café in lieu of the theater?" Franz asked, but people were already spilling out the door. Marie indicated her lack of enthusiasm with a look of distaste for the crowd about the café.

"What about the Café Bauer then? Or the Linden Casino?"[8]

Marie shrugged her shoulders, and they began to stroll toward the Café Bauer. While Unter den Linden was crowded, most people walked along the promenade, between the colonnade of linden trees. Franz and Marie walked on the north side of the street next to the shops and cafés. They talked for a while, taking in the incredible scenery and walking as they had always walked. Indeed, the mildness of the evening was so infectious that they avoided walking too quickly, often stopping at windows and peering in at the displays. When they reached 29 Unter den Linden, Franz stood before the window display. Inside were neatly arranged bolts of cloth and wire mannequins. In the deeper shadows of the room, several large tables could be seen. Some of the finest suits in Europe had been cut on those tables by some of the most skilled tailors in the world. Franz had spent many a late evening, after he had seen Marie home, in front of this very store. It was Heider and Jean-Jacques, the most esteemed tailors in all of Berlin.[9]

"When I get out of the army, I'm going to open up a shop just like this."

"On Unter den Linden?" Marie asked.

"No. I was thinking somewhere on Charlottenstrasse, across from the university."

"Wouldn't that be expensive?"

"Well, yes, it probably would be expensive, but a tailor's shop needs a good location."

"Of course, Franz," she smiled. "But do you have the money for a shop like Heider and Jean-Jacques?" It was her father talking through her, and she knew it, but she continued to press Franz because she wanted to test the extent to which he had thought about his future.

"You'd be surprised how much money I've managed to save in the army."

"How much?"

"What kind of a question is that?"

Franz withdrew from her but Marie pressed on.

"Do you have enough to start your own business?"

"Of course not, but I will work for a tailor and refine my craft and save enough money to open my own business." He could feel his neck pushing against his starched collar. "And eventually I will own my own shop."

"And when will that be?"

"I don't care if it takes me twenty years. I will get it done."

Marie's probing had taken some of the luster out of Franz's eyes, and he slackened his pace. She had wounded his pride. Then, regaining his composure, Franz began to walk briskly in the direction of the Brandenburg Gate, adjusting his collar. They spoke no further until they arrived at another café. A little sign outside read "Café and Bar, L. Hoffman."[10] Through the small window in front, they could see a few candles lit within. It looked more like the tavern where Franz used to take his meals in Wedding than a proper café. "It looks quiet," Franz remarked, and without consulting Marie, he made his way down a cobbled alley toward the door of the establishment.

The tavern, for that is what it was, had managed to survive in the midst of the most glamorous part of Unter den Linden. Frank ordered beer and sauerbraten with potatoes; Marie opted for coffee. She had been on the verge of crying since their scuffle in front of the tailor's shop, and as a result she had lost her appetite. Why had she pressed him so much? It was a terrible thing to do, especially on the last night of their lives together. She was having a hard time forgiving herself when Franz asked, "Are you worried about our future together?"

After recovering from the initial shock of the question, Marie could barely hold back the tears. She turned away from him and replied blankly, "No. No, that was not what I meant at all."

Franz felt like he was about to burst out of his uniform. "I'm sorry to pester you, Marie. But what did you mean?"

"We can't see each other anymore." She was trembling all over and avoiding his gaze. Franz stood up and walked around the table to look at her directly. As he did so, she covered her face with her hands and began weeping. "I'm . . . so . . . sorry."

"Look at me, Marie."

But she shook her and said, "I can't."

Standing up again, Franz carefully put on his hat. Marie sat with her shoulder turned away from him, sobbing as before. The few patrons of the restaurant stared at her rather rudely. Her hat sat slightly askew on her head. Franz stood in front of her as if to cover her shame. He called the waiter and paid for their dinner, apologizing stiffly. When they made it out the door, Marie ran down the alley, unable to control her grief.

"Shhhh," Franz whispered after her, and stroked her shoulders awkwardly.

"Oh, I don't care. I don't care who hears us. I don't care about Berlin."

Franz laughed nervously. "I do. Someone may report me to the authorities," he returned in a low whisper.

Somehow this comment caught her attention. How could she be so thoughtless? People see a woman and a soldier carrying on, and what will they think? "Of course, of course. You're right."

Franz removed the handkerchief from his breast pocket and offered it to Marie. As she took the starched square of cloth, Franz had an idea. "I know where we can go. Follow me," he said, extending his hand.

Somehow this gentlemanly gesture of kindness only made matters worse. Marie could only think that he was relieved to be rid of her; it was the only explanation for his calm. He led her away from the bright lights of Unter den Linden down darkened streets lit by kerosene lamps. When they reached the Spree River and crossed the bridge, Marie finally blurted out, "Where are we going?"

"You'll find out soon."

The river was black, and the few barges docked along the bank disrupted the otherwise uniform sheen of the water. Franz and Marie followed the curve of the river north along Schiffbauerdamm toward Wedding and continued along the northern canal. By this time Marie had almost forgotten her grief in her curiosity about where Franz was taking her. Just before the bridge at Invalidenstrasse, Franz led her down a small staircase to a landing by the black waters of the canal.

"I used to go fishing here on Sunday evenings when I worked in the mill. Especially in the spring, when the west wind blew all the smoke away, I used to come down here and fish late into the night. I never caught anything, of course. I don't think there's any life left in that water. But it was enough for me just to hear the splashing of the water on a warm spring evening."

Marie looked down at the still water, which seemed to be covered in a slick of oil that coiled slowly about the massive piers of the bridge. Droshkies and horse-drawn buses rattled above them, oblivious to their quiet conversation. It made her sad to think of a lonely young Franz Frank, gaunt from a twelve-hour day of work and poverty, coming down to this desperate little spot on the canal that birds and fish had long since forsaken. The calls and rough talk of laborers unloading coal barges drifted up from Humboldhafen just south of them. Marie moved closer to Franz and gazed out into the blackness of the canal where the water was spotted by the reflection of the yellow lamps. It was hard not to think that the canal was somehow diseased with the pocks of the reflected lamplight oozing an oily discharge. It was hard to not think that something had gone horribly wrong.

Franz craned his neck north and pointed over the bridge. "I used to live about a quarter of a mile north of here when I first came to Berlin."

Marie climbed up a few steps in order to get a sense of where he had lived. A thick yellowish haze of smoke draped Franz's old neighborhood. More and more buildings crowded the streets beyond the Invalidstrasse bridge. Just the thought of all those rooms and all those people in the rooms turned her stomach. She stepped back down the cobbled steps gingerly and smiled nervously at Franz. She had no idea what to say.

Removing his hat and stroking his hair, Franz first looked at the river with an odd, formal gesture, as if by solemnly placing his hat on his breast he was about to give testimony to the water. He turned to Marie in her beautiful brown silk dress—there was a wind down the canal now fluttering the ribbons of her hat—and got down on one knee.

"Marie Weichbrodt, will you marry me?"

When something unexpected happens, something so entirely contrary to one's expectations, it somehow seems inevitable, as if fate itself had blinded one temporarily in order to reveal itself more fully. Marie threw herself into Franz's arms. She stroked his light brown beard. She kissed his neck. And she could feel his heart beating like a drum beneath his jacket.

"Yes. Of course I will, yes."

And then, as if to acknowledge the authority of fate, she looked into her fiancé's deep-set eyes and asked, "Why did you wait so long to ask?"

IV

The following morning Franz woke up before dawn, his head still swimming from the momentous event on Thursday night. There was so much to do now! He had to buy an engagement ring, and he had to earn enough money to buy a house. He refused even to consider marrying Marie until he had a proper home. Living with either of their families was out of the question. Rather than become indignant about Herr Weichbrodt's rejection of his faith and social status, Franz felt ashamed of his poverty instead. After all, Herr Weichbrodt was right; his daughter deserved far more than what Franz's meager savings could provide. The first thing he was going to do was march down to Heider and Jean-Jacques and ask for a job.

The barracks were practically empty. Private Frank was always among the handful of soldiers to remain in the barracks during leave. In the pre-dawn darkness — he was able to sleep only a few hours that night — Franz laid out his uniform carefully over the bed and then set an iron on the stove at the opposite end of the barracks. After adding some fuel to the stove, he waited for the iron to heat up. He still couldn't believe it; she actually said yes! He had never done anything as risky as that in his life. He knew that Marie didn't want their relationship to end, despite what she had said at the restaurant, but he didn't know until he was on his knees that he wanted to marry her. But it was so obvious to him now as he stared at the glowing coals in the stove. Of course, he had wanted to marry her; he had wanted to marry her since he first saw her outside Brandenburg Gate. He just didn't know that she wanted to marry him. He wasn't certain and there was nothing he liked less than uncertainty. But it was so obvious to him now! He shook his head at the incredible capacity for self-deception. "We're blind. That's all there is to it. We're blind," he muttered quietly to himself and chuckled at the happy inconsequence of his understanding.

Removing a long wooden board from the utility closet, he set up an ironing table by the stove and covered it with a thick cotton canvas. Methodically, he brought his jacket and his pants over to the table separately and ironed each piece to a crisp perfection. Following the most important night of his life, this was decidedly the most important day. It was imperative that he secure some kind of work at Heider and Jean-Jacques. In his mind, he reviewed all the questions he would be asked to test his knowledge. He considered all the steps for preparing a morning coat. While his tailoring experience was more or less limited to military uniforms, he had thoroughly researched the various methods for cutting and preparing topcoats, frock coats and vests.

He calmed himself by examining the hem of his coat in a mirror and brought out a ruler to measure the precise length of his sleeves. Satisfied by the appropriate proportions of his uniform, Franz set out again into the streets of Berlin just as the sun was rising over the city. There is something miraculous about momentous decisions—the way the most ordinary things are transformed by the light of resolution, the way a lamp or an undistinguished storefront one has passed a thousand times before quite suddenly becomes the locus of the most promising possibilities. The promise of love, marriage, and a future, can penetrate the dull objects of labor and domesticity and reveal their purpose and their humble grace. Franz was happy walking down the narrow lanes of Berlin toward Unter den Linden, where he would meet his fate. The old ladies with their carts full of asparagus delighted him; he imagined there would be evenings coming home to a plate of lovingly prepared *Spargel!* Even the ubiquitous urchins peddling dirty pails of black coal held a certain charm; they too would one day be relieved of their odious chore and find satisfaction in a bowl of beef stew. Mercy, kindness, charity, justice—these were the pillars of the world and it was only a matter of lifting one's eyes to see their bounty.

Filled with optimism and faith in human nature, Franz continued on his way until he came to the door of Heider and Jean-Jacques. He entered rather noisily, stumbling over the threshold. The front room was empty except for a neatly dressed man with a well-trimmed mustache standing erect behind the counter. Franz looked around at the room paneled in maple and wondered where all the tables he had seen the night before had gone. The man regarded Franz skeptically. "Can I help you, Private?"

Franz stood at attention. "Yes, sir, I would like to speak to Herr Heider."

The man stroked the lapels of his dark wool morning coat and looked at Franz more carefully. "I'm sorry, Private. I don't think Herr Heider was expecting you."

Franz remained near the door. He felt as if his fingers were popping out of his gloves and his neck were overflowing his freshly starched collar. It was difficult to move forward, but eventually he managed to bring one foot in front of the other. He was desperate to assume a less formal air. "Well, yes, sir. He wasn't expecting me. Nonetheless, is he available?"

"I'm afraid he is not available, Private."

"Well, then, sir, I was hoping I might speak to Herr Jean-Jacques."

"He is not available either." The man then walked behind the long counter, closer to where Franz was standing, and added, "Can I help you with anything?"

"Sir, I was hoping to speak to Herr Heider about a job."

The man appeared interested. "Really? May I ask what kind of tailoring experience you have?"

"I have spent the last two years in the army, sir, and I have been appointed the official tailor of my regiment."

"You can sew a soldier's uniform?"

"Yes, very well, sir."

"Well, as you can probably tell, Private, our customers are not interested in purchasing soldier's uniforms."

"But I would like to learn."

"What would you like to learn? Cutting or tailoring?"

"Well, I would like to learn both."

"I'm sorry, Private, but at Heider and Jean-Jacques we hire either cutters or tailors." The man paused for a moment, looking at Franz carefully. "Where are you from, Private?"

Franz stood at attention again. "From the seventh company of the kaiser's infantry, sir."

"I understand that, Private. I'm asking where you came from originally. Bavaria?"

"I apologize, sir. I misunderstood your question. I am from East Prussia."

"Oh yes, I see. You must be from Ermland."

For a moment, Franz imagined a sign that read "Ermland" emblazoned on the back of his uniform so that all could read it but him. How did this stranger know that he was from Ermland? Before he could affirm this assessment, the well-groomed tailor picked up the thread again. "I have a suggestion for you, Private. If you walk about a half a mile north of here, you will find a street filled with companies looking for young tailors just like yourself."

"Yes, sir, I know the street you are referring to, but I would much prefer to work for Heider and Jean-Jacques."

"But you can't get the necessary experience for Heider and Jean-Jacques in the army."

"Can I get the necessary experience in Wedding, sir?"

The man stroked his neat lapels again and gave out a short laugh. "Of course not, Private. This is an exclusive tailor. We only hire tailors that have been professionally trained in the best schools."

Pausing momentarily, Franz picked it up again. "Of course, sir. Excuse me for being so presumptuous, but where can I find out more about a school like that?"

Before Franz had finished his question, the man sighed, walked to the end of the counter, reached down into a cupboard, and pulled out a large catalogue. After flipping through several pages somewhat emphatically, he found the page he was looking for. "Here. There is a school here in Berlin. I received my training in Paris, but I have been told this is a reputable school."

The advertisement for the school simply listed its name and address. The Berlin Tailoring Institute was located just north of the Spree and east of Friedrichstrasse, about a ten-minute walk from Heider and Jean-Jacques. "Thank you very much, sir. You have been a great help. I only hope that I can return the favor to you sometime."

"It was my pleasure, Private," said the man, smoothing the vest beneath his lapels.

Franz had to stop himself under the linden trees and pause for a moment. He had heard about the Berlin Tailoring Institute when he was apprenticing; tuition cost forty marks a year. How in the world could he come up with that kind of money on a soldier's salary? He would have to work before he could pay for school, and he would probably have to work the night shift at the steel mill so that he could attend classes during the day. It would be years before he could marry Marie. The impossibility of the situation was dawning on him. He had saved what he considered was a great deal of money, but not enough to get into the tailoring business. He needed a job now that he was about to be married.

In a final act of desperation, Franz decided to go to one of the banks on Friedrichstrasse to inquire about a loan. Once inside, he filled out an application and was introduced to a loan officer, who politely offered him a chair.

"Herr Frank," the banker said, "we have no security that you will be able to pay back the loan. Possibly your father would co-sign the loan or pledge some property to the bank, just in case you can't make the payments in a timely fashion? I am sorry but we can't just lend money to a man whose only job is as a private in the army. If you got some money or someone with money to sign for you, then we would consider making a loan."

Franz countered to the banker, "But I know I am ready to start a tailoring business, sir. I have been making civilian suits on weekends for men in our unit for over a year. They like my work, sir. I can do it. I will gladly make a suit for you to show you what I can do."

The banker smiled and said, "Thank you, Herr Frank, but I don't think my superiors would regard my suit as evidence that you can succeed at running a tailoring business. I am sorry."

It was a devastating blow. How was one to get ahead in this world? In order to make money, one needs money, which Franz didn't have. How was a man supposed to find his way in the world without money? And on top of all this, he hadn't even bought the engagement ring yet! There was no chance of his going to school, and there was no way he would marry Marie under such circumstances. In all good conscience, he could not possibly ask Marie to live in one of those miserable tenements in Wedding. Perhaps her father was right; she has no business marrying a Catholic country boy, because he simply cannot provide for her.

In his dejection, Franz found himself wandering back to Wedding. He walked past the steel mill, where he received jeers from a few of his old work mates, and he stopped off in one of the beer halls that beckon the workers on the street opposite the plant. While he didn't normally drink much, Franz lingered over beer and soup all afternoon and nervously smoked several cigars. It was over. There was no way he was going to marry Marie. He even considered returning to Derz after the army and living with one of his brothers for a while until he was able to rent one of the small cottages on the outskirts of town. By the time he left the beer hall, the street was crowded with workers. It was a familiar feeling, trudging home elbow to elbow with thousands of people he'd never seen before. He had never quite gotten used to that feeling in the two years he worked at the steel mill, but he had no choice now; he would have to get used to it.

v

It was several weeks before Marie heard from Franz again. They had agreed on that fateful night that she would contact him in order to determine when they would next meet. After Franz had proposed to her, they continued to walk along the canal, discussing their future to-gether. Marie explained that it would be better if they didn't have much contact until she was able to smooth things over with her par-ents, and she didn't know when that would be. She told Franz that she would get in touch with him sometime in June so that they could see one another, perhaps surreptitiously. She also informed him that if absolutely necessary, he could address a letter to her that looked as if it came from one of the textile manufacturers. It was on a Tuesday that his letter arrived. It was very brief and asked that she meet him near Brandenburg Gate in the Tiergarten on Sunday afternoon. The tone was so formal that she began to worry that something was wrong. The three weeks since she had accepted his proposal had been strange, full of conflicting feelings about her loyalty. She knew she had made the right decision; she was in love with Franz and knew that she would never discover another person like him. She didn't care what financial sacrifices her life with him involved; she was totally committed to this man. But she still hadn't been able to discuss it with her parents. She wasn't even able to talk to Anna or Stefan about it. Convinced that her parents were wrong about Franz, Marie struggled to address her deliberate deception. As far as her parents knew, she was no longer seeing the young private, and her peculiar and somewhat secretive behavior of late was easily explained as the grief that comes with young love. But Marie felt frozen; whatever moral ground she had was lost by her deliberate deception. She resolved then to speak to her parents openly before meeting Franz that Sunday about her love for Franz and her intention to marry him.

While Marie anticipated that such a conversation would be difficult, the sudden freedom that came with a clear conscience obfuscated the reality of her parent's disapproval. After dinner that night, when she announced her intention to marry Private Frank, Herr Weichbrodt let the cigar fall from his fingertips to the floor, his lower jaw dropping in his disbelief. The room was noiseless. The rest of the family gazed at the burning cigar on the floor, but no one dared pick it up. Finally, Herr Weichbrodt reached over the arm of his chair to retrieve the cigar. Stubbing it out thoroughly in the ashtray on the table, he folded his hands over his stomach and sighed heavily. It was his wife who broke the silence.

"Marie, I thought we discussed this a month ago."

"I know mother, I should have told you then."

"You deliberately deceived me so that you could go see that . . . that . . ."

Marie lowered her head in shame.

"All those tears, Marie, those were tears of deception?"

"No, mother. I didn't know then."

"Didn't know what, young lady?"

"I didn't know how much I loved him."

Looking toward her husband, who sat like a sphinx at the end of the table, Frau Weichbrodt said, "Wonderful. It appears that we have raised our own Juliet."

No one had ever disobeyed Herr Weichbrodt. When he made decisions, not even his brothers ever dissented. As he sat motionless in the tall, carved chair at the end of the dining room table, his daughter pondered his improbable posture. With hands still folded neatly across his waistcoat, Herr Weichbrodt appeared to be probing an infinite space just below his chin, visible only to him. When it seemed impossible to retrieve him from his moody distance, his wife began clearing the table. Marie stood up to help, but before she could pick up a spoon, her mother informed her coldly that she wouldn't need her assistance and that it would be better for everyone if she excused herself. As Marie closed the door to her bedroom, she could hear, amid the clatter of plates, her mother sobbing in the kitchen.

It was awful. Whether things were worse or better than she had anticipated, one thing was clear as she peered out the window of her room looking for evidence of the stars: everything had changed and there was no going back. Remarkable that things could change so quickly. Not only had she disobeyed her father; she had betrayed him. More importantly, they would never look each other in the eye again; yet somehow she had already accepted this as a kind of penance. But with penance came absolution from guilt. Despite the anguish she had caused and despite the lump in her throat and the ache in her heart, she felt better. She was hiding nothing from her parents, the people for whom she had the greatest respect in the world. Yes, it was true, she may have forever lost their respect, but it was enough for her now that she had not lost her own integrity.

VI

The rain came down in sheets that Sunday, so there was almost no one in the park. As a result it wasn't difficult to locate Franz. He stood beneath an awning near the information building, his boots still perfectly dry and shining with an almost metallic gleam. He had obviously arrived before this sudden shower. His buttons were polished to perfection, and his uniform was neatly pressed, as always. Even his cap appeared crisper. It rested heavily on top of his head, the brim shading his eyes. As she approached him, Marie was sure that it was a new cap, as it didn't fit his head at all.

"A new cap for you, Private?" she said, kissing him.

"Yes, my old cap was starting to lose its shape."

"Well, this one doesn't quite fit."

Even in the shadow of his umbrella, little red spots began to appear on his cheeks, whether from embarrassment or anger she could not tell. "But I quite like it. It's a fine cap, Franz."

"It doesn't really matter. Let's get out of the rain," he said gruffly.

They walked over to Café Bauer, where all the Sunday promenaders seemed to have gathered in lieu of Unter den Linden. When Marie suggested that they go somewhere else, Franz responded somewhat hotly that he "just wanted to sit down." So they waited half an hour in the crowds for a table to clear while Marie tried to make small talk with Franz. Eventually she grew annoyed with his clipped manners and wondered why he had invited her out on a miserable afternoon. After all, hadn't she risked the trust and respect of her family for him? By the time they were seated and had ordered coffee, Marie had had enough of his stony behavior.

"What's wrong with you, Franz?"

He gazed up at her face, feigning innocence. "Nothing."

"You send me a curt letter telling me that it's important that I meet you today, and when I do meet you, you behave as if you are doing me a favor by attending a funeral in your own head."

Franz stared at the crowd behind her head and coldly replied that he couldn't marry her after all. Marie grabbed his hand and removed his glove so that she could feel his skin. He obliged mechanically. "What's wrong, Franz? Tell me. Look at me. What are you saying?" To which he answered that there was nothing wrong except that he had made a terrible mistake and that he had asked her to marry him in a moment of passion. Each time he tried to withdraw his hand from hers and put his glove back on, Marie stubbornly refused and held onto him more tightly. The more tightly she squeezed his hand, the less he remembered his original intention of remaining aloof in breaking off the engagement. Of course, she deserved an explanation, and as he gradually raised his eyes to meet hers, the gentleness and generosity of her love struck him like the flow of a swollen river.

"You can't marry a man like me." When he spoke it was as if a lid had burst open within him. "You can't marry a man like me because I can't possibly provide for you in the way that is fitting and proper. Your father was right. I can't marry you. I can't take you back to Wedding. What would you do but waste away in those awful tenements like all the other poor wives? I won't have that. But *I* can't have anything other than that. This uniform may suggest otherwise, but I'm a poor Catholic from the country, nothing but a farmer's son. I left home because there was no work there for me, no work

Marie Weichbrodt Franke, circa 1885.

and no way to make a living. And I know there's nothing for me to do here but waste away in the factories, and I won't have you go there with me."

She looked at him with her pale, moist eyes and leaned forward over the table, squeezing both of his hands. "When I saw you that afternoon over three years ago, it was *you* I fell in love with and not your charcoal suit. And in just the same way, when I accepted your proposal, it was *you* that I accepted, not your uniform. It was your strength and courage that I admired, not the starch on your collar. It was you. It is you. And so whatever we have to do, we'll do it together. I don't care if I have to push a cartful of coal all day, because I know now that my life without you is not worth living."

Franz leaned forward in his chair, his face now only a few inches from hers. Like the harvest moon rising above the picket of chestnuts behind his house in Derz, her face entirely filled his eyes and his mind with its luminosity. She was so beautiful that he could no longer entertain the petty objections he had so carefully prepared before meeting her this afternoon. It was as if the very curve of her cheek and the tender shape of her lips had anticipated such silly resistance and had pushed Franz to the boundless region of the heart where gloom can yield to laughter.

VII

It was still raining when they left the crowded café, but the air was warm, and Franz's umbrella was broad enough to protect them both as they strolled through the rain-soaked streets. "Let's walk to the park," Marie requested, and as they made their way to the Tiergarten, Franz was drawn again to the handsome window display in front of Heider and Jean-Jacques as if he needed some kind of punishment to counterbalance his extraordinary fortune in meeting a woman like Marie. "Oh, they won't take me here," Franz sighed and began to describe his adventures of a few weeks before. "This is what started it all, right here," Franz concluded. "I wouldn't have asked you to meet me if I hadn't come here and realized that my chances of becoming a real tailor were gone before I was born."

"Come on, let's move on. I would like to take a look at the gardens in this rain," Marie said, pulling on her fiancé's arm. It was true what she had said earlier; she loved him, and it didn't matter what they did as long as they did it together. But she knew that brooding over life's limitations couldn't be good for anyone, so she ushered Franz somewhat forcefully away from the windows of Heider and Jean-Jacques.

"Before we go, do you mind if I stop in the tobacconist's up ahead? I'd like to pick up some cigars."

"Not at all," Marie replied somewhat absently. She was worried that Franz might forever brood over his station in life and that he might always judge himself to be a failure. When they stepped into the tobacconist's, Marie felt a strange resentment as she looked around the store. Everything was so neatly arranged; cigars of varying sizes rested in their handsome boxes under glass cases. There was a separate area for newspapers and magazines, which were carefully displayed so that the covers could be seen. How was this poor tobacconist able to raise enough money to open a store on Unter den Linden? His father must have owned the store before him. Perhaps his father even owned the whole building. Nevertheless, Marie leafed through some of the magazines while Franz purchased his cigars with great care. Before she was done, Marie noticed one magazine that simply read "America" across the top and showed a picture of the Brooklyn Bridge spanning an unfathomable distance. At the bottom of the magazine, in letters as large as the title, was the word "Liberty," as if it were another name for America. Marie lingered over the picture of the incredible structure, which with its spiderlike cable seemed to be pulling the opposite shores together. It was staggering to think that the thinnest threads of wire could bridge such an incredible distance. On the counter was a large cardboard poster with an outline of the American continent, and in bold red, white, and blue letters were the words "Land of opportunity, free land, jobs, own your home!!! Ships sail every week from Bremmerhaven to New York City. Reasonable fares, on the GERMAN-AMERICAN LINES! In the last five years 600,000 German citizens have made the voyage to their new homes!"[11]

Neither made any comment about what both had seen. On her way out of the store, Marie made a point of saying thank you to the tobacconist in his short red vest, complimenting him on the cleanliness of his establishment.

As they left the tobacco shop, the rain had reduced to light drizzle, and a patch of sunlight could be seen in the distance. Both were deep in thought as they walked into the Tiergarten. At the same moment they both started to talk: "Did you see . . . ," said Marie, just as Franz was saying, "I was thinking . . ." Then they both burst out laughing and hugged each other.

"You first," Franz insisted.

"What do you think about America?" she asked without warning. "Did you see that magazine on the rack?"

Her light brown hair looked damp and made an oval frame about her face. Franz brushed aside her hair as they continued walking. "What magazine?" He could see her mind working now.

"The one that said 'America' across the top."

"Yes, I did. The one with the photograph of the Brooklyn Bridge on the cover?"

"Apparently the bridge has recently opened."

"Yes, I read that the chief engineer of the project was born in Prussia. Roebling was his name. I just read about him this past week."

"Really? A marvelous structure. Who could imagine that those little threads could hold up an entire bridge."

Frank nodded and stroked his beard several times, trying to imagine how Roebling had managed to accomplish such a feat. "Apparently Roebling died during the first year of construction, and his son replaced him as chief engineer."

As they emerged from the canopy of linden trees and into the gravel square, the sun broke through. The air was warm, and an almost lurid green beckoned them through the Brandenburg Gate, so lush were the gardens beyond them. Well-established rivulets worn into the gravel flowed past them as Franz put his hand to Marie's arm lest she step into a puddle. Marie turned and looked at him closely. She removed his hat and appeared to examine the shape of his skull, like a phrenologist, for indications of his character and perhaps indeed his future. She gazed on his brow, which sloped ever so gently downward at an angle that suggested genuine humility, but as she saw the play of light sparkle in his eyes, she began to imagine his brow as a kind of protection, an armor as it were, not only to ward off the elements but as a cover for his tremendous energy and enterprise.

"Now it's my turn," said Franz. "I was just thinking about that poster on the counter. Can you imagine that 600,000 Germans have gone to America in the last five years? That's about half the population of East Prussia. I was just wondering. If that many people have gone, it can't be that difficult."

Marie jumped in. "I was thinking the same thing." As they walked on, their step became more spirited. They gestured with their arms to reinforce their words. Everything was on the table. Could they make it to America? The hope of a new life together and the myriad of unresolved issues that such a move involved tumbled out as they talked. How could they afford it, not knowing any English and leaving both of their families? And yet, despite these difficulties, an irrepressible excitement kept them considering the project.

They went directly to a bench before the gate and sat down like two children who hadn't seen each other for weeks, with so much to tell each other. Their conversation continued for the better part of an hour. Franz related the desperation he recently had felt with the recognition that there was no prospect for him to get a meaningful position as a tailor in Berlin. No one would lend him money to start his own business.

Marie was nodding her head in understanding as they began walking again.

"Let's move to America," she concluded. "Think about it, Franz. There's nothing here for us, and nothing's going to be here. You said it yourself that you don't want to rot in one of those factories once you leave the army. Why not go to America? We could move to America, and you could open up your own tailoring shop, or, think of this, we could even own our own farm. Wouldn't that be wonderful? Our own farm. I've read about the corn and the apple trees there and the fertile soil. Oh Franz, let's go to America."

They stopped at the gate and Franz took a deep breath. It would be wonderful. There was certainly nothing to keep him here. But it was hard not to think that if only he had had the opportunity, he would have been able to make a great life in Germany.

"Franz, did you happen to see what it said on the bottom of the magazine? It said 'Liberty.' Do you know what liberty is? Of course you don't. Because we've never had it. You don't need to know anyone in America. We just need to know each other. That's all we would need. We would never be bothered again by the money and by whether or not you're good enough for me or I'm good enough for you or whether you're Catholic or I'm Lutheran. In America, we can forget about all of that. Nobody there cares, because they don't have hundreds of years of wars over religion in their history. Don't you see, Franz, that we can strip ourselves free of all the problems of Germany? Everything that has hurt us and made us miserable this past year will be gone."

Franz listened intently to his wife-to-be. Of course, she was right; he had no future in Germany. That was the whole reason he brought her out here in the first place. But it was strange to imagine himself leaving, hearing the bands playing *Must I Leave My Native Town,* and seeing all those people leave the Old World behind. And when he arrived on the shores of America, he would become a stranger again. How lonely those first months in Berlin had been, how awkwardly he had walked along the banks of the canal, aching to be home, to be somewhere he could call his own. How awful it would be to live through that again in a place where not a word of German was spoken. But it was a chance to begin anew, and it was the only chance he and Marie had together.

Franz turned away for a moment and cupped his hands to light a cigar. Puffing away, he looked up at the sturdy Doric columns of Brandenburg Gate and then looked down the grand canopy of linden trees where he had courted his fiancée and had seen so many of his hopes dashed. He broke into a smile as he took off his cap and ran his fingers through his hair.

"You're right. It's time to go."

LOOM OF AMERICA

Franz's trip to the United States determined whether it was prudent for Marie to follow in their great adventure. The discovery of Marie's letter confirmed many aspects of their courtship that directed me to the archives in Berlin. This love letter, though brief, conveys the intensity of feelings and courage that they both experienced.

BERLIN, JULY 9, 1884

My eternally beloved Franz,

I have received your sweet letter with longing and I have gathered from it that you are healthy, but dear child that you are so sad makes me happy, also for me it has been already too long. I am also already counting the days as I will certainly not allow the waves to deprive me of my dreams. Dear Franz can you write me and if it so happens that I shall die at sea, then you can worry . . .

Dear Franz I am definitely ready to board the ship on August 30, therefore please send me the ticket as soon as possible. I still do not have the letter . . .

I have to close as my time is short and my eyes are tired. Dear Franz you cannot believe how hard it is for me now.

With much love and kisses I will remain until death your beloved wife.

Marie

I have not yet received the money from your agent.

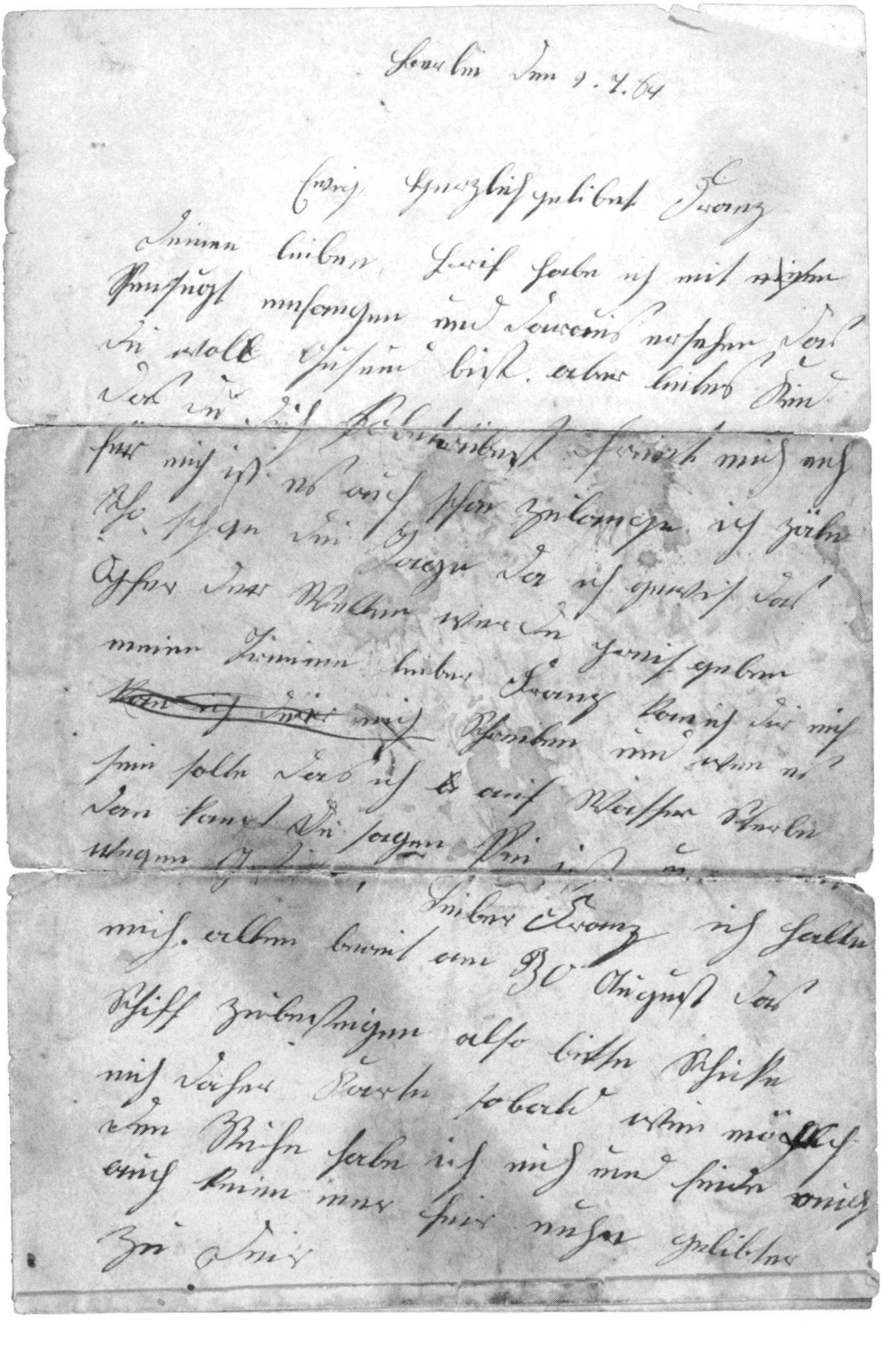

Berlin den 9.7.64

Mein herzlichgeliebter Franz

Deinen lieben Brief habe ich mit [illegible] Sehnsucht empfangen und daraus ersehen daß [illegible] bist. aber liebster [illegible]

[illegible]

Lieber Franz ich halte mich [illegible] am 30 August das Schiff [illegible] also bitte [illegible] sobald als möglich [illegible]

Zu Dir [illegible] geliebter

I

By the time Frank received Marie's letter, he couldn't believe it had been only three months since he had last seen her. An era had passed since then—an interminable purgatory of anticipation, chastened by doubt and fear. Mother Sherman, an old German woman with thick ankles and sagging stockings, kindly informed him that a letter had arrived that day, July 31, 1884, from Mrs. Franke.[1] Mother Sherman ran Sherman House,[2] the boardinghouse on Washington Street in Springfield, Illinois, where Frank and Marie had decided to cast their fate. As she shuffled in her slippers down the long hallway of the boardinghouse, Mother Sherman could have easily been mistaken for one of those women pushing carts full of vegetables on their way to the covered market in Wedding. Her hair was always tied up in a scarf, and coins jingled in the great pockets of her apron even as she stood behind the kitchen counter. While Frank feared Mother Sherman for her stern commands and short temper, he found a strange comfort in her presence. Indeed, he might have died of homesickness and the daily grating of English in his ear had it not been for the sound of Mother Sherman's German in the evening: "Lights out! Time to go to bed, Mr. Franke."

"So when is Mrs. Franke due to come to Springfield?" Mother Sherman asked as Frank sat down to a plate of beef, corn, and turnip greens. Touching the letter in his coat pocket to assure himself that it was still in his possession, Frank answered that he expected her to arrive at the beginning of September.

"That's good. That's good. Perhaps your appetite will return with her arrival," she chuckled, elbowing one of the other guests.

All the guests at the boardinghouse were German men with the exception of two married couples staying down the hall from Frank. One Irishman had been staying there when Frank first arrived back in April, but he left as soon as his wife arrived at Springfield Station. The men of Sherman House gathered each evening at 6:30 sharp to eat dinner, which usually consisted of beef and a side dish or some variation of beef such as spaetzle floating in a light beef broth. Beef was so cheap and plentiful here relative to Germany that Mother Sherman saw no reason to serve anything other than the dressed beef that arrived in refrigerated cars from Chicago every day. If you weren't seated at the long wooden table in the dining room by the appointed hour, you were not allowed to eat dinner. Mother Sherman didn't care if work prevented your getting home by 6:30; those were her rules, and if you were going to live in her house, you had to abide by them. An awkward camaraderie existed among the men of Sherman House, but it was mostly borne out as a respectful silence. Occasionally, a few of her guests could be found in the tavern across the street, but in general the men of Sherman House were not in the mood for talking or carousing. They were all working and waiting to save up enough money to send for their wives and family members back home. As soon as that hoped for reunion occurred, there would be no return to Sherman House, except in passing to remind themselves of their good fortune through the memory of the terrible loneliness that once greeted them with the morning sun. "I used to live there," they would sigh, and shake their heads in disbelief.

Throughout dinner, Frank kept touching the letter Mother Sherman had dutifully given him, worried that he had somehow managed to misplace it during the course of the meal. It was one of those depressingly hot evenings in Springfield when the trees wheeze with the noise of locusts and the air is still and thick with humidity. Without the aid of cold beer it was incomprehensible how the early Illinois settlers tolerated the heat. Berlin could get hot, but only for a day or so, and compared to Springfield it was relatively dry. As one of the tailors at Buchner's, where Frank was working, explained, they were now in the bottomlands of America where all the water east of the Rockies and west of the Appalachians ended up. "Good for corn," he concluded, "but not so good for a cutter cutting wool suits."

After dinner, Frank sat in the dining room smoking a cigar with the other boarders and listened distractedly to the talk of business schemes and dreams of owning a home in Vinegar Hill, the German neighborhood just west of downtown Springfield. It was too hot to enjoy a cigar, and it was impossible to think of anything other than the letter in his coat pocket, so by 8:30, just as the sun was setting, Frank took leave of his fellow boarders and made the long, lonely walk down the darkened corridors of Sherman House to his modest room on the third floor. It was a bare existence there. The little iron bed sat squarely in the middle of the room between two small windows that looked out onto the dirt roads of Springfield. The noise of the tavern across the street often provided welcome relief to the creaking of the pine boards beneath his pacing feet. He would stop before the window and try to pick out the German conversation amid the din.

Frank walked to the sink opposite his bed and hung his hat on the single hook next to it. He washed his face and hands with the warm water provided by Mother Sherman, and looking into the small, dingy mirror above the sink, he examined his whiskers. He proceeded to check the cut of his coat, determined that there were no sweat stains from the heat, and finally retrieved the letter from his coat pocket. He then hung his coat in the wardrobe next to the sink. The sun had sunk below the prairie horizon, but the sky would hold its last light for another hour at least. It was quite beautiful, especially on a clear night such as this when a lonely cloud drifted into the frame of his window and gathered all that western light into its transient form. It came like a messenger whispering above the tender oaks of Springfield, "Time, space, pleasure, pain—this too shall pass."

On a small nightstand he kept candles, money, a copy of the Bible, and a few magazines featuring the latest methods in tailoring. With the exception of his clothes hanging in the wardrobe, it was all he had in the world. Soft shadows filled the corners of the room. Frank placed the letter like some sacred object not fit for daily exposure in the top drawer of the night stand and carefully lit a candle. Before opening the letter, he read a passage from the Bible at random as a kind of thankyou offering for this unexpected letter. Although he didn't deserve it, the evidence of Marie's handwriting was enough to restore his sense of hope. The passage came from the Gospel of Mark (2:21), where Jesus, responding to the skeptical Pharisees, says, "No man also seweth a piece of new cloth on an old garment: else the new piece that filled it up taketh away from the old, and the rent is made worse." If she had been with him now, he would have told her that that is exactly what he had been trying to say to her all along when he was assuring her in the days before he left Germany for good that everything would be fine. But she wasn't with him now, and the pettiness of his thought struck him as unworthy of their love.

Frank removed the letter from the drawer and saw that it was postmarked July 9 in Berlin. The letter was addressed to Mr. Frank Franke. When they were married in Berlin just before Frank sailed to

America, the couple decided that they would changed their name to Franke. "Once I move to America I can no longer go by Franz," he had said to her. "I have to take an American name — I will be called Frank Franke." Marie happily agreed, admitting that she preferred Franke to Frank as a last name, but asked him for his patience when it came to calling him Frank rather than Franz.

"My eternally beloved Franz" the letter began, and with each syllable he read came a greater pounding in his heart. He ached to see his wife again. Sitting on his bed, bent over the candlelight, he read the letter over and over until each letter of each word seemed to free itself from the page and floated before him as a portent of things to come. Was it somehow inauspicious that she had addressed him as Franz rather than by his American name Frank? It was awful that she wrote that she might be taken by the waves. His own journey had been grim, and the months since then had been an exquisite torture of counting hours and days and weeks until she came. It was impossible to know the country that lay outside his window, for America had become exclusively an experience of time. How could she even think that she might not survive the voyage!

Frank got up from his bed and began pacing the pine planks of his room in a familiar pattern, still clutching the letter. He began at the door, walked to one corner, abruptly turned about, scratched his beard, and then made his way across the planks to the opposite wall. Over the course of five minutes he covered the floor as if his room were a loom, and the motions he made across the planks guided the warp of the new fabric that would be woven by his life with Marie. When he had made the final turn around his bed, Frank repeated the pattern as before.

His journey to America had been inauspicious. Two days before he left Berlin, Marie expressed genuine regret that it all had to come to this, their leaving everything behind for something so completely unknown. "But it's not unknown," he had objected stiffly to her at the café. "I will go to Springfield and find a job as a tailor, and together we will eventually open up a business together. You will be the bookkeeper and I will be the tailor."

It had all been so neat in his mind. "America is the land of liberty," he had told her in 1883. "You saw it for yourself. America is all about liberty, and liberty in America is the freedom to run your own busi-

The Steerage, 1907, photo by Alfred Stieglitz. Collection of Richard Franke. Courtesy of the Georgia O'Keeffe Foundation. I often wondered if my grandfather might have been on a ship such as this one. He did wear a straw boater at one time.

ness." At that point Marie began to weep, saying that she would never make amends with her father, that he would die before she ever saw him again. What could Franz say to her? This was the second time he had left his family, and this time it was for good. There was no chance that he would ever return to Derz, but it was clear that their situation required sacrifice. Only sacrifice could redeem their impossible love. Only sacrifice could give them the life they deserved. There was no chance for them in Berlin, and he knew that now. And if it was their tie to their families that had to be severed, then that was the price that had to be paid for their freedom.

By the time he boarded the train for Bremen in April of 1884, Franz had convinced himself that Marie no longer loved him and that she would return to her family instead of taking the great sea journey. There was no ground for such anxieties, for he had never known Marie to back out of anything. But why should she suddenly feel all this regret, especially now? If anything, now was the time to look ahead and forget about the past. So it was with some bitterness that he had watched all the families gathering at the docks in Bremen, wishing their fathers and husbands and children and mothers farewell, with the bands all playing behind them and the waters of the harbor lapping against the great ship's side, beckoning them out to sea. He had been anticipating that moment as such an exalted one when he would finally be free of the shackles of Germany, free to pursue his destiny on his own terms as he gazed from the deck of that great ship at the receding shores littered with the business of being Germany. Instead, when he got out onto the deck, he could see no one waiting at the shore to see him off, no one to bid him farewell, no one with a fluttering scarf to wave him bon voyage. For all he knew, Marie was back in Berlin, planning her new life without him. As the ship finally sailed out of the harbor, the thread of the waters behind the vessel served not as a reminder of his ties to whatever lay back on shore but rather of his isolation in this uncharted world when those threads were totally swallowed up by the vastness of the open sea. He had become an orphan and a stranger in the world. And with the dull sway of the ocean rocking the boat from side to side, he was seasick. His nausea lasted nearly the whole way to America. It was only in the most placid waters that he found any comfort at all.

The trip from New York to Chicago had been hardly more comfortable. With few seats available, he had spent most of the journey sitting on his suitcase between railroad cars. Sleep was a distant memory until he got to Chicago, where he spent the night before boarding the train to Springfield the following morning.

Looking out of the train window that morning and seeing the first spring shoots of tenderest green coming up from the fields and farms,

First Presbyterian Church, 1884, on the northwest corner of Seventh and
Capital Streets. Courtesy of Sangamon Valley Collection, Lincoln Library, Springfield, Illinois.

it was as if he had chosen the perfect place to forge a new life. Flat,
and nearly featureless, the Illinois prairie extended beyond the visible
horizon like the ocean he had just crossed, uninterrupted by buildings
or trees. Nowhere was to be found even a path among the rippling
green. The train roared through the morning, and he could have gone
on forever in that nowhere, for the pathless prairie is the land of or-
phans, and only there can a man such as Frank Franke find peace.

When he got out on the boardwalk of Springfield Station, he was
surprised to find the city as crowded as it was. Expecting something
only somewhat larger than Derz, he marveled to see so many people
strolling around downtown in the middle of the day. Still exhausted
from his journey, Frank inquired at one of the German taverns where
he might find a place to stay and was informed of Sherman House just
down the street.

Pacing the planks of his darkening room, Frank recalled the feeling of walking down the muddy street; it had been the only time during his journey that a feeling of lightness propelled him forward. The

air was warm, and a faint smell of manure lingered about the wagons full of hay in the street. Springfield was both more and less civilized than he had anticipated. The taverns and tobacco shops reminded him of the comforts of Berlin, but the deeply rutted muddy streets and the haphazard boards strewn together to form a crude sidewalk belied the pioneer struggle to order an unruly and even capricious natural world, which constantly threatened the daily routine of the city.

Within a week of his arrival at Springfield, Frank found work. He woke up one morning in early May, polished his shoes, ironed his suit, and found the nearest tailor. When he walked up the narrow staircase above Hall and Herrick's, Joseph Buchner, the sole proprietor of Buchner's tailor shop, greeted him warmly, and within a half an hour Frank was told that he had a job.[3] What an extraordinary feeling that was! Everything he had heard was true; the muddy streets of America *were* paved with gold, and opportunity was no further than a stroll down the block. Although he started off slowly at Buchner's, mostly taking orders and doing the inventory, by June he was being trained as Buchner's main cutter.

It was only a month before he would see Marie. He had sent her the travel money almost two weeks ago. After she arrived, everything would be exactly as they had planned. They would march down to the city hall and get married before an official of the state of Illinois, using their new name. Marie would then find a job as a bookkeeper, perhaps even for old Buchner, and within a year or two they would buy a house and start a family. It was incredible to think how easy it would be, how everything they had ever wanted in Germany was right here for the taking. To even think of her arrival made his stomach queasy for fear that it would all somehow fall apart.

And just then, as Frank was wearing down the pine boards of his room with worry and anticipation, the sound of Mother Sherman's voice came as welcome relief: "Lights out! Time to go to bed, Mr. Franke."

The candle barely produced a flicker of light. Frank carefully placed the letter back into its envelope and returned the envelope into the top drawer of the table that held all his worldly possessions. With a moistened fingertip, he extinguished the guttering flame, and as his head hit the pillow, a gasp from somewhere deep within his chest whispered, "Oh, Marie."

II

The fall of 1883 had been hard on Marie, with Franz working overtime every week to save up for the trip to America. She was lucky to see him once a month, and that was usually on Sunday afternoon in a noisy corner of Victoria Café or some tavern on Friedrichstrasse. The rest of the time had been almost intolerable. She still lived at home and she still counted flounces every Friday afternoon for her father; but her family rarely acknowledged her, aside from giving her direct orders.

Franz's short missive from Wedding requesting that they meet at Café Bauer offered no explanation as to why he never had written to her from Derz. In fact, he had been utterly consumed with plans for leaving Berlin and leaving Germany forever.

Shortly after their conversation at the café in February, Franz had decided to leave for America earlier than they had originally planned, which meant that he was working around the clock and almost never saw Marie, except on their wedding day. Franz had begun to worry that it would be unseemly for a woman to travel all the way to America without the cloak of marriage to protect her dignity. Marie had agreed, and they were married down at the city hall on a Friday afternoon, in March 1884, just before Franz left.[4]

Nothing could have prepared Marie for the trauma of his actual departure. Just three days before Franz was to take the train to Bremen, Marie's father approached her as she was rolling up a bolt of silk at the end of the day. She had not spoken to her father, other than to reply to his orders, in more than eight months. Her brother Stefan, who was now old enough to have an active hand in the family business, was the only family member still sympathetic to her. Even Anna, who was probably more scared of her father's disapproval than actually disappointed in Marie's decision, refused to acknowledge her sister other than to pass the butter at dinnertime. But Stefan had courage and occasionally took Marie out to lunch, and they would talk about the beach at Swinemünde. Stefan never really liked Franz—she knew that—but he obviously felt bad about how ostracized his sister had become. And it was precisely this sympathy that prompted him to talk to his father about Marie.

After Herr Weichbrodt had pondered his son's overtures "to find a way to save the family," he thought of the perfect solution. Fresh from an evening shave, he approached his daughter.

"I have something I would like to talk to you about, Marie," he began, and ushered her into his office.

"Sit down," he said calmly, as if he were about to enter into some business negotiations.

Herr Weichbrodt sat behind his great oak desk, which, except for the ink blotter, was entirely cleared of papers or ledgers. Having lit a cigar, he stood up, walked toward the window, and began to talk aimlessly of business matters.

"We have a large shipment coming in from Swinemünde tomorrow. You'll be able to take care of it, I assume."

"Monday," Marie said curtly, straightening herself in her chair.

"No, the order will need to be processed tomorrow," Herr Weichbrodt insisted.

"I have plans for tomorrow," Marie admitted, in a tone that indicated she was talking about Franz Frank.

"Yes, that's what I've been meaning to talk to you about," Herr Weichbrodt said, catching her tone. "It seems to be that you are unhappy, and before you interrupt your father, let me say what I mean. We are all unhappy about this unfortunate circumstance. I know, I know. You fell in love with this young man. But just because you have made a mistake doesn't mean that you have to wed yourself to this man as punishment for your sins. Please don't tell me that this is about religion or a lack of charity. Private Frank is simply not the right man for you."

Marie looked at her father as if she were looking through him to the turret on the other side of the courtyard.

"Listen to me, Marie. Not everything is solved with love. Life is full of unpleasant surprises—and when those surprises come along, it's best to be with the right people."

"Who's better to be with than the one you love?" Marie asked defiantly.

"But you don't love Franz Frank. Not with a love that lasts."

Although mostly numb to her father's remarks, this one seemed to strike a nerve. "How would you know what kind of love I have for

Franz? You haven't even spoken to me since we announced our engagement."

Herr Weichbrodt assumed a ponderous expression in reply and held it for several minutes. When he finally started speaking again, Marie studied his face closely. "I have a simple proposition," he started. "And before you give me an answer, I would like you to consider it carefully. Now, I understand that you have feelings for Private Frank, but it is foolish to think that you can spend the rest of your life in America with him. It's foolish, Marie. Therefore, I'd like to give a gift of money to Private Frank. Take this and give it to Private Frank," he said as handed her an envelope. "It's for his journey to America. But take it only with the promise that you will not follow him."

Marie looked directly into her father's eyes and let the envelope drop to the floor.

"Marie, I'm not asking you anymore. As your father, I forbid you to follow that young man to America. I've already discussed it with a lawyer and with the minister. You can get your marriage annulled, and no one will ever know the difference."

At this point Herr Weichbrodt pulled on the tails of his coat and sat back down at his desk. He stubbed out his cigar in an ashtray that he kept in the top drawer of his desk and leaned forward, saying: "I care very much for you, Marie. I do not want to lose you, but with your stubbornness you have forced me into a position where I have no other choice. Give the money to Private Frank, or you are never welcome in this house again."

Without glancing either at her father or at the envelope on the floor, Marie stood up and walked out of the room.

III

Marie went straight upstairs to her room and began packing a suitcase. She took enough clothes for a week—hairpins, a hat, a brush, a Bible, and all the money she had in the world. Calmly walking into the kitchen, where her mother and Anna were preparing dinner, Marie stood behind them momentarily until they turned around. She set her suitcase on the ground, leaned forward and kissed her sister on the cheek. And then she kissed her mother.

"Good-bye, Mother. Good bye, Anna. I have to go now."

And with that, Marie struggled down the stairs with her great suitcase amid a flurry of protests and questions from her mother. Ignoring them, she walked out onto the street and quickly found a carriage for hire. She ordered the driver to take her to the nearest boardinghouse.

The next few days with Franz were wonderful but difficult. Of course, she had to find a job now that she was on her own, but that would have to wait until she saw him off. Franz had to work on the weekend—"the more I work now, the less time it will be before we are together again," he told her—but they still had the evenings to be together. Late on the Sunday afternoon, they met again at Café Bauer after most of the afternoon's patrons had left. Marie had spent most of the day in a daze. Not wanting to see her family at church, she found a church on the other side of town. It was quite chilly after the service, but she did not want to go back to the boardinghouse, which, after only two nights, was already assuming a prisonlike air. So she decided to stroll among the hedges of her adolescence in the Tiergarten for the balance of the day. By the time she met Franz, she was relieved to see someone she knew again, especially him. He no longer wore his private's uniform but had replaced it with another uniform of sorts— topcoat, waistcoat, and wool trousers—which he wore with the same sense of purpose and dignity as before. She found a profound assurance in his sense of propriety, which was marked by sincerity, as if it had a moral fiber to it, as opposed to her father's propriety, which now struck her as false and motivated strictly by appearances.

Throughout the day she had gone over the conversation with her father again and again. How outrageous it was that he would offer money for Franz to go away, that you could just buy someone like another piece of cloth! She should have left home long ago, right after they announced their engagement. She couldn't imagine how she had endured such a servile and oppressive existence for so long. But nor could she imagine how she would leave it now. How dreadful the next several months would be! How long would it take Franz to send the money for her ticket? It was terrible to think that it might be months before she even heard from him. It seemed absurd that they had to travel halfway across the globe just to be together.

Marie was relieved to speak her mind that night as they lingered long over coffee and dessert. It seemed so long since she had last held

Café Bauer, Berlin, at the corner of Friedrichstrasse and Unter den Linden.

his hand, and she found great comfort in talking about her worries and hopes and fears. While she was able to express her fear that she would never come to any reconciliation with her father, she did not mention that she had decided to move into the boardinghouse. That would just be another thing for Franz to worry about before his journey. Besides, it was more important that they enjoy each other before Franz left.

On the night before Franz left for Bremen, they treated themselves to a fine meal at the Kaiserhof, one of the grand hotels of Berlin. Franz insisted on it, and they spent a wonderful evening forgetting their present troubles and focusing instead on just being together. The next morning they met at Café Bauer for the last time. Franz carried a small suitcase and was dressed to perfection. He had spent the early hours of the morning pressing his shirt and pants, so he looked as much the private as he had done on the day he walked into her father's dry goods store several years before. His beard was neatly trimmed, and he wore a newly purchased broad-brimmed hat for his journey. "American style," he commented when removing it in the café.

It was a sad departure at the train station. While Franz was typically reserved, Marie was unusually so; they barely spoke to one another before Franz boarded the train, resigning themselves to a desperate clutching of hands. It was hard to believe it was actually happening, that they were going to leave everything behind. In some ways it was much worse for Marie, who faced an unknown delay before their reunion in Springfield. In tears, Marie watched the train crawl out of the station and disappear. She sat there for while, numbed by the prospect of what lay ahead, and it was not until she felt hungry that she realized she had to go out and find a job. She got up and walked slowly out of the station.

IV

The rest of the week was marked by a terrible headache, which had struck Marie on the day Franz left. Having no luck at finding a job, she walked back to her boardinghouse and lay in a darkened room for hours, refusing dinner because of the nausea that consumed her. It was the loneliest night of her life, and the pressure on her head felt like a lead ball rolling from one side of her head to the other. She feared she would die in that room, and that without papers to identify her, no one would be able to inform her family or Franz, who was now cast about on the ocean waves. For the first time in her life, she felt she was a foreigner and might die on foreign soil, in that dreadful little boardinghouse in the middle of Berlin.

The pressure persisted into Wednesday, but she had discovered somewhere in the course of the night that if she propped her head up at precisely the right angle, the pressure and the nausea abated somewhat. That immobilized her, so she couldn't even get up for breakfast or tea. Finally, about mid-morning, someone knocked on her door, then turned the lock. It was the house mother, who kindly brought a hot bowl of beef broth to her bedside.

By Friday afternoon, she was able to walk outside for a few hours before returning to her room. It was good to be out again, to feel her strength returning, but Berlin seemed strange to her now. She could no longer conceive how people summoned the energy to load up wagons and train cars and polish the brass railings of the stores along Unter den Linden. How could life persist amid this din? Even when the first tulips dappled the Tiergarten, Marie could no longer see the pleasures of Berlin. They did not exist for her, just as her family no longer existed.

After recovering from her headache, Marie found a job at a tobacconist's near the boardinghouse. The pay was meager, but it was enough to pay room and board. Without Franz, there was no need to visit the theaters or the cafés any longer. It was enough to sit in her empty room, read from the scriptures, and hope that Franz had made it to Springfield safely.

Almost two months passed and she still hadn't received a note from Franz announcing his arrival. Of course, she would have to go home to find such a letter, and despite her anxiety to hear from him she was incapable of going there right now. It would be months before Franz would send the boat fare anyway, and in the meantime she had found a way to endure this interval through a steady, solitary routine. Although it seemed inevitable that she would go back home sometime, she wanted to enjoy the peace and quiet for now.

It turned out that she did not have to go back; Stefan showed up in the tobacco shop one afternoon. Marie embraced her brother and asked what brought him there.

"You," he said kindly.

"What do you mean? How did you find out I worked here?"

"I've got eyes and ears all over this city," joked Stefan.

"Seriously, how did you know?"

"I just asked the woman at the boardinghouse."

Marie was still puzzled. "But how did you know about the board-inghouse?"

"Father found out. I don't know how, but one night over dinner he mentioned that you were staying here."

"So, did he send you here?" Marie asked.

"No. I came here to give you a few things," Stefan said as he handed her a thick envelope tied with string.

"What is it?"

"Well, there's a letter in there from Frank Franke. I'm assuming that this is our same Private Frank with a new American name."

Marie was ripping open the package to find the letter when some money fell to the ground. "What's this, Stefan?"

Blushing, Stefan admitted that "it is a little something to help you through this difficult time. I figured you would need it for your journey." And then added, "Anna intercepted the letter before Father could find it. When I heard where you were staying, I thought I would bring the letter."

Tears welled up in Marie's eyes. "It is very kind of you to come, Stefan," she said. "Thank you so much for everything. But I have to get back to work."

"I understand, Marie. But listen, you must come home, regardless of what your plans are. I know Father made an offer for you to stay in Berlin and I'm sure the offer still stands."

Marie watched her brother walk out the door and down the street. She was sure that her father had not put Stefan up to this, but she was still angry when she was reminded of his offer. She went back to her room that night and with great anticipation read the short note from Franz stating that he had arrived safely in Springfield. He had gotten a job there already and would send the money as soon as possible.

In order to survive a time fraught with uncertainty, it is sometimes necessary to forget the purpose of your struggles and to limit your purview to the struggles themselves, to accept the anguish as the very terms of existence. Marie had done just that in the months following Franz's departure. Suddenly to be reminded that the goal of her joy-less endurance had been getting nearer and nearer was like emerging from months of life underground. After reading the letter from Franz, life teemed with a sense of possibility again. Everything had color and texture and taste. She wrote Franz a short note that night gratefully acknowledging receipt of his letter and noting that he should send further correspondence to her new address. She ended the note with a promise that she would write again soon.

It was with renewed purpose that she considered visiting her parents the following morning. After all, she would be gone within a few months and would probably never see them again. She had to see them before she left, but she wondered if now was the time. By the time she left for work, however, her thoughts had turned to Franz and to Springfield. The letter had confirmed that it was a real place and that it was the place that she would call home. Whenever she thought of Franz, she imagined him not in a town but at the edge of a great field; perhaps there was a little orchard there filled with cherry trees and apple trees; perhaps there were sunflowers as far as the eye could see. For the first time in her life, she felt that she understood what freedom was.

v

It was not long after Franz's letter arrived that new anxieties surfaced. They began as minor obsessions, but by the end of June they would often send Marie into a panic. She spent hours wondering what would happen if the money were lost in the mail. Franz would have to send more, but that might delay her for another two months, probably until October or November. She had read frightening things about the gales of autumn and was sure that if she were delayed, she would find herself tossed overboard. There was so much to worry about now as there was so much to lose! She might never enjoy the freedom she had envisioned. She might never be able to reunite with Franz. That would be tragic. She wondered whether she deserved such punishment. She had disobeyed her father, and while she stood firmly by her position, she feared misfortune.

It was with this sense of foreboding that in the evening of July 9 she sat down and wrote another short note to Franz. If only he had been around, just talking to him would have calmed her down. He would have assured her that things would be fine. Even more than his assurance, she missed his ability to listen, his deep-set eyes looking at her, the ponderous way he stroked his beard—everything about him, everything she was afraid of losing. She sealed the letter and posted it the following day.

Louis Tuaillon, *Amazon on Horseback*. Sculpture at the eastern edge of the Tiergarten.

Her anxieties persisted and were only made worse when she received the money order from Franz at the beginning of August. Convinced that something terrible would happen on her journey, she knew that it was time to see her family again. She made reservations on the ship departing from Bremen on August 14, which meant that she would leave Berlin on the 13th. She wrote her parents with her departure date, explaining that she wanted to see everyone before she left. Her mother replied with an invitation to dinner on the night of the 12th. With the exception of Stefan, who still visited her on occasion at the tobacco store, Marie had not had contact with her family since the day she left.

The days leading up to the dinner were an emotional time. Marie spent her evenings strolling the streets. She revisited the site of Franz's proposal. She sat on the benches under the linden trees, recalling a conversation or an afternoon together with him. She made a last trip to the Tiergarten to take a final look at the marvelous woods and the statue of the girl on a horse, which had inspired her as a young girl. The city she wanted so desperately to leave was tugging at her now. It would have been easier to make an offering to the city of her youth, to place it on the altar and be done with the past. But with nothing tangible to offer and no place to offer it, she studied instead the haunts of her courtship and her lonely adolescence for evidence of something she could take with her and something she could leave behind. Ever the bookkeeper, she had to admit that what she left behind here would not necessarily show up in another column of the balance sheet. She was leaving her world, and that was her only certainty.

Marie wore her most formal dress—the brown silk one—to dinner with her family in an effort to make an impression of strength, certainty, and dignity. A hired carriage took her back home, just the way she had left. Anna opened the door with tears welling up in her eyes, and fell into Marie's arms. It was going to be a difficult night.

The meal itself was delicious: rabbit, potatoes, and greens. It was as if through their distinctly German preparation, Marie's mother was trying to make a last plea to her daughter to stay home. Herr Weichbrodt frowned at his plate most of the evening and hardly said a word. The conversation was stifled, as her mother always tried to steer it clear of the fact that she wasn't going to see her daughter anymore. After they had cleared the plates, Marie returned to the dining room, where her father sat smoking.

"Well, I have some packing to do still," Marie said. "I should probably go. I think I'll go upstairs and say goodbye to everyone there first."

Herr Weichbrodt continued to puff away, hardly acknowledging his daughter.

When Marie returned from visiting her cousins and her aunt and uncle, she found her family still seated at the dinner table. Herr Weichbrodt, who had not removed his coat, was twirling his mustache. Everyone was waiting for someone else to say something. Marie stood in the dining room looking at her family for the last time. They were all sitting in the same order around the table that they had been accustomed to since first moving to Berlin.

"Well, I suppose it's good-bye then," said Marie.

Stefan was the first to get up and embrace his sister. "Good bye, Marie," he said, and sat down again.

Before Anna stood up, she burst into tears, asking why Marie had to go. "Because I have to," Marie explained calmly, stroking her sister's back.

She next turned to her mother, who gave her a small cameo depicting the profile of a mysterious woman in the manner of a Greek goddess. She said to Marie, "It's for your journey," and kissed her on both cheeks.

Finally, when it came time to say good-bye to her father, Marie was bracing herself for a stern farewell. He stood up, it seemed, for the first time all evening and extended his arms to receive his daughter. He held her there for a moment as she shed tears onto the lapels of his jacket. She could feel his heart thundering away. She couldn't bear to look at him as she walked out the door.

VI

Marie was grateful that Anna and Stefan had decided to see her off at the station the following morning. Completely absorbed with the prospect of her travels, more specifically with the prospect of the waves, Marie welcomed the company of her brother and sister. But when Anna begged Marie not to leave and even accused her of destroying the family, Marie boarded the train with a renewed sense of purpose. There was no turning back now.

Distraction came the following day as well in the incredible press of people boarding the *General Werder* in Bremen.[5] It was as if the whole city had come out for the ship's departure. People from every walk of life streamed aboard the ship, while the rest stood at the docks waving their scarves and playing martial music. As she stood out on the main deck and gazed at the smokestacks that reached up to the low cloud cover hovering over Bremen that morning, Marie was sure she would never again lay eyes on her native shores. Feeling superstitious about the waves, she decided it would be best to wait in her cabin while the ship departed.

As evening approached and there had been no noticeable disturbance since the ship had left Bremen, Marie went upstairs to the main deck for some fresh air and to see what she could see. Fearing that she might break her good luck with the waves, she stepped nervously onto the main deck, but the glorious orange globe of the sun beckoned her from beyond the ship's smokestack. There were small children playing tag, while leagues of travelers shuffled about in the light of the setting sun, some of them talking quietly among themselves as if returning from a funeral. Here and there people erupted in song as well, while others sat alone, preoccupied by the idea of departure or destiny. Making a crooked path across the deck, Marie approached the railing and watched the sun begin its final descent. Expecting to see the churning waters of her oblivion, Marie looked at the sea below. It was dark already in Swinemünde, where the surf surely boomed in protest against the rocks and the gravelly shore, and somewhere out in the vast trenches of the sea, unseen creatures navigated the depths endlessly. Between those two places, however, she stood on the deck marveling as the ship's prow cut through the placid waters. She could feel something men and women had sought in the outer reaches of civilization; it was live and elusive and for a moment enveloped her like the moist air of the sea; the only name she had for it was freedom.

VII

Frank Franke woke up earlier than usual on September 7, 1884, and looked out the window of his small room. It was still dark, but he could see the silhouette of the trees above the houses just west of downtown. He took out his washing bowl and sprinkled water on his face. Removing his pants from his wardrobe, having hung them carefully the night before, he began to dress himself. Before leaving the room, he sat on his bed, said the Our Father, and reached for the most recent letter from Marie announcing her estimated arrival date in New York. Assuming that the ship was on time and that she had arrived in New York on August 29, Frank knew she would be in Springfield any day now. Optimistically, he had gone down to the railroad station two days ago to wait for the first train from Chicago before going to work. He could forego Mother Sherman's breakfast for the third day in a row; there would be plenty of opportunities for breakfast later.

Frank stepped out of Sherman House in the early dawn and walked straight to the station, where no other soul waited. He sat beneath the awning there in his new wool suit and stared at the point where the train tracks curved north out of town. It was absurd to think she would be arriving on the early train, but the little ritual had a calming effect. He simply stared at the railroad ties and thought of Marie for an hour before work and forgot about all the practical troubles that lay ahead: Where would they live? When would they be able to afford a new house? Would he be able to earn enough money to support children?

The Chicago train arrived fifteen minutes late, and after the last person departed there was still no sign of Marie. Frank stood up, dusted his suit, and went to work.

Since he had received Marie's letter, things had gotten better. Life was better still when he learned in a later note that she had received the money and was scheduled to arrive in New York on August 29. For the first time he was enjoying life in Springfield or, perhaps more accurately, he could see how he was going to enjoy life there. Work at Buchner's absorbed almost all of his time and energy. Because there were only three other tailors at the shop, Frank had been asked to do some tailoring after months of only cutting. There was no doubt about it; it was a promotion not in pay but in responsibility and opportunity. There was still a great deal to learn about tailoring, and to work directly with a man as experienced as Mr. Buchner was the best opportunity he could have hoped for.

Frank had to work a little late on August 29, so that by the time he showed up at the station for the evening train from Chicago, a conductor told him the train had arrived on time and was now on its way to St. Louis. It had taken Frank over a week to get from New York to Springfield, but there had been some delays, including an unanticipated night in Chicago, so none of this was surprising. Perhaps Marie too encountered delays or perhaps she had gotten ill during her trip and had to stay in New York to recover.

What he dreaded most at this point was another letter explaining that she hadn't been able to board the ship or had been robbed of her money and so could not afford the train ticket to Chicago. His heart sank a little as he crossed the wooden planks leading up to Sherman House, wondering whether Mother Sherman didn't have a letter buried somewhere in one of her apron pockets. He stood outside for a moment and watched the elegantly dressed young men and women walk toward the nearby theater. A wagon with the name "Blauman Coal" painted in blue across its side was delivering coal to the tavern across the street. It had been a hot summer, but the air was cool and moist this evening, and there was nothing that he might enjoy more than a stroll along the outskirts of town where the dewy grass would soak through his shoes. It was almost half past six, however, and Frank didn't want to miss another meal.

The door of Sherman House stood ajar, perhaps to let the late summer air in. Frank opened the door completely, and as he did so, the light of the evening sun struck the well-varnished hallway floor. A young woman sat next to the registration desk in a white dress appointed with blue flowers along the hem and collar. As he doffed his hat, she stood up suddenly and made a motion toward him. She was beautiful, more beautiful than any woman he had ever seen. She fell into his arms. The air was soft, and the light seemed to be coming from beneath her feet. She was stroking his cheek, and tears were streaming from her pale blue eyes. "Don't ever leave me again," she sobbed.

Frank and Marie Franke exchanged vows once again—this time according to Illinois law—the following day, September 8, 1884, at the city hall in Springfield. Within three weeks, they said their final goodbye to Mother Sherman and the lonely tenants of Sherman House. They rented a small apartment not far from Joseph Buchner's tailoring shop and called it home.

The Catholic church in Lemkendorf, East Prussia.

WARP AND WOOF

I

It was 1906. Mist was still rising from the river, now in a pattern discernible above the surface of the water, now lost to a sudden breeze as quickly as it came. A pair of barn swallows tailed one another in a display of aerial acrobatics in the early autumn air that afforded them such swift and easy passage. The first patches of yellow and red were just beginning to blush on the tips of the maples just beyond the banks, with the noise of ducks and geese converging somewhere over a nearby cornfield. The boys began to fidget. They had been on the river for a few hours, paddling about from one side to the other. Blue stem and buffalo grass on the shallow side of the upcoming bend stood tall. The dry stalks rattled at the slightest breeze, or at the lighting of a house sparrow on the dry, but still pliant leaves. Massive cornfields, heedless of deviation in the nearly featureless landscape, stopped sharply at the river; a simple geometry of columns and rows disrupted into a tumble of abbreviated stalks. A great stand of oaks graced the river's edge, and through the oblong colonnade it made, the shaggy outline of a solitary cottonwood could be discerned. Further off, the roofs of barns and houses appeared to bob gently like puny ships on the horizon, pitched not so much by the waving fields of corn or clover as by the very flatness that granted the eye such extraordinary distances.

The three boys would remember the feeling for the rest of their lives. It was something like the boredom of right field on a long hot afternoon with the ever-distant possibility of a line drive to keep you on your toes, to keep you looking. A man may wake up one morning with his heart full of longing and say, "I am leaving, I am leaving for California," because he doesn't know what else to do with the burning in his chest and is convinced that only a glimpse of the Pacific will satisfy his terrible thirst. So it is with the fisherman, whose vision of a million fish running beneath the hermetic surface of the water drives him to the river. Although the futility of such a vision was evident in the little cyclones that would stir the tree crowns quite suddenly and disappear into the still air as quickly as they came, the idea of a swift, silver thing hidden somewhere in the waters was enough, more than enough to compensate for the impossibility of fulfillment, more than enough incentive to keep looking.

Frank Franke kept stroking his beard, looking ahead and then behind for any disturbance in the water. His feet were still wet from the launching. He looked at his three older sons but didn't say anything. His fourth son, Milton, sat in his lap, nodding off occasionally. Frank's right hand remained on the line, while his left hand circled his chin. This was how his father did it, and so it was how Frank learned to fish. Right hand on the pole with the line wrapped in his hand except for the extension of his index finger forward onto the taut line, like a feeler, just as a spider that seeks to know every dumb whir of its prey through the tiniest vibrations of its web. What was left for the other hand to do but comb the thatch of his beard, so as not to get too dependent on both hands, so as to take some of the waiting off on his chin? None of the boys knew this. He hadn't told them yet. On occasion, he would see Carl mimicking his movements, stroking his beardless chin, but he knew that Carl didn't know because he hadn't told him yet. *When thou doest alms, let not thy left hand know what thy right hand doeth.* His father used to quote these words of Christ every time they went fishing back in Derz when he was a boy. And then Herr Frank would explain that the apostles were fishermen and that fishing was thus a sacred activity, like almsgiving. It was peculiar logic but had become so familiar that Frank had all but forgotten what made it strange. So he continued to stroke his beard out of habit.

Frank rested his elbow on the side of the boat. It was a wooden boat painted white with a light blue stripe along the side. Although he didn't own it, Frank came to think of it as his boat. He rented it from a German farmer, always the same boat, when he fished the Illinois River. There was nothing particularly special about it. It was a standard rowboat that, if pressed, could seat six, but seated two or four comfortably. There were three wooden benches separated by even intervals across the length of the boat, two oar sockets in the middle for rowing alone, and hooks along the side for extra oars. Raising his elbow from the side of the boat, Frank straightened his slouching shoulders with a quick jerk of his spine as if to assure anyone that might be looking that he was stretching. He ordered his sons Carl and Otto to row to the other side of the river where the water moved faster. Bill, his third son, pulled in his line, set the long bamboo pole along the inside length of the boat and leaned lazily on the bow. The youngest son, Milton, although he was not old enough to understand any possible strategy in moving to the other side of the river, watched his family intently from the lap of his father between naps.

All the children thought of their father as old. In part, this was due to his powerful presence, or more precisely, the enormous authority he held over them. Such authority made him seem old, beyond the baffling hierarchy of father and son. Primarily, however, they all thought of him as old because of the long gray beard he favored. In fact, Frank was only forty-six years old. But the only people that looked like him were the last soldiers from the Civil War, whose presence on the streets of downtown Springfield suggested tools of a former age, perfectly usable but somehow made obsolete by the argument of progress. These old soldiers barely needed to speak to one another because they already knew each other's stories, and when they did converse, they would tell each other the same story of bygone days that they had told before. To the boys, these men with their funny-looking beards, their broad-brimmed hats, and their weary smiles seemed to represent an age more ancient than the days of chivalry. Although their father was born but a year before the Civil War began and five thousand miles away in East Prussia—it may as well have been China to them—he retained something of the old soldiers' air. There were many other Germans around town, but few that looked like their father. Especially when he went fishing and he wore the gray three-piece suit—the same suit he went to work in—beneath his big straw fishing hat, their father looked as though he belonged to a period in history the boys could only dimly recall from tedious afternoons in school. In any case, he looked old, out of time, and when he tipped his hat to one of those other Germans on the street, even on occasion to one of the old Civil War soldiers, the boys sensed an expression in that exchange that could only be described as loss.

On this particular day, Bill was on the bench up front in the bow; Carl and Otto sat on the middle bench, rowing on either side. Although only thirteen, Bill was already bigger than his older brothers Carl, almost nineteen,[1] and Otto, fifteen. His brown knickers were already dirtied from a slip on the banks of the river, though somehow he had managed to spare his shirt and tie. The tails of his white shirt dipped below the bench and grazed the top of a mason jar filled with lemonade; it was impossible for Bill to keep those tails tucked in his knickers.

His oldest brother was the exact opposite in appearance. Carl's features were finer, sharper than Bill's, which were mild and almost gentle. Of all the Franke children, Carl least resembled his siblings. Frank Franke's face was long, emphasized by a long, prominent nose; Carl's nose, by comparison, was dainty. While his eyes had the same shape as his mother's and the dark brown color of his father's, Carl did not look like either of his parents, except for the downward turn on the left side of his lips when he held his mouth closed, which was identical to the curl of his mother's mouth. His carriage, however, bore a studied resemblance to his father. Carl walked like his father, held his hands like his father, and dressed as immaculately as his father, if a bit more fashionably. Frank always taught his children to dress well, no matter what the circumstances were. He would quote scripture as justification: Jesus told his disciples to wash themselves and keep a clean appearance while fasting so that no one would know of their sacrifice except God. But, in truth, there was another reason for preaching such fastidious appearance. It came from his days in the German army when Frank was lifting himself out of poverty. As long as one is presentable, people are less likely to ask about one's origins. Furthermore, the art of tailoring involves not only fitting and fashioning jackets and pants but the implicit belief that a well-tai-lored suit can raise a man's spirits and that an accurate cut can actu-ally provide a standard to which the customer can raise himself. Of all the children, Carl took this belief most to heart, with the result that he never left the house without a hat, coat, and tie, even if just to buy a loaf of bread. A well-dressed man commanded respect, and, as the representative of the rich tradition of the Franke family, Carl thought it his duty to encourage the honor due to his family.

Because there was such a large age gap between Milton and his older brothers, Otto was effectively the middle brother, and his tem-perament lay decidedly between Bill and Carl. Sharing his older brother's habit of impeccable appearance—his hair was always neatly parted, and his clothes were freshly pressed even as he sat on the fishing boat that morning—Otto took his father's penchant for order to an extreme. He was methodical to the point of obsession, and it was precisely this depth of need that distinguished him from Carl and, incidentally, connected him to his brother Bill. Already a prom-ising mechanic, Otto eschewed the social graces of his older brother for a single-minded dedication to true order, which resulted in an emerging pragmatism that he could share with his younger brother. As long as a thing was doing what it was supposed to be doing, there was order. Decorum was his older brother's territory; Otto just wanted to make sure that things got done. It was precisely this focus that gave Otto an altogether rougher expression than his brothers. It was perhaps that burning for an order beyond what the world can offer that made his pressed white shirt seem like an awkward prop, but the wiry frame beneath the starched collar and wool pants gave him an intensity that his brothers lacked.

A bucket of river water swimming with minnows was placed as near to the middle of the boat as possible, just back from where Otto and Carl were sitting. Next to the bucket sat a tin can full of dirt and night crawlers in case the fish weren't taking the minnows. Beneath the backbench of the rowboat, Frank kept the tackle box. Although it had been quite cool when the day began, it was already beginning to warm up. Even Milton, who was so cold that morning, began to make noises about the heat, and poked his blond head out from beneath his father's beard. Whenever they went out, Milton stuck to his father. Only three years old, he already had a special connection to his father.

Frank, younger by ten years or more than most of his own brothers and sisters,[2] felt a special affinity for his youngest son, who had to contend with the stormy egos of adolescent siblings. Both Frank and Marie doted on Milton, but no one in the family minded. Marie was forty-six now, and there was little chance of another Franke child coming along.

Frank sat at the stern with his feet forward, Milton beside him. He navigated with gestures of his left hand, barking at Carl to pull harder, to straighten out the boat, to make a straight course to the other side of the river. Otto just buried his oar deeper in the water, never looking up, almost if he was studying the water for something he'd lost. When they found a shady spot among the weeds near the far bank, Frank told them to stop. The waters gathered near an outcropping of rocks and oaks. They remained in the calm shallows and cast their lines on either side of the boat into the weedy waters in hopes of landing a bass.

Still they had no luck. They had some bites, but caught only a few small fish. In short, they had no keepers. They needed a real fish in the boat to justify their trip. Every dark or shiny spot on the surface of the water held hope for the boys, and every ripple made them grow more impatient.

"They're just not biting today," Carl said, disrupting another half-hour of no fish on the stringer.

Frank knew that the boys wanted to quit, but he had no intention of leaving the river without at least a dozen or more bass for dinner. What kind of fisherman could he call himself if he were unable to bring home a halfway decent catch? What kind of father would he be if he couldn't get his sons to stick with it, to show some patience, and to bring home bragging rights as fishermen for the women at home?

Otto pulled his line in and recast further up the river, letting the current carry his minnow and sinker downstream without allowing either to touch the river bottom. When a few empty cans floated toward the boat, Frank ordered Carl to steer them in with the end of his oar; anything that upset the majesty of the river, especially when he was fishing, troubled Frank. Just as Carl was leaning over the side of the boat to pull in the cans, Bill stood up on the uneven planks that tapered near the bow.

"Over there, look, look!"

Pointing out a bass jumping on the river, Bill promptly received a wet slap from the broad side of Carl's oar on his shoulder.

"Get down or you'll tip the boat, you idiot!" Frank shouted. Bill felt the hard tug of Carl's hand pull him down by the collar of his shirt. Sure enough, the boat pitched wildly at first, but gradually righted itself.

No one said anything. Frank shook his head as if to say, "How many times do I have to tell you this," while Carl just looked disgusted. It was a look both treacherous and humiliating, as only an older brother in possession of sheer physical advantage can produce. Bill felt stupid and angry. He cast toward the shallow waters and stewed in his humiliation and growing indignation. There was a time when Carl had played a trick on their father. Everyone knew there would be trouble, but as long as Carl was willing to do it, the others agreed. At first Mayme, Carl's twin sister, had resisted, warning Carl of what would come, but he prevailed. Their father was lying on the couch in the long summer afternoon, dreaming of breezes sweeping down from the Baltic Sea. Carl tiptoed over to the couch and lofted a paper triangle tied to a rubber band into the thicket of their father's long beard. He then scurried back and hid among the rest of the kids. Untwisting in his beard, the rubber band made a buzzing sound, and within a minute, their father woke. Normally a man of few words, he sprang up from the couch, fire in his eyes, and strode toward his children with a flurry of questions: "Which one of you did this? Was it you? Was it you? Or was it both of you?" This was sprinkled with phrases in German that no one understood. Finally, he lined up all the children, military-style, with the exception of Milton, and asked each one whether he or she had done it or knew who had done it. All of them, even Bill, who had had his doubts about the whole thing in the first place, answered with a firm no. And they all got the paddle.[3]

And now, here was Carl, acting totally superior, as if he had never done anything stupid or out of line in his life, letting out his line just like his father and stroking his beardless chin just like his father.

Carl turned to Bill and smiled mockinglyy. Bill lunged at his older brother.

"Stop!" Frank shot them a hard, cold look.

Neither Carl nor Bill would look directly at their father. They felt his eyes upon them, but pretended to let go of their own accord. As

Carl let go of Bill's shoulder, Bill gave him a short shove in the back for good measure. When Carl discovered the faint traces of Illinois River mud on his freshly pressed shirt, he could barely contain himself. It was an offense not only to him but also to the business and his future. It took everything in him to resist tossing Bill into the river. He eventually settled on boxing Bill's ears.

Their father let it go for a while, still hot from Bill's having stood up in the boat in the first place. Finally, Frank struck the side of the boat with his pole and glared at Carl. It was at this prompting that Carl ceased boxing his younger brother's ear and recast into deeper waters.

II

Along with his twin sister Mayme, Carl was the eldest of the siblings. As the eldest male, he was both blessed and burdened.

There were many things that Carl's father had left behind in East Prussia when he set sail for America. He left his family and his hometown. He left Catholicism and many of the old ways of life. But on this day Frank would uphold one of the old customs, firm in his resolve to do so.

Back in East Prussia it was customary that the firstborn son would inherit the family's estate, however large or meager it might be. There was both a practical and a religious purpose to this tradition. At the beginning of the nineteenth century, when Napoleon was swiftly conquering Europe, he established the Code Napoleon wherever his armies marched. Born of Enlightenment ideals, the Code was largely liberal, guaranteeing personal liberty, equality before the law, and private property. It also eradicated the privilege of primogeniture, thus guaranteeing a family's estate to be equally divided among the children. Because of his determination to meet the Russian army decisively, however, Napoleon bypassed East Prussia, so the code was not adopted there. By the time Franz was born in 1860, only three generations after the Code was established throughout most of Western Europe, the estates of the western part of Prussia were reduced to a sliver of their former vastness. As each generation grew, so the original estate was cut up among siblings, their children, and their children's children. As a result, the East Prussians took particular pride in primogeniture, and the great estates of East Prussia bore witness to

The cemetery at Derz.

their judicious decision, maintaining the integrity and pageantry of old ways rarely, if ever, seen west of Berlin.

There was a religious origin to primogeniture as well. Throughout the Bible, the firstborn son had rights to the father's blessings. In effect, this meant that the first son would inherit the property. This ensured the integrity of the estate and provided evidence for the ancestry of the Messiah. The Gospel of Luke offers a clear genealogy: Jesus was a direct descendant of David and, in turn, of Abraham. Thus biblical precedent justified primogeniture, with one troubling exception, rarely referred to among the Catholics of East Prussia. Anyone who had some familiarity with the Bible knew that Jacob, the very name of Israel, was not, in fact, the first son of Isaac and Rebekah but came out of the womb on the heel of his brother Esau. Jacob tricked Isaac into believing that he was Esau in order to receive the father's blessing. This was an outlandish form of treachery; almost unforgivable, yet it was forgiven and even sanctioned by the Lord himself. It certainly presented a conundrum for someone unschooled in theological debate.

Until he was thirteen, Franz attended Catholic school in Lemkendorf, a small town a few miles down the road from Derz, as did all the children in Derz and Lemkendorf. Franz's family attended Mass at the church. His Father's family had been baptized there for generations, and the church cemetery held the remains of his forebears.[4] There Franz learned to read, primarily from scripture, and to write. He was also taught the rudiments of the sciences, mathematics, and history. At the end of every school day, and after Mass on Sunday, the students were required to review stories from the Bible. At times, one of the priests from the parish would come in and paraphrase a story, sometimes quoting directly from the Bible. At other times, the students were ordered to read from the Bible themselves, while one of the nuns kept a strict eye on them.

Frank never forgot the day he first heard the story of Jacob and his deception. He was only fourteen years old, recently confirmed and in his last year of catechism. He had already come to understand his lot in life. He would either become a priest or head off to Berlin for factory work. He understood that he neither had the right to acquire the meager property of his parents nor would ever find the means to purchase any property. As much as he loved the rivers and lakes surrounding Derz, he realized that a life of wandering and day labor among the potato fields and cabbage plots was not for him. Frank was approaching the hour of his decision: the priesthood or Berlin.

He knew very little about Berlin. Grim stories about the city circulated among his extended family and the migrant field workers. Rather than the more common image of a bustling, modern city, Franz's primary impression of Berlin, as described by his relatives, was that of a grayish yellow fog hanging over the city and covering everything, from the factories in Wedding to the buckets of dirty brown coal in every tenement courtyard. The endless crowds of people hurrying every which way, whether for food or work or church. As for the living conditions, there were apartments no bigger than a chicken coop for a family of ten, and courtyards so foul even a pig would raise its snout at the stench. Certainly there were stories of wealth, but of wealth beyond the opportunity of villagers, and so mostly outside of their interest. In the end, Berlin to them was a necessary Gomorrah: full of corruption and vice, yes, but also full of jobs for people like them with little education and no place else to turn.

On the other hand, there was the priesthood. Franz had great respect for priests, as any child growing up in Derz did. Priests not only

had the privilege of saying Mass every day but were instrumental in
every village celebration, be it a wedding or baptism or harvest festival.
Priests were at the heart of village social life, and they commanded a
great deal of respect from everyone. Even the wealthiest villagers
sought the blessings of the pastor. And for a person in Franz's position,
the priests had it pretty good. They had to teach and tend to the congregation's needs, performing the sacraments sometimes at odd hours
of the night, but never once did they have to break their backs lifting
potato sacks onto a wagon bound for Allenstein. The church always
took care of them, modest as their needs might be. In the end, however, Franz recognized that he had no vocation. He certainly believed
in God and stood firmly behind the church, but when it came to
thinking about a life, he felt no passion, no calling, for the priesthood.

Franz had never questioned the fact that his eldest brother would
inherit his parent's house and the small plot of land behind it. This
had been a foregone conclusion. And then came that day when he discovered Jacob's story.

It was the feast of Corpus Christi, and everyone was dressed in his
or her finest apparel. Franz wore a jacket that his older brother August had outgrown, a high collar mounting his chin and a large bow
tie nearly the size of his face. Although cracked near the toes and split
in the back above the heels, his boots were immaculately polished.
He had spent the whole of the previous evening polishing them for
the occasion. After Mass, all the villagers of Derz and Lemkendorf assembled in front of the church and began the procession. In their
First Communion clothes, the children led the procession with
flowers falling from their fingers to make a carpet for the approaching Eucharist. Three makeshift altars were placed around the village
square and another altar on the road leading from Lemkendorf to
Derz. Altar boys, clergy, and prominent citizens with guild and society banners of silk followed. Franz's family gathered beneath the ban-
ner of The Brotherhood under the Invocation of the Lord of Transformation.[5] The procession approached each makeshift altar in the
square. The priest followed, bearing the Holy Eucharist in a mon-
strance beneath an embroidered silk canopy held by four posts. The
procession parted as the priest approached the altar. There the
Blessed Sacrament rested while the congregation kneeled to pray and
sing in adoration.

O saving Victim opening wide
The gate of heaven to man below!
Our foes press on from every side;
Thine aid supply, Thy strength bestow.
To Thy great name be endless praise,
Immortal Godhead, one in three;
O, grant us endless length of days
In our true native land with Thee.
Amen.[6]

Along with the harvest festival and Christmas, the feast of Corpus Christi was one of the best holidays of the year. Everyone in the village came out for the procession, even those who didn't attend church regularly. Something about the banners and the music made people want to join in. It was also the last holiday before the frantic activity of the growing season.

After the procession, Franz went back to school for catechism. One of the priests from church came in to explain the meaning of Corpus Christi to the students. Given that the rest of East Prussia was predominately Protestant, and given the recent attacks on the Catholic Church coming from Chancellor Bismarck himself, the priest was adamant about teaching the difference between Catholics and Protestants. The feast of Corpus Christi was an obvious time to demonstrate those differences. Most of this, however, was lost on the students. Their main concern was whether or not they would have to go further away in order to attend a German school rather than the Catholic school in which they had grown up.

As soon as the priest finished his explanation of the feast, the class picked up where it had left off the previous week. They were going over all the stories from Genesis in order to have a proper understanding of the genealogy of the people in the Bible and to understand how Christ fulfills that genealogy. The priest read directly from the Bible, sometimes paraphrasing, at other times pausing for commentary. He began with Jacob's story.[7]

Jacob was born on the heel of Esau. Isaac and Rebekah knew Jacob was to be the favorite son, despite the fact that he was the second son. God told them so. Rebekah remembered this, but Isaac seemed

Adolph Menzel, *Corpus Christi Procession 1880*. Bavarian State Collection, Munich.

to forget over time. When he was still young, Esau came home exhausted after a hunt. Jacob appeared with food, and Esau begged for some. Jacob said he would feed him only on the condition that Esau should forfeit his birthright. Blinded by his immediate corporal desires, Esau agreed and gave his birthright to Jacob.

Here the priest interrupted the story to explain that the birthright represents the name and profession of religion and that Esau's relinquishment of the birthright is a lesson in the vanity of earthly satisfactions. He who is willing to throw away the responsibility of religion for a trifle does not deserve its privileges.

The priest continued: Now Isaac was old and blind and ready to bestow his blessing on Esau. He called Esau and told him to go hunting and to bring some venison, of which Isaac would eat and then bless Esau. As Esau went off to the fields, Rebekah fetched Jacob and insisted that he should deceive Isaac by disguising himself as Esau and so secure the blessings of the father. Rebekah prepared her own venison and sent the disguised Jacob to Isaac. When Isaac asked, "Are

Altar of Lemkendorf Catholic Church in 2000 (LEFT).
Church pews that Frank Franke occupied 1860–1875 (RIGHT).

you my very son Esau?" Jacob replied with a simple, "I am." After a series of questions, Jacob obtained the blessing of the father.

When Esau returned, he wept bitter tears before his father. Again,
the priest interrupted to comment: "The day is coming when those
that now make light of the blessings of the covenant, and sell their
title for a trifle, will seek those blessings in vain."

Half the class was dozing at this point, some of them struggling
to keep their eyes open for fear of getting a rap on the knuckles,
some staring slack-jawed at the bright light of the afternoon just beyond the window. The other half of the class twitched and shifted
in their seats. Franz was simply bewildered. The tension was palpable. The students were ready to leave. It was the last afternoon before they would begin the almost ceaseless work of the growing season, and the priest was well aware of this. The sun was shining, the
day was still long, and there would be great dinners that evening—
chicken or goose or, in the most fortunate houses, lamb. The priest
dismissed the class early, and the students squeezed through a tiny
doorway to get back into the light of day. Franz was slow to get up
from his seat, but he had no intention of asking the priest any questions.

A few friends waited for Franz outside the church. He told them to
go on without him, that he planned to walk by one of the creeks just
off the road to Derz to see if his brothers were fishing there. In truth,

he knew his brothers would be fishing at a small lake outside of Derz. He just wanted to be alone.

The story of Jacob and Esau troubled Franz. It went against every notion of fairness he had ever learned. Yes, Esau was wrong to throw away his birthright, but wasn't Jacob wrong to bribe it out of Esau? And, even more so, wasn't it wrong of Jacob to lie to Isaac about who he was?

It was still early in the afternoon, so he walked out beyond the fields to follow the creek for a while. The sky was perfectly clear, and the earth warm and soft beneath his feet. From just above the creek bed he could see the scrubby potato fields where he had worked with his father the previous week. A mellow breeze came in through the ash trees along the banks of the creek, cooling the air to an ideal temperature. The story raced through his mind again; the creek was quiet as he hopped among the rocks and fallen branches. If God knew that Jacob was to be the greater of the two sons, then why didn't he make Jacob the first son instead of Esau? As it is, the story lacks consistency, and God appears to break his own rules by privileging Jacob, who has to lie to obtain the birthright. It simply didn't make any sense.

Franz stopped for a moment and grabbed onto the trunk of a tree as if to brace himself. The sun shone in discrete rays through the trees. Several beams gathered at one point on the creek, and Franz moved in for a closer look. Trout swam effortlessly through the stream, some pausing to take a fly off the surface, others darting among the sunken rocks.

"How can anyone justify the ways of God to men?" Franz whispered.

He felt as he had never felt before. He was angry but his anger had no object. A slab of limestone carpeted in moss lay in the middle of the creek, water pouring on either side of it. Franz sprang from another slab on the bank of the creek, but as soon as his foot met the slick mossy rock, he fell flat on his back. Flecks of foam gathered around his pant leg. His wrist hurt, and his right shin was bleeding. He stood up in the water, his brother's coat sopping from the damp moss. All the fish had cleared from that part of the stream. The wind barely stirred above him. Whatever noise there was before, whether it was water or crickets or the buzz of his thoughts, suddenly stopped. Everything looked strange. The creek kept changing colors, but the more it changed, the more it appeared the same. He imagined his mother and father. They were eating soup at the dinner table. It was an old pine table, darkened with the years, nothing special about it, yet it now looked earthen, almost tomblike, a crude mausoleum of four columns of clay and a mud slab across. His father's hands looked smaller than normal. In fact, they seemed positively tiny. Frank stood in the creek for several minutes staring into a middle distance. In his mind, he could see his parents as clear as day. He watched his mother washing the pot for soup by the well down the road, his father going over the same old ground with a shovel and a plain pick. They were both so small and frail.

Leaning forward, Franz dipped his cupped hands into the moving stream. Several times he let the water fall on his face. The cool water felt soothing on his wrist. Having cleaned his cut thoroughly in the stream, he walked straight across the creek, not even bothering to look for a dry path. His boots squelched and leaked at the seams. He walked diagonally across the field toward where he thought the road was. An inconsolable loneliness overcame him. He tried to slough it off. A summer breeze blew his straw hat off his head.

Eventually he found the road to Derz. Looking behind him for the church in Lemkendorf, he let his eyes follow the treetops to the steeple. The cross appeared dimly over the village. Above, a pair of crows circled. The sky was so blue, Franz could barely believe his own eyes. He wished he had never listened to the priest tell the story. He wished that it was yesterday and that he didn't know what he knew now.

III

As Frank sat in the boat with his sons, the water was quiet. Then the bass was there. None of them saw it, but it was as if he knew it, understood exactly what his father had spoken of, that you can feel the fish approaching like an electric current in the water. Otto would remember that feeling for the rest of his life. The feeling was the line, the anticipation of where the fish would be, what the fish was thinking, but the feeling was the knowing, knowing as if conversing for the very first time. The line moved of its own power.

A few ripples were still bouncing back and forth between the banks from a grain barge that had passed them a few minutes before. Otto's father leaned forward and spoke at almost a whisper, half in German, half in English, instructing him on how to bring in the fish. It wasn't as if Otto had never caught a fish before. He'd been fishing with his father a dozen times or more. Bass, carp, gar, blue gill, sunfish—he'd caught them all before. His father had been with him, had seen him. But this time things were different. Otto knew it. And his father knew it.

It was the knowing that was different. Frank had pulled in his line and noticed that his minnow was dead and half-mangled. He had then set his pole inside the boat and leaned forward to the middle of the boat in order to grab another minnow. Leaning over the minnow bucket, he had caught something out of the corner of his left eye. Otto's arm was twitching slightly. He wasn't moving the pole noticeably, but Frank could see Otto's arm muscles twinge rhythmically. Then in a quick, confident motion, Otto jerked his pole to ten o'-clock and had the bass. Just as Frank had taught him.

For a moment he was elated, letting out a guttural "whoop" over the river. Then he leaned over Otto's shoulder and settled into a half-whisper, almost as if to compensate for his unusual shout a moment before. His voice was gravelly.

"Not too fast, not too fast. Feel his strength. Let him swim. Tire him out. You don't want to lose him."

By this time Bill had pulled his pole inside the boat and was watching intently. Carl ignored the whole scene and cast into the river near the spot Otto had originally hooked up in the hopes that there might be more fish where Otto landed his. Frank continued, now mumbling to himself between instructions.

"Just as I said, just as I said. You know what to do."

Otto calmly pulled in the fish. It was a beautiful eighteen-inch bass, perfect for pan-frying. Frank was nearly beside himself. He kept slapping Otto on the back and laughing. Bill was laughing too. Their patience and persistence had yielded the most precious fruit. Otto held the flipping fish in place on the bottom of the boat and removed the hook from the its mouth adroitly. Frank handed him the chain as Otto held the bass in his right hand, his thumb placed carefully over the fins so as to avoid cutting himself. With his left hand Otto opened the bottom link of the chain, deftly stringing the fish through the gill and out of the mouth. He set the fish down and tied the string around the oar socket. Frank had ceased slapping and mumbling. Otto picked up the fish and gently placed it back in the river.

Carl was watching now, mesmerized by the skill and dispatch with which Otto handled the fish. It was as if he were watching a black-smith pounding out horseshoes, or a glassblower making a simple gob-let—activities so familiar, so much a part of the craftsman's trade as if to be second nature and thus pleasing and somehow reassuring to wit-ness. But where had Otto gained such experience? He'd been with him on nearly every fishing trip. He knew that Otto was good, a natural some might say, but Otto was in full possession of himself today.

As Otto turned back toward the others, his father smiled at him and put his right hand forward. He shook his son's hand proudly, warmly. Otto was sheepish, his head buried in his chest, his arm flap-ping from his father's enthusiasm. It was the proudest day of his life.

IV

By the time they took a break for lunch, Otto had caught two more fish. Bill and Carl caught two apiece, albeit significantly smaller than Otto's catch, and both were a little miffed at their brother's fortunes, but Otto's unflappable demeanor helped to reduce tension. He nei-ther gloated over his prowess nor spoke too much about his luck. In short, he gave them nothing to work with, so they gradually came to accept his success. Frank, on the other hand, was frustrated by his own failure to catch any fish, but he still felt pride at his son's accom-plishment. He also recognized a connection, if only for a moment, between himself and Otto. Something about the way Otto went about his business—calmly, efficiently, and without a shred of arro-gance. Something about the knowing that passed between them. Yes, he had taught him, as he was teaching Carl and Bill, as he was teach-ing his daughters too, and as he would come to teach Milton. They would all learn, he was sure of that. With Otto it was different only in that he could see himself so clearly thirty years earlier in a tiny row-boat with his father and brothers. When he saw Otto's arm twitch-ing, he could see his own arm. When he watched Otto pulling in the fish, it was as if he were pulling it in himself.

They pulled the boat up to a sandy spot on the bank. Bill got out first and then Carl. Frank lifted Milton from the back bench and handed him to Carl, who was standing on the shore, one foot still in the water. Frank then held the boat for Otto as he stepped on shore. Carl and Otto pulled the boat three quarters of the way out of the

Helen, aged nine, circa 1906.

water and followed Frank and Bill up a low bluff, where they were met with a flurry of questions.

"How many did you catch? How many did you catch? I caught three big ones. Do you want to see? Over there, down by the river." Helen twirled about her older brothers in a long, white summer dress embellished with floral embroidery. Helen's smile, her ten-year-old enthusiasm, and her delight to be in other people's company infected everyone she met.

"So? How many did you catch?" Elizabeth asked the boys with skepticism.

"We did just fine," Carl told her abruptly. "There'll be plenty tonight."

"Can we see?"

"Not now. I'm starving. Have you made lunch yet?"

To which Elizabeth responded by pointing to a low willow where her mother and her older sister Mayme had spread two patchwork blankets and all the fixings for a picnic. The girls had agreed to meet the boys at the appointed hour. While Helen wanted to go fishing in a boat, both Elizabeth and Mayme preferred to stay away from their father on fishing expeditions — it could be such a challenge — and so remainded in the relative safety of the sandy banks. The morning had been successful for them: Elizabeth and Helen each caught three good-sized bass, while Mayme landed two. Their mother kept an eye on them from the shade of the willow, reserving her energy for cooking the fish later that evening. The three of them made quite a vision along the gently rippling surface of the Illinois River. With the tall, faded grasses swaying beside them, Marie's daughters in their white dresses looked like the three Graces come to bless the river with their bamboo poles. It was a pleasure to sit by the waters, just listening to the wind stirring the willow leaves; there was no need to upset the quiet by catching more fish.

It turned out to be a perfect day. The long, hot, busy summer had afforded few opportunities to get away on a Saturday like this. While Carl, Mayme, and Otto went to work every day, Elizabeth, Bill, Helen, and Milton were still at home. On top of cooking and cleaning — which usually took Marie through morning, noon and night — there was also the bookkeeping. Ever since Frank had opened his own merchant tailor's shop in 1894,[8] Marie did all the bookkeeping for the business.[9] A fabulous accountant, she brought an almost military rigor to the books, which delighted Frank. While the work required none of the tediousness of doing the books for Weichbrodt Imported Dry Goods, she still had to squeeze it in after the dishes had been washed. The business had been growing steadily over the last ten years. They had seen Frank's former employers Buchner and S.J. Willett retire,[10] so that many of those customers came to Frank. While not doing as much in the way of tailoring suits from whole cloth, Frank seemed to be cuffing pants and letting out the waists for all of Springfield's businessmen. In short, business was good, and life was very busy for the family, so a sunny afternoon under a willow in early September was no less than a blessing.

A trace of the morning's chill remained in the air as Mayme laid out the plates and cups and little silverware sets wrapped in gingham napkins. While there was no specific identifying feature, Mayme bore a significant resemblance to her mother. Rather than the shape or color of the eye, it might have been the hint of worry on their faces that connected Marie and Mayme in this way. Or perhaps it was the fact that both were the eldest daughters. Mayme and Carl, though twins, neither looked nor acted alike. Instead, they stood like sentinels on either end of the family; Carl bossed his brothers and sisters around while Mayme followed to make sure they weren't making too much of a mess.

Elizabeth raced ahead of her brothers to assist her mother and Mayme in setting out cured German sausages, a jar of mustard, a half-gallon jar of pickles, two loaves of dark pumpernickel, a small wheel of cheddar, and the last of the season's peaches. As the boys came under the shade of the willow, Elizabeth gave each of them two sausages and two pieces of pumpernickel. Elizabeth bore some resemblance to her older sister but not to her mother. Her nose was more prominent, like her father's, and her lips were fuller, like Mayme's. Yet there was something about her eyes, a mildness that she had in common with Bill and brought the pale blue eyes of her mother to mind.

Otto was the first to take up a knife; he split his sausage in two, spread mustard generously across the pumpernickel, and set the sausage on top for an open-faced sandwich. Everyone else soon followed, Elizabeth passing two large mason jars filled with lemonade. After saying grace, the whole family sat down on the two patchwork blankets and began eating. The wind picked up a bit, but was never consistent enough to be called a breeze. Frank stared at the boat down below the sandy banks and gazed out at the river. They were looking east, back toward Springfield. The land was perfectly flat, as if God himself had swept away any deviations in the landscape that might mar the perfect line formed by the conjugation of heaven and earth. The farmhouses looked even smaller from their vantage on the bluff. A few grain elevators and steeples were the only things piercing the horizon line. At the farthest limit to the eye, an assembly of buildings and cranes marked the spot of the latest strip mine.

Bill had consumed both sausages before his father had prepared his own sandwich. The lemonade was still slightly cold and very tart.

Bill was eating plain bread with mustard now, wondering if he might be lucky enough to get a third sausage.

"When I first came here almost twenty years ago there was still prairie grass over there," Frank announced suddenly, gesturing to the northeast. "It came right up to the edge of the river where those cornstalks are now. I remember descriptions of the prairie grass in the advertisements in Berlin—like the ocean, they said, but ready to be farmed."

"What advertisements?" Carl asked, sipping his lemonade.

Looking south and gazing north along the river, Frank replied, "At that time, there were advertisements all over Berlin—in the papers, in magazines, in the beer halls. There were men whose sole job was to hand out pieces of paper selling land in Illinois, Wisconsin, and Missouri. The advertisements were always the same—best farmland in the world, the Promised Land, a new Eden. Some of them had descriptions of the waves the prairie made. Some of them had descriptions of Chicago. I'd never seen the ocean at that time. We were saving up money to come here. When I finally got here in 1884, I took the train from Chicago to Springfield. I remember looking for those prairies all the way from Chicago. What I saw most were cornfields, sometimes fields of clover. I was so glad to be here that I didn't care if the prairies had vanished. But I remember coming out here with Mr. Buchner to go fishing. He was the man I first worked for when I moved here. It was around this time of year, maybe a little bit earlier. We took the train over to Beardstown and then rented a wagon to get to the river. I remember when I first saw that undulating mass of prairie grass, I couldn't believe my eyes. The grass was so tall! We came on the wagon through a path in the prairie. It was like being in the woods. It wasn't like the ocean. Maybe from a distance, maybe from the noise it made. The sound was like waves rolling against the side of a boat. Mr. Buchner told me that this was the last stretch of prairie in all of Illinois, that everything else had been turned into railroad property, farmland, or a site for a town.[11] It was funny. When I was in Berlin, I always thought of what it would look like. I always thought of these prairies. I don't know why, somehow the descriptions stuck in my mind. It wasn't like anything I thought it would look like. That beautiful expanse of grass grew out of the deepest black loam soil I had ever seen. It was beautiful. I remember that."

The children were taken aback. They had never heard their father speak like this before. They could barely recall a time when they had heard anything other than commands from him. Even Marie was surprised by her husband's sudden gregariousness. It was strange, even a little disconcerting. He had always been so focused on work or problems with the house—fixing something or working late into the night on a customer's suit or shirt. It was as if the children had been on a sea journey for years and caught a sudden glimpse of a continent they hadn't known to exist previously. Their father had had a life completely unknown to them.

Carl, sensing the opportunity, pressed a little further.

"What was Berlin like?"

Frank seemed annoyed by the question. He turned away from Carl, saying, "Oh, it was nothing. Big city, like Chicago. It was dirty—terribly dirty." And the conversation appeared to have come to an end. They sat for a while like that—Carl a little uneasy at his father's apparent displeasure, and Marie still curious about her husband's sudden divulgence of their past life. Bill finally broke the silence and asked for a peach. Elizabeth reached into a basket and pulled out a big, juicy one. She handed it down to her younger brother and then she distributed peaches to everyone. Mayme carefully cut up one of the peaches and offered it to little Milton, who was now sitting in his mother's lap.

Marie reminded Frank that they had to catch the four o'clock train out of Beardstown, which meant that the boys had to be out of the boat by three. Frank checked his pocket watch; it was still only noon, so they had plenty of time for more fishing. Carl spoke up again, asking where and how they would fish after lunch. After some consideration, Frank thought it might be best to throw an anchor somewhere toward the middle of the river. Far enough away from the middle, he said, so that they wouldn't meet up with any of the barge traffic, but close enough so that they could cast into the deepest water. "It might be getting too hot for the good fish," Frank concluded.

Finishing his lemonade, Bill noticed something out of the corner of his eye. At first he thought it was a gigantic fish leaping from the river. He set his empty cup down in a patch of dry grass and perceived instead the dark silhouette of a slender-necked bird stepping gingerly among a stand of cattails on the far bank just north of where they

were. A cool wind came from the direction of the bird. He studied it for a while not knowing what it was. It appeared from this distance to have long, dark cords of hair dangling from the back of its neck. After a series of awkward stops and starts among the waterweeds and cattails, the bird finally took off, straight over the river. As soon as it crossed the middle of the river, it began a smooth turn south, its great, almost awkward wings in utter contradiction to its graceful silhouette. It was flying low on the river, eye level to where they were sitting. Bill watched the bird as it flew along the river, pointing it out to the others but without saying a word.

"Great blue heron," Frank told them.

Carl asked him again what it was.

"It's called a great blue heron. We've seen them here before."

Carl wasn't sure. "We've seen that bird before?" he ventured, uncertain whether his father was testing him.

"Yes, we've seen that bird before. We've even seen that bird on the Sangamon River before. I've always liked that bird. It reminds me a lot of the storks in East Prussia—long slender bodies, great wings. You know what storks are, right?"

Helen stood up and proudly declared, "Storks bring babies."

Her father chuckled, recalling the all-encompassing fascination with procreation from his Catholic school chums back home.

"Yes. Storks bring the babies. Every year they bring babies."

He paused for a moment while Elizabeth handed out more peaches. Marie followed the great bird's flight down the river, pointing it out to Milton.

"No. Storks are real birds," Frank resumed. "They nest all over East Prussia. They leave in the winter and come back every spring. My father would plant cabbage every year as soon as the storks returned. And they come back to the same nests. There was a stork's nest on the church we went to when I was growing up. The nest sat in the middle of the roof, right on the crest. They never took the nest down, not even when they patched the roof or swept the chimney. And every year, sure enough, the storks would return to the same nest. Their offspring returned to the same area and raised families

(FACING) This stork's nest in East Prussia is said to have been
continuously occupied in the summer for over one hundred years. Photo taken in 2000.

(TOP) Boat house, Washington Park, circa 1907. Courtesy of the Lincoln Library,
Springfield, Illinois.

(BOTTOM) The Franke family on the porch, circa 1905.
Standing: Carl aged 19, Elizabeth aged 16, Frank aged 45, Mayme aged 19.
Sitting: Bill aged 12, Milton aged 2, Otto aged 14, Helen aged 9.

too. And then, once harvest was over and the rain began, the storks went south to Egypt for the winter. When my father and I went fishing after the spring thaw, he would always say that everyone should live like the storks."

Frank stood up and tossed the peach pits into the tall grasses behind the horses and wagon, which they had borrowed from the old farmer. After washing his hands in the river, he brushed off his pants meticulously and smoothed over any creases in his shirt. The boys followed suit, their father examining each for an overlooked blade of grass. Marie smiled, looking at her husband and children. It seemed that they had talked about doing this for years, but could never find the time; either one of the children was sick or work kept them at home in Springfield. Of course, they often took little trips to the Sangamon River—sometimes Frank would just take the boys—but they could rarely go anywhere with the whole family.

"We'll see you in a few hours," Frank said tipping his hat.

As the boys walked down to the boat, Helen called out to them from the bluff: "I'll bet you a nickel we catch more than you do!" She was carrying her bamboo pole and pretended to cast into the river.

They walked back down to the shore single file, laughing, with Carl bringing up the rear. Helen waved to them from the bluff with her irrepressible smile and went back to the willow to help her mother and sisters.

v

As they were launching the boat, Frank noticed a stain on Bill's shirt. He halted the launching to ask him what it was. It was obviously a mustard stain, but Frank wanted Bill to acknowledge the fact. Bill looked down and said in genuine disbelief, "Is it mustard?"

"Of course it's mustard!" Frank fired back. "That's the second shirt you've dirtied today. You won't get any more shirts if you keep on like this. I make that shirt for you and what do you do? You spill the mustard on the front of it. I make the shirt for Carl, the shirt he wears for work, and you smear it with your dirty hands. You don't think. You don't listen. Soon there'll be no more shirts!"

Bill was silent, on the brink of tears. He did everything he could to hold them back, but his father's sudden rage took him by surprise, especially since it was directed only at him. Why had he even bothered to go fishing? Of course he had to go fishing—he couldn't stay up there with the girls—he'd never hear the end of it from Otto and Carl. But he had no idea that there was mustard on his shirt. It must have fallen on him while he was eating the piece of bread without sausage. Or maybe it happened when he had his second sausage? It didn't matter now, so he summoned all his courage standing there on the sandy bank of the river. A single tear welled up in the corner of his eye.

Quickly, Carl turned to him and nearly burst out laughing. He then elbowed Otto, and Otto made a few honking noises through his nose. Bill wanted to lash out, but he watched his father's wrath rising.

"You two, into the boat, now!"

Frank shoved Carl in the back and threw the tackle box at him while tripping over the middle bench of the boat. Veins were popping across his forehead, his face flushed red. Otto scurried into the front of the boat, careful to stay out of Frank's way. Bill was next. Relieved that some of the attention was off him, but careful not to fan the flame any further, Bill stepped gingerly past Otto and never even looked at Carl.

Frank pushed off the sandy shore and hopped into the boat as it drifted away. His left foot caught the edge of the water. He looked at his wet boot in disgust and told the boys to row over to the other side of the river, toward the spot where they had seen the heron alight during lunch. Frank could bring his children into line with a few stern remarks. But with Bill, he thought, it seldom seemed to have any effect: discipline seemed to elude Bill.

The river was brown with the color of the clay along the bank. The heron side of the river was a mixture of cattails, big bluestem, and Indian grass. The heights of each plant were different, but several stands of grasses gathered to form a wave pattern. Frank decided to fish the shallow water for a while, contrary to good sense and the height of the sun.

After they had all settled into fishing, Frank began to speak again. This time he was more gentle, but more direct as well.

"It's time to stop acting like this. Carl, you're the oldest—you're a man now—I expect more from you. You work at the shop; you have responsibilities. I can't have this kind of horseplay from you. It's time to grow up, Carl. You're not a child any longer."

"And you two," Frank continued, looking at Otto and Bill. "You have to listen to your brother. He's the oldest, and your mother and I can't always watch you like a hawk. Eventually, Bill, you will work in the shop for your brother, so you have to respect your brother. Things will change. Soon you'll be out of school and working at the shop. There's a lot to learn, but the only way to learn is by listening. If you do, you can make enough money to buy a house and a fishing boat."

None of this was news to them. Even little Milton understood that Carl was in charge when his mom and dad weren't around. But it was the first time they had ever heard their father articulate his expectations so specifically. Carl felt simultaneously proud and burdened at the prospect of his responsibility. His mind raced for a moment. He saw himself taking orders, handling customers, strolling by the Springfield courthouse at lunchtime, reading the newspaper with purpose—all the things he understood adulthood to be about. Being a tailor wasn't the most prominent position in town, but it was important nonetheless. People always needed clothes and needed them to fit properly. There was a certain pride in the craft of tailoring that suited Carl. Anything he could do to help the family suited his purposes. His ears, therefore, burned with embarrassment when he recalled his behavior earlier that day. They burned even more as he turned and saw his father's expressionless eyes scouring the river for evidence of fish.

Otto hardly gave the upbraiding a second thought. It was true, he had never heard his father so clearly say that he and his siblings would be working for Carl in the future, but all of them had understood this for as long as they could remember. Otto, however, was confused by the prevailing mood. He was used to being scolded—that was how he understood his father. Frank Franke was a taskmaster and a disciplinarian. But the stories of Berlin and East Prussia remained with Otto. It was strange to think of his father as anything other than what he was now.

Frank was terribly irritated by his sons' behavior—he couldn't recall that he had ever been so disobedient to his father or mother—but eventually his thoughts got lost in the cattails. No longer concerned about Carl or the business, he began circling his chin and pulling his beard with his left hand again.

He was reminded of his last fishing trip before he left Derz and what his father had told him. He left in the fall of 1878. The final harvest was complete, and he had stayed through the harvest festival. Nothing in his life would ever compare to those festivals. They were

Road near Derz, June 2000.

like the warmth of sunlight on the skin after spending months in the dark. There was an ease to the feast that couldn't be repeated at Corpus Christi, or Christmas, or even Easter. There was music and food and dancing, but the music was sweeter, more mournful and more joyous all at once, and the food tasted so wonderful that everyone sang its praises through the winter. If there was a world beyond the boundaries of streams and fields on the outskirts of town, if there was a heaven beyond the heaven that shone on them dancing at harvest time, it did not matter to them, for they knew that tomorrow would be a day devoted to sleeping and eating. Not until well after he had left Germany and was struggling to establish his own tailoring business did Frank realize that it was the simple, back-breaking exhaustion that made the harvest festival more buoyant than the rest of the holidays in Derz. Everyone in the village had to work day and night during harvest to get everything done. Once the cold autumn rains began, there was no turning back—it was winter and four months of darkness. The difference, however, and the reason he was never to experience that feeling again, was that all the villagers were exhausted in the same way at the same time. And they all knew they would have ample days to sleep, once winter was almost upon them. It was a fatigue totally different from the exhaustion after a twelve-hour day at the tailor shop, when there is no one to share the misery with at home, when the children are already in bed and the soup is cold, and unless the sole proprietor gets up early there is no one to take care of the next customer. The first night of the harvest festival had passed. Franz and his father rose late, but earlier than the rest of Derz. Neither of them particularly cared about catching fish that day; they merely wanted an excuse to walk around, to look at the water, and to walk through the woods. As they walked along the main road through Derz heading toward Lemkendorf, Franz's father began talking very plainly. He first expressed his regret that Franz did not choose to become a priest. But following that, his father took on a decidedly different tone. He was generous, open—almost apologetic. He wondered aloud about what was happening to Derz and East Prussia. The Frank family had been in that area northeast of Allenstein for as far back as the church records would take them, probably four hundred years.[12] Suddenly, he had seen nephews and cousins leave the area for factory work in Berlin and Allenstein. He wondered about the cause of such a change, whether Chancellor Bismarck was behind it, trying to make life for Catholics more miserable. He worried that this might be the beginning of the end of the Frank family in Derz. Of course, he had assured his son that he was not to blame. He well understood the situation but had trouble hiding his disappointment.

The rowboat bobbed gently as a barge passed. Frank looked at each of his four sons and thought of his three daughters. How had he been able to make it from there to here? Life was hard in Berlin, but those four months waiting for Marie were a slow way to madness. He wondered about his brothers and sisters still in Derz. Little had changed, no doubt, but he suddenly had the urge to contact them, to invite them to America and introduce them to his family.

Frank could still picture his father as clearly as the day he left Derz in 1878. He could barely restrain himself from shuddering at the recollection. He pitied his father at that moment, and he hated that feeling. He was proud then, excited at the prospects of a new life in Berlin, but as he walked with his father toward the little lake where he and his siblings had fished so many times, he couldn't help feeling that all this world was passing before his eyes. His father continued to recall particular events from when Franz was still a boy. The air was clear and bright and the leaves on the trees were brilliant in their autumn colors. As they approached the lake, his father placed his hand on Franz's shoulder in a gesture suggesting a blessing and asked him to make a promise. He insisted that Franz not get married until he had enough money to buy his own property. His father urged him to make the money in Berlin and eventually to come back and buy a small piece of property in Derz. Not knowing that he would be able to fulfill only half of the promise, Franz agreed wholeheartedly and the two men embraced. The father was glad. Franz's chest swelled with pride. They walked on to the lake and fished that whole afternoon, never speaking of the promise until the day Franz left Derz and Germany for good.

VI

The rest of the afternoon proved to be good fishing. Frank and the older boys ended up catching a few decent-sized bass each, and Bill was happy enough to help string the fish alongside the boat. Among them they caught eighteen fish, plenty for a good family meal. Since it was almost three o'clock, they rowed back up the river to the spot where they had left the girls.

Helen stood on shore, not far from where they left her a few hours before. She struggled with two stringers full of fish and held them up proudly. There must have been almost two dozen. Her father smiled and removed his hat. It was official: the girls had won. Helen gleefully proclaimed victory before her older brothers as they pulled the boat ashore. She explained that the boys needed more practice and that each of them owed her a nickel.

"But we never shook on it," Carl explained.

"That's not fair!"

"Fair is fair, Helen. You have to shake on it before it's official."

"Fine. I guess you won't be getting any of our fish then."

Her father laughed: "I suppose you are going to do the cleaning then?"

Bill and Helen walked over to the willow tree with three stringers of fish. As Bill and Otto pulled the fish off the stringer, their mother promptly wrapped it in that day's newspaper. Mayme and Marie had already folded all of the blankets and washed the dishes, so Carl and

Family picnic in the park, a form of family recreation, circa 1908.
Frank and Milton on the left and Helen at the head of the table.

Elizabeth began loading up the wagon. It was only a short trip
through the fields and up the river road to Beardstown where they
would return the wagon to the old farmer. They climbed into the
wagon, Frank and Marie up front to drive the horses. The dry grass
crackled under the wheels and the leather reins creaked as they made
their way along the ruts. The children were quiet, and stillness lay
over the fields now golden in the light of the sun. The cottonwood
rustled, turning an almost silvery shade of green. As they drove
through the fields and the roadside crickets sang as they passed, it
seemed that they were the only people on earth. Their little wagon
ascended the high bluff along the river, and it was as if they had come
from the plains of Moab to view the Promised Land for the first time;
like palm-leaves of Jericho, the tall ears of corn bobbed gently in the
breeze. Scratching his full beard with satisfaction, Frank looked back
at his contented children. Here he was, Frank Franke, miles from anywhere, but no longer a stranger in a strange land.

PATTERNS

The family business went through several mutations in the first two decades of the twentieth century. Grandfather's tailoring business was transformed into a dry cleaning and tailoring business in 1908. The photograph shows the first site for the cleaning plant at 313 East Monroe Street. The building remains there today, albeit with a different facade. Over the succeeding fifty years Franke cleaning establishments were located at many locations in Springfield, but Monroe Street always had one or two active stores. At one time or another there were stores at 313, 315, 321, and 625 East Monroe Street.

The first place of business was at 313 East Monroe Street with Paris Cleaners on the left and Franke Tailors at the door to the right.

(TOP, LEFT) Bill and Milton on a bike at 314 West Adams Street,
across from the old high school.

(TOP, RIGHT) *Left to right:* Frances, Mayme, Bill, Helen, Milton, Elizabeth.

Quiver Beach in July. *Left to right:* Frank, Elizabeth, Dorothy, Mayme,
Bill, Milton, an unknown person, Anna, Helen, and another unknown person.

I

Two bankers stepped into Paris Cleaners a few minutes past 8:30 a.m.
on Monday, April 22, 1914, each with a briefcase in hand and a suit
over his arm. A bell on the door lightly jangled, causing Elizabeth to
look up from sorting the previous evening's pick-ups, which Otto had

(TOP, LEFT)
Standing: Frances, Bill, Helen.
Sitting: Mayme, Julius, Elizabeth.

(TOP, RIGHT)
Carl's Riverside gun club.

Carl skeet shooting.

(BOTTOM)
Carl and Dorothy entertaining.

(TOP) Franke-sponsored YMCA camp.

(MIDDLE) Quiver Beach guests on a hot summer day.

(BOTTOM) Carl, Dorothy, Mayme, and Charles.

Dorothy at the ready

been late in bringing back. Frank sat beneath a bright lamp at a tailor's table a few feet back from the counter. Just to his right was a doorway that led to a large room where the pressing machines were kept. When Frank saw the bankers, he carefully set down a pair of pants that he was letting out at the waist and walked around the sewing machine to the front counter. Elizabeth, too, got up from her sorting and greeted the bankers.

"Mr. Bunn, Mr. Easley,"[1] she nodded. "How do you do today?"

"Very well, Elizabeth. Another Monday, another week," Mr. Easley replied.

Frank stood behind Elizabeth at a slight distance and observed her interaction with the bankers. He wore a long, dark gray, double-breasted coat over a waistcoat. His ample beard draped down well below his necktie, so that he looked more like a Russian mystic than a Prussian tailor. His rigid posture and formal demeanor, however, were more like those of an aspiring cadet in the kaiser's army. The bankers respectfully nodded in his direction, and Mr. Easley, laying on the counter a charcoal gray suit with a high waistcoat, moved to the left side of the counter in order to address Frank directly.

"Now, Mr. Franke, I have a wedding to go to in St. Louis next weekend. I noticed two of the buttons on the sleeve were cracked."

Carl and Dorothy's honeymoon photos,
circa 1912, taken in Chicago and Denver
and at Colorado Springs at the
Garden of the Gods.

"Sure, that won't be a problem, Mr. Easley. How does the suit fit?"

"Well, it seemed to fit OK when I tried it on yesterday."

"What about the jacket? How did that feel?"

"It felt fine."

"Why don't you try it on again before you leave? It will only take a few minutes. We want to make sure you look your best."

Without hesitation, Mr. Easley set down his papers next to the counter and put on the gray coat. Frank opened a gate at the counter and ushered Mr. Easley back toward the tailor's table. Pulling out a

Elizabeth, circa 1914.

wooden platform, he told Mr. Easley he could change in the bathroom.

Meanwhile, Elizabeth took care of Mr. Bunn. She fastened a separate receipt with a safety pin to his blue suit and hung it on a large rack with wheels in the room behind the cash register. Her light brown hair was carefully tied up in the back, but a few strands occasionally dangled, which she brushed aside from her eyes. The simplicity of her white blouse and long pleated skirt, combined with the strain of her father's scrutiny, gave her an almost puritanical air. When she returned to the counter, she smiled at Mr. Bunn and asked if there was anything else she could do for him.

"No, no. I'm just waiting for Mr. Easley."

Mr. Easley stood on the small wooden platform while Frank pinned a few points on the back of the jacket, making several sharp chalk marks. Then he asked Mr. Easley to step down from the platform, adjusted Mr. Easley's coat, and stood back a moment to observe the sleeve length. Taking up a ruler from his table, Frank began measuring the distance from his customer's thumb to his sleeve.

"Say, my wife told me that your mother and father are going to Germany this summer," Mr. Bunn ventured to Elizabeth.

Checking the sleeve length against Mr. Easley's shirtsleeves now, Frank turned his ear toward the conversation.

"That's right," Elizabeth returned. "They leave a week after my older sister Mayme's wedding."

"Yes, Mrs. Bunn and I are very much looking forward to the wedding this weekend."

"We are too, but there is still so much work to do."

"I'm sure," Mr. Bunn said emphatically. "The reception is at the house?"

"My mother insisted on it. She said that's the way they always did it in Germany and she wouldn't have it any other way for her daughter," Elizabeth replied, turning her fingers around a safety pin.

Mr. Bunn smiled and assured her, "Well, so it must be. I'm sure it will be a lovely wedding. This is the third Franke wedding, isn't it?"

"You have a very good memory, Mr. Bunn," said Elizabeth. "Two years ago our oldest brother, Carl, married Dorothy Sheplor in a splendid wedding at the Methodist church. And last year Otto married Anna Englund in the same church. With Mayme being married this year, that makes three weddings in three years."[2]

By now, Frank had finished with Mr. Easley and was helping him with his jacket. Mr. Easley thanked him and said, "Sounds like you have a busy week ahead of you, Mr. Franke. Who is the lucky groom?"

"Charles Creighton. Young man from Champaign. Although he works for a ready-made clothing store, he is a fine young man," said Frank with a wink, and led Mr. Easley back toward the bathroom. When he emerged, Mr. Easley handed Frank the rest of the suit and walked back through the gate and around the counter.

"Well, that's wonderful news, Mr. Franke. Congratulations," Mr. Easley said. "As for the trip—sounds like quite a journey. How long are you going for?"

"Oh, it takes over two weeks to get there, including the train to New York and the ship to Bremen," Frank replied, standing rather stiffly behind the counter now with the noise of the presses drifting in from the back of the store. "Once we arrive, we plan to stay for six months." And then Frank added, almost bashfully, "It's our thirtieth wedding anniversary this September, so we plan to celebrate back in Germany."

"Wonderful, wonderful. I bet it's changed since you were there last. How long has it been since you've been back to Germany?"

"I came to this country in 1884. My wife came four months later. Neither of us has been back since then. So, it's been thirty years."

"Thirty years . . . Do you still have family there?"

"Yes. Both Mrs. Franke and I have family there."

"Well, I hope you and your wife have a wonderful time," Mr. Easley said as he extended his hand to Frank.

"Thank you very much, sir. I will have your suit ready for you by Wednesday," said Frank, shaking Mr. Easley's hand.

"And I look forward to seeing you on Saturday," Mr. Bunn added, leaning over the counter to shake Frank's hand too.

Frank nodded in assent, "Until then."

"Good-bye."

As the bankers were walking out, Otto was coming into the cleaning area. He held the door open, said hello to the bankers, and picked up two sacks full of clothes he'd spent the morning picking up. As he struggled through the doorway, knocking the bell off the door, he was met with harsh words from his father.

"What happened last night? Elizabeth is behind schedule now. We have customers coming in, and there's no one to take care of the register, no one to handle the customers. Why were you so late last night? When did you finally get here?"

Frank made quite an impression, looming behind his tailor's table, his beard the only part of his body that visibly moved. Elizabeth offered her hard-working brother a look of warm sympathy, her eyes expressing that she wished there were something she could do. The sounds of men and women operating the presses in back grew louder in an almost rhythmic succession of steam release. Otto sighed, picked up the fallen bell, and began to explain.

"I went to the North End plant to drop off the Andersons' drapes. When I got there, Bill was having trouble with a pump in the cleaning machine. We started looking into it . . ."

"I don't care about what was wrong with Bill," snapped Frank. "You were supposed to be here by five o'clock yesterday, so we could sort these things and have them cleaned this morning."

Exasperated, but with no time to explain as he knew there were people waiting for his instructions in the back of the shop, Otto replied, "It won't happen again." Pushing his sleeves above his elbows, Otto hoisted the sacks onto his shoulder and walked through the doorway.

Frank's beard continued to vibrate, but Elizabeth was not sure if he was addressing her.

Helen and Milton, circa February 1911.
Old Springfield High School, across the street from 314 West Adams Street.

"You know, your mother and I leave for Germany in two weeks. What am I going to do about Otto and Bill? You have to make sure that they stay on schedule. And where is Carl? It's almost nine o'clock. Half a tailor's business is done before nine o'clock . . ."

He continued like this for a few minutes, trailing off into a mumble at his table. Elizabeth heard him but made no reply. A few minutes later, Carl walked through the front door, ever the man of fashion. Lighter gray pinstripes and a light gray vest punctuated his dark gray suit; a watch chain dangled from his pocket. He doffed a gray hat and adjusted his tie, smoothing it into his vest.

"Where have you been?" Frank shot out from behind his desk.

"I was meeting with new clients this morning at the café," Carl replied, walking toward the small office behind the cash register.

"New clients? We don't need clients, we need customers."

"I met with the manager of the St. Nicholas Hotel. He has agreed to let us handle all their uniforms and give us the first recommendation to hotel guests for their cleaning needs."

Still upset, but recognizing the importance of the agreement, Frank shrugged his shoulders and headed back toward his table, muttering "That's good."

Like a breath of fresh air, Helen entered the front room from the plant in good spirits and in a long, trim skirt striped in two shades of blue. Except for the ruffles on the high-necked collar, her white blouse was plain, which provided a dramatic contrast to the liveliness of her face. Even in a bad mood, Helen looked as if she were about to laugh. The light of the room seemed to gather about her blue eyes, which were both mischievous and compassionate. It was nearly impossible to remain angry or sad in her presence. After greeting Carl, she handed him several sheets of paper with the balances of accounts. Carl glanced at the papers and asked if she had checked them against last month's accounts. Satisfied with how they looked, he handed the papers back to her.

"Bill has to become more efficient," Carl sighed to himself, although loud enough for others to hear.

Elizabeth glanced at Helen as she was walking away. After a few moments she said, "You know, Carl, I ran into Mr. Herndon yesterday at the bank. He went out of his way to say how happy he was with Bill and the service at the North End plant."

"When I was his age, I . . ." Carl began to complain, but Elizabeth cut him off.

"Carl, when you were his age, you were in Chicago."

Carl stopped in his tracks. Feeling the sting of this comment, he began to recount his successes to Elizabeth, how he had put this business together, how this was the first dry cleaner in the city, how they have some of the most modern facilities in the country. Elizabeth waited patiently, realizing that she had hit a sore spot. When Carl was finished, she ended the conversation by apologizing and telling Carl that she was only trying to say that Bill was doing a good job and that the employees at the North End had nothing but good things to say about him. But Carl did not acknowledge her apology. Instead, he walked into his office and closed the door behind him.

Elizabeth regretted her comment almost the moment she spoke, knowing that Carl would give her the cold shoulder for the rest of the day. Carl resented any mention of his time in Chicago, not so much because his dreams of becoming a merchant tailor were dashed—in hindsight he realized he had no interest in tailoring—but because he had failed his father.

II

In the fall of 1907, Carl had gone to Chicago in order to attend tailoring school.[3] He was twenty years old and understood that as the eldest son he had a responsibility to advance the family business. After finishing seventh grade when he was thirteen, he had worked full time for his father at the tailor shop. Carl had learned a great deal about the business by the time he left for Chicago, including some elements of the trade, having spent the previous four years as a cutter. While he enjoyed working with his father, he wanted more experience; he wanted to learn about tailoring and above all, he wanted to learn about how to manage a business. Frank, however, with Milton and Helen still very young (4 and 10, respectively), felt the financial pressure to take on as much business as possible. Mayme (20), Elizabeth (18), Otto (16), and Bill (14) all still lived at home at 314 West Adams Street. Everyone worked: Mayme was a milliner at the Boston Store, where many of the ladies of Springfield bought their hats; Elizabeth was a stenographer for J. W. Scott; Otto was an apprentice at the Illinois Watch Company; and Bill, still too young for a regular job, helped out his father at the store.[4] All the children began working when they turned fourteen. Although Frank and Marie valued education and were especially proud of their Prussian education, none of their children went beyond the seventh grade, with the exception of Elizabeth, who attended one year of high school and later would go on to business school, and Helen, who eventually would graduate from high school. It was unusual for any of the children of first-generation German parents in Springfield to go to high school, regardless of their educational interests. As long as you could read, write, add, subtract, multiply, and divide, that was enough. And college was reserved strictly for the privileged. Because things were so tight at home with the children and chores, Mayme only completed the third grade and started working at home, even pitching in at the tailor shop until she got a job at the Boston Store. Everyone helped out financially, but Frank, ever vigilant, especially when it came to money, worried that the tailoring business wasn't bringing in enough income to adequately provide for his family. He concluded that he simply did not have time to train Carl properly as a tailor. In order to take on as

Chicago, State and Monroe Streets, circa 1911,
looking east toward Wabash Avenue.

much business as possible, Frank needed his eldest son Carl as a full-time cutter.

As time went on, however, Frank sensed his son's growing frustration at his lack of training. Carl never openly complained, but would frequently look over his father's shoulder, attempting to learn how to tailor. Finally Frank decided to sit down with Carl to discuss the family business and Carl's future. After a series of conversations, they both agreed that Carl should go to tailoring school and Frank should hire a temporary cutter.

So Carl set out for Chicago in 1907 with his father's blessing and his family's support. Chicago was the fastest-growing city in the world at the time. Like German peasants fleeing the countryside for Berlin, people poured into Chicago from the small towns along the former frontier; from the still devastated states of the former Confederacy; from Germany, Ireland, Poland, Bohemia, Italy, Lithuania—from anywhere in the world where people were desperate for work and willing to put up with marginal living conditions in hopes of a job and a better life. Almost every day, new buildings sprouted on the prairie, some of them hardly more sturdy than a lean-to, while others were feats of engineering. Indeed, in flat Chicago, mountains were built brick by brick. Black clouds over Packingtown were a constant reminder of just how much meat was on the move. Bubbly Creek and its strange, attendant odors made some question whether the slaughterhouse was worth the jobs and money it brought to the city. Upton Sinclair's *The Jungle*, published a year before Carl came to Chicago, caused a national sensation when the horrors of bologna and Bubbly Creek cast a pall over the thirty-six-year-old city.

But Carl had no intention of remaining in Chicago. As much as the opulence of State Street dazzled him, Carl was firmly committed to returning to the family business once his training was complete. It was, however, the first time he had spent any time away from his family, and in the beginning he found the experience exhilarating. Here he was in a brand-new city—the newest city in the world—bustling along in a massive grid of traffic and skyscrapers he had only previously read about. Trains arrived every hour, bringing travelers from all over the country, some of them visiting, some of them just passing through. Every day, new merchandise was displayed in the shop windows at Montgomery Ward's and Marshall Field's. Every evening, workers from a brewery down the street sat on crates outside Carl's building and talked and played cards until all hours of the night. Carl made the best of his first month there, meeting friends, staying out late—wasting time, as young men are wont to do when they first leave home.

By Thanksgiving, he knew that he was in trouble. He lived in a small room at the end of a long hallway in a boardinghouse with fifteen other tenants. Because all but one of them worked at various jobs in the city and seldom were there to do much more than sleep, Carl had become terribly lonely. There was nobody to talk to. The days in November had grown colder and shorter, so his chance to interact with the workers down the block had faded away. He loved those first evenings in Chicago when he could brag about his accomplishments and the family business in Springfield to anyone he met. It was like sustenance to him. At home he had always enjoyed a privileged position as the eldest son. He was used to being looked up to, to organizing his brothers and sisters in their daily tasks. Now he was the low man on the totem pole; with the fierce competition in tailoring school, his skills paled against those whose handiwork received the admiration of the teachers and the other students. To make matters worse, the money he came to Chicago with was running low. He longed for the comforts of home, and even school began to lose interest for him. When the time came around for his final examination in tailoring school just before Christmas, Carl was completely unprepared. Between the initial excitement of the city and loneliness of its long nights, he had managed to while his time away without learning much about tailoring. As a result, he failed his final examination.

After a week of wandering up and down the lakeshore, wondering how he was going to tell his father about the exam, he ran into two of his fellow tailoring students at the Berghoff Restaurant and Bar—Tom, his friend from the boardinghouse, and Ned, a young tailor from St. Louis. Tom motioned to Carl to sit down with them. They ordered beer and bratwurst and talked about school. Eventually Tom asked Carl how he had done on the exam and what he was going to do next. Carl stared into his beer glass. He barely touched his bratwurst, and when he did, it was only to move it from one side of his plate to the other. After a few minutes, Carl finally admitted his failure and told them that he was going to return to Springfield to work in his father's business.

Sensing Carl's frustration with his prospects, Tom pulled out a piece of paper and handed it to Carl. It was an advertisement for a dry cleaning school in Denver. Carl glanced at the ad and handed it back to Tom with an air of indifference. Tom explained that he saw the ad at school and that he was thinking about going to Denver.

Carl knew a little about dry cleaning from a class he had taken at tailoring school on various methods for cleaning clothes. The ancient Romans made use of absorbent earths and powders, such as fuller's earth to remove grease stains from garments. Since it did not involve the use of water, the technique became known as "dry" cleaning. Modern dry cleaning was developed in France in the 1820s by Jean-Baptiste Jolly of the French cleaning and dyeing firm Jolly-Belin. Legend has it that Mr. Jolly was working late into the night when he spilled camphene, a lamp fuel, onto a dirty cloth. When he returned to his desk the next morning, he noticed that the cloth was clean where the fuel had spilled. For a time, the new solvent cleaning processes were carried out by hand in copper bowls used traditionally in wet cleaning. Pullars, of Perth, Scotland, introduced the first power-driven machinery for dry cleaning in 1869. With the incredible growth of the coal-gas industry at the end of the nineteenth century, a number of inexpensive organic solvents became available, namely naphtha.[5]

As Tom continued to discuss dry cleaning, Carl began to understand why he had suggested the school in Denver. Dry cleaning, completely new in the United States and non-existent in Springfield, was the best way—in fact, the only way—to truly clean wool fabric. Executed with machines and presses, dry cleaning was less a trade than a business, and the possibility for it to become a lucrative business was very real given the recent population growth in Springfield. By the time the Berghoff Restaurant closed on that fateful night, Carl had discovered a way out of his dilemma. Of course, he would still have to face his father and explain that he failed the examination, but now he could do so with a plan. He would go to school in Denver, and upon his return he would establish a dry cleaning business with his father. In the back of his mind, Carl knew that it was a long shot, but he kept reassuring himself that it was a great idea. Anything was better than coming home empty-handed.

Carl took the train from Chicago down to Springfield on the day before Christmas, carrying less than what he came with: a suit his father had made for him, five shirts including the one on his back, two pairs of pants, a watch, a bible, a towel, and a razor. It was the same train that his father had taken nearly twenty-four years earlier when, with an even lighter suitcase than Carl's, Frank first came to Springfield in 1884.

Arriving home for Christmas with the family, Carl found a warm house and food that tasted better than he remembered—goulash, potato pancakes, spaetzle piled high, sauerbraten, sausages, and hot apple strudel to finish the meal. After his parents had retired, Carl relaxed by the fire with his brothers and sisters. He told them impressive stories about the big city, the endless traffic, the new skyscrapers, the stores, and the friends he had met. And then, after bragging about his new-found sophistication, Carl, in a moment of unusual openness, told them all how much he missed them and how happy he was to be back home.

The next day he went to work with his father. As it was the day after Christmas, there was very little business, so Carl thought it best to explain what had happened in Chicago. Frank was so disturbed by the news that Carl had to repeat the entire story just to be sure that his father understood. After Carl reconfirmed his failure of the examination, a few minutes of silence passed. Frank then resumed his work on a suit jacket, making no further comment.

Carl was horrified. Even in the worst scenario he had considered—his father venting his terrible wrath—he never imagined a response such as this. Carl panicked and several times begged his father to speak. In his shame, he could hardly work. Carl had to face his father's disappointment directly rather than through the veil of rage. Now he wasn't even worth speaking to. Carl resembled his father in so many ways—being proud, demanding, hardworking, stubborn and short-tempered—that to fail to win his father's respect was devastating. For the entire afternoon, no customers came in to break the silence and no words were uttered between the two men.

On the walk home, his self-respect in tatters, Carl had nothing further to lose, so he asked his father if he knew anything about dry cleaning. Frank said he knew of it from his tailoring days in Berlin as a way to clean wool and other fine material without destroying it, but he didn't know much about the business or how it had developed since then. Carl explained the basic idea and mentioned the school in Denver.

"After all this, you want to go to another school? In Denver, no less!" his father responded.

The following morning a general gloom hung over the breakfast table. It was time for everyone to return to work, and Frank's mood seemed peculiarly foul. Marie served eggs and toast with jam; she too was a little gruff, especially with Carl, since she had heard the news from Frank the night before. A little puzzled by their mother's shortness, Carl's siblings stole glances at one another for confirmation of the mood, searching for events of the day before to see if they had unwittingly contributed to the tension at the breakfast table. Before anybody could probe matters further, Frank pushed his plate forward and got up from the table. Two corners of toast remained on his plate, his full cup of coffee giving up the last of its steam.

Carl and Bill rose too. Bill looked at Elizabeth and then stared at the floor bug-eyed in mock fear to indicate a plea for help. Within minutes, they were in their coats, hats, and gloves and out the door with their father.

It was bitterly cold that morning. A steady, harsh wind blew in from the northwest. The thin covering of snow from two days before Christmas squeaked beneath their feet. Sunlight reflected brightly from the frost on the trees, and a mixture of steam and smoke wafted from every house in Springfield. High above the capitol building a thin wisp of white smoke stood out sharply against a crystal blue sky. Except for the periodic rasp of a crow, there was no noise and no motion on the street. Bill hunched his shoulders forward, bracing himself against the cold.

"Straighten up! We are on our way to work," Frank directed Bill, who dutifully obliged and even opened his collar a bit to test the bitter air.

When they arrived at the store, it was still early. Bill was always the first one at the door, but on this day, with the heat between Carl and Frank at a slow boil, Bill made an extra effort to move out in front of them. He waited for his father and Carl as he hopped up and down outside the door, which noticeably aggravated the both of them. He opened the door without a word.

Like everything else in Springfield that morning, the store was frigid. Frank set Bill to work on getting a fire in the stove while Carl put water in the kettle for tea. The stove stood against the back wall of the store. Although nearly thirty years old, it looked almost new. One of Bill's tasks at the store was to make sure it was spotless. He spent hours every day scrubbing the seams of the stove with a wire brush, removing all traces of soot. Any clutter, any speck of dust, his father would tell him, gives the wrong impression to customers. A clean store was essential to a successful business because it signified quality. "Mark my words," he would invariably add.

Frank explained to both his sons what had to be done that day. Bill had some cleaning and organizing to do, such as straightening the bolts of cloth that lined the back of the shop, gathering the "cabbage," the excess cloth appropriated by a tailor when cutting out clothes, for a patchwork blanket, cleaning the mirrors in the dressing room, and, of course, keeping the stove free of new soot. Carl's assignment was to help Frank at the cutting table. The customer wanted a three-piece navy pinstripe suit. Carl went to the back of the store to retrieve the appropriate bolt of cloth, which he then hoisted onto the six-by-four-foot cutting table. Frank unrolled the material over the table, which was regularly scored to create a half-inch grid over its entire surface. Two-yard sticks bordered the top of the table, with forty-eight inches marking the right border, and two metal lamps were suspended from the ceiling directly over the cutting board. Sunlight from the front window, however, provided most of the light to work by. Frank reached into a large flat drawer under the cutting board and pulled out what looked like a leather ledger. The book contained all the measurements for his current customers. He then asked Bill to bring up a roll of paper from the back of the store. Unrolling a large piece of paper over the fabric, Frank began measuring all the cuts and marking the paper, carefully explaining every decision to Carl.

When they had finished cutting three suits, it was lunchtime. Business was slow, for most people in Springfield were still at home with their families or away visiting relatives. Frank took the large jar of soup that Marie had made the night before, poured it into a pot, and placed it on the stove. He then refilled the kettle and set it to boil. Carl gathered more wood from the pile, opened the stove and put more wood on the fire, while Bill went to the bakery just down the street for a loaf of rye. Once past the window of the store, Bill ran down the icy sidewalk, almost slipping at the corner of the street.

As they watched the soup begin to bubble, Frank asked Carl a few more questions about dry cleaning school.

"Now about this school in Denver, what would they actually teach you there?"

"Well, they teach you everything about dry cleaning," Carl replied somewhat nervously, "how it works, how to do it, how to obtain the cleaning machines and presses, how to handle the waste—everything you need to know to start your own business."

Frank opened the stove with a pair of metal tongs and stoked the fire. He sat back and stroked his great beard slowly. His eyes wandered around the store and settled on the milk carriage across the street, where the milkman was unloading. The neat rows of milk bottles looked like Prussian soldiers poised for marching. Carl sensed that his father was actually considering his proposal. Frank finally grunted and walked to the front of the store. Genuinely puzzled by this behavior, Carl stirred the soup and tried to guess what his father was thinking. Frank was rubbing away the frost and condensation that had built up on the corners of the front window. As he finished, he waved to the milkman and walked back to the stove.

"So what do you know about this school?" he resumed.

Carl sat up straight. He spoke clearly and deliberately but tried to appear matter-of-fact. "It came highly recommended by the tailoring school in Chicago. They provided advertisements for the school, and when I spoke to one of my teachers about it, he told me that several nearby dry cleaners had gone to the same school in Denver."

Frank took his turn stirring the soup. "How much does it cost?"

"Fifty dollars for tuition, room, and board."

Frank winced at the price but made no further comment.

Bill returned from the bakery and stamped his feet on the front mat, a fresh loaf of rye under his arm. The three of them sat at a small table by the stove. After dividing the soup into three bowls, Frank tore off a hunk of rye and handed the loaf to Bill. By now, the water in the kettle was boiling. Frank poured the water into a small dark pot over a perforated ceramic basket, which Carl had filled with new tea leaves. They ate quietly together, soaking the soup up with bread.

Despite his dismay at Carl's failure in Chicago, this new idea was a way to deal with a problem that Frank had had on his mind for over a year. The trouble with tailoring was the new competition from the catalogue stores in Chicago—Sears Roebuck & Co. and Montgomery Ward. Even businessmen were beginning to wear ready-made suits. These, of course, could never compare to the quality and craft of a well-tailored suit, but it was impossible to compete with the prices. Although he didn't like to acknowledge it, Frank's dream of creating a family business was beginning to fade. When he had arrived in Springfield, the first thing he saw as he left the train station was a sign reading "Hesse & Son, Carriage Makers." It represented everything he wanted from America: a business to call his own and a legacy to leave to his family. It was the mark of a successful life, he thought, and so did every other German immigrant in Springfield. The tailoring business, however, which had been so lucrative just twenty years ago, could no longer support his whole family. But if dry cleaning caught on, if the people of Springfield took their wool suits and coats to be cleaned, the combined business might yield an adequate income. It would be the family business he had always dreamed of: F. Franke & Son, Merchant Tailors and Dry Cleaners! Bill and Otto could work the machines while Elizabeth and Helen handled the customers and the bookkeeping. Carl could manage the money and the accounts, and even continue his work as a cutter; Mayme could bring her hat-making skills to tailoring; and when Milton was old enough, there would surely be work for him.

But Frank was getting way ahead of himself, and he knew it. Ever cautious, especially when it came to business, he knew that Carl's idea had to be tested. It was one thing to claim that dry cleaning was the wave of the future, but it was another thing altogether to have the first, the second, and finally the regular customer walk through the door. Nonetheless, by the end of the afternoon when the three men were walking home together, Frank openly discussed the dry cleaning business with Carl. He was still somewhat skeptical about particulars—how much money they would need to start the business, how much of a loan they would be able to obtain, and whether or not the school in Denver was truly credible—but Frank no longer questioned the potential success of the business. Even when he was still in Berlin, he recalled that "French cleaning" was the only way to get a wool suit clean. The idea of a mechanized version of dry cleaning made perfect sense.

So it was decided.

In the month before going to Denver in the spring of 1908, Carl had to survive the revelation to his siblings of his embarrassment in Chicago. The final assignment of the tailoring course had been to design and tailor a gentleman's formal evening suit with tails and satin lapels and trim along the seam of the trousers. Carl was very nervous about the exam, and in a moment of panic he had cut off the tails of the jacket. In a few weeks it became an old story around the dinner table, and it never lost its humor for Carl's brothers and sisters.[6] Yet none of it bothered Carl now. He endured the teasing with a new sense of purpose. He was going to Denver to learn how to set up a new business that would make any family proud.

In the fall of 1908, Carl returned to Springfield from dry cleaning school as planned. He and his father carefully constructed the new business plan at night, and continued the tailoring work by day. Carl even had a name for the firm: Paris City Cleaning Company, F. Franke & Son. Within two months of Carl's return, Frank had established contacts and obtained the necessary loans. Paris Cleaners officially

Paris Cleaners: first business card.

opened its doors for business at 313 East Monroe Street in January of 1909. The dry cleaning, which Carl ran, was on the left side of the store, and the tailoring, which Frank continued, was on the right. At first, Carl cleaned all the suits by hand. He would place the clothing on a large table, almost the size of a cutter's table, and rub the suit with a cloth soaked in naphtha. Then he would take a rack of clothing still damp with naphtha and thoroughly dry the clothes in a dryer in order to remove any trace of the petroleum smell. Within six months, Carl had enough work to hire another full-time employee to help with the cleaning.

As soon as the business opened, Frank never looked back to the initial disappointment of Carl's failing his examination. Carl, however, never forgot his shame. Like his father, Carl was a proud man and didn't take jokes about his tailoring career lightly. As the train was pulling away from Springfield on the way to dry cleaning school in Denver, Carl had looked out the window at muddy fields, unplowed and unplanted. They appeared exactly as they had done when he came in from Chicago just before Christmas, and Carl winced with shame as he recalled the day after Christmas. Looking straight into the low bank of clouds as if he could see through to the light of the sun, he vowed to God and to himself that he would never again disappoint his father. His life depended on the success of the business. And he would never let anything come between him and his commitment.

III

A man opened the door, and a woman walked through, the bell ringing loudly this time. Carl came out of his office, smiled at the customers, and disappeared into the back of the plant in order to reconfirm some of the numbers that Helen had given to him earlier that morning. Elizabeth approached the counter.

"Good morning, Miss Elbe, what can I do for you this morning?" she said.

Removing two silk blouses from her bag, Miss Elbe responded, "Just a few blouses. I was hoping you might be able to remove a stain on the right sleeve of the white blouse. I don't know where it came from."

"It doesn't look too bad. We shouldn't have any trouble removing it."

"Thank you."

The man, elegantly dressed in a well-fitted suit, now approached the counter. He removed his broad-brimmed hat and smiled at Elizabeth.

"Hello Elizabeth. How are you today?" said the poet Vachel Lindsay.

"I'm doing well, Mr. Lindsay; how are you?"

"I couldn't be better."

"What can I do for you?"

"Well, I'm here to pick up my suit. I'm giving a reading at the public library this evening. You should come if you have the chance. It's at 5:30." Mr. Lindsay began pumping his fist in a syncopated rhythm, as if he were conducting a symphony.

"It sounds wonderful, but I have to work this evening," said Elizabeth, and then added, "You know, I saw your poem in the paper the other day."

"Oh, yes. *Yankee Doodle*—it's from a new collection of poems I am working on—a collection that I conceived of as a kind of higher vaudeville. You know, poetry that has something for everybody in it. What did you think?"

"Well, I'm not much of a judge of poetry, but I thought it was interesting."

He shrugged his shoulders, but then quickly regained his confidence.

The poet Vachel Lindsay, 1913.

"I gave a reading of a poem called *The Congo* last month in Chicago. The great poets William Butler Yeats and Carl Sandburg were in attendance. They both seemed to approve," he said, raising his eyebrows.

Elizabeth nodded quickly and said, "Yes, Helen tells me that your new book will be published in the fall."

"*Yankee Doodle* is a part of that collection. I have a few poems to finish, but it's basically ready to go. For now, the book is simply called *The Congo and Other Poems*."

Elizabeth smiled and then walked into the back room to fetch Mr. Lindsay's suit. As she returned, her father rose from his table and headed for Carl's office, looking toward Mr. Lindsay. The poet bowed his head deeply, somewhat ostentatiously. A little taken aback by this sudden gesture, Frank nodded at Mr. Lindsay.

"The suit fits beautifully, Mr. Franke!" Mr. Lindsay called out. He stepped back from the counter, ran his hand across the sleeves of his coat and held onto his lapels.

Frank turned toward the poet courteously, if a bit suspiciously. "Anytime you need a new suit, Mr. Lindsay, please come to me," he said, and walked into Carl's office.

"I certainly will!"

Mr. Lindsay turned back to Elizabeth as she handed him his suit. He removed a dollar bill from his wallet and pushed it toward her.

"Did Helen see it? What did she think?" Mr. Lindsay asked rather suddenly.

"Did she see what?" Elizabeth replied with a puzzled look.

"The poem— *Yankee Doodle!*" He was now marching in place with a slight gimp.

"Yes, in fact she was the one who showed me the poem in the first place." Elizabeth said, laughing at his gimp. "She is a great admirer of your poetry."

Mr. Lindsay stopped in his tracks. "As I am a great admirer of her. The life of our nation depends on the Helen Frankes of this world."[7] He held his hat over his chest in a pledge of allegiance. Elizabeth was shaking her head and laughing harder now as she handed him his change.

Releasing himself from his pose, he asked, "Is she here this morning?"

"She is, but she had to step out momentarily."

"Well, do me the favor of reminding her of my reading this evening. I gave her an invitation last week, so she already knows, but do remind her."

" I certainly will. Will that be all, Mr. Lindsay?"

"No, that won't be all, but that will be it for now," he replied, tipping his hat.

As soon as the poet had left, two other men entered Paris Cleaners, one after the other. Elizabeth waited on both of them. Frank, with a piece of paper in his hand, returned to the front of the store, followed by Carl, who asked where Helen was. Frank explained that she had gone to the bank.

Elizabeth worked unceasingly for the rest of the morning, handling customers until just after one in the afternoon. When things let up for a moment, she gathered all the clothes from the morning and hung them on the large, movable rack. She wheeled the rack past Carl, who was now leaning back in his chair scratching out numbers on a pad in his office, then past her father, who was working on Mr. Easley's suit, through the doorway, and into the back of the cleaning area.

Otto was on his knees holding a wrench and looking underneath one of the presses. The floor was made of gray concrete slabs; each press occupied a single slab. Lights from the ceiling dangled down over each press and provided an orangish yellow glow to work by. A network of pipes across the ceiling knocked periodically from the steam heat they carried. The noise was almost rhythmic.

There were nine presses in all: four toppers, four leggers, and one silk machine, each made by an Illinois company called Prosperity. The toppers were designed specifically to handle coats and the tops of pants; the leggers, for the legs of pants. The silk machine handled large silk dresses and gowns. The men and women who ran the presses worked from 7:00 a.m. to 12:30 p.m., when they took a half-hour lunch break. The workday ended at four o'clock.

Next to each press was a hamper filled with recently cleaned garments. To the right was a rack for pressed clothes, like the rack Elizabeth was pushing. The workers arranged each article of clothing onto the padded bottom of the press and clamped it in place with a lever. The person operating the press then hit the steam pedal, which was connected to a pipe descended from the network on the ceiling, and released steam under seventy-five pounds of pressure. (It was the steam pedal that accounted for most of the noise in the room). All the pipes were connected to a large boiler at the back of the plant. There were two steam pedals on each of the machines, one releasing steam from the top of the press and the other from the bottom. Another pedal controlled a vacuum, which was run by a small, one-and-one-half-horsepower motor. The vacuum removed all the moisture from the steam on the clothing: one pedal for the top and the other for the bottom. As soon as one part of the pants or dress was pressed, the whole process began again. It was exhausting work which, to be performed efficiently, demanded dexterity and timing. The worker was on his or her feet all day, operating pedals and shifting clothes across the board. The room was always hot because of the steam, even on cold winter days.[8]

As Elizabeth stood by the press at which Otto was working, she noticed one of the men who was working so quickly, so naturally, that the machine had virtually become an extension of his hands and feet. Reaching into the hamper next to the topper, he removed a dark blue suit coat, which had been tumbled dry by one of the dryers in back only an hour before. Adroitly arranging the back of the coat around the press so that it pressed flat on the board, he quickly clamped it in place, hit the steam pedals, followed with the vacuum pedals, and finished by releasing the clamp. He made his way around the coat methodically, with each step of the process marked by the loud hiss of the steam being released, followed by the dull roar of the extractor. The total effect was mesmerizing, but the efficiency and elegance with which he worked gave the lie to the aches and pounding in his feet at night. As she waited for Otto to look up from his press, Elizabeth stared at the worker almost as if she were seeing this activity for the first time.

Although Otto had only been working at Paris Cleaners for two years, he was already in charge of training all the floor workers on the presses and the cleaning machines. It all came naturally to him. Mechanically inclined, fastidious almost to a fault, and beautifully coordinated, Otto was the perfect dry cleaning chemist and plant floor manager. He could fix all the machines—he had an almost intuitive feeling for the valves and pumps—and he kept the plant as clean and orderly as a Prussian barracks.

Elizabeth interrupted Otto from his task and asked him if he was ready for another batch of clothes. Otto did not move from beneath the press. He just shook his wrench in the direction of the cleaning machine in back. Elizabeth wheeled the rack past the other workers, who were sweating from the hot steam. There were always more clothes to be pressed, always more skirts to be pleated. As Elizabeth walked to the back room, where the cleaning machines were located, Otto followed her and began sorting through the clothes on the rack, loading only light items into the machine. Generally, the clothes were separated by weight rather than color. Often lighter than men's clothing, women's clothing was usually presorted. The sorter also distinguished the loads by material: wools, cottons, and silks. Otto then threw another bin of presorted blouses into the cleaning machine, which contained a large perforated steel basket that held the clothes. Elizabeth took out a white blouse that earlier in the morning had been tagged for stains. She spotted the garment with a sponge soaked in a water-based solvent and dried it with compressed air. After examining the spot, she dabbed it again with the solvent and dried it. Satisfied with the result, she tossed the blouse into the machine, along with the rest of the load.

Before starting the machine, Otto examined the pump from the storage tank to the machine. Then he noted the thickness of the cake that had developed on the pump filter. Judging it safe to proceed, he started the machine. As the clothes began to rotate in the basket, Otto and Elizabeth could hear the sound of the solvent spraying out of the pumps. Otto's attention was fixed on the machine for a moment, as if his gaze would ensure its operation. Just then Helen came in from the back office to ask how much solvent Otto thought they would have to buy for the next month. Elizabeth interrupted to tell Helen that somebody had asked for her earlier that morning.

"Who was it?" Helen asked quickly, already anticipating the response.

"Oh, I can't remember—just somebody who was asking about you."

"Elizabeth!" Helen could barely contain herself.

Otto was visibly disturbed. "Yeah, I know that guy," he said distaste. "What's his name? Vachel something?"

"Vachel Lindsay—he's a poet!" exclaimed Helen with enthusiasm. "He's going to publish a new collection of poems in the fall. In fact, he's giving a reading tonight at the public library. He gave me a copy of some the poems about a month ago. One of them was published in the paper the other day."

"Yes, I read it when you showed it to me. It was certainly unusual," Elizabeth acknowledged.

"A poet? No wonder he's so strange," Otto started. "I ran into that guy the other night. I was checking on one of the machines at the North End plant because I was worried about too much static building up. It was late. I couldn't sleep, so I went over there. After I closed up, who did I see but Vachel Lindsay wandering around the streets all by himself? At first I thought he was drunk, because his face was all screwed up, and he seemed to be talking to himself. He was looking up and down the street, and he kept looking back toward the Capitol building. He was the only other person on the street— not even the paperboys or the milkmen were out yet. I was a little worried about him, so I walked up to him and said hello. He looked startled, like he didn't see me approaching him. But he was looking right at me!" Otto mugged a dumb stare at Helen and continued.

"Anyway, I asked him if he was OK. He muttered something and turned to walk the other way. I grabbed him by the shoulder and asked him what he was doing out there. So he opens up his hand and holds out a lilac from Mrs. Steinkuhler's yard and tells me that he's looking for the ghost of Abraham Lincoln. I thought to myself, 'What kind of nut is this guy?'"

"He's not a nut!" Helen protested. "He's romantic."

"Romantic, nut—either way, that guy is strange."

Heedless of Otto's judgment, Helen went on: "He walked all the way from Springfield to New Mexico last year. He worked on farms and traded his poems for food and a bed."

Otto was bewildered. "You mean people actually paid for his poems?"

"Yes, and he got into all sorts of adventures on the road. He wrote poems while he was going from town to town, and then he would perform them. He's recited whole poems from memory for me. He's really good!"[9]

Helen set her notebook on a chair next to one of the dryers, stood back from Otto and Elizabeth to give herself room for a performance, and began reciting a few lines from a poem that Vachel Lindsay had recited to her a month before. She cleared her throat and began:

With a silk umbrella and the handle of a broom
Boomlay, boomlay, boomlay, BOOM
THEN I had religion, THEN I had a vision
I could not turn from their revel in derision
THEN I SAW THE CONGO, CREEPING THROUGH THE BLACK
CUTTING THROUGH THE FOREST WITH A GOLDEN TRACK.[10]

Helen was hunched forward, gesturing with every line, pumping her fist and laughing. Otto and Elizabeth just looked at her. She stood up straight, slightly embarrassed by her brother's exasperated look.

"You had better stay away from that guy," Otto concluded. Helen finally waved him off and picked up her notebook. She headed toward the back office. "Boomlay, boomlay, boomlay, BOOM" could be heard trailing off under her breath.

Elizabeth shook her head and walked back toward the front of the cleaning area, the remainder of Otto's comments drowned out by the sound of the pressing machines. Carl was standing at the end of the room in the doorway near the entrance to the cleaners, squinting at the ceiling through his pewter-rimmed glasses and then down at the floor. Otto soon rejoined the workers, keeping time with steam, pressing suits and blouses and whatever else Springfield was wearing that week. Some of the workers had just returned from their lunch break. Words couldn't be discerned above the din, but an occasional hand gesture indicated a conversation, if fragmented by the noise and the work. From the spot where Elizabeth had paused momentarily, she saw the lights from the ceiling forming a grid across the room, their little filaments burning brightly above the presses. Steam shot out of the top of the unit in front of her as one of the workers adding more coal to the boiler at the back of the room.

As Elizabeth walked toward Carl, he seemed lost in thought. Elizabeth wondered whether he was still smarting from her comment earlier in the morning. "He'll get over it," she said to herself as she noticed another customer entering the store.

IV

April 27, 1914, was a beautiful spring day. Mayme's wedding reception was a big success. Everyone the Frankes knew was there, all the extended family and their spouses and, in a few cases, their spouses' parents. Old friends of the family were there, including Mrs. Sutter, the baker's wife from East Prussia; the grocers Mr. and Mrs. Steinkuhler; Mr. Geitl, one of the first car repairmen in town; the housepainter Mr. Thielken and his wife; Mr. Buchner; Mr. and Mrs. Willet; and, of course, the Bunns. Some of them, living just down the block, arrived on foot, while others, like Mr. and Mrs. Steinmetz, pulled up in front of the house in a new Model A. Many friends from the German Methodist church came too, some of them bringing gifts and food, and others with letters for their relatives back in Germany, to be delivered by Frank and Marie.

It had been threatening to rain before the ceremony, but the clouds were breaking up to patches of blue. Even sunlight began to play on the roof of the Capitol building, which was in full view of the Frankes' yard. A bed of daffodils and red and yellow tulips along the side of the yard provided the appropriate mood for the festivities. Tomato, cucumber, and spinach were just beginning to sprout in

Marie's little garden plot near the back of the yard. Marie had started the seeds indoors a month before, and when the temperature rose the weekend before the wedding, she felt confident enough to plant the seedlings. Since the garden was to be Elizabeth's responsibility while Frank and Marie were away, Marie had offered persistent advice on its proper maintenance, none of which Elizabeth minded except for the occasional but lengthy digressions about life in Swinemünde and the little vegetable patch there. Trees in the yard were still well in bloom and their blossoms showered the backyard when the wind suddenly gusted. It was an altogether pleasant day, if only a touch humid.

Elizabeth was in charge of the arrangements. Marie was technically in charge, but Mayme and Elizabeth had insisted that their mother make an effort to enjoy herself, as the reception was in part a going-away party for their parents. So Marie did her best to meet with guests and not worry too much about the details. Helen and Milton had the responsibility of greeting newly arrived guests and directing them around the side of the house to the receiving line in the backyard. Bill, having acted as an usher during the ceremony, was first in line in a freshly pressed navy suit, a dark red bow tie and—now that they were outside—a straw boater. Otto and Anna were next in line. Otto stood erect, greeting guest after guest, his hair as impeccable as the fold of his shirtsleeves under his dark blue vest or the seam of his khaki-colored pants. His wife Anna, seven months pregnant, looked more relaxed, her white blouse dangling somewhat carelessly over a long dark skirt.

Carl and Dorothy would have been next in the receiving line, Carl being the best man, but Carl was busy directing a few men from the cleaners to set up another table in the yard for drinks. He had paid for all the refreshments, including coffee, lemonade, and a keg of Reich beer, which Mr. Schafer had yet to deliver. Wanting to make sure that everything was being attended to properly, Carl paced back and forth along the garage wall in his morning coat and top hat. Mr. Schafer was supposed to have delivered the beer via the alley before the reception. Carl periodically checked his watch and looked for the Reich truck. Dorothy stood in Carl's place greeting people as they walked by. Her beautiful dress was made even lovelier by a glow that seemed to surround her—she had just found out the day before that she was pregnant and had yet to tell anyone.[11]

Frank and Marie stood next to the bride and groom, beaming with pride—especially Marie, a first-time mother of the bride. She wore a dress that Frank had made, based on a pattern from one of the most fashionable boutiques in Paris. Embroidered with silk on both the waist and the skirt, the blue taffeta shimmered in the afternoon sun while the plaits over the shoulders gathered luxurious shadows. Although he generally worked only on men's suits, Frank had made an exception for their wedding anniversary. With the sun above and slightly behind her now, Marie's delicately tied hair looked like a tawny halo over her head as she kissed the guests in succession. The high collar she wore was punctuated by an old brooch given to her by her mother before she left Germany, an exclamation point for the day's events.

In his morning coat, gray trousers, and silk top hat, Frank was the picture of success. He had walked down the aisle proudly with Mayme, greeted and talked with people about the trip to Germany and about the incredible success of Paris Cleaners. Now he waited in line for another round of greetings. As he stood there looking at his children and their spouses, at Helen and Milton happily ushering more guests to the receiving line, his well-fitting waistcoat could hardly contain his immense satisfaction. His life was all but complete. His firstborn daughter was married; his comfortable house was paid for, and he was about to return to Germany triumphant. The world, it seemed, was at peace. In the yard next door, a bright orange oriole lighted on a crabapple tree whose branches sagged with full white blossoms. Not knowing where it came from or where it was going, Frank took the sudden appearance of this bird as a sign of his blessing. When he had first set out on his long journey from Berlin to Springfield, never in his wildest fantasies could he have predicted a more perfect day than this. When he and Carl had established Paris Cleaners five years before, never did he imagine, despite his aspirations, that he would actually bring the family together in the same business. Not even his father or his father's father had been able to achieve that. Yet here he was at his daughter's wedding with three of his sons standing next to him—two of them (Carl and Otto) with wives and their own homes—and each of them working for the family business that was a model for other families on Vinegar Hill. When he saw Helen opening the back door for Elizabeth, who was carrying a huge platter of sauerkraut, Frank couldn't help but smile.

Just then Carl came back into the yard directing a man wheeling a dolly that held a keg of beer toward one of the back tables. Carl straightened his tie and rejoined the receiving line. As he was whispering into Dorothy's ear, he felt his father's hand patting him on the back.

As Frank leaned slightly forward from the receiving line, Bill caught his father's long beard in the corner of his eye. After greeting the Vogels, good friends of the family, Frank first looked toward Mayme and Charles and then toward Bill and Otto. His two sons immediately pushed out their chests, making sure their spines were vertical. It was instinct. All the Franke children had the instantaneous response of standing up straighter as soon as their father looked at them. All had endured their father's curious, if somewhat severe, posture remedy of lying flat on the cutting table of the tailoring shop to be measured for growth. If they hadn't grown since the last measurement, their father would tell them that they had been stooping over too much and exhort them to "stand tall."[12] Milton was still in training. All had their complaints about the ordeal, but it served as common bond of humor and humiliation, especially as their father was unafraid to correct them in public if necessary. But none had had it worse than Bill. By the time he was sixteen, Bill stood at least a head above the rest of the family. Easygoing and unassuming, Bill struggled with the posture regimen, and it became a bone of contention between him and his father. It wasn't out of disrespect that Bill found himself slouching on occasion; he simply lacked the Prussian predilection for an upright posture.

Elizabeth now came out through the back door with Helen close behind her. They were bringing more food; this time Elizabeth carried a large baking dish filled with smoked sausages, and Helen followed with a plate of dill pickles and hot German potato salad. One of the women from church came out a minute later with a half-dozen loaves of fresh rye. Thus began the procession of food from the kitchen to the long tables covered in gingham tablecloths. Milton helped too, bringing turnovers, jellies, and pancakes. One of the guests even showed up with a German cured ham. It was an altogether abundant display, with nearby guests oohing and ahing as more dishes were laid on the table.

Still greeting new guests, Charles stood between his father-in-law and his bride. As he watched Frank and Marie laughing with friends, he couldn't help thinking of his own parents. His father had died fourteen years before in 1900, and his mother just four years before in 1910.[13] He regretted her absence the most. By the time he was fifteen, his father's health was already failing. The youngest in his family, he remained with his widowed mother. They grew close, but his mother was always urging him to find a wife. Even Charles had given up on the thought by the time his mother died. He had obtained a position as a salesman at a clothing store in Champaign and was quite satisfied with his prospects there. But Champaign was a small town, and by his mid-twenties he still hadn't met a prospective bride. Most of his friends were already married, and the few available women that were left in town showed no interest in him. Charles, a reserved man, had resigned himself to bachelorhood.

V

Well before he met Mayme, Charles and several of his coworkers played in a local baseball league in Champaign. They often took the Saturday train to the Illinois River, where they practiced as a team, had a picnic, and went fishing. On one Saturday afternoon two years before Charles's wedding, this group set up a baseball diamond in a field along the river. It was an ordinary summer afternoon—sunny, hot, with a little breeze coming off the river. Tree pollen hung above the great oaks by the field, making a haze over the river and across the field.

Toward the end of a lazy game of baseball, a young man emerged from behind a stand of oaks along the river with a long, bamboo fishing rod in his hand. It was Carl, well dressed as usual, in tailored tan pants with dark brown stripes. His flowered tie was set off by a chalk-white long-sleeved shirt with a stylish, starched, oversized collar. A straw boater topped off the ensemble. Carl watched the game for a moment and finally struck up a conversation with Charles, who was standing along the first-base line harassing the infielders. By the time the game was over, Carl had set up an appointment for Charles and Mayme to meet on the following weekend in Springfield.[14]

This was not the first time Charles had been set up on a blind date, but it was his first date in Springfield. So the following Saturday he took the Inter-urban to Springfield. He was skeptical about his prospects with Mayme, as he hadn't had much luck before. By lowering his expectations, he would avoid disappointment. Nonetheless, he brought flowers with him from Champaign and a box of chocolates for Mrs. Franke, and he wore his best clothes. Working at a clothing store always gave him this distinct advantage: he could afford the smartest suits in Champaign. On this day he was wearing a neatly tailored cream-colored suit, a blue silk tie, and a straw boater with a blue and green striped band.

Carl was gracious enough to meet him at the train station and walk with him back to the house in order to meet Mayme. It had stormed earlier in the morning and clouds still hung over Springfield. The day was hot and humid, and Charles was sweating as they walked. Carl was discussing the cleaning business with him.

When they arrived, Frank was sitting with Milton on a swing on the front porch sipping lemonade. He wore his big straw fishing hat and was considering trimming his beard for coolness. Charles and Carl climbed the steps as Frank stood up to greet them. Carl introduced them, and after a few minutes of small talk he and Charles made their way through the living room to the kitchen, where Bill, Helen, and Marie were seated. Charles nervously shook hands with them and offered a box of chocolates to Marie. She was delighted by the gesture, passing the box around the kitchen table. She then asked Charles about his job, Champaign, his family, and whatever else came to mind. Although she awed him a little, Marie had a calming effect on Charles. She could already sense that he was the right man for Mayme and quickly decided to do everything in her power to make him feel welcome.

Mayme had had plenty of dates with promising young men, but none had worked out. Naturally, Marie had begun to worry about her eldest daughter. They had struggled with one another over the years as eldest daughters and their mothers often do, but Marie wanted nothing but the best for Mayme now.

Mayme thought of her relationship with her mother as an estrangement rather than a struggle. As the result of something that had occurred many years before, Mayme could never regard her mother without suspicion, fear, and shame. One Easter Sunday, the whole family was getting ready for church and a long day of festivities. Half the family waited on the porch, watching a light spring rain drizzle over Springfield, while the other half finished getting ready. Mayme was at that age of physical awkwardness when she was never satisfied with her appearance and was mortified by the prospect of someone's noticing her growing pains. She was fourteen years old and, try as she might, her hair just wasn't doing what it was supposed to be doing that morning. She was so embarrassed that she even threatened to forgo church. Finally, her mother ordered her to go to her parents' bedroom and bring a hair comb from the top drawer of the dresser. Mayme was furious but managed to control her anger. In the bedroom, the overcast light filled the room with a bluish hue. Opening the drawer, Mayme immediately began rifling through all the trinkets of her mother's youth: jewelry, brushes, brooches, empty picture frames, German coins, a pin from Berlin, a tiny American flag, and an assortment of boxes. She knew her family was waiting for her, but she couldn't help lingering over the fragments of her mother's life. Until then, Mayme had only understood Marie as her mother, yet here were bits and pieces that indicted a life beyond motherhood. She did find a hair comb, but it didn't look suitable, so she continued searching the drawer for other combs. It was then that she decided to explore one of the boxes.

It was a large wooden box covered with red morocco and studded with nails that made an attractive pattern across the top. The box barely fit in the drawer. Mayme removed it carefully and set it on top of the dresser. She could hear someone coming up the front stairs as she opened the box. A fine piece of white silk lay over an indiscernible lump. Removing the veil, she moved in for a closer look. A shriveled brown thing lay at the bottom of the box like an abnormally large prune. Whoever was coming up the stairs was now at the top. Mayme reached into the box and picked up the object in question. It was unmistakable: at the end of a large strand of the leatherlike, shriveled material Mayme discerned a tiny head. She turned it over in disbelief. Its tiny cheeks had sunk into its little skull, a shrunken idol of what horrific faith she shuddered to imagine. She closed the box and stuffed it back into the drawer. Her body trembled; her head spun; she felt faint. Carl came into the room and said, "Come on, everybody's waiting downstairs." She was visibly shaken, and Carl asked if she was all right. As she descended the stairs, she kept repeating to herself, "I don't know . . . I don't know . . . I don't know."[15]

Two years after they had married and settled in Springfield, Frank and Marie were about to become parents. On September 1, 1886, Marie gave birth to twins. Willie died at birth, while his sister Mary struggled for her life, only to die seven weeks later on October 19. It was a devastating blow for Marie. For two months leading up to Christmas, she was sick with fatigue and convinced that the death of her babies was somehow punishment for dishonoring her family back in Germany. Shortly after New Year's, however, she was pregnant again with Carl and Mayme. In a later pregnancy, when Marie miscarried in her seventh month, she was reminded of the grief of losing her first two babies. All of the guilty feelings about her family returned, so that she could not bear to bury the child. She had prepared the tiny fetus by washing it in vinegar, but when it came time for burial, the thought of her poor baby suffocating under the earth sickened her. Having wrapped it up and sealed it in a box, she secreted the box into the barn, retrieving it only after the worst of her grief. That was when she noticed that the fetus had been shrunken by the dry weather and cured by the vinegar.[16] The little body became an effigy of her grief, and to part with it would have been to dishonor the souls of her lost children. Frank made no objection to keeping the tiny casket in their bedroom dresser. He had been so distraught by Marie's grief that anything to ease the pain seemed acceptable.

Without such information, the memory of the fetus continued to haunt Mayme through her adolescence. She never told anyone in the family, and like her mother before her, she secreted the image into the barn of her memory. But the image returned to her, usually at night, just before she fell sleep. The mystery of its origin grew stranger and more horrible, and she often wondered what other hideous things might be hidden in that room. It was as if the shrunken baby represented only the beginning of the strange practices of her mother, hidden until now. As Mayme matured into adulthood, she tried to convince herself that it was all just some German peasant tradition or that perhaps she hadn't seen the fetus at all, that she had been mistaken all along. As much as she tried, however, it was impossible not to feel disturbed about her mother's private life. Subsequently, Mayme grew more distant from both her mother and the rest of the family.

Sensing this distance, Marie worried about it a great deal. She realized she made demands on Mayme, always expecting her to be perfect, but she couldn't help herself. At birth, Mayme was weaker than her twin brother, and Marie was desperate to correct that weakness. She couldn't get Mayme to gain any weight, while Carl grew normally. A doctor who was a customer of Frank's had suggested that Mayme might be having problems with the mother's milk, that Marie might try feeding little Mayme some goat's milk. That afternoon Frank walked down to the end of Adams Street to the outskirts of Springfield to the farm of a fellow German of his acquaintance. He bought the first goat he saw, slung it over his shoulders, and walked all the way back into town. He and Marie kept the goat in the backyard and Frank milked it every morning. The milk helped. Mayme gradually took on weight.[17] But Marie continued to worry about Mayme and not only about her physical wellbeing. She wondered if Mayme was emotionally weak as well. In order to ensure that her daughter grew stronger, Marie always disciplined Mayme more than the other children. At the end of third grade, she kept Mayme at home to help with the family.

Mayme would never forget the day her mother taught her how to crack eggs into a bowl and then run her index finger around the inside of the shell so as to not lose any of the egg white.[18] When she was old enough to cook, clean, and take care of the other children, Mayme had to do it all without Carl's help. He was usually at work with his father, and, besides, he was not expected to assist with household chores. Although Mayme was, in fact, born a few minutes before her twin, Carl was considered the firstborn. Mayme was just the eldest child.

By the time she was sixteen, Mayme was working at Boston's as a milliner.[19] It was a liberating experience, and she quickly became one of the best milliners in town. Even her father, very reticent when it came to praise, saw her handiwork and liked it so much that he expressed his pride. As Paris Cleaners grew, Frank would have welcomed Mayme into the family business. By then, however, Mayme was firmly established as a milliner. She loved the work and really had no interest in tailoring. Despite his disappointment, Frank understood his daughter's decision. He spoke to Marie about Mayme. Both he and Marie were proud of Mayme and recognized how demanding

Mayme and Charles early in their relationship, circa 1912.

of her they had been. Since she would not share in the family business and had yet to be married, they decided to give her a diamond. Frank spared no expense. He bought her the best diamond he could afford and brought it to her as a kind of peace offering, an installment on her inheritance as a member of a successful merchant Prussian family. She had no expectations of such a gift and was puzzled by the timing, but she accepted the ring graciously. As she grew older, she came to understand the gift as a token of the enormous sacrifices that her parents had to make. They needed to give her something. And later, in a way that meant a great deal to her, she realized that the diamond was recognition of her as a person, outside of the family and the family business.[20]

Despite her genuine respect for Mayme as an adult, Marie continued to worry about her daughter's chances of getting married. Mayme was already twenty-six. So when Charles came into her kitchen that day with a box of chocolates and a bouquet of flowers, Marie seized the opportunity, and Charles proved more than willing to go along with the plan.

The first date began awkwardly. After Charles had met the whole family, Mayme finally emerged from the bedroom. She wore a long blue dress and a straw hat, which she had made for the occasion. It had a wide brim and a large crown and was draped with several brightly colored ribbons. She was shy and nervous, and so was Charles. They sat in the living room, watched by everyone else. Charles occasionally broke the silence with an awkward comment on the weather. When he finally remembered the bouquet of flowers, Mayme was more pleased than he could have imagined. Not that it was an unusual gesture, but she was touched by the young man's thoughtfulness. After a few more minutes, Charles asked if she might like to walk downtown and have some lunch. By the end of the day they were still uncertain about each other but felt willing to meet again. They went for a picnic the following weekend on the bank of the Illinois River. Charles had taken the early train to Springfield and spent most of the morning talking to Marie, asking about her life in Germany, what was new in Springfield, and whatever else came to mind. From then on, Marie was Charles's greatest advocate. She was careful not to sing his praises too loudly but to slowly persuade Mayme that Charles was the man for her.

Mayme needed little persuasion, however. By the end of their third date, which consisted of an evening stroll along the banks of the Sangamon River, Mayme detected a gentleness and kindness in Charles that she felt sure she could live with. Within six months of their first date, they were engaged to be married.

VI

Charles stood at the end of the receiving line with Mayme, now his wife, nervously shaking hands with many people he had never seen before. His tuxedo was tailored to perfection, courtesy of his father-in-law. He was clearly relieved that the ceremony was over, and whenever the opportunity presented itself, he leaned toward his his bride and kissed her tenderly on the cheek.

Mayme appeared to take it all in graciously, thanking people for attending and laughing with friends. But she was not accustomed to being the center of attention, and had been all nerves just before the ceremony. As she began to walk down the aisle with her father, she had turned her head to look at him. He marched as only a Prussian would on the day of his eldest daughter's wedding: tall, proud and straight-backed. Yet just before they reached her husband-to-be, she noticed her father's great shaggy beard move a little. There was no sudden breeze in the church. In that moment, Mayme detected a gentle smile cross her father's face. He was proud of his daughter on this her wedding day. It was the first time he had ever shown any emotion or sign of approval in what Mayme had done. She had to fight tears of happiness as she and Charles made their vows.

There was majesty to Mayme's appearance that afternoon that belied any hesitation or turmoil. She was the picture of the bride. Being among the best milliners in town, Mayme felt it her responsibility to fashion a wedding hat fit for a queen: it was ivory-colored, wide-brimmed, with a net ribbon that encircled the crown and swept down into a white veil. The crown was rounded, low, and decorated with lace appliques and fresh lily of the valley. The whole effect was light and airy. Many attending the reception described it as "elegant and angelic."

Mayme's dress, though also magnificent, held less of her own distinctive touch. The skirt was from her mother's wedding dress. The original bodice was too large and, Mayme thought, too worn and out of fashion. But her mother insisted that Mayme wear at least part of the dress as a way of maintaining continuity between mother and daughter. Since Mayme had to have a hat for her wedding, as opposed to a simple veil, they agreed that the skirt was the best article of clothing with which to establish this continuity. When they were married, Frank and Marie had dug into their savings for the material for Marie's dress. It somehow symbolized for them how far they had come since leaving Berlin. And here they were, thirty years later, about to return to Germany for the first time. How right it would have been, Marie believed, for her first daughter to bid her farewell in Mayme's original dress.

Compromise, however, has its own poignancy. The ivory satin skirt, draped into a modest train, was embellished with three-leaf clovers that picked up the light and gave the garment a rich glow and texture. The bodice was based on a pattern Mayme had picked out in a fashion magazine. Her father, of course, was instrumental in choosing the right material, fine silk brocade, and, indeed, in making the piece. Mayme had added the faux pearl buttons down the front. The high collar and sleeves were trimmed with intricate ecru lace left over from a hat Mayme had made for Mrs. Bunn. So stunning was the effect that Charles gazed at his bride in apparent disbelief. Even Marie, who was never slow to criticize Mayme, had to agree with the final decision.

The food continued in a steady stream from the kitchen and onto the tables in the backyard. Several people from the church helped Elizabeth in the kitchen. Some of them brought bread, noodles, potato salad, pickles—everything for a German feast. Elizabeth was busy with the final preparations and ordering people around. She had been up since five in the morning and had spent the previous day cooking with her mother as her helpful, if somewhat taxing, guide. Fewer than fifty people attended, but in those final moments before they all sat down, Elizabeth felt as if she were cooking for a small army.

The food was traditional German, in honor of Frank and Marie's return to Germany. By far the most important dish was sauerbraten. Little else mattered, as long as the sauerbraten had the proper tang. Growing up in Derz, Frank rarely ate beef. He was raised on potatoes, cabbage, and turnips. When his family ate meat, it was usually goose, lamb, or pork, and that was reserved for a special occasion, such as a Church feast or harvest festival. In fact, Frank could recall only three or four occasions in his childhood when he had eaten beef. The few cows around Derz were almost exclusively reserved for dairy. Arriving in Berlin in 1878, Frank discovered a world of beef. It was not a cheap meal, but was certainly more available than it was in Derz. As a result, Frank had developed a taste for sauerbraten, a passion he shared with many of the wedding guests. Marie's sauerbraten was legendary, so the pressure on Elizabeth was significant. Getting sauerbraten right involved several days of preparation. Most recipes called for beef cut from the upper back hip to be marinaded in vinegar from red wine for two to three days, but Marie insisted that the marinade consist of a mixture of red wine and vinegar. Elizabeth put the beef into two large pots, covered them in the vinegar-wine mixture, and placed them in the cellar on Wednesday evening. Early Saturday morning, she dried the meat and rubbed it with coarse pepper. About an hour before the wedding, she placed the beef back in the pots with the vinegar and wine, added more wine, onions, carrots and potatoes and left them to simmer while she went to the wedding. One of their neighbors, Mrs. Detig, agreed to stay behind to watch the food during the ceremony and help with other preparations.

Helen, circa 1914.

Elizabeth sliced the sauerbraten, while Helen arranged the slices on two platters with a bowl of sour cream for each platter. The last of the dumplings and red cabbage were boiling on the stove. Elizabeth wondered whether she could stand up any longer, but at that moment three of the women from church came back into the kitchen and whisked away the last of the dishes and Elizabeth along with them. Before they came out of the back door, Elizabeth paused for a moment at the bottom of the stairs, wiped her brow with a dish towel still in her hand, and smiled at Helen descending the stairs with a large bowl of steaming red cabbage.

"Are you ready?" Elizabeth called up to Helen.

"Sure."

When they walked into the backyard, Elizabeth received a hearty ovation. Most of the guests understood how much work the reception involved, and the food looked wonderful. Helen set the cabbage next to the sauerbraten at the end of a long table piled with food, and the guests wasted no time in lining up for their share.

Frank stood at the end of the line next to Mr. Steinmetz. After briefly discussing Mr. Steinmetz's new Model A, Mr. Steinmetz asked Frank about their trip to Germany. The conversation quickly turned to politics.

"Have you been following what is going on in the Balkans?" Mr. Steinmetz asked as he picked up a plate at the end of the table. Frank, always an avid reader of both the German and the English papers in Springfield, replied that of course he had read of the war in the Balkans.

"Aren't you in the least bit worried about a situation developing while you are back in Germany?" Mr. Steinmetz continued, helping himself to potato salad.

"No, not in the least bit," replied Frank.

"Really?" Mr. Steinmetz looked at Frank incredulously. "As I understand it, Mr. Franke, all of Europe is drawn into this mess. In fact, just the other day I read an editorial that suggested that it could involve not only Austria, Serbia, Germany, and Russia, but also France and England. Because if Russia supports Serbia, which of course they do, they would be supported by France. And if Germany attacks France, they might do it through Belgium. This would bring Great

Britain to France's side because Belgium and Great Britain are already allies."[21]

"You must have read the same article I read the other day. Was it in the *State Register*?" Frank asked.

"Yes it was. What's more, this journalist confirmed the general view in Germany that war is inevitable."

"Well, war may be inevitable, but the question is what kind of war and when," Frank replied, taking several slices of sauerbraten. After spooning out a dollop of sour cream, he continued: "When I was in the army, the chancellor led us to believe that war was always imminent. The training was constant, and the French were always the assumed enemy. Yet, in the three years that I spent in the army, I never saw any combat. Besides," Frank added, "when the time comes, France won't have forgotten 1871. The Prussian army is quite simply the best army in the world, and if France is any ally to Russia, she will surely let Russia know what kind of opponent lies behind the Austrian lines."[22]

Frank was referring to the Franco-Prussian war of 1870–71, in which the Prussian army attacked and defeated the French at Sedan in the northeast of France and went on to occupy Paris in 1871. The overwhelming victory not only confirmed Prussia's reputation as the mightiest army in Europe, but also, through Prussia's annexation of Alsace and Lorraine in the subsequent peace treaty with France, encouraged all the German states south of the Main, including Bavaria, Wurttemberg, Baden, and Palatinate, to join the new German Reich. In other words, the swift and decisive force of the Prussian army in France and in Austria just five years earlier in 1866, combined with the canny political maneuvers of Chancellor Bismarck, unified Germany and created a new economic power in Europe.[23]

Mr. Steinmetz now followed Frank to the line of guests waiting behind the beer table in the shade of large cottonwood. Mr. Schafer had the honor of tapping the keg and dispensing it; he had a joke for each guest as he handed out the glasses. Mr. Steinmetz picked up the conversation where it had left off.

"Well, Frank, that was before my time. My family came here in 1880, when I was three years old. All I remember of Berlin was the dank smell of the room we lived in. My mother used to tell us we lived in the basement of one of the Berlin tenements, but I certainly couldn't tell you what it looked like, let alone anything about the Prussian army or the unification of Germany."

Frank smiled like a soldier about to recount a boot camp story. "Oh, I could tell you something about the room where I lived in Berlin. First of all, there were seven other people in the room, not including myself—all in a room no bigger than our parlor."

Steinmetz interrupted, "Yes, my mother said that we lived with another family in this room and when my brother had asthma, she would have to carry him a mile before she could get him to some fresh air."

"And that would have been the least of her troubles," Frank went on more gravely than before. "We didn't even have a toilet on our block. You had to walk all the way to the end of the block, walk through the first tenement on the left and find your way into the basement. I won't even tell you what you would find there."[24]

"Well, let's hope some things have changed in thirty years," said Steinmetz, picking up a glass from the table. "Where exactly will you be traveling in Germany?"

"We'll spend most of our time in Berlin, I suspect. Most of Mrs. Franke's family is there and I have a number of relatives there, but we do plan on returning to Derz, the village where I grew up. We'll see my brothers and sisters, go fishing, and visit with friends. We also plan on visiting Mrs. Franke's hometown."

"And where is that?" Steinmetz asked.

"Swinemünde," Frank replied, nodding to Mr. Schafer as he was handed a glass. "It's northeast of Berlin on the Baltic Sea. It can be quite beautiful in summer."

Feeling a tap on his shoulder, Frank turned around. Otto explained that it was time to sit down, as the toasts were about to begin. Frank turned back to Mr. Steinmetz, who was already nodding in assent. "It sounds like a wonderful trip. We'll talk later."

Otto ushered his father to a long table surrounded by four smaller ones. Frank sat at one end and Marie at the other; the rest of the wedding party filled the long sides, with Mayme and Charles taking the middle. In a gesture that—given her somewhat modest and, at times, serious demeanor—suggested the extent of her delight that afternoon, Marie picked up her napkin and waved to Frank across the length of the table. He smiled at her as he smoothed the ends of the white tablecloth over the table.

After everyone was seated, Carl stood up with a beer glass in hand. He tucked a small piece of paper in his back pocket. He cleared his throat and walked toward the house, so that everyone could see him. Bill visibly winced at the approaching pomp. Carl began.

"Almost thirty years ago to the day, my father arrived in New York with one thing on his mind: he had to get to Springfield. It was his destiny to bring the name of Franke to these shores and establish the business that is second to none in our city. Though from a family of position and a brilliant military career, my father came to this chosen city. His wife, my mother, followed him upon receipt of assurance that Springfield was the community of the future. Of course, they were married and proceeded to have seven children. They worked very hard and raised us to have a profound devotion to honor, truth, honesty, diligence, and a commitment to excellence."

Frank looked at all of his children. Tears were welling up in Marie's eyes. Even Bill bowed his head.

"What could be a more joyous occasion for my mother and father and for all of us here than the celebration this afternoon of the marriage of Charles and Mayme? We have watched them through their courtship, and I can speak for the whole family in saying that we eagerly look forward to a life of their company."

Carl paused for a moment to look at the bride and groom. Mayme, who had had her problems with Carl over the years, was touched by her twin brother's words. As Carl raised his glass, she choked up again.

"Therefore, I would like to raise a glass for both couples this afternoon—for my mother and father and for Charles and Mayme," Carl resumed. "To thirty years of love and devotion, and to the happiest days of our lives!"

A cacophony of clinking glasses and clapping hands ensued. Carl walked back to the main table, knocked glasses with his mother and kissed her dutifully on the cheek while Mayme and Charles were swarmed with beer glasses from every direction. Carl finally came over to them, clinked glasses and sat down.

Then the pastor rose from his seat and took Carl's place near the house. After grace was said, the roar of conversation resumed, and people began to eat. The sauerbraten was just right, so much so that several guests even got up from their table to complement Elizabeth on its success. "A true successor to Frau Franke's sauerbraten," they said, at which Elizabeth blushed. Frank and Marie took in the scene contentedly. The afternoon sun was full and warm now, and the guests, who knew each other from church or work or the neighborhood, began to get up from their tables and talk to others. The conversations soon turned toward Germany. Elizabeth nodded at Helen, and both rose. Helen tapped Mrs. Sutter on the shoulder and told her that it was time. The three of them went down into the cellar. Mrs. Sutter, the baker's wife, was an expert cake maker. Frank and Marie had known the Sutters from since first arriving in Springfield. The Sutters lived just down the block from the Frankes at 228 West Adams.[25] One day in 1885, Frank went to the bakery where Henry Sutter worked. It was a German bakery, so Frank naturally spoke to Henry in German. After taking Frank's order and handing him a loaf of pumpernickel, Henry asked Frank if he was from Allenstein. With a look of surprise, Frank told him that he wasn't but had often gone to the market there as a child to sell cabbage and beets. Then Frank, assuming his local accent had largely disappeared during his time in Berlin, asked Henry how he knew where he was from. Henry explained that his wife, Ottilie, was from Ermland as well and that he had become quite expert in identifying people's birthplaces by their accents. The two couples soon discovered that they now lived in the same neighborhood, and they became fast friends.[26] Before Henry died in 1910, Ottilie baked most of the cakes for her husband's bakery. Although she hadn't done any commercial baking since the bakery closed, she hadn't lost her touch, especially when it came to the butter-cream frosting.

Mrs. Sutter had brought the cake over early that morning with Otto's help. When she came up from the cellar, followed by Elizabeth and Helen, the crowd hushed a moment to behold the cake. As Mrs. Sutter set it in front of the bride and groom, Mayme couldn't hold back her delight. The cake was not large in diameter, but consisted of three thick layers stacked neatly on top of each other to form a conical pyramid. Each layer was marked with different piping along the edge. It was a lemon cake with white frosting and sugar-coated violets. Mayme had always dreamed of eating violets on her wedding day.

The bride and groom stood up and with very little ceremony cut the cake. Elizabeth, however, insisted that they feed one another the first bite for good luck, and everyone at the table soon chimed in agreement. While Mayme and Charles were performing their wedding day ritual, Bill silently got Otto's attention and pointed to his pocket watch. Otto rose promptly and waved toward the house. Bill followed. Otto then led Bill around to the front of the house, where they began discussing the next phase of the reception.

"I thought they were supposed to be here by now," Bill said, somewhat agitated.

"No, I talked to them yesterday afternoon and told them we would go get them when we're ready," Otto explained.

"So where are they?"

"Just down the street. We can go down now and help them with their instruments."

Otto was referring to a well-known band in Vinegar Hill that played German music at weddings and other social events in the German neighborhoods of Springfield. In summer they could be heard on Friday nights in the beer garden of a tavern just a few blocks away from Paris Cleaners. Bill and Otto both knew some of the musicians, and they thought it would be a nice way to send Frank and Marie back to Germany.

The band brought their instruments to the yard by way of the alley, so that none of the guests would see them coming, especially Frank and Marie. No one else in the family knew about the music except for Elizabeth, who had a way of finding out everything that was going on in the family. As the musicians approached the back gate, Otto asked them to pause for a moment. Bill was smiling in anticipation as Otto went in through the gate. Back in the yard among the wedding guests, Otto cleared his throat loudly. A few of the guests turned toward him. He was nervous. "I'd like to make an announcement," he called out over the disparate conversations, clasping his hands behind his back. "As many of you know, in a few days my mother and father will return to Germany for the first time since they came to Springfield in 1884. Thirty years is a long time, and we are all very excited for them. This has truly been a wonderful day, for Mayme and Charles and for our families. So we can't bid my parents a German farewell without a proper march."

At that moment, the steady beat of a snare drum rattled from the alley. Bill came in first, walking in step to the beat, hamming it up for the guests with every step. The drummer followed with the snare drum strapped to his shoulder. The accordion player, flutist, and violinist were close behind, playing a lively version of a German march. Not surprisingly, almost all the hearers knew the tune, and they stood up in unison, clapping to the drum beat. Frank was shaking with laughter as he went over to Marie's end of the table and stood next to her. The band circled around the yard twice until the march was completed. The musicians then stood along the fence, while several of the guests, directed by Otto and Bill, helped clear the tables off to the side of the yard. The band played a quiet, measured song, with the accordion taking the lead. The violin made a low whining sound. Several older couples, including the Steinkuhlers and the Thilkens, sought out Frank and Marie and brought them to the center of the yard. The band repeated the first eight bars of the German folksong *Kegel-Quadrille* as Mrs. Steinkuhler grabbed the nearest couple to make a total of five couples, with Frank and Marie in the center and the other four forming a square around them. Joining hands, the four outer couples circled around Frank and Marie at a swinging gallop. Without missing a beat, Frank skipped toward Mrs. Steinkuhler, hooked arms with her, twirled her around, headed across the circle to Mrs. Thilken, and twirled her around in turn. Marie followed Frank's lead and skipped toward the Steinkuhlers. Once Marie got back to the middle of the circle, the dance repeated with the other two couples. Frank was clapping his hands to the first beat of the bar and stomping his foot to the second. The couples were now dancing in a reverse chain. The song came to a break, and all five couples joined in a waltz. The whole song was then repeated, with the Thilkens in the middle position, while Frank and Marie ducked out and sent Mayme and Charles in their place.

One by one the guests shook hands and laughed with Frank and Marie as they watched their children stumble through the dance. People congregated around the keg while others urged the dancers on with clapping. Marie watched Mayme and Charles dancing in the center of the circle now. It was strange to think that she and Frank had come all the way from Germany only to dance the same dance here in America. It would have been beautiful to dance like this in Swinemünde or even in Berlin, but it was not meant to be. A low bank of clouds was coming in from the northwest, still miles away. Spring had arrived. But as surely as the buds bloomed, a late frost could bring all their petals down again. And if not frost then heat or a sudden storm, leaving the blossoms choked or whirled in a tangle. "There will be rain tonight," she said to herself as she watched the turning of the dancers, "rain raining on the rooftops and rain on the city where I have lived." A freight train could be heard in the distance, heading north to Chicago at a steady clip, and for a moment the accordion's drone harmonized with the horn of the train.

When the band started in with a different song, the older couples set their beer or lemonade down and formed a large circle. The men stood behind the women with their hands on their hips and hopped up and down, turning in a circle. The women, feigning surprise, did a little waltz on their own. The drummer noticeably quickened the beat as if to signal all the young people to join in. The circle widened. There still wasn't enough room in the yard to form a full circle, so the Franke family volunteered to form an inner circle, with Charles and Mayme in the center.

The violin resumed the melody with greater force and speed, and the men resumed hopping in place. The younger couples watched the older couples. After swinging their arms and bending their knees at the appointed time, they all took a small step forward and began hopping on one foot. Some of the older men dangled their handkerchiefs in front of them as they hopped on their left foot and then on their right.[27] The circle turned. The men were now in front of the women and the whole dance repeated. There was no sign of letup.

Eventually, however, the older couples retreated to their seats, leaving only the seven Franke children and their partners on the dance floor. Mayme and Charles beamed with joy, but it was Otto and

Anna's graceful movements that everyone noticed. Otto loved to dance; it was as if his body was another instrument in the band. Soon, he was leading the dance. Handkerchiefs waved in a circular motion, and the tempo increased. As Marie turned to Frank, Frank waved his handkerchief in front of her face almost childishly. If she hadn't known better, Marie could have sworn that they were all bidding her farewell as the crab tree shook white petals from its boughs, sending them down on the guests like confetti.

2. J.

EMERGENCY PASSPORT.

THIS PASSPORT IS ISSUED TO

Frank Franke

IN ORDER THAT HE MAY

PROCEED TO *U.S.A.*

*Fee
1066*

Embassy
of the

United States of America,

HAMBURG BERLIN GERMANY

To all to whom these presents shall come, Greeting,

*I the undersigned, Ambassador Extraordinary and Plenipotentiary
of the United States of America*

hereby request all whom it may concern to permit

Frank Franke

a Citizen of the United States accompanied
by his wife ——————— safely
and freely to pass and in case of need to give
them all lawful Aid and Protection.

Given under my hand and the
Seal of the Embassy of the
United States
at **HAMBURG**
the *15th* day of *August*
in the year *1944* and of the
Independence of the United States
the one hundred and *39th*

Description

Age *57* Years
Stature *5 Feet 7½ Inches Eng*
Forehead *high*
Eyes *brown*
Nose *prominent*
Mouth *medium*
Chin *square*
Hair *grey*
Complexion *ruddy*
Face *oval*

Signature of the Bearer
Frank. Franke

No. 09665

OLD HABITS

The most important vacation for Frank and Marie was to Germany in the summer of 1914. It was their thirtieth wedding anniversary, and the only time they returned to their homeland. This trip was a pivotal event in their lives; with the outbreak of World War I while they were in Berlin, they faced some very complex problems. Without his emergency United States passport, Frank most likely would have had to serve again in the German army in 1914.

I

Frank always liked Berlin. To be sure, his first years there were marked by abject poverty. He lived with his cousin's family of eight in a small dark room lined with cots floor to ceiling. He owned only one pair of workpants and struggled daily to keep them clean, which, in the coal-brown streets and dirty factories of 1880s Berlin, was no small task. During his first winter there in 1879, he ate turnip soup at least once a day, usually twice. On better days he would find an actual slice of turnip floating in his soup bowl. But the soup didn't bother him so much as the fact that he was always eating with fifty other people hunkered over their steins of beer, puffing away on cigars and groaning over the day's labor. It was the noise that got to him, and the fact that the water used to extend yesterday's soup tasted like the very coal that covered his clothes, his face, his cousin's family, and the floor of the power plant where he worked. It was an inescapable condition of Berlin, and particularly of Wedding, the working-class neighborhood where he lived before serving in the army.

Nonetheless, Berlin retained for Frank an aura of excitement, of mystery, and of youthful possibility that he was never to discover anywhere else. St. Louis was a sleepy river town by comparison. And while Chicago shared Berlin's wild and muscular magnificence, it marked something so different for him that he could hardly compare the two cities. After all, memory consists less of past events than of a tableau of the past. Berlin was the theater of Frank's true education. He found his first freedom in Berlin. He discovered the bitterness of beer and coffee in Berlin and, when he had a little more money, the pleasures of beef. There he learned the satisfaction of progress, of making his own way, step by step, in the world. There too he knew the sting of exclusion, that of both class and religion, and encountered forces much larger than himself—indeed, forces almost unaccountable in their pervasiveness.

It was a different story for Marie. For her, Berlin held far more ambivalence. That is why, when they arrived in the Hamburger Bahnhof from Bremen on May 18, 1914, Marie asked Frank if they could stay in a hotel a few days before visiting her sister Anna. She wanted to remember their Berlin before returning to the one she had tried so hard to forget for thirty years. Frank, ever punctual, especially now when he was eager to get into the good graces of Marie's family at last, objected at first. Marie was quick to point out that she had written to her sister that they would be arriving in two days. She claimed that she had done so in case they encountered any problems in their travels. In fact, she realized she would need a day or two to get accustomed to the city again. Eventually Frank agreed with her plan, and hailed a porter. They walked through the grand station teeming with people. Just as they remembered, there were newspapermen selling a hundred different kinds of papers. Men and women with pushcarts sold ham sandwiches and sausages. There were flower girls and coffee stands. There was even a man walking through the station with a bucket sloshing with beer and a ladle for any takers.

As soon as they were out on the street, the porter found them a motor cab. Frank waved the cab on and opted for an old horse-drawn taxi. He was feeling nostalgic, even a touch romantic at the prospect of two days of revisiting the streets of their courtship. Besides, a horse-drawn taxi would give them a better view of the Berlin that had erupted in their three-decade absence. Moved by this unusual display of affection, Marie could barely contain her excitement as she stepped into the carriage, assisted by Frank's sturdy arm. Inside, the driver asked Frank where they were going. Looking at Marie with an almost sly smile, Frank asked, "Should we?" Marie grabbed his arm and nodded her head yes. She laughed at her own disbelief. Leaning forward, Frank said to the driver, "To the Kaiserhof, please." And down the street they went.

The Kaiserhof was the oldest grand hotel in Berlin. When Frank and Marie had left in 1884, it was the only grand hotel to match the elegance of those in Paris or London. They had never spent a night there, but on the evening before Frank left for America they had eaten in the hotel restaurant. The romance of that evening had temporarily quelled their travel anxieties, and its memory had helped carry both of them across the Atlantic, despite the five-month difference in their arrivals.

Now after thirty years of marriage, Marie held Frank's hand and peered out the window of the carriage. It was an altogether different Berlin. Certainly plenty of things were exactly as she remembered. The peasant ladies in head scarves, selling spring's first local asparagus, still stood on the corner with wheelbarrows and crates. Beer halls still dominated the corners of every street. Marie could even see a young man sweeping up nut shells and cigar butts in one of them. The preponderance of new buildings, however, made the city seem cleaner than before. On nearly every block in the city center, she could identify something new: a café; a restaurant; a new department store; Tietz, the largest department store in Europe, glazed with two stories of plate glass; new government buildings; theaters; and, above all, more and more banks. There was an elegance and refinement to the new Berlin that she couldn't recall from the Berlin she had known with Frank. Women's hats were even bolder, men's suits more stylishly fitted.

But none of this quite added up for Marie. She told Frank to look outside, asking, "What makes it seem so different?" After all, there had been no major changes since their departure except for the absence of Bismarck; Germany was still Germany, perhaps cleaner, wealthier, and more orderly than when they left.

Frank, leaning forward and looking up to the top of one of the new department stores, murmured, "Just about everything is different."

It was true in more ways than one, but Marie was interested in something specific. The mood was different. Was it simply that with all the automobiles and streetcars and people dashing from one side of the street to the other, life in Berlin had accelerated and, hence, become more anxious? Marie wondered if there was a threshold to the pace of a city beyond which there was no turning back. She sensed that Berlin had crossed it and was forever changed. It was impossible to imagine living in Berlin now.

As the carriage wheeled past the Brandenburg Gate, Frank pointed to the top of the Siegesäule, the triumphal arch on which two pigeons were perched. Marie looked up at the new monument, but the austerity of the Doric columns brought back such a powerful set of feelings that she could hardly speak, let alone consider the significance of the Siegesäule. Designed by Carl Gotthard Langhans and built in 1789, the Brandenburg Gate was a symbol of the emergence of Prussia as a European power. Langhans designed the neoclassical gate in order to give full view from the city to the garden. The guardhouse and customs office flanked the magnificent colonnade, consisting of six fluted pillars set on plinths. It represented the best and worst of Berlin to her. All the oppressive pomp of the kaiser's regime and German military culture could be summed up by the Quadriga, the Victory statue that crowned the gate. Yet it had been a familiar sight on so many Sunday afternoons as Marie strolled under the linden trees with her family. The simple lines of the Doric columns ordered the very memory of her youth.

When her family first moved to Berlin, Marie hated the city. She missed her life in Swinemünde. She missed the fall hunts with her father and her cousins, the tall grass soaking her boots up to her knees. She missed the excitement of harvest, the sleepiness and tranquillity of a long Baltic winter. She missed Sundays at the sea, climbing on rocks, the salt taste of the air and picnics on the beach. Compared to Swinemünde, Berlin was a giant root cellar. The air was always heavy, moldy even, and some days, with the smoke and tubercular scents wafting up from the Spree, it could be downright oppressive.

Her parents sent her to the best Lutheran school for girls in the city. She had to walk nearly two miles through the crowded streets of

Berlin to get there in the morning, but she made a point of walking through the Tiergarten even though it added twenty minutes to her commute. There, under the linden trees, she felt free. The air was cleaner and at certain points along her walk, all the street traffic was out of earshot. She could never entirely escape Berlin, however. Soldiers were always on display along Unter den Linden, and even in the most remote corners of the grand park she could see the scaffolding to the latest stately building being erected or, worse, catch a whiff of the Spree. But she learned to appreciate even these intrusions through the lovely veil of leaves and manicured hedges that framed the Tiergarten. Near the end of her walk through the Tiergarten stood Brandenburg Gate. When Marie first saw it with her father, she was utterly perplexed. She stared long at the burly Victory goddess atop the gate until her father tried to explain the significance of the goddess and the history of the statue. Given her good Lutheran education, Marie immediately objected to what seemed a clear violation of the first commandment. Her father laughed and assured her that the artist had no intention of erecting idols. Over time, Marie grew to dread the gate, for the oppressive shadow of the colonnade marked the end of her morning sojourn in the garden and the beginning of a long day in school. Her first year of school in Berlin had been especially difficult. She didn't know anyone and kept mostly to herself. She often had to hold back her tears when her father or one of her uncles came to pick her up. As Marie grew older, the gate meant different things to her, and eventually she came to regard it as an endearing emblem of her new city. It was all that was good and bad about Berlin—the stateliness, the grandeur, the rigidity, and the pride. Most of all it was the gate of her solitude, a place sometimes fraught with questions and fears and at other times filled with tedium.

All such associations would and did change for her forever, from a single day under the shadows of the Brandenburg Gate.

II

Sundays in Berlin were among the finest things civilization could offer. Despite the carnival atmosphere, there was still innocence to the city's progress in the 1870s that blessed the pageantry of the Sunday stroll with novelty and an infectious exuberance. The Weich-

Brandenburg Gate, circa 1890.

brodt family got up early on Sunday mornings and put on their finest clothes to go to church. After the service, they walked over to the Viktoria Café, on the corner of Friedrichstrasse and Unter den Linden, and ate a late breakfast. It was Marie's favorite family ritual, an element of urban living she'd grown quite attached to. Her father, elegantly dressed in the latest serge suit, would order kidney or sausage and eggs and twirl the ends of his mustache while reading one of the many Berlin newspapers. Marie's mother preferred a bowl of hot cereal and coffee. She too read the papers with great interest, all the while conversing with her children. Stefan was invariably bored with the whole procedure, while Anna sat content just contemplating the menu. For Marie, every Sunday morning was a moment of delicious indecision. So many things to consider: Should she reawaken last week's taste for French crepes? Or should she follow her father's lead with the kidney? In her heart of hearts, she wanted a piece of the chocolate cake so carefully displayed under the glass case by the cash register, but knew that her mother would never approve. Marie had no need for newspapers at that time. Just watching the people on their way to a stroll under the linden trees was news enough, and when she grew tired of looking, the warmth of the sun through the great panes of glass provided all the interest she required. Sunday was the only day Marie really got to relax; when she was younger, it was school all week, and once she was finished with school at the age of sixteen, she was working at the family business six days a week. More importantly, Sunday was the only day she had even the slimmest hope of meeting a young man. This made breakfast in the café and strolls in the park endlessly fascinating and, of course, by evening, disappointing to the point of heartbreak.

The particular Sunday that changed everything was in September of 1880. At that time, Marie rarely walked among the linden trees and hedges because of her obligations to work and to the family. She was twenty years old and had yet to meet someone she could call her young man. Her parents had kept a very watchful eye over her youth but recognized that it was getting time for Marie to find a husband. They tried to set up meetings with the sons of friends from church, but the results were often painful and embarrassing. Simply put, Marie was shy and had a very difficult time making conversation when she found herself meeting someone new. Her adolescence in Berlin taught her to guard her solitude and privacy. When the city was at its most oppressive, she turned inward to recall the wide-open seascapes of her childhood. While expanding her imagination, such habits of withdrawal often left her overwhelmed in unfamiliar social situations. Her mother began to worry about her, and the family made a concerted effort to find themselves at large gatherings, whether on Sundays after church, or at the opera. This particular Sunday marked the ninth anniversary of Germany's victory over France in 1871.

Few events could draw a bigger crowd in Berlin than a march, except perhaps the public appearance of the chancellor himself. In this case, there was a long military procession, followed by the chancellor and the kaiser, with their own cortège, so practically all of Berlin showed up.[1] The Weichbrodts took an early breakfast and then set up a picnic in the shade of the linden trees, just inside the Tiergarten, opposite the Reichstag. Marie's mother had packed a hamper of ham sandwiches. Along Unter den Linden, temporary drink stands were set up where everything from beer to punch and coffee could be bought. Makeshift bands played all kinds of music—Bavarian folk songs, Prussian military marches, and Mozart serenades. All of Berlin paraded under the shade of the linden trees, bedecked in their finest; the audacity of the women's hats was matched only by the luster of the men's meticulously polished black boots.

Marie took in the festivities with genuine excitement. Since she first began working full time in the family business, she found herself longing for the childhood freedom of Swinemünde. The days in the store could be long and dreary. Anytime she found a mistake in the books, it would take hours, sometimes days, to reconcile the discrepancy; she'd spend whole afternoons counting the flounces she had just counted the day before. If she protested to her father that only one or two flounces were missing or that a minor discrepancy turned out to be another counting error of the manufacturer, he would smile in satisfaction. Nothing made Herr Weichbrodt happier; he would rub his hands together almost with glee as he approached a more complete understanding of exactly what was in the store at any given moment. "One day," Marie's father liked to tell her, "we will know exactly what we have, and when we do, we can be assured that Weichbrodt Dry Goods is the best-run business in all of Berlin." After those long afternoons in the back office poring over inventory sheets, Marie would go upstairs to their apartment, and work started all over again. She had to help her mother with the cooking. "It is only proper," Frau Weichbrodt always told her, as if the mere mention of the word "proper" were explanation enough. Proper behavior often meant cooking for as many as fifteen. Because relatives were always coming in from Swinemünde and because Uncle Helmut's family lived upstairs, it meant peeling a lot of potatoes. As a result, Marie had begun to lose her sense of joy. There was nothing to look forward to, no prospects of meeting a man. She had bought a few romance novels from a bookseller near the university and read them by candlelight, but they had only increased her sense of disappointment.

The picnic in the Tiergarten was a well-earned treat. Stretching her arms behind her, Marie planted her palms firmly in the well-manicured lawn. Several children were playing a version of ring-around-the-rosy in front of her. Two soldiers chewed on thick sandwiches beneath a statue of one of the Hohenzollerns. An older man with a bushy mustache after the manner of the kaiser, wearing a magnificent red coat and a row of medals on his chest, made way for the parade by insisting that the citizens clear off the parkway. All the ladies, including Marie, wore flowers in their hats: big, bright roses, some of them drooping in the warm September sun. Gentlemen with top hats and cigars escorted the ladies at a leisurely pace. A young man leaned against a black lamppost, reading a newspaper. A black and white springer spaniel kept sniffing at the bottom crease of the paper. The young man folded up his paper and shooed the dog away. He then resumed reading, and the dog returned. Turning his head in search of the owner, the man bent down to pet the dog. He wore a dark gray, somewhat shapeless coat with gray pants and a black felt cap. He couldn't be much older than twenty, twenty-five at the most. Just by the way he scratched the dog's ears and rubbed its chin, Marie knew he was from the country. No native Berliner would be so at ease with a strange dog. After a few minutes, the young man returned to his paper, and the black and white spaniel lay down at his feet. A friend for life, or so it seemed. Just then the police came on horseback to clear a pathway through the street. Although most of the crowd had already obliged, the police managed to create perfectly straight rows of citizens to greet the kaiser. Miles of bunting hung from the buildings. Some of the bands played *Hurrah! Hurrah! Germania!* while people in the crowd began to sing along. Suddenly figures appeared in the distance, and a low roar could be heard. Seven soldiers mounted on horses moved forward cautiously. Marie could hear the roar of the crowd grow louder as the soldiers approached the Brandenburg Gate.

Now three of her little cousins had joined in the circle of ring-around-the-rosy. Inexplicably the game stopped, and the children scattered. One of the well-dressed gentlemen nearby approached Marie, top hat and umbrella in hand, and sternly asked her to mind the rowdy children, adding that they should be better behaved in honor of the chancellor and the kaiser. Apologizing profusely for her negligence, Marie promptly called her cousins over and scolded them. They obliged and sat down next to her.

The mounted soldiers approached, followed by the Prussian Guard marching in perfect unison. The crowd shouted with excitement. The marchers were machinelike in the precision and rigidity of their movement; their uniforms looked almost as if they were made of steel. These mustachioed young men were the pride of Germany. Their unmistakable, pointed helmets flashed a myriad of tiny reflections back onto the canopy of leaves dappled with light. Behind them, with fountains of red and white plumage ascending from their silver helmets, marched non-commissioned officers holding aloft eighty-one captured French flags and eagles.

Marie's cousins were getting fidgety again. Standing up, Marie smoothed out her long blue skirt and discreetly checked her blouse for blades of grass. She then asked her mother to watch the children while she tried to get a better view of the procession. She moved closer to the young man, who was standing upright now with the dog still by his side. While merely glancing in her direction, he seemed to Marie to be looking directly at her. Marie stood counting the soldiers nervously as they marched by. Her heart pounded as she kept him in the corner of her eye. She was out of breath and beginning to flush. After the officers had passed, another set of mounted guards followed. Two enormous horses pulled a carriage gilded with baroque festoons. Field Marshal Count Helmuth von Moltke and General Albrecht von Roon stood up and greeted the adoring crowd. All the gentlemen removed their hats and shook them in the direction of the carriage, while the ladies waved their kerchiefs. Marie too dangled a scarf in the direction of the procession. The black and white spaniel approached her playfully, apparently distracted by the fluttering scarf. When Marie turned toward the dog she noticed with surprise and dismay that the young man wasn't looking at her at all. She realized that he was looking at the trees or just staring blankly at a small café on the other side of Brandenburg Gate. It was as if the wind had been knocked out of her. Disappointed again, she let her scarf hang limp.

Thousands of soldiers in full battle dress, crowned with laurel wreaths, then marched by. The crowd broke into applause as the soldiers passed in perfect lockstep, twelve men across. Marie's cousins and some of the other children began twirling around her again, but this time in a more restrained manner in order to avoid the attention of disapproving onlookers. Marie, however, was close to tears. The soldiers' steady pace appeared to quicken and their march became even more rigid, more uniform. Women held their children close to them while the men straightened their coats and stood solemnly regarding the distant figure of Chancellor Bismarck in a royal coach.

Marie now stood apart from her mother and father. Her cousins dutifully lined up next to her. Two of the boys began shoving each other and Marie quietly scolded them. Finally, one shoved the other so hard that he tumbled into Marie. She lost her footing and fell over, her hat careening backward. She wasn't hurt, but her cheeks burned at what she considered her clumsiness. Before she could scold the children, the young man in the gray suit helped her back on her feet and handed back her silk hat with the rose intact. There was hardship around his eyes, but the eyes themselves seemed limpid, and even a bit playful. He was leaner than he looked from a distance. His hands were rough, and his suit was worn at the knees and at the elbows, but he was well groomed with a short, almost tawny beard. He said not a word, but looked straight into her eyes. She thanked him, but he didn't acknowledge her thanks. She knew it wasn't seemly for a woman to stare directly at a stranger, but she couldn't help herself. She then looked at his hat. Realizing what she was implying, the young man immediately removed his hat and held it out in front of him. Marie laughed. The chancellor was passing at that very moment.

They waited next to each other, looking over the crowd, while the kaiser followed in a carriage more lavish than Bismarck's. He wore a shiny silver helmet that came to a sharp, golden point—a royal version of the Pickelhaube worn by the Prussian Guard. The kaiser and the empress sat amid the rich white silk of the open carriage. The empress waved a dainty kerchief to the crowd, while the kaiser merely saluted as the carriage rolled past Marie and the young man. More soldiers followed, but the crowd had had enough and soon began breaking up. In a moment of unprecedented boldness, Marie turned to the young man and asked him what his name was.

"My name is Franz Frank," he said, removing his hat again.

"Well, thank you for your assistance Herr Frank. I am Marie Weichbrodt."

Franz smiled at her with his eyes. She had an urge to kiss him right then, but such impropriety would have been scandalous, so she nodded, smiling broadly.

III

Franz, for his part, did not stop thinking about Marie after the festivities. It was one thing to see a pretty girl in the park, but he always had an excuse for not talking to them. They were too attractive, too wealthy, or too clearly not interested in him. In some respects he was right to be cautious about whom he approached. Berlin was a deeply divided city. Its very modernity provided the fuel for such divisions. New industry brought peasants from all parts of Germany, which meant that Catholics from Prussia and southern Germany and Protestants from the north mingled in close quarters: they worked together and often lived near one another. Members of the Jewish merchant class were firmly established, and although they interacted with German society in business affairs, they were still largely excluded from the corridors of power and lived, for the most part, in separate parts of the city. The result for young Franz was a confusing mixture of social taboos, which he didn't fully understand and felt keenly in the form of simple slights and, in some cases, outright hostility. As a rule, he kept to himself. He worked long hours, six days a week, and on Sundays he would go to Mass early with his cousin's family. Afterwards, he would eat lunch at a café and walk along the Spree. Usually he ended his Sunday by sitting on one of the benches in the Tiergarten for an hour while the sun went down, and then ate dinner at one of the beer halls on the way back to Wedding.

He had no idea what he was going to do with his life. He had finished working at the steel mill and had started as an apprentice at a tailoring shop. He knew he had to serve in the army. All young men were required to serve in the army if they did not pass a set of entrance examinations to the university. Franz was not even given the opportunity to take the examinations; such opportunities were reserved for the upper and upper-middle classes. Although economic circumstances forced him to leave Derz, Franz wanted to learn a trade. He had started an apprenticeship in tailoring, but he still hadn't landed a real job. At this point in his life, the only thing he was certain of was his desire to complete his three-year military service.

All week long, Franz thought of the young woman he had met at the parade, but he had convinced himself that there was no chance he would run into her again. Yet everywhere he turned, whether in a tavern or on one of the public buses, he kept thinking he was catching a glimpse of her. He even thought he saw Marie in the hall of his tenement as he walked out of his room on Thursday morning. He followed the mysterious woman out onto the street. When he caught up to her on a bus, he realized it was the daughter of a family down the hall, a woman he'd seen almost every day since he'd been in Berlin. It was then that he committed himself to find the woman he'd met in the park.

The following Sunday morning, in the near dark of his apartment Franz put on his suit. His cousin was sleeping in the lower bed. Without a sound, Franz closed the door and walked down the long hallway past rooms of other tenants to the one window on the floor that faced the courtyard. He took out a small mirror from his pocket and began brushing and straightening his suit, which had belonged to his father and was the only one he owned aside from his work clothes. His mother had made it from a gift of cloth from his grandmother. It was a simple navy blue suit, but well-fitting and normally reserved for church holidays. In the dim light of the tenement hall, it looked worn and gray.

As he walked out of the tenement, the spray of chicken blood from a freshly slaughtered chicken narrowly missed him. Franz complained loudly and told the man to go down to the market or at least down to the river. The butcher just pointed at Franz and laughed. Several of the tenants, including the landlord, kept chickens, goats, and, on one occasion, an ox in the courtyard. Sometimes the smell of coal smoke and the chicken coop mingled to create an odor more noxious than either the smoke or the chickens could be on their own. Most of the time it was just chicken traffic that proved difficult to negotiate in and out of the tenement. But the diurnal goings on particularly annoyed Franz this morning. He stepped defiantly past the birds, though careful to avoid the ones bloodied by the reckless butcher, and sprinted into the street.

Berlin looked like a ghoulish ruin of modernity that morning. A pale blue light flickered behind the smokestacks and electric plants of Wedding. People were hauling buckets of dirty brown coal up and down the tenements while an unguided team of dogs drew a wagonload of cabbage through the narrow street. As he heard the church bells chime, Franz cut through six double arches of the long courtyard of one of the tenements and emerged at the front steps of St. Stephen's, the church he'd attended since his arrival in Berlin.

He arrived at Mass exactly at seven o'clock to find the church about half-full. Concentrating on the liturgy was impossible. As often as he tried to focus on one of the scenes depicted in the windows, whether it was St. George slaying the dragon or Christ walking on the Sea of Galilee, his mind was distracted by his plans for the day. He would scold himself for getting his hopes up and then further scold himself for allowing his attention to stray. His mind returned to the image of the young woman's face from the week before, a face that opened up a boundless horizon. He received the Eucharist mechanically, as he had done so many times as a child in Lemkendorf when anticipating a Sunday afternoon of fishing with his father. When the Mass was ended, Franz resumed his normal air of purpose and headed straight for the horse-drawn bus.

From the top of the bus on the way to the Tiergarten, he was now able to take in the scenery. Businessmen, civil servants, professors and their families were walking to or from church. Peasants were coming in from the country with wagonloads of the fall harvest. Children were buttoned up for Sunday school, and workmen plodded along the sidewalks with the familiar weariness that comes when one only has a single morning of rest for an entire week of work. As the bus wobbled over the Wilhemstrasse Bridge, Franz spotted a woman who looked exactly like his mother. As the bus passed her, he heard her singing a light country tune like those his mother had sung to him when he was a child. A shock of recognition shot down the back of his neck. He started sweating, shifting back and forth in his seat. He felt guilty, as if his mother had sent her doppelgänger to Berlin to reprimand him. When the bus stopped near the Tiergarten, he got off and walked into a church where a Mass was already underway. The priest was finishing his sermon. When the choir began the Credo, Franz walked reverently toward the vigil candles, crossed himself, and lit one of the candles. An infant cousin had died recently back in Derz. Frank prayed for the infant and thought of his mother. He now felt a little guilt at his inattention to the earlier Mass, something that would have disappointed his mother.

Magdalene Frank was a deeply devout woman who took to heart Christ's dictum to love neighbor, stranger, and enemy alike. When Frank was still a boy, she was once walking with several other women after a twelve-hour day of harvesting asparagus on a farm outside Lemkendorf. All she had eaten that day was a crust of stale bread softened by a cupful of watered-down potato soup. The landowners sent her home with a few spears of asparagus and a freshly baked loaf of bread. As the women returned to Derz late that evening, they ran across a group of day laborers from Minsk, lonely young men wandering the countryside desperate for work. The women ignored the laborers' crude remarks and passed on. Further down the road they saw another man lying in a ditch. He was not dead, nor was he sleeping, but lay in a stupor of drunkenness and hunger. Several of the women passed, barely acknowledging his presence. Others looked away. Magdalene, however, blessed the man quietly and without thought or hesitation placed her loaf of bread on his chest and his right hand over the bread. This story was firmly implanted in Franz's memory and would often come to mind while he sat in church.

The organist's fingers flew across the keyboard in a burst of liturgical music. Franz was startled. He'd been kneeling for more than half an hour and had lost sense of where he was. The Mass was coming to an end, and he joined the procession with the rest of the congregation, saying his last Ave Maria as he crossed himself on leaving.

Resuming his former purposefulness, Franz practically sprinted to the Tiergarten. The day grew brighter. An autumn breeze descended on the city, blowing much of the soot and smoke southeast along the Spree. The linden trees shook gently, not quite ready to shed their leaves. The day was almost perfect.

Franz found the exact spot where he had stood a week ago. Leaning against a tree, he unrolled a day old newspaper. However many times he tried to start an article, he'd seem to see her out of the corner of his eye. He would look up and in some instances even follow a familiar-looking hat through a crowd, half-knowing he was chasing shadows. Then it occurred to him that perhaps he shouldn't be standing there at all. Better to keep his distance, and find a less exposed spot from which to observe the scene. Of course, she would think him feeble-minded or even crazy if she found him there at the exact spot. So he fell back from the avenue and found a bench. He returned the newspaper to his pocket, sat down on the bench, and watched the procession of Sunday strollers, hoping at once to catch another glimpse of Marie Weichbrodt. The promenaders were out in full force that day, strolling with a jauntiness usually reserved for the first warm Sunday of spring. Whole families marched up and down the avenue in tight groups, congesting the traffic. Small orchestras amused audiences lunching on ham sandwiches and wurst. Women flaunted befeathered hats. Army officers sporting their campaign ribbons saluted one another, their boots gleaming as if dipped in a bath of black ivory. Students, too, were out on Sunday, headed for the Café Bauer, the Library, the Royal Academy of Art, or the Aquarium. Frank observed everything with a watchful eye. A nun; three ambassadors; a young man with an enormous bucket of beer; an old woman selling librettos for the evening performance at the Opera; young nurses from the Spree Valley strolling the avenue with children; and anonymous dozens streamed by, waiting in line at drink stands, gawking at the brightest shop windows. But nowhere among them could Franz discern his Marie.

The dinner hour was approaching, and only Franz and a few workmen remained on the sidewalk. Franz sat quietly, his hands folded. He looked up at a monument to a man he did not recognize. Some prince or king, undoubtedly. Leaning back, his hands behind his head, he watched the leaves stirring. It was too much to expect to run into her again. He shouldn't be disappointed. Nothing had happened that might lead to disappointment, he assured himself.

He crossed the Spree for the fourth time that day. A band was playing old songs to a crowd of people in a beer garden. He thought about drinking a beer and then thought better of it. Seeking out the loneliest streets, the ones without lamps or ones with lamps someone had forgotten to light, he made a slow way back to Wedding.

IV

After checking into the Kaiserhof and making dinner reservations, Frank and Marie decided to take a walk through the park. The difference that thirty years had made to the city mattered little to Marie when she asked Frank if he remembered the day they met. He recalled it precisely, right down to the black and white spaniel that had followed him all the way back to Wedding that day. The two of them now crossed a busy intersection and made their way into the familiar shade of the linden trees.. Although both of her parents were dead, Marie was sufficiently nervous about seeing her family again to consider calling the whole thing off. She could make up some wild excuse and just travel the German countryside with Frank, reliving their courtship. After all, that was the real reason they had come back to Germany. It was for them. It was their thirtieth wedding anniversary. Of course, in the back of her mind Marie knew that this was not entirely the case. She had returned, in part, for a reckoning. Indeed, as much as it clashed with her sense of propriety, Marie wanted to show her family how well she and her husband had done for themselves in America. She was proud of their life together and wanted to let her family know that she made no mistake in marrying "Private Frank," and that the real mistake was her family's attempt to block their union.

They sat down on a bench where the Princess Café used to be. After a night at the theater, Frank and Marie used to sit there and split a piece of cake or have a late dinner when the rest of Berlin was heading to bed. In some ways, those were the best days, the most innocent days of their lives. They hungered for each other's affection and met whenever they could. At the beginning of their courtship, the Weichbrodts' disapproval of Franz's Catholic background made it all the more exciting. In the moments before sleep, Marie would often compare their situation to that of other star-crossed lovers in history and would imagine the trials of their love and the sacrifices she would have to make. She would tell herself that only such great sacrifices could reveal an iota of her love. All for love, she would tell herself, all for love.

In fact, Marie had exaggerated her parents' disapproval, and she came to realize this only when she had children of her own. The passions of youth allow for no ambivalence. Her parents' concerns about Franz's background and economic future had appeared judgmental. Marie looked at the sidewalk in front of the old Princess Café (now Café Stenwyk) and the lights that flickered above the entrance, and brooded on the curious arrangement of things. The most important decisions in life happen before you can understand the complexity of other people's persuasions. Yet we commit ourselves to these decisions, and their incision into the fabric of life becomes the very shape of our lives. The passion of a few minutes at a parade in Berlin can take you all the way to America.

Frank and Marie continued to walk all afternoon. Although still exhausted from their morning trip from Bremen, they made their way through new Berlin with fresh eyes. Every time they thought they'd seen enough, they would discover a café or a restaurant they used to frequent in their courtship. Few were still exactly the same, but the sight of each of them uncarthed another memory buried by the years. Berlin now was decidedly a world city. Great banks stood on almost every corner in the center of the city. Streetcars and subways rumbled from every direction. Businessmen and clerks dominated the sidewalks with their charcoal gray suits and black bowlers. The streetcars and cafés were filled with them, their noses buried in one of the daily papers.

Dining that evening at the Kaiserhof, Frank and Marie descended the grand staircase of the hotel in Springfield's most fashionable apparel; Frank wore a navy wool coat with a high collar and a white silk scarf modestly pinned. Marie played the grande dame of Springfield in a one-piece princess dress of fine batiste, yoked in Val lace and ornamented with medallions of Swiss embroidery. The meal was splendid. It tasted even better than the dinner they had enjoyed there thirty years before. A few minutes before the appointed hour, Frank had gone down to the restaurant and explained to the maitre d' that it had been thirty years since their last evening at the Kaiserhof. As a result, they were presented with one of the finest meals in Berlin. Little specialty dishes prepared by the chef kept appearing. They had never had a seven-course dinner before, and it took them all evening to complete it. It began with a trout terrine, followed by a light cream of asparagus soup. Next came a goose liver served in a pastry shell shaped like a goose, and then roasted rabbit with a mélange of vegetables circling the plate. The delicate rack of lamb with small potatoes was the chef's finale. They ate slowly, recounting with almost every bite another detail from the night that had brought them there thirty years before. Finally, a variety of chocolate animals were served, followed by the requisite coffee to round out the evening.

A well-dressed couple sitting at the table next to theirs smiled at them from time to time. The man was splendidly dressed in a black suit with a vest and a high starched collar. His wife appeared to float in her mescaline dress shrouded in an embroidered silk net. The high collar of the dress, trimmed with a row of delicately beaded braids, gave her a swanlike appearance, especially in conjunction with her relatively unadorned turban. All eyes had watched them as they entered the room and walked slowly to their table. Frank had been talking about a friend of his from the army and an assignment they shared when the man leaned over and politely tapped Frank on the shoulder. "Excuse me sir, I couldn't help hearing you mention the name Hutten in association with the Second Guards Regiment, Infantry, Seventh Company. Did you know Sergeant Joseph Hutten?"

"I knew him very well," said Frank. "Sergeant Hutten and I entered His Majesty's service at the same time. We both came from East Prussia."

"Remarkable," the man replied. "I was in the very same regiment." Straightening his back, he stood up rather formally. "Forgive me, sir. I am August Hauptführer and this is Frau Hauptführer."

Frank paused for a moment before introducing himself. "Delighted to meet you again. I am Frank Franke and this is Frau Franke," he said, as he stood up to shake hands. It felt odd to introduce himself with his American name.

After inviting Frank and Marie to join his table, Herr Hauptführer resumed the initial conversation with Frank. "It's strange, Herr Franke. I have no recollection of you in our regiment. None whatsoever."

Frank, being the company tailor, remembered Hauptführer's name perfectly well. Being a Protestant from the eastern part of Prussia, Hauptführer was one of the regiment's most highly prized soldiers. "Well, it was a rather large regiment," Frank replied awkwardly, avoiding further explanation.

"It's nothing compared to what they are building up these days."

Frank was puzzled, but then explained: "We just arrived in Berlin from America this morning. This is our first time back in Germany in thirty years since I left the army."

Herr Hauptführer's eyes sparkled, a smile broke out on his face, and he immediately ordered a bottle of champagne for the table. "This calls for a celebration! Waiter, let's have a bottle of Lutter und Wegner Sekt, the house's finest."

After the somewhat uncomfortable introduction, the evening proceeded beautifully. The two couples laughed together and toasted Berlin. They talked about Springfield and Chicago and New York. Specifically the Hauptführers were interested in American business, skyscrapers, Indians, and the Wild West. Eventually the conversation returned to the old regiment. "Of course, you've both heard that war is inevitable," Hauptführer declared somewhat eagerly.

"We knew from reports in the paper that a serious situation was developing due to the conflict in the Balkans," Frank began. "Though I admit that I thought the Springfield papers were overestimating France's resolve. And as for the Russians, I used to see Russian soldiers come through Derz, looking for work when I was growing up." Then, with all the pride of the kaiser's army, Frank added, "Needless to say, I was never impressed me with their discipline."

Frank paused a moment for Hauptführer to smile and nod in agreement and then resumed: "But when you say inevitable, how soon do you think there will be a declaration of war?"

Taking up his champagne glass, Hauptführer hesitated. "I suspect as soon as the Austrians declare war, we will declare war," he said. "But when that happens is anyone's guess. For my part, I see it as a wonderful opportunity. As you well know, Herr Franke, there is no better-trained army in the world than the German army. Despite the great progress in our country since you left, young people today lack focus and leadership. They have no common goal. When you have a moment, visit the university while you're here. You'll know exactly what I am talking about. These children have never faced the hardships of our generation. They've never had to work for anything; everything's been handed to them. I can think of no nobler goal than coming to the aid of the fatherland in a time of crisis."

As the night went on, Frank and Marie were convinced that all of Berlin was giddy with the possibility of war, at least according to the Hauptführers. They also learned from a discussion of the latest building projects and train lines that their old leader, Sergeant Hutten, had become a sergeant major and that he personally oversaw all the enlisted personnel from the northeastern part of Germany. Hauptführer, Frank learned later, was a textile manufacturer. Having completed his service in the army, he went to work for his father, whose business served as a broker between textile manufacturers and large clients such as the army. In the early 1900s, Hauptführer had the opportunity to acquire a small factory. With assistance from his father and a loan from the bank, he made the purchase. Their firm grew to be one of the bank's largest customers, and Hauptführer's father became a bank director. Hauptführer himself had replaced his father just a year ago. Life in Berlin, Hauptführer said, had been nothing but opportunity for him, and he was ever grateful to both the kaiser and Bismarck for laying the foundation for such unimaginable prosperity.

"I've come a long way for a simple boy from the country," Hauptführer concluded, raising his glass to Frank.

After the two couples had bidden each other good-night, Frank and Marie took a short walk in the park before going to bed. Frank was a bit withdrawn. Arm-in-arm with Marie, he walked silently, sighing from time to time. Marie asked him what was the matter. He just shook his head. The truth was, he didn't know how he felt and he wasn't sure that anything was the matter. The conversation with August Hauptführer had awoken something in him that he hadn't felt since he entered the army. He wanted to know about everything. He wanted to learn all that had happened in Berlin since he left. At the same time he felt embarrassed by this desire. What was Berlin to him now anyway? Nonetheless, there was something to Herr Hauptführer's tone, something about all that pride and presumption and privilege, that challenged Frank. An old comrade who wouldn't have lowered himself to speak to Frank in the army had become an important German business success. Although Frank himself had created one of the most successful businesses in Springfield, he wondered whether his old city hadn't somehow bested him.

v

Frank and Marie woke up late the next morning and went to Café Bauer for coffee and pastries. They had nothing to do that day, and neither was in the mood for sightseeing, so they decided to have a leisurely breakfast at the café and read up on news in Germany. It was something they had always dreamed of doing together in Berlin. An activity so simple and harmless, to be sure, but one that suggested their arrival as an urbane couple of leisure.

Marie was worried about seeing her sister Anna. They had been close as children, and continued to be so throughout Frank and Marie's courtship. Just before Marie left for America, however, Anna had accused her of breaking up the family for the selfish purpose of "some ridiculous romance." It was a betrayal. Anna remained, nevertheless, Marie's primary link to the rest of the family. They kept in touch over the years with a letter at Christmas and usually one in the spring, but Anna's letters had become more infrequent, especially after their father died in 1903. Many of Marie's relatives had expected her to return to Germany when their father was ill. They had presumed that since Frank owned his own business, money would not be a problem. Anna had considered her letter to Marie about their father's illness to be a call that could not be ignored. But much as Marie wanted to see her father before he died, it was impossible. With six children at home and Milton on the way, Frank and Marie simply couldn't leave for the three months that a transatlantic voyage would take. Nonetheless, Marie felt pressure from her family to make the long journey back to Germany, and she deeply resented it. After all, it was the Weichbrodt family that had driven Frank and her to America in the first place. Regardless of the extenuating circumstances, Marie was again reproached after her father's death. She and Anna drifted further apart, and before she knew it, ten more years had passed. In 1912, just two years before returning to Germany, Marie began writing to her sister again. Eventually, Anna wrote back. They were both older now and eager for reconciliation. Yet the insinuations and subtle condemnations lingered in the letters. It was as if her father were writing through Anna. Would it be OK for them to attend church with the family, or would Frank have a problem with that? When Marie wrote back saying that they had been German Methodists since they arrived in Springfield, Anna replied that she had never heard of German Methodism.

Sitting in a sunny spot of the café with a cup of coffee and a pastry, Marie tried to forget family matters for the time being and catch up on what was happening in Berlin. The Hauptführers were quite right: almost every article mentioned the inevitability of war along with the ennobling aspects of a national effort. Other articles reported on the latest developments among the young socialists of Berlin and their demonstrations for voting rights and against factory conditions. "This must be what Herr Hauptführer had in mind when he told us to visit the university," Marie said, showing Frank one of the cover articles.

They spent the rest of the day like that, reading, walking, and pointing out new things to each other. There were monuments; it seemed, on every corner. Statues of Teutonic knights and the long line of Hohenzollerns dominated the main walk through the Tiergarten. At first marvelous, the sheer abundance of edifying monuments soon grew wearying. Normally accepting of Prussian self-satisfaction, even Frank wondered why they needed such pomp at every turn. At the end of the day they headed for an old café Frank liked to frequent for soup and sauerbraten.

The following morning at the Viktoria Café, Marie sipped her coffee slowly. Frank checked his pocket watch and returned to an article in one of the Berlin dailies about the coming conflict. Although Frank shared the Berliners' confidence in the German army, he began to wonder if they weren't a little too eager for war. He checked his watch again and looked at Marie, who was gazing aimlessly out the window. Finally, he'd had enough.

"OK. It's time to go."

"She lives on Schmollerstrasse, you know," Marie replied casually, still sitting comfortably.

"Exactly," Frank shot back, exasperated.

"She lives on the *north* end of Schmollerstrasse, on the Kupfergraben. That's a twenty-minute walk or a ten-minute cab ride at the most. We still have almost two hours before we need to be there."

Frank had clearly been mistaken about where Marie's sister Anna lived. He had assumed that Anna had never left the old neighborhood. But of course, her husband was an attorney and they had moved to a more stylish address. Nevertheless, Frank continued to press Marie into leaving the café. "Besides," he tried to persuade her, "I thought it might be nice to walk through the Markt-Halle and find some flowers for her."

"Oh Frank! Still trying to impress my family after all these years?" Marie smiled and then added, "It's a wonderful idea. I've wanted to go there ever since we arrived. Just let me finish my cake."

Frank had a difficult time unwinding, but eventually he returned to his seat and watched Marie finish her almond torte. It was as if Frank had assumed all the anxiety that Marie had felt in anticipation of seeing her family. She appeared to be utterly at ease, taking in noisy, matter-of-fact Berlin as if it were a Sunday picnic.

On leaving the café, they headed for the Markt-Halle. Although there were outdoor markets throughout Berlin, they were both thinking of the same place where they used to shop. It was a simple covered market in the center of Berlin and it was the largest, noisiest market in the city. They approached the flagstone forecourt, slippery with debris from the vegetable stands. An uneven procession of housewives laden with net bags and wicker baskets marked the path from booth to booth. Every edible bird, beast, or vegetable under the sun was on display. It had been too long since Marie had set foot in a real market like this. Thirty years of corn and cabbage in Springfield had blinded her to the delights of a true German market. Frank followed her to the stand where crustaceans were purveyed by a heavy, wool-clad lady. Mushrooms, cabbage, cured meats, oranges all the way from Spain, fresh peas and asparagus, yards of rhubarb and green fennel, long strings of dried Turkish figs, great chunks of beef and plate-sized sole fillets, and a profusion of dark purple beets: these were the foods of Marie's childhood. This was the part of home she regretted leaving. She walked along the stalls, questioning the stout farmwomen with aprons full of money from the day's sales: "What price for the figs? How fresh is this fish? Where did these turnip greens come from?"

Aside from chefs and servants, Frank was the only man in the market. It was a weekday and still midmorning. Many of the housewives looked at Frank with suspicion. After some time poking among the produce tents, he persuaded Marie to find a flower stall. Having settled on the one she liked best, Marie bought a little pot of pansies for Anna. They then made their way back to the hotel to retrieve their bags.

Before they left for Anna's house, Marie asked Frank to wait a moment while she crowned her head with one of Mayme's latest creations, a broad-brimmed white hat with a large ostrich feather spilling over the right side of the brim. Her blue suit with white piping around the cut of the collar went perfectly with the hat. Marie looked like a Parisian lady off to a lunch, Frank told her as he held open the grand door of the Kaiserhof. They were still early, so Marie asked that they pause for a moment. Frank protested, arguing that with traffic and their baggage they were sure to be late. "Frank, I just need a few minutes," pleaded Marie. She took a deep breath and closed her eyes as if she were trying to remember every detail of her last conversation, thirty years earlier, with her sister. Frank said nothing further. He took a long look down the busy street. It appeared unusually busy, even for eleven o'clock in the morning. His thoughts drifted home to Paris Cleaners, four thousand miles away. There was really nothing to worry about; the business would be fine. Elizabeth and Helen could keep an eye on Milton better than he could. And if there were any problems with the machines, Otto could surely fix them. Nevertheless, he felt pressure in his throat, as he had on the afternoon when he said good-bye to his parents for the last time. He wondered why things seemed so quotidian at such moments. No birds of augur or sudden burst of sunshine on the pavement, no tea leaves to suggest the shape of a conflict resolved. Nothing but a Berlin police officer in his crisp uniform straightening a stack of papers by the kiosk and a steady stream of traffic, each person apparently lost to his concerns. Life pressing on.

When they pulled up to the gate of Anna's house, the driver set their bags on the inside of the courtyard. Spring vines had already climbed a foot up the brick walls. It was one of those plain, solidly built houses from the Schinkel period. Originally designed for the burgeoning merchant class of Berlin, the buildings provided welcome relief from the rococo curlicues of Potsdam or the heavier neoclassical facades of downtown Berlin. For Marie, however, these houses held a particular significance. And she knew the same was true for Anna. As a teenager, Marie used to walk past houses like this one. In fact, she was sure she'd taken this very street home from the family store on Schönhauser Allee. Anna and she would look at each house and pick out the one that would be their favorite to live in. On cold nights especially, with a harsh wind biting their ankles, they would often stop to look in at the warm glow of lamplight emerging from a living room and the steady puff of smoke from a chimney. They would create a story about each house, who lived in it, the length of the dress worn by the mistress of the house, the preparation of the leg of lamb the residents were eating that night, and where they were going the following morning. Anna and Marie's conversation on the way home was often sparked by the light of a single room.

A jostling could be heard coming from Anna's house. The great front door swung back into the shadows of the broad front hallway. Anna wore a simple gray skirt, a stylish white blouse, and a dark wool fisherman's sweater that looked exactly like the one her father had worn as a young man in Swinemünde. It was difficult to tell what the years had done to her. She stood in the doorway smiling, clasping her hands nervously. Her round, light blue eyes and oval face were pure Weichbrodt. With the fine wrinkles about her eyes, the touch of gray in her hair, and her heavier carriage now, she could have passed for Marie's mother. Marie bounded up the stoop to meet her sister. Anna

Adolph Menzel, *The Departure of King William I for the Army*.
Alte Nationalgalerie, Staatliche Museen zu Berlin–Preussischer Kulturbesitz.

opened her arms, tears welling up in her eyes. They hugged and kissed and burst into laughter every time they stopped to look at one another. It *had* been thirty years.

Frank came up the stairs, bags in hand, laughing nervously. He stood stroking his beard while the sisters embraced. Finally Anna approached Frank, kissed him on both cheeks, and invited him and Marie inside. Her home was richly furnished with broad hallways and tastefully decorated in the Biedermeier style. After Anna had given them a brief tour and shown them to their room, they all reconvened in the living room, the sun shining through the front window despite the heavy curtains. The travelers sat on the salmon-colored divan and were served tea and oranges by Anna's maid while they talked about their journey. Everyone was nervous, and there were long pauses in the conversation. It was mostly small talk about the weather and the latest theater in Berlin. On occasion Anna would veer into reports about the extended family and then fall silent when she approached a subject she deemed too sensitive to be discussed so soon and so openly. Marie could tell that Frank was uneasy.

Inevitably, they discussed the military buildup. Anna was eager for war, seeming almost bored by years of prosperity. Much like August Hauptführer, she argued about the newest generation of Germans and how they utterly lacked direction and the sense of sacrifice on which she and Marie had all been raised. Frank shifted on the couch and frequently looked out the front window onto the quiet street or stared at the molding on the ceiling in a half-ponderous gesture of reflection. In an attempt to make him feel more comfortable, Marie invited him into the conversation several times. But as soon as he began to speak, Anna abruptly changed the subject. After an hour of this, Frank stood up and asked to be excused. He went to the front hallway and noticed a small sign screwed into the right side of the staircase that read, "For the master's family only." He looked at the maid, who was entering the living room to clear away the plates and teacups. He chuckled and went upstairs. "Some things haven't changed," he said to himself as he opened the door to the bedroom.

VI

Anna's husband, Friedrich, came home late that evening. He had been drafting an addition to some court documents due the following morning. He apologized several times, greeted his distant in-laws graciously, and asked them to be seated for dinner. Well-mannered and immaculately groomed, Friedrich had an altogether calming effect on the group. Thin but firm of build, he had something of the ambassador about him: polite, interested, but never so obtrusive as to be anything but pleasant company. The rounded pewter-rimmed spectacles perched on his long nose accentuated his angular face, while his thick mustache softened that effect and gave him a benign appearance. Having never met Frank or Marie, Friedrich had the advantage of being without memories or old grudges to inhibit him. So his conversation with Frank wandered quite naturally from inquiries about the American legal system to a discussion in the differences in operating a business in Germany and America.

Anna had arranged two days of rest for her American visitors, and on the following Saturday evening he insisted on throwing Frank and Marie a proper German party. All of Marie's relatives had been invited to see how their American cousins had fared. Naturally, this meant many preparations and huge quantities of food and wine. It also meant that Frank and Marie would be subjected to extreme scrutiny.

Not every Weichbrodt had remained in the family dry goods business. After the death of their father, several had started businesses of their own, and their children were now entering new professions: lawyers, doctors, clerks, and civil servants. All of this came as a surprise to Marie, because she recalled a stronger sense of family unity in the days of her adolescence. Then, aunts and uncles and cousins were frequently at the house, eating, preparing for a wedding, or sitting down for Sunday dinner. She and Frank had raised their children differently, for their circumstances were different. No matter how obedient her children were to Frank, they led, by comparison to her siblings and herself as they grew up, independent lives. The Weichbrodts of her generation, on the other hand, stuck to one another as if it were a code of honor. Although the Frankes were supportive of one another—Carl watched out for Mayme and had introduced her to Charles; Bill looked out for Otto, Elizabeth, and Helen; Helen babysat for Milton; and Elizabeth seemed to always be in the middle of it all—family cohesion had changed. Obedience remained but took on a different role and represented a different power. With the exception of Mayme, all the children returned to the family business as soon as they were asked, but once they came together, chafing began. There had been disagreements in the Weichbrodt household as well, but nothing a meeting with their father wouldn't resolve immediately. Since they lived above the business, the building was the locus of everything in the family. They seldom had reason to venture further than the end of the street, to go to the grocery store. In this sense, the family was extremely close-knit and insular; the only opportunity to meet outsiders was provided by church or by new customers. Marie was the only child who had ever disrupted and broken free of the strict order of the Weichbrodt family.

Marie had always believed that something happened to her on the way to America that left her fundamentally changed. It was only now that she realized the change had already taken place before she left Berlin. Her resistance to her family had changed her. She wondered whether her children would ever be able to appreciate the stability of life created by the strict enforcement of Prussian culture that she enjoyed while growing up. In America there was the church and all the neighbors in Vinegar Hill, but that never quite added up to the cultural pressure of authority she knew while growing up. For the first time since leaving Germany, Marie envied the clear order of the old ways.

The homecoming party began about four in the afternoon on Saturday. Having spared no expense on the celebration, Anna and her maids ran around all afternoon making last-minute preparations. There was wine and beer and even champagne for a toast later that evening. Once again, Frank and Marie found themselves standing dutifully at the door, greeting guests. Everyone Marie could think of was there, even cousins from Uncle Helmut's family whom she had not seen since she left Swinemünde at the age of twelve. The biggest surprise, however, was her older brother Stefan. He appeared quite suddenly in the hallway of the house. When Marie spied him, she ran to him immediately. She was thrilled to see his familiar gait, but startled by his aspect. Stefan resembled her father uncannily, in both his broad physical stature and his temperament. He looked like the successor to the business, if not the financial captain, certainly the decision-maker. Marie had neither spoken nor written to Stefan in thirty years, except for a letter of condolence when she learned that his wife had died. Everything she knew about Stefan came from Anna. For reasons that were not entirely clear, Marie understood that Stefan had quit the family business in 1900 and struggled on his own since then. His face was pallid, almost gray. Lost was the vigor in his face and shoulders that he had inherited from their father. While he still wore the familiar Weichbrodt mustache, the ends were no longer twirled to exquisite little points. Instead, they drooped over his upper lip and fluttered at his labored breathing. Marie embraced him gingerly. Although only five years older than Marie, Stefan had become an old man. They had spoken only a few words before he asked to sit down and catch his breath.

As the evening went on, Marie reconnected individually with each member of her family. She marveled at how little had changed in some cases, and how much had changed in others. What was missing, to her relief, was the resentment she had dreaded. Nowhere could she detect a backhanded compliment or an incriminating observation. Her family actually seemed happy to see her again.

As people seated themselves for dinner, Stefan asked Anna's son Martin for a glass of wine. When Martin returned, Stefan asked to be helped to his feet. He stood rather feebly and raised his hand. No one took any notice. Finally he asked Martin to get everyone's attention, as he was about to make a toast. Martin barked out, "Excuse me! Can I get your attention? Uncle Stefan would like to make a toast."

Anna hurried across the room. "No, no! Not yet." She was flustered. "Why don't you wait until everyone arrives?" she suggested.

Stefan was annoyed. He rubbed his nose and muttered, "I'm fine, you know."

"Of course, you're fine. I'm just saying. Let's wait until all the guests arrive. Then we'll start our toasts."

Stefan sat down and frowned into his wineglass. Anna had no idea whether more people would show up. There might be a cousin or two missing, but that wasn't the point. The point was, as she explained to her son, "You never know how much Stefan has been drinking. Please keep your eye on him and try to persuade him to give up the idea of toasts this evening."

From across the living room, Marie was aware of the conversation between Anna and her son but couldn't imagine why her sister would want to delay her older brother from making a toast. And, furthermore, why was Stefan so obliging? Marie had never known her brother to be so sheepish. She subsequently learned from Aunt Charlotte, Uncle Theodor's widow, that Stefan had taken to drinking over the last ten years. He had started his own competing dry goods business in 1900, four years after the death of his wife, but by 1902 his store had closed. No one knew why. He later came back to the family business and asked to reinstate his partnership. A group of younger cousins had taken over the business when Stefan's father died, and they told Stefan that he was welcome to work for them but not as a partner. He was devastated. Stefan declared he would never set foot in the store again without an offer to become a partner. "It's been ten years and they've never called him into the store. I think they have sore feelings from when they were younger. At any rate it's been hard on Stefan. Rumor has it that Friedrich is his only support. Otherwise, he'd be living in Wedding," Charlotte concluded.

"Poor Stefan," Marie whispered.

"Indeed."

The time had arrived for toasting. Everyone stood up at the long banquet table that stretched from the dining room through the broad pocket doors and into the living room. At the end of the table, Friedrich stepped forward and raised his glass: "To the American branch of our family." They raised their glasses, and each of the cousins and uncles and nieces and nephews dutifully clinked glasses with Frank and Marie. Anna whisked in the servants, and before anyone had time to make another toast, they were sitting down to dinner.

The food was a picture of a German feast with spaetzle in a rich broth, sauerbraten, asparagus, sausages, lamb, and roasted potatoes, all on platters that were passed from one end of the table to the other. Anna was the supreme hostess for such occasions. The guests obliged by complimenting her on every dish. After Marie had described their journey back to Germany, the conversation turned to the conflict in the Balkans. War had come to seem inevitable. Even Marie's cousin Max, who still worked at the family store in Swine-münde, was eager for Germany "to take its rightful place in history." Some argued that their nation needed a place to direct its power. Other, more sophisticated opinions offered the balance of European power as a justification for war. Anna threw up her hands, explaining that she neither understood nor appreciated this new taste for war but that she would unhesitatingly support her kaiser in his decision. Joseph, another of Marie's cousins and one of the newer partners at the store, questioned the concept of loyalty to the kaiser, pointing to various scandals and political ineptitude over the course of the last decade.[2] All, however, whether young or old, man or woman, believed in the moral superiority of Germany over the rest of Europe. France and England had cast a spell of decadence; it was Germany's sole responsibility to restore a moral order to civilization.

After the family had aired its opinions, Friedrich took a more measured response. "As the situation is developing now, I'm not confident that it will be an easy victory for us. Consider if Austria takes action against Serbia. This will bring France and Russia into an alliance. Now I'm certainly no military expert or strategist, but that sounds as though we will have to wage war on two fronts."

He was met with a shower of protest. Johan, Marie's second cousin Gertrude's son, who was currently serving in the army, raised his voice. "I've been training for the last eight weeks with the newest group of recruits. You should have total confidence in your army, Uncle Friedrich."

"What would you know about the army anyway?" was heard from the opposite end of table.

Friedrich shot back: "You don't need to have marched a hundred miles through East Prussia to know that an attack on opposite fronts weakens your position."

Friedrich was one of the few men in the room who had not served in the army. He had attended the university and then law school. Most people, including the men of the extended Weichbrodt family, who had all served in the army, assumed that social position exempted you from army service. In Friedrich's case they were absolutely right; his mother belonged to an old Junker family, and Friedrich was directed to the most prestigious education Europe could offer. As a result, any time the army was mentioned, some of the old social tensions flared.

Anna tried to rein in the conversation: "I don't know why we should talk of war this evening. After all, my sister and her husband didn't make the long journey back to Germany just to hear about politics. Please, can't we discuss something more edifying?"

Finally Paul, one of Marie's cousins who had worked side by side with her in the store when she was still a girl, spoke up: "There is nothing more edifying, especially for the young people at this table, than a discussion of the moral responsibilities of war."

This was followed by the buzz of various conversations. After a few minutes, Martin's three-year-old daughter Heidi piped up from one end of the table: "Grandma!"

"Yes, Heidi?" Anna tried to control her surprise and irritation.

"What kind of cake are we having?"

Anna glared at Martin and his wife, Alexandra, who jumped up and ran to the end of the table near the kitchen, but it was too late. Little Heidi, with two red ribbons dangling from either side of her pretty face, called out at the top of her lungs, "Grandma! What kind of cake?"

"That's enough young lady. We have chocolate cake and pineapple pudding, but there will be none for you," said Anna, taken aback by her granddaughter's cheekiness. Heidi then turned to one of her cousins and said more quietly, "I like orange pudding better." At which Anna tried to suppress a smile. When others at the table began to chuckle, Anna relaxed and laughed openly. The rest of the table followed her lead. Soon the servants were clearing the dinner plates in order to bring in the pudding, cake, and champagne. Stefan, who was sitting next to Heidi and the newest generation of Weichbrodts, took the opportunity to tell them a story about when he was a boy in Swinemünde. "I was fishing with my father just north of town. Mr. Klugge, the local blacksmith, lent us his rowboat for the afternoon. My father was a great fisherman, you know. He had this wonderful walnut pipe he smoked whenever we went out on the water—the kind with a great black bowl that dips down below the chin. He would smoke all afternoon."

"I think the children have heard that story Stefan." Anna interrupted.

"No, they haven't. Not this one," he shouted. His anger was out of proportion to his sister's interjection. Then he leaned over the table with considerable violence, bumping into one of the servants who was removing a bowl of roasted beets from the table and causing her to drop the bowl on the clean white tablecloth. Stefan hardly noticed the spill, and gazed down the table to the end where Frank and Marie sat quietly observing it all.

"Can you hear me down there Marie?"

"Look at what you've done!" Anna could no longer hold back her disgust. Stefan looked at the sleeves of his jacket and then watched the bright magenta circumference of beet juice expand slowly out from the bowl.

"I'm terribly sorry. Please, let me clean it up."

Turning the bowl right side up, Stefan rather clumsily shoveled the spilled beets back into the bowl with his hand. He removed a dirty handkerchief from his left breast pocket and began blotting the beet juice from the table. Marie watched Anna closely as she marched to Stefan's end of the table and said to him, quite politely, "Please, Stefan, there is no need to clean it up." She handed the bowl and two plates to the servant.

Marie could see Stefan apologizing, his head nodding. Anna returned to her seat. Each guest, even the children, had a champagne glass. The children were served water while the rest were given champagne. As soon as the servant filled his glass, Stefan stood up, stuffing the now bright pink napkin into his gray trousers.

"I would like to make a toast to my lovely sister Marie and her husband Frank." His voice was thin and somewhat breathless.

"Stefan, would you please wait a moment," said Anna.

"No. I've waited long enough. My sister has been home for a week now and I haven't been allowed to see her." The veins in his neck swelled with every word. Turning toward the rest of the guests, he asked, "Do you mind if I welcome my sister back to Berlin?"

No one objected.

A minute of silence ensued. The gray pallor returned to Stefan's skin; he looked small and gaunt in his gray suit, and his knees were shaking. Marie held her breath as he began to speak. "It's just wonderful to be here this afternoon. So many new faces." As he said this, he looked toward the children he'd been sitting with during dinner. "Dear God, it's been ten years since I've seen some of you. I don't know why we don't get together like this more often, but I can think of no better reason than to celebrate my sister's return." Marie lowered her head, smiling at the kindness of her brother's welcome. "Our family never liked Franz, but as I've been thinking about it, I never really knew why I didn't like him." Stefan paused for a moment, apparently looking for words. "Oh, we were such fools! Stubborn fools." The veins stood out on his neck, and he hung onto the table for support. "Whatever America you found, I'm sure it didn't come without your strength and sacrifice. It is good to see you again Franz." Stefan then raised his glass in Frank's direction.

Frank was totally unprepared for this declaration. He had barely uttered two words to Stefan before he left for America. Despite Marie's pleas that Stefan attend their modest wedding at the municipal court in Berlin the week before Frank left, Stefan had refused to see them that day, as did the rest of the family. So the explicit acknowledgment of the wrong that had been done so many years ago came as a great surprise to Frank. He was moved by Stefan's awkward and perhaps drunken recognition. Buttoning the coat over his vest, Frank stood up solemnly and bowed toward Stefan. Anna stood up and raised her glass as well, but Stefan continued, his voice even more tremulous than before. "I know my father would have been proud of these two. Just look at them. They've made it and they've made it back. That's more than I can say for myself."

"Please, Stefan," Anna called across the table. There were tears in his eyes. In an almost clownish gesture, he refused his sister with a wave of the hand and continued. "Why is it that the last time I've seen anyone was father's funeral? It's not like I live in America. What has happened to us? I used to see you every day!" He was looking at his cousins. Some of them shook their heads and looked at him coldly, while others refused to look at him altogether.

"I don't need to go on like this. I'm sorry. This is a celebration. My sister has returned. My dear little sister has returned triumphant! I can only hope that the next time we see one another will be as joyous as this."

"Hear, hear!" cried Friedrich, rising from his seat. Everyone followed his lead. Stefan was coughing through his laughter. Charlotte approached Marie and whispered in her ear, "We all worried that he would be drunk. But his heart's in the right place."

Marie made no reply. She just looked at Stefan, who had turned toward the hallway in an apparent effort to find the bathroom. His hands were still trembling.

"Poor Stefan."

VII

Three weeks after the homecoming party for Frank and Marie, the Austrian archduke Franz Ferdinand and his wife were assassinated in Sarajevo on June 28, 1914. Frank and Marie were traveling in East Prussia through the Mazurian Lake district when they heard the news. They were staying at a small lakeside inn northeast of Allenstein, not far from Frank's birthplace. Frank wanted Marie to visit the area before he returned to Derz to introduce her to his family. They had left Berlin two days before the archduke was assassinated. "We'll see you in a month," Marie told Anna, waving good-bye from the train window. The journey to Allenstein that had taken two days in Frank's army years was now a mere six-hour trip.

Shortly after they arrived in Allenstein, Frank secured a driver. He had assumed that they would make it up to the old inn by horse and carriage, but there were only automobiles waiting outside the train station. Not a single carriage was left in Allenstein, or so it seemed as they drove through the town that Frank had long ago considered living in when he was still farming in Derz.

"Good Lord!" Frank sighed as they passed the outskirts of Allenstein.

"What is it?"

He pointed through the window of the car to a smokestack emitting a plume of ash-colored smoke.

"This was hardly more than a farm town thirty years ago. We came down here to buy supplies, sell beets, that sort of thing."

Sugar refineries and sheet metal plants littered the outer ring of the town. Marie shook her head. Except for a few peasant cottages on the outskirts of town, it could have been Illinois. Soon they were in the familiar country of Frank's youth. He breathed a sigh of relief as he gazed out to the flat yet rugged landscape. Little lakes and fishing holes began appearing on either side of the gravel road. Marie was more curious, as if this oddly familiar landscape might somehow afford her special insight into her husband. She had never been to East Prussia. She had been hearing about it all her life, but this was the first time she had breathed the fabled East Prussian air.

VIII

Before they were married in Berlin in 1884, Franz had written to his parents that he would like to come home with Marie and introduce her to the family. Since his parents had been strongly opposed to their marriage, he doubted that they would agree to meet her. Still, it was important to give them an opportunity to meet their future daughter-in-law. When he received their response, Franz refused to show the letter to Marie and burned it. "At least your parents had the decency to sit down to a meal with me," Franz later lamented to Marie at the Princess Café. "At least they had the courtesy to shake my hand."

Franz's parents loved their son dearly but detested Lutherans for what they perceived as the ultimate betrayal. This dislike had its roots in religion and class. In their defense, Franz knew how difficult the *Kulturkampf* had been for them.[3] The church they attended from birth was all but shut down due to Bismarck's new regulations in 1873. Franz remembered the day very well. Everybody in the town walked to nearby Lemkendorf. They gathered around the church and the school while a state official came to town in a carriage flanked by two soldiers of the Prussian Guard. Many of the townspeople swore they could see the official laughing and sneering at the crowd as the carriage approached. He looked like a miniature version of Chancellor Bismarck in his greatcoat and epaulets as he stood stock-still, waiting for the pastor to approach him. He handed the pastor an official writ with the kaiser's seal on it. The writ simply ordered the pastor to shut down the church school, which had been in operation for over one hundred years. That the school would be shut down was widely known months in advance. Bismarck had been railing against Catholic education for two years before he convinced parliament to shut down all Catholic-run schools. Before the state official returned to his carriage, he looked haughtily at the crowd and said to them, "It's time for you people to become Germans."

From 1873 to 1876, Franz had to receive all his education at home; children could attend Sunday school, but that teaching was restricted to religious instruction. A state official came around regularly to make certain that math and grammar weren't being taught at the church. For most children this meant that they received no education, because the German schools were simply too far from Derz for them to attend, and their parents were too busy in the fields to teach their children how to write. Although Franz had finished with his formal education, his parents insisted that he continue to practice his writing every day and asked him to read aloud to them from the weekly paper. The closing of the school in Lemkendorf had merely confirmed the suspicion of many of the Derz villagers that Berlin and the members of parliament were no friends to Catholics. Normally unflappable, especially when it came to news of the opinions forming in Berlin, Franz's father, Joseph, took great offense at this official disruption of his quiet life in East Prussia. He signed petitions urging members of parliament to reconsider their position, and became very active in the German Catholic party. In short, the edicts of Chancellor Bismarck against Catholic education only served to strengthen Joseph's Catholicism and by extension, that of his family.

When Joseph and his wife condemned their son's marriage proposal to Marie, Franz considered severing all ties to his family. He discussed this with Marie one December evening in 1883 while strolling through the Tiergarten. As firmly as she was committed to the marriage, Marie didn't want to be responsible for a schism in Franz's family. She begged him to return home, at least to say good-bye to his parents and the rest of his family. After proclaiming the virtues of simply leaving Germany, without any letter or explanation, Franz saw the wisdom behind Marie's calm and persistent pleading. They were, after all, his parents. He loved them very much and wanted their approval above all else. What little he possessed had come from them, and, more importantly, everything he knew—his work ethic, his values—had come from them. How could he not return to Derz and attempt to make amends?

Franz made the trip in January of 1884. He and Marie had decided that they would go to America that year. If all went well, Frank would send a letter to Marie in Berlin inviting her to Derz to meet his family. But he never wrote that letter. Upon arrival in Derz, he discovered that much had changed in the five years since he left in 1878. Many families had followed the same path as Frank had, leaving the farm for the city. Furthermore, as his brother explained to him, fewer and fewer farms were producing anything other than potatoes and beets. Potatoes had always been a staple around Derz since first introduced in the late eighteenth century, but beets were in greater demand as more sugar refineries were being built near Königsberg. As a result, other crops such as turnips and asparagus had been gradually marginalized, or restricted to small family gardens.

What Franz had not considered was how much he himself had changed since he moved to Berlin. He was tougher, prouder, but also more open-minded than when he left, and he was to recognize this very clearly during his visit with his family. His parents were suspicious of what they considered to be the liberalizing effect of Berlin on their son. His brothers and sisters regarded him with a mixture of genuine happiness, overall disapproval of his choices, and a touch of envy that he had not only managed to leave Derz but he was about to quit Germany for good.

He returned to Derz the same way he left: on foot. He was able to take a horse-drawn bus from Allenstein to Lemkendorf, but then walked the familiar road to Derz. On reaching the main street in the village, he saw a few children playing in the snow in a nearby field. The town was quiet. Near the blacksmith's shop, a number of men were standing around talking. Franz waved to them. They merely watched him pass. Continuing through the village of his birth, Franz imagined a hundred eyes staring at him through curtained windows and half-open barn doors. It was cold, and the road was by turns muddy and frozen. Franz's knapsack was pinching his shoulders after the five-mile walk from Lemkendorf. As he approached his family's house at the outskirts of town, he noticed the front door was ajar. On opening it, Franz expected to see his family huddled around the fire, busy at various tasks. There were a few dying embers in the stove, but no one appeared to be home. Dropping his knapsack, Franz sat down on his favorite chair in front of the stove. He threw a log into the stove and stoked the few remaining embers. When he was satisfied that a new fire was burning, he carefully closed the stove door with a crude pair of iron tongs made by the blacksmith whose shop he had passed a few minutes before.

The room was almost completely dark. It was two o'clock in the afternoon, so the workday was nearly done. Where were his parents? He knew his oldest brother Joseph lived at the other end of town, in which house he didn't know. His recently married sister Anna lived in nearby Fleming, but Franz assumed that she would be in Derz for his return. And there was still Rosa, August, and Anna. They all lived at home but were nowhere to be seen that afternoon. Franz pushed his boot against the stovepipe and, leaning back in his chair, stared at the odd constellation of pots and pans hanging above the stove.

A silhouette appeared in the back doorway against a dusky blue winter evening. The shape of the broad-brimmed felt hat was unmistakable. It was his brother August, who had grown a full beard and looked like an old potato farmer, with dirty patches on his knees and tall boots covered in mud.

"I see the army doesn't do anything for some people," August said.

"What do you mean?" Franz asked, smiling at the familiar voice.

"You're slouching in the exact same way as the day you left."

Franz stood up and embraced his brother warmly. August then ushered him out to the muddy yard and across to a barn in the neighbor's yard. The path was slippery with snow and ice.

"Where is everybody?" Franz asked cautiously.

August made no reply. Several lamps lit the barn from within. Frank's whole family, with the exception of his bother Joseph and his sister Anna, was there in the barn. His mother, Magdalene, looked up momentarily and smiled. Frank approached the circle of his family. In the center of the circle a mare was foaling. His father, Joseph, sat on a chair next to the mare. The local vet was assisting. Franz's siblings quietly approached their brother to greet him. They explained that the foal should arrive any minute. They had been in and out of the barn all day.

Joseph had bought the mare two years earlier. The family had never owned a horse before, but Joseph found it so useful that he decided to try for another. Franz was surprised that none of the letters had mentioned the mare. The family stood around for half an hour until Magdalene invited Franz into the house. She put water on the stove to boil and asked Frank to peel some potatoes while she prepared the rest of the soup. They talked for a while about Frank's service in the army until the conversation fell silent and Frank concentrated on the remaining potatoes. After dropping an onion and the potatoes into the boiling water, Magdalene finally asked Frank about "that woman you've been running around Berlin with." He patiently explained to his mother that the woman's name was Marie and that she was his fiancée. Magdalene looked to the heavens and crossed herself three times. That was enough for Franz. "Look, Mother, I love her. I never knew I could feel this way until I met her. I'm going to marry her with or without your blessing. And after we are married, we are leaving for America."

He was visibly shaken. His mother turned to face him. "You're not really leaving, are you, Franz?"

Franz nodded solemnly.

"But what about your brothers and sisters? What about your mother and father?"

He nodded his head at each question and calmly responded. "I've thought about this a great deal and have come to the conclusion that there's no place for me and Marie in Germany. America is a land of opportunity. A lot of Germans have gone before us and are doing very well."

"I'm not so sure there's enough room for you in America either."

"If America has anything, Mother, I can assure you it has space." Franz was growing more agitated.

"Fine. You should go to America. Forget about the rest of us. Forget about our lives and our land. It may not be much, but that's what God gave us. And what God gives is more than enough for us. But for you, it's a different story."

Franz was furious. He stormed around the kitchen. He walked out the door and turned around the yard a few times as he heard noise coming from the barn. Returning to the kitchen, he saw his mother stirring the soup kettle.

"What am I supposed to do?" He had never raised his voice at his mother before. She stared back at him coldly. "What about me?" he continued in the same tone. "Should I stay in Berlin and work in a factory for wages that are not enough for two of us to live on? I tried to borrow the money to open a tailor's shop and they laughed at me. Those bankers don't give a fig for me or for God. All they care about is money. Is that more virtuous than making a life in America? At least in America there's the opportunity to make my own way, to serve no other master than God."

"You can't know the will of God," Magdalene said gravely.

"Nor can you, mother. Didn't God give us choices to make? And if he did give us choices, we are responsible for making those choices. Aren't we born free in Christ?"

"Yes, we are born free to accept our responsibilities. Remember," she added, "I was young once, just like you."

Franz smirked. "You don't know the half of what I've seen. Misery has a face. Shoveling coal into a furnace in Wedding is what misery is."

Magdalene stopped stirring the soup. A bitter smile crept across her lips. "Yes, your poor father and I don't know any better than to stay on this pathetic little patch of earth, scratching the dirt and praising God for what little we have."

It was as if Franz were talking to a stranger. His mother's sarcasm appalled him, and it would be years before he understood what she meant. After a moment, Franz declared, "Going to America isn't a sin, nor is marrying a Protestant girl from Berlin. And if it is a sin, then I'm a sinner, so help me God."

"The devil needs no coaxing. The devil needs no coaxing," said Magdalene, and fell silent.

"The devil what?"

After a long pause, Magdalene said, "Our discussion is over. You will have to wait until your father comes in." She returned to stirring the pot more angrily than before, adding more potatoes. Franz stared at her. She looked worn and tough and intractable. He walked out the back door again and toward the barn, arriving just in time to see the birth. The foal came out all legs and lay knock-kneed and shaky on a thin mattress of hay. Joseph guided the mare away from the foal, which now splayed its legs. August instinctively moved toward the foal in order to help it up. The vet told him he should let it struggle to its feet on its own. The whole family watched the foal stand. As it began to take a few steps, the mare moved toward it. It was breathing very rapidly. The vet asked August for a blanket and more light. The foal took two steps and fell into a bundle of hay, knocking over a pitchfork. The noise startled the mare, and August seized her rein while Franz attempted to calm her by stroking her mane. She struggled fiercely to be free of their hands. The vet moved quickly to cover the foal with the blanket and then directed Franz and August to let go of the mare. Joseph, Anna, and Rosa winced at the sight of the struggling foal. When released, the mare calmed down and gingerly moved toward her offspring. Franz stared at the foal's vibrating rib cage. It looked so vulnerable lying there with its eyes staring blankly at the circle of people. Within a few minutes the foal stopped breathing. The mare had already given up. The vet looked at Joseph and told him the foal was dead.

The rest of the week in Derz was decidedly gloomy. The northwest winds brought more than a foot of snow from across the Baltic Sea. The Christmas season was long over. The days were short and cold, and there was little to do but sit around the fire. But there was little conversation, for everyone in the family knew about Franz's decision and none knew how to feel about it. As a result, petty arguments erupted, which were invariably repressed by a glare from Magdalene. It was too cold to go outside and no one was in the mood to read or be read to. Rosa and Anna sat next to the stove knitting sweaters, while August and his father tried to work in the barn.

In the coldest corner of the house, Franz sat wrapped in a thick wool blanket staring at his boots. He could not move or speak and was at a loss what to do with himself. He was numb from thinking of what he now considered untenable options. He came home resolved to leave Germany. Now, after the conversation with his mother, Franz found himself paralyzed by the prospect of leaving on such terrible terms with his family. Of his siblings, Rosa worried most about her brother's condition. She had never seen him like this, and feared he had come down with something far worse than discouragement. To her offers of soup and tea, he would simply respond, "No thank you, Rosa."

August and his father were attempting to repair a hole in the roof of the barn but discovered that they needed to replace one of the supporting beams, which had rotted. Joseph came in from the cold and looked at his wife, who nodded toward Franz's corner of the house. Joseph approached his son, held out his hand, and asked Franz to accompany him five miles through the snow to Lemkendorf in order to obtain the tools and supplies needed to repair the roof.

The first part of the walk was silent, for which Franz was grateful. His father trudged ahead of him in tall leather boots; a great wool coat and an old rabbitfur cap, which now matched the color of his long gray beard. Snow clung to the branches of every tree along the road. The fields were a continuum of gentle, undulating whiteness, interrupted only by deer tracks. Low clouds crowded the sky, providing little relief from the biting cold of the past several days. The two men now walked side by side, following the grooves of a recently passed sledge. As they came to a bend in the road where they had so often turned off to find their favorite fishing hole, Joseph stopped and pointed to the top of an old oak, which marked the bend. A stork was stretching its gangly wings on one of the high branches. Joseph gave Franz a puzzled look and said, "Must be lost."

When they reached Lemkendorf, they met an old friend of Joseph's. They sat down by the fire and drank strong tea before doing any business. When Franz and his father left, they had everything they needed—Joseph carrying the tools, Franz the beam—no questions asked and no haggling over the cost. As they walked back to Derz, Joseph addressed Franz sternly. "Your mother tells me you are moving to America."

"Yes, sir." Franz kept his eyes on the ground.

"And you are planning on marrying a Protestant girl from Berlin."

"Yes, Father. I wrote to you about her."

"Well, I didn't want to believe it. Your mother has been sick over this for months now."

"I gathered as much."

"I don't think I need tell you this, but know that if you do decide to go through with the marriage without our approval, you will not be welcome in our home."

Franz, still balancing the beam over his shoulder, fell knees-first into a powdery bank of snow.

"Are you OK?"

Nodding, Franz took his father's hand and got back on his feet.

"I slipped."

Father and son looked into each other's eyes. Joseph's brown eyes were dull, lifeless. A look of disgust curled around the corner of his mouth. Franz tried to suppress the lump in his throat. There was nothing he could do. Straightening his shoulders he declared: "I'm going to America to make a life with a beautiful woman named Marie. I love her more than my own life. I'm going with or without your blessing."

Joseph never spoke to Franz again, not even to wish his son farewell the following afternoon. There were no tears and no apparent regrets. Franz said good-bye to his family and left the house. After walking a little way, he turned to look back. Perhaps August would walk with him to Lemkendorf; perhaps even his father would embrace him one last time. But there was no one. The houses in the village were sealed up in preparation for another cold winter evening. An old man and woman led a horse through the snow. A few men stumbled out of the local tavern and found their way into other rooms of the town. As Franz well knew, it would be months before some of them stood under a warm sun again. In the gray, dying afternoon, Franz took a last look at the village of his birth. Kicking the snow from his boots, he turned east toward Lemkendorf.

IX

For a week following the assassination of Archduke Ferdinand in 1914, even the countryside of East Prussia swarmed with rumors of subterfuge and war. Everywhere they went, Frank and Marie found themselves discussing the event with total strangers, farmers by the roadside and old fishermen normally impervious to worldly affairs. From all quarters, so it seemed, came the cry for war.

Since none of Frank's family had remained in Derz, he and Marie decided to go directly to Frank's sister Rosa's house in nearby Freiburg, some ten miles north of Derz. They found a driver to take them from the Mazurian Lakes all the way to Freiburg. The drive, on treacherous roads, including a long stop to change a flat tire. Frank, however, was oblivious to the time. He could have ridden all day in sheer delight, pointing out to Marie the simplest things along the road—an old tree stump, a field surrounded by neatly planted plane trees, a dry riverbed, a stork's nest here and there. Whatever they passed reminded Frank of his childhood in Derz and revived long-forgotten stories.

When the travelers arrived, Rosa and her husband Andrew were harvesting leeks in a small plot behind their farmhouse, a modest timber house similar to the one Frank had been raised in. Both Rosa and Andrew wore the traditional garb of peasant farmers. Rosa's hair was tied up in a red scarf; she wore a simple white blouse and a dark green skirt. Andrew, in shapeless brown pants, wore a fuller and longer beard than Frank's, and a straw hat even broader than Frank's fishing hat. He was hoeing the soil about the leeks. When the driver pulled up by the house, Rosa put down a neat bundle of leeks and came running behind a row of corn.

"Franz, is it really you?"

Frank barely recognized his sister, and approached her very cautiously.

When Frank arrived in Springfield thirty years earlier, he didn't write to his family. After his departure from Derz in January of 1884, his father fell ill. Joseph struggled for several months and finally regained his strength just as Frank was leaving for America in spring. Within a month of recovery, Joseph fell ill again and died shortly afterwards of pneumonia. Frank knew nothing of the illness. Anna simply wrote to him, "Father died on June 6, 1884. The funeral followed two days later. Everyone from the parish attended. Anna."[4] Frank received the postcard in late September 1884, two weeks after his marriage in Springfield. His eyes moistened as he read it. He felt a mixture of anger and profound guilt; he had presumed that he and his father would find a way to reconcile their differences. He was truly an orphan now. He never wrote back to his family and heard from them only once, five years later, when his mother died. But in preparing for his son Carl's wedding in 1912, Frank began to feel an absence of continuity in his life. As a result, he resolved to resume contact with his family with the goal of returning to Germany with Marie for their thirtieth wedding anniversary.

Now standing on the porch of his older sister's cottage thirty years later, Frank saw tears in his sister's eyes and noticed her uncanny resemblance to his mother. Years of regret and loneliness welled up in him. He took a deep breath and fell into his sister's arms.

X

During the first week in Freiberg, people streamed in and out of Rosa's house: brothers, sisters, cousins, and even old friends from Derz. It was all comfortable and familiar, as if nothing had happened, as if Frank had simply returned from a long stint in the army. Everyone was warm and cordial to Marie. As far as Frank could tell, about half of the people he used to know had left the area, most of them driven to Berlin by economic circumstances. The great estates of East Prussia could no longer support their old agrarian ways. The new techniques in farming had become so efficient that fewer laborers were required to plow the fields and gather the harvest. Nevertheless, many of the old folk remained in the area, including all of Frank's brothers and sisters. All week long Rosa was cooking and offering soup, ham sandwiches, or fresh berries to the guests as they arrived. And all the guests brought something with them to share: cookies, sweet and savory pies, tea, leg of lamb, roasted goose, beer, fresh fish. It was like the harvest festivals of Frank's youth or the feast of Corpus Christi, when everyone in town would meet at the church and bring food and eat and celebrate for several days. The only thing missing was music and dancing. The old stories and conversations, however, the peculiar lilt to the East Prussian accent, were music enough for now.

In the evening Frank and Marie often walked by themselves among the oak-lined roads and meadows, Frank elaborating on stories recounted from earlier in the day. For years, Marie hadn't seen her husband so enthusiastic, even joyful. He was the man she remembered strolling through the Tiergarten thirty years ago, who would speak to her so passionately of the bass that swam in the limpid creeks of Ermland.[5] As they came to a pond one evening, Marie asked Frank to sit down with her on a flat slab of limestone surrounded by tufts of grass. Although it was nine o'clock, the sun was still fairly high above the horizon. After remarking how much she missed the late summer evenings of northern Germany, which they had all but forgotten in thirty years of Springfield summers, she asked him what he was thinking about at that moment, something she had often done during their courtship. Frank smiled and squeezed her hand. Insects hovered over the pond, and fish pierced the surface of the water to feed on them. Fanning himself with a straw hat, Frank listened to the buzzing of the crickets and tree frogs. There was a calm about his expression and a softness to his features in the evening light when he said, "I'm thinking about how glad I am to be here with you."

Marie's eyes sparkled. She wrapped her arms around Frank's shoulders and whispered, "Me too."

XI

The following day, Frank borrowed a neighbor's horse and cart and drove with Marie back to Derz. Clouds dotted the eastern horizon as they set out in the morning. Frank, preoccupied by the anticipation of his return to Derz, drove the cart over the dirt road at a modest pace. Until now, sensing the emotional magnitude of the occasion, Frank had decided not to think about it. So he wasn't so fearful as unnerved, unnerved by the fact that despite a week of conversations at Rosa's house, no one had talked about what was going on at Derz. The village had merely been mentioned in passing, as part of a story. Frank had been so pleasantly surprised by the visit with his family thus far that he hadn't asked about Derz for fear that it would bring up the unpleasant topic of the deaths of his mother and father. He was getting along with everyone, and that was what mattered most to him now. As they approached the village, however, Frank found himself confronting the difference between nostalgia and reality.

The main road through the village was as empty as he had left it in the winter of 1884. He and Marie were approaching Derz from the north, a way Frank had formerly come into town only on rare occasions, such as when he and his brother August worked on the Rodds' family farm north of Derz. As a result, everything looked unfamiliar. Marie saw the puzzled expression on his face and asked if anything was wrong. The cart was moving very slowly. With his left hand on the reins, Frank rubbed his knees nervously. Without acknowledging Marie's question, he continued looking at the little cottages along the road.

Reaching the main square, Frank reined in the horse. There was the well he had gathered water from a thousand times or more. Tufts of grass and weeds grew from between the stones his father had hewn with his grandfather nearly seventy years before. A little sheepdog approached their carriage from behind the door of the old blacksmith's

Derz farmers in 2000.

shop and timidly sniffed Frank's shoe. When he bent down to pet the dog, it scurried back behind the door from which it first emerged. Frank then turned the cart and headed west to the end of town.

"Where are we going?" Marie asked.

"This is it."

"What do you mean?"

"This is it. This is where I lived." Frank was in a daze, looking around him at what appeared to be abandoned homes. Removing his straw hat, he mopped his brow with a handkerchief. It was getting hot. At the end of the road they saw a farmer approaching. A short tawny horse was pulling a wagon full of hay. They waited in the square until the wagon stopped. Frank did not recognize the driver, who was dressed just as Andrew had been on their arrival in Freiberg: shapeless brown pants, a white cotton shirt, and a broad straw hat. The man's face was milder and more rounded than the typical East Prussian face.

"Good morning!" Frank hailed the farmer, who nodded back to him in response. Overcome by a sense of disbelief, Frank shed his normal formality and asked the farmer, "Where is everybody?"

The farmer looked puzzled. "What do you mean?" he asked in a thick Polish accent.

Frank got down from the cart and walked toward the man. "I'm sorry. My name is Frank . . ." Stumbling for a moment, he reconsidered. "My name is Franz Frank. I grew up in Derz and left here in 1878. My wife and I moved to America in 1884. This is the first time I've been back since then."

The farmer, noticing Marie's brown Panama cloth skirt and linen shirt, said dryly, "It looks like it did both of you some good."

Frank shook the farmer's hand, which was thick and rough with strong, stubby fingers.

"Jacob Milosz," said the farmer in the same dry tone

Frank resumed his initial inquiry. "When I was a boy growing up, there were almost nine hundred people in Derz. On a hot summer day like this, you'd see women and children walking up and down the street all day on their way to the well and back. Others would be playing, some working, some talking, but there were always a lot of people."

"There are maybe half as many people here now, I'd guess," said Jacob. "Most of them are out by the Hoffman estate."

"The Hoffman estate?"

"I suppose it was rather different when you were here. Let's see, I was here in '95; so, yes, the Hoffmans bought all their land around 1890."

"Who sold it to them?"

" I don't know. I came here in 1895 from Königsberg."

"So where did everyone go?"

Jacob climbed down from the wagon and adjusted the harness on his horse. "Most of them went to Berlin I guess. Or maybe to America."

The sun was high. Little cyclones of hay twirled around the village square in a gust of warm wind.

"Why didn't you go to Berlin?" Frank finally asked.

Jacob replied that he probably would have made more money in Berlin, but money was not the most important thing to him. He had moved to Königsberg with his wife and daughter for work. Two years after their arrival, the women both died from consumption. "It was the filthy air," he said. When he could no longer bear the sight of the room where his wife and daughter died, he decided to try his luck in

Berlin. Fortune met him two weeks before he had planned to leave, however. He met a farmer in a local Königsberg tavern. They started to talk, and after Jacob had spoken of his sorrows, the farmer offered him a job in Derz. Jacob left Königsberg the following day with the farmer without saying good-bye, "as there was no one left to say good bye to. The farmer ended up leaving the farm two years later," said Jacob. "He had some cousins running a business by the docks in Bremen. I'll never forget him. Nicest thing anyone has ever done for me."

Looking around the shabby village square as if to express his satisfaction, Jacob continued his story. "My parents were both farmers, and I suspect their parents were as well. I decided that night it was better to return to the work I knew, the work that was in my blood, than to try to find work in Berlin. I thought if I didn't, all my parents work would have been for nothing."

Frank stood motionless gazing at the farmer's gentle eyes.

"That may still be true—their work, my work, all for nothing," Jacob added with a grin, "but at least there's room to breathe out here."

Frank looked down the road to the cottage where he grew up. He looked behind him to the sun, whitening the sky with its brilliance. He finally turned to Marie's smiling face and nearly broke down. It *had* all been for nothing. All of his parents' work, all of his own work, buried in the silence of the earth. Derz was gone, along with its old ways. People had inhabited this little village since the Crusades, and now they were all moving to Berlin or to America. Suddenly, it was all gone.

Frank thanked Jacob and both men took their leave. Jacob opened the sliding door of the blacksmith's former quarters and drove the wagon in. After tying up the horse by the well, Frank walked arm-in-arm with Marie down the main road through Derz to his old house. No one else was on the road. Despite the sun blazing on the tall grasses, the village seemed desolate. Marie noticed Frank growing anxious.

"Where did it go?" Frank asked himself loud enough for Marie to hear.

"Where did what go?"

"My house."

"What do you mean?"

"My house, my house! The place where I grew up. It's not here!"

Frank looked around and he saw several of his neighbor's cottages missing. He ran into an open area of tall grass and weeds. "This is where our kitchen was," he said turning back to Marie. "I used to look out a window right here at night when I couldn't sleep. My mother would hold me while we counted the stars. It was right here," Frank said, framing the trace of the old window with his index fingers. He moved further away from the road into the field. The grass was shoulder-high. "This is where we slept when it got too hot to sleep inside. August and I stayed out here practically the whole summer."

Marie stood on the road, shooing away flies. There was something comic about her husband gesturing to her from the middle of a field. Pointing to various clumps of weeds, he gave a tour of the vanished house: "This was where the stove was . . . This is where I slept." Marie couldn't help smiling as her husband traced a rectangle in the grass. "This was our garden." And walking to the spot where the front door of the cottage once was, Frank turned to Marie with tears in his eyes. "This is where I left them. This is where I said good-bye."

XII

Obsolescence is a fact of life, especially in America, where resources are abundant and traditions are few. What would be the point of preserving a building that was poorly built in the first place? Frank and Marie had come to accept this aspect of American life. After all, the absence of tradition was, in part, the source of the financial freedom they enjoyed. Nevertheless, it was unthinkable that what was once such a permanent site of Frank's psychic landscape could be so completely erased. The inflexible nature of his parents' home was the very thing that had driven him to America. Yet the grasses bore no trace of what once seemed permanent. There was no sign reading, "Here lived Joseph and Magdalene Frank."

The following morning, Frank's sister Anna came to Rosa's house with her husband, Franz Rodd, and their daughter Barbara. As they sat down to breakfast, Frank asked Anna and Rosa about the house. Anna looked at Rosa and chuckled. "I suppose that must have been a bit of a surprise for you yesterday."

Rosa then explained that the house burned down more than twenty years earlier. Their old mother had fallen asleep one afternoon without closing the stove door. Fortunately a neighbor saw smoke coming from the window and was able to rescue Magdalene. Several cottages were burning, but all they could do at that point was to try to contain the fire. Hundreds of people gathered with buckets of water to ensure that the fire got no nearer to the rest of the village. It was nearly two days before it subsided. All told, seven cottages were burned to the ground. After the house was destroyed, Magdalene went to live with Anna and her husband. By that time their son Franz was seventeen and their daughter Anna was fifteen, so they were able to take care of Magdalene when she was dying.

"For a while we thought Mother died of heartache from the loss of the house, but I was telling the story to a doctor a few years ago and he said he was sure she died from the damage done to her by smoke inhalation," Anna concluded solemnly.

"Why didn't anyone tell me?" Frank asked, and immediately regretted asking.

"What? So you could ignore us for another twenty years?" said Rosa coldly.

Anna followed, "I told you that Mother died. I told you that Father died. Did you want a weekly bulletin from us? It wasn't enough that you left Father for dead with a broken heart?"

Rosa got up from the table and began clearing the dishes, Barbara assisting her. After a moment Frank looked at Anna and said, "What I meant to say is, why didn't anyone tell us before we went back to Derz yesterday."

Anna snapped: "I know exactly what you meant, and so do you."

"What do you mean?"

Frank himself was no longer sure what he meant. He held his tongue awhile and then excused himself from the table. After pacing back and forth in front of the stove, he felt compelled to speak. "You've no idea what it was like. You've no idea what my conversation with Father was like. You've no idea how Mother spoke of Marie. You don't know how hard it was for me to leave Derz in the first place—it was even harder to leave Germany, even harder to go to America. Can you even imagine what it was like not to know a single person and hope to God some soul would have pity on you and offer you a crust of bread and a roof over your head?"

Frank was trembling. His beard quivered.

Anna spoke more gently but with no less conviction: "Oh Franz, no—I couldn't know what you've been through," she began and stood up from the table as Rosa rejoined them. "I've often lulled myself to sleep imagining Illinois. Sometimes I've even wished I'd gone myself before everything changed, before Mother died, before the children came. But then I thought, 'What would happen here?'"

There again was the question that had been plaguing Frank ever since his return to Ermland. He could hear his mother saying the same thing. But what did she know about choice? Their entire world was handed to them, and all they had to do was to live in it. They were simple people. Simple people with simple needs and never a thought beyond next week. What did they know about factory work? Hard work they knew, but what did they know about the kind of work that exacts a pound of pride for every hour?

Anna continued more warmly than before, looking at Frank with an expression reminiscent of his mother. "Of course, no one is irreplaceable. Nothing lasts forever, and with war almost upon us, who knows what will happen to these trees and this rocky soil? It's not very hard to pick asparagus, scrub beets, and sweep the floor. That's my life. That's all it's ever been. But if no one stays to take care of things, it will all go away." She stopped as if struck by a sudden recognition. Frank moved toward her and held her hands. They were small and dry. He could sense something in her—was it resentment or forgiveness? In the end, words failed them both. Rosa smiled at them.

"It's been a long time," she said, echoing the words that had hung on Frank's lips throughout his return to Germany. "It's been a long time. I don't care what happened, Franz. None of us cares. August lights up every time your name is mentioned and speaks with pride about your business. Magda and Joe don't care. Let the dead bury their dead. We're just glad to have you back. It's been such a long time."

XIII

The assassination of the archduke was followed by a flurry of diplomatic activity, which was reported almost hourly in every paper from Munich to Berlin with all the misinformation and divergent facts to be expected from such rapid speculation. The thing consistent in all the reports was that war was inevitable, and Germans everywhere rallied around a once unpopular kaiser.

After a week in Ermland, Frank and Marie slowly headed south through Bavaria and toward the Swiss Alps. They tried to avoid the anticipation of war, but when they reached Switzerland, they were forced to make an early return to Berlin. Frank and Marie were staying at a small Swiss mountain inn near the Austrian border when the news came of Austria's official declaration of war on July 28, exactly one month after the archduke's assassination. It was all over the morning papers: Germany had issued an ultimatum to Russia to demobilize within forty-eight hours or face war. After a brief conversation with Marie about what they should do, Frank decided to place a phone call to the American consul general in Berlin, but was not able to get through.

"We have to go, Marie." Frank said gravely as he began to pack their suitcase.

"Right now?"

"Yes, right now!" Sensing Marie's aggravation, Frank asked her to sit down. "Let me explain something. After I completed my military obligations in 1883, I was put on reserve. You have to report your whereabouts to your superiors in case you are called again to active duty. If you don't, you can go to jail or face a heavy penalty. Naturally, I reported to them that I was going to America, and they granted me a two-year leave of absence from military obligations."

Marie was puzzled. Frank scratched his beard nervously and paced around the room. "They could have me arrested!"

"Frank. What do you mean? You're not a German citizen anymore."

"To the U.S. government I'm not a citizen, but to the chancellor I am. To his people I'll always be a German citizen, subject to military service."

"That's ridiculous, Frank. You think they're going to track you down after all these years?"

"You don't know the German army." Frank was pacing more nervously now.

"Fine. We'll go back to Berlin to make sure our papers are in order."

"Back to Berlin! That's where it's going on. They'll probably put me on active duty again."

"You really think they're going to want a fifty-four-year-old man to fight in this war?"

"It may be ridiculous. It may be unreasonable. But I think it's time for us to go home."

Late in the morning of July 28, they were on the train to Berlin, to retrieve their luggage and ensure that Frank had the full protection of his American citizenship at the embassy there. The train pulled into Stettin Bahnhof at eight o'clock in the evening; Marie's sister Anna and her husband met them. Crowds of people waited by the newspaper kiosks for the latest editions. With a thick piece of chalk, a laborer had scrawled on one of the columns in the station: "DEATH TO THE SLAVIC HORDES." With regard to the French, a more sophisticated sloganeer had written across the lockers: "LET THEM EAT HORSEFLESH." The mood on the street was one of excitement and confusion; traffic was at a standstill. Almost everyone was walking in the direction of the kaiser's palace on Unter den Linden.

After trying in vain to find a cab or some other way back to the house, they decided to put Frank and Marie's baggage in storage for the evening and to walk to one of the cafés along Unter den Linden. By the time they arrived at the Brandenburg Gate, a mob had formed and was heading toward the Russian Embassy. All along the street and into the Tiergarten, people were singing the national anthem, waving flags, and dancing to sentimental songs. "Just like the old Berlin," Frank said to Marie as they walked down the street with the thousands of revelers. A group of young men sprinted past them, carrying two-by-fours.

The following morning, July 29, it was reported that the Russian ambassador and his party had been stoned. Others, accused of being Russian spies, were beaten to death by the mob.[6] When Frank and Marie returned to the station to retrieve their luggage later that day, they were surprised to see that the celebrating from the night before had hardly ceased. Crowds gathered in the cafés to listen to the bands playing folk tunes. Thousands of soldiers arrived at the station and were promptly offered great platters of sandwiches and sausages and little squares of chocolate. Berlin had been instantly transformed into the headquarters for the German army; regiments were on the move; groups of general staff officers raced about the city in their well-fitted coats and epaulets. Huge crowds of civilians carried banners about the streets, eager to please the kaiser and prove to the world that

Germany's hour had arrived. Before the end of the day, Frank visited the U.S. embassy, only to find it closed. Panic seized him, aggravated by the patriotic demonstration of a group of older men dressed in ordinary foot soldiers' uniforms. He was back at Anna's house within an hour and immediately sought out Friedrich, who explained that the American embassy in Berlin had closed indefinitely.

Next morning, Frank placed a phone call to the American consul general's office in Hamburg. Unable to get through, he sent a telegram asking for instruction. He then waited with Marie at the Viktoria Café for a response, drinking coffee and reading the news for an hour. All traces of criticism against the kaiser had disappeared from the papers. Germany was united by the war effort in a manner that only those of Frank and Marie's generation could recall from the early days of unification. Soldiers marched through the streets, Berliners throwing flowers at their feet.

The reply from the consul general was hardly reassuring. Frank and Marie were advised to leave the country as soon as possible, though passage to the United States was difficult to obtain. The telegram confirmed that the embassy in Berlin was temporarily closed. It also stated that German military officers were responsible for reviewing exit visas and that several German-born American men had been arrested for attempting to leave the country on the charge that they were avoiding military service.[7] Therefore, the consul general advised that they present themselves to the embassy in Hamburg in order to obtain emergency passports.

Frank and Marie had originally purchased a return passage out of Bremmerhaven, leaving on November 15, which would have given them a six-month anniversary trip. Frank went to the steamship company's Berlin office that afternoon to change their reservations. Four ships sailed to the United States each month. Since all were fully booked for the next two months, the agent put them on a waiting list and advised them to call daily to see if tickets had become available. Any openings had to be taken within a few hours or would be passed on to others.

On the morning of July 31, Friedrich and Frank went to the center of Berlin, where at the corner of Friedrichstrasse and Unter den Linden thousands of men were assembled. The excitement in the crowd was palpable as people pressed closer to hear officers of the Prussian

Guard read the mobilization orders for the German army from strategic points on the street. It was now official: Germany was at war. As they returned home, even the once skeptical Friedrich was swept up in the call to serve the fatherland. There was no use in questioning the policy of the government; it was time to support the troops. Despite a rising feeling of patriotism, Frank remained focused on securing safe passage to America. After all, he had already completed his service to Germany. He was needed back in Springfield.

On the morning of August 5, the day of the invasion of Belgium, Friedrich returned from the newspaper kiosk with several papers in hand, one for each person in the house. Sitting together at the breakfast table, Friedrich and Anna read the reports with great interest. It was now inconceivable to them that they had once questioned the prudence of war. They had no doubt that their sons would soon become heroes in the noble service of Germany, and would return from Paris within a month or two with stories to last a lifetime. Germany absolutely had to fight Russia and France, and now was the time to do it.

Frank and Marie read the papers with considerable anxiety. At the urging of Sir Edward Grey and Winston Churchill, the British had sent Germany its own ultimatum: withdraw from neutral Belgium or face war. Everyone was shocked by what was portrayed as the ultimate betrayal. True as several journalists had warned of just such a sequence of events months before the assassination of the archduke. The Germans had to recognize that they might be facing several enemies at once if they supported Austria in war. But as Friedrich discussed the immediate future, Frank and Marie marveled at how quickly everything had changed. In less than a week, Germany was at war with Russia, France, Belgium, and Britain, and the kaiser was promising soldiers that they would return by the fall with all the perfumes of Paris in their rucksacks.

The couple remained at Anna's home another week, waiting to hear from the steamship company and taking in the peculiar atmosphere of wartime Berlin. Although Frank could never feel entirely at ease in the midst of such massive mobilization, the atmosphere was high theater. Marches and patriotic demonstrations continued every day. Berliners lined the street as soldiers marched to the station with flowers in their gun barrels, garlanded by their wives, mothers, and even total strangers who were swept up in their support of the troops. People were overjoyed at the prospect of a swift victory. They all felt, for the first time in their lives, that they were a part of something historic.

Enthusiasm for war is quickly overcome, however, by the reality of rage and brutality. Marie noted this one evening after they walked into a demonstration calling for British blood. The undercurrent had been there all along, but total hatred of Britain was manifested that night. Rumors of treachery and deceit ran through the crowd and fed the instinct to hate. Marie was troubled by it. When she mentioned her feelings to her sister and her husband, she felt even more disturbed by the isolation of her position. Three of Anna's sons had already been called to serve as officers. Subsequently, she was in no mood to question the civility of wartime Berlin. Frank tried to put things into perspective, arguing that the blood thirst was temporary and, given the nature of the British betrayal, understandable. "It's like the American sport, baseball," he tried to reassure her. "You try to get the blood boiling before the big game."

On August 10, after daily visits to the steamship company, Frank secured two tickets to New York City, departing August 14 from Bremmerhaven. On August 11, he and Marie were on the train to Hamburg. Both were relieved to be going back to Springfield. Their final farewell party from Berlin, quickly brought together by Anna, was subdued and somewhat disappointing. Marie tried to say goodbye to her brothers and cousins, but most of them were too busy preparing for war or were already enlisted and training for battle. Anna promised she would stay in touch, and Friedrich insisted that they would come to America when the war was over. But they never did. No one could anticipate the horror of battle that the young men on both sides would soon be experiencing. The emotional disease of world war had barely touched the families. The initial symptoms were just emerging.

The lines in front of the American consul general's office in Hamburg stretched down the block and around the corner. Fortunately, Frank had brought with him his certificate of naturalization as a United States citizen and his German military passport issued in 1883. After nearly a day of waiting, an emergency passport was issued to Frank Franke and his wife. The American who issued the passport cautioned Frank to be careful in his discussion with the German officer. Anything out of the ordinary could cause a passenger to be pulled out of the line and subjected to a rigorous investigation, which meant missing the ship.

Arriving at Bremmerhaven on August 14, 1914, Frank and Marie presented themselves and their baggage to the customs officer. Frank began his conversation in English to establish his American citizenship. The young officer understood what he had said, carefully looked at his documents, and then addressed him in German. Frank responded politely in German but returned to English when appropriate. The officer looked skeptically at Marie but never spoke to her. It was excruciating. Frank was sure that he was about to be called back to serve in the German army.

After a long and awkward pause, the officer said, "I hope you enjoyed your vacation in Germany, and I wish you a happy voyage home. My first assignment three years ago was in the unit in which you served in 1883, the Second Guards Regiment, Infantry." Then, with dramatic flair, the officer stamped the passport three times and told them to board the ship.

They were among the last U.S. citizens out of Germany after the outbreak of the war.

FRAYED

On Friday, March 26, 1915, the Illinois State Journal carried the obituary of Marie Franke.

OBITUARY OF
Marie Franke, March 25, 1915
MRS. MARIE FRANKE SUDDENLY CALLED
IS STRICKEN WITH ATTACK OF PARALYSIS AND DIES THE NEXT DAY

Decedent, Who Was the Wife of Frank Franke,
Apparently Had Been in Good Health Until Short Time Before Her Death.

FRANKE — Died, at 4 o'clock Thursday morning, March 25, 1915, at her home, 314 West Adams street, after a stroke of paralysis suffered the night before. Mrs. Marie Franke, aged 56 years, wife of Frank Franke.

Funeral services will be held Sunday afternoon at a time to be announced later. Interment will be made in the family lot at Oak Ridge cemetery.

Every member of her immediate family, with the exception of one daughter, Mrs. Charles Z. Creighton of Champaign, was at her bedside when death occurred. Mrs. Creighton arrived in the city yesterday morning not knowing that her mother had died.

Several friends had called on Mrs. Franke Wednesday morning and she was apparently in the best of health until her husband, Frank Franke, arrived home in the evening. She complained of her throat and said that she thought she was losing her voice, when suddenly her whole right side was stricken.

Physicians were called, but Mrs. Franke failed to regain consciousness after the first shock. Mr. and Mrs. Franke spent five months in Germany recently, where she was born, returning to their home here last September. She had three brothers and one sister in Berlin. The sister has six sons who are all fighting with the German army. Mrs. Franke had received many letters from her sister, since her return from Germany, telling of the war.

Mrs. Franke was born [in Swinemünde, Germany] May 6, 1860 and came to this country when twenty-one years old. She resided at [Springfield] ever since. She was a charter member of the Nast Memorial German M.E. church, founded twenty years ago, and she was always an ardent worker in all Christian matters.

She is survived by her husband: four sons, Carl D. Franke, William, Otto and Milton Franke, all of this city, and three daughters, Mrs. Charles Creighton of Champaign and the Misses Elizabeth and Helen Franke of this city, besides three brothers and one sister in Germany.

I

It was not until Christmas 1914, when she received a postcard from Anna announcing the death of Anna's son Martin and the enlistment of her other five sons in the German army, that Marie fully understood how serious the situation in Europe was. Of course, from the sheer fever of those August days in Berlin when the war first broke out, Frank and Marie had known that they were witnessing something extraordinary. But six children fighting a war was another thing not least because all of them had been educated at the university. "Oh Anna! . . . Oh Heidi, that poor little girl! And just think of his wife Alexandra. She was so lovely, wasn't she? . . . It's awful. It's just awful . . . What if it had been you, Frank, years ago, just after you opened the tailor shop?" she asked her husband one evening before Christmas, knowing full well that she wouldn't get an answer. Especially sensitive to the vagaries of fate, Marie was prone to this kind of speculation since their trip to Germany. Instead of internalizing her anxieties, she concluded that it was better to speak freely of them, regardless of any response. So sometimes she just talked to her husband. And he, in his turn, had concluded that nothing was required of him other than to listen. "That poor family . . . It's just awful."

Carl and Dorothy, a few weeks before their wedding, 1912.

Should any one of her own sons die on the battlefield, Marie knew she could not bear it. What could possibly seduce men into butchering one another? Although Anna wrote of her pride of Martin's valor in the trenches, Marie could only imagine her poor sister lying shattered on the divan, the procession of friends and relatives offering little comfort and rarely easing her grief. "Poor Anna. Poor, poor Anna."[1]

As the war had progressed through the fall of 1914, Frank grew more silent about his predictions. When they first returned to Springfield, Frank had assured Carl and Otto that the war would be over soon, that the German army would handle the French as surely as they had done more than forty years before.[2] By Christmas, however, Frank reserved all military speculations for himself, and when saying grace at the family dinner, he solemnly prayed for the safety of his nephews in Germany.

In many respects, it was a typical Christmas dinner. Ever since Carl had married Dorothy,[3] Marie always insisted that she prepare a feast for the whole family at the old house on Adams Street, whether on Christmas Eve or Christmas Day. The return to Germany, however, made this Christmas especially important to her. As their lives returned to normal and Frank went back to work, Marie had more time to consider what the trip had meant to her. Certainly there were

issues she would have liked to resolve with her family, and she especially regretted not seeing her brother Stefan more often, but as she
came to understand, such things take time. Relationships, once severed, are slow to heal, and she hoped the healing would come now
after so many years.

This year brought the added significance of two new granddaugh-
ters: Marjorie, Carl and Dorothy's daughter; and Frances Marie, Otto
and Anna's daughter.[4] The Christmas meal was prepared exactly as
Marie's mother used to do in Swinemünde: the main dish being goose
cooked according to a traditional Austrian recipe, which imbued the
meal with the essence of Christmas, so Marie thought, because the
Austrians had practically invented Christmas. The secret was placing
the mashed potatoes inside the goose while it roasted. As the goose
fat was rendered in the oven, it dripped down into the potatoes, with
delicious results. These potatoes were a perennial favorite, especially
with Bill and Otto. The rest of the meal was more standard fare—
sautéed cabbage, Prussian-style pickled beets with onions, and chocolate pudding for dessert—but cherished as a seasonal tradition.

After Frank had said grace, Bill and Otto began singing the praises
of the potatoes, eating as quickly as possible to ensure that they had
adequate second helpings, just as they had done when they were boys.
Marie shook her head, laughing. A modest chandelier lit the table and
the faces of the guests with the warm glow of candlelight. Her husband sat at the opposite end of the table in his light gray vest and
dark tie with a shred of purple cabbage in his beard. She sat in the
middle of it all, with her back facing the kitchen where Helen, Milton, and the new babies ate at the kitchen table, occasionally fussing.
A general silence prevailed while they all ate, and Marie put down her
fork and knife for a moment to gaze at her family: Otto, Anna, Carl,
and Dorothy flanked one side of the narrow table, with Mayme,
Charles, Bill, and Elizabeth on the opposite side. They were all in
their holiday best. The girls wore the latest French serge dresses, except for Dorothy, whose dress was of silk crepe de chine, trimmed
with tiny gilt buttons. As always, Carl was immaculate in a high collar
and an expensive dark gray pinstripe suit, his outfit completed with
gold cufflinks, tie pin and watch chain to match. Charles, wearing a
dark gray vest and red bow tie and sitting rather stiffly next to
Mayme, occasionally brushed over the few wisps of hair that still cov-

ered his head. Bill and Otto were in their usual uniforms. For Bill, this meant a white shirt and a bow tie, which was hidden now by the napkin dutifully tucked into his collar. For Otto, it was also a white shirt, but with a gray vest and a short striped tie after the manner of his father. Despite concerns about her sister Anna and grief at the death of her nephew Martin, Marie was glad to be back home in Springfield. It was good to be with *her* family.

Of all the children, Bill most resembled Marie's father. The trip to Germany had confirmed this, not so much in Marie's memory of her father as in reconnecting with her brother Stefan, whom she always thought the spitting image of her father. Yet Bill's ambling gate, his sense of humor, and his casual grooming stood in direct contrast to her father's fastidiousness. Even as a boy, Bill resembled his maternal grandfather, which made it difficult to scold him. When Bill came home with mud on his trousers, Marie had to struggle with a triple consciousness: the immediate responsibility of issuing punishment; her memory of herself as a child and the fearsome impression her father made when angry; and, finally, what her parents must have felt when they had to punish her. She could see herself raising her voice at Bill with a vehemence that the deed did not merit. Seeing her father's eyes in her son and the slight pout of his mouth, she would hold back. It was as though she were seeing her father as a child. Then she would remember being scolded by her father. Was she correcting the mistakes of her past through Bill? Or was she somehow seeking revenge on her father? The confusion made her react more gently to Bill, but invariably she would think of the other children and of her need to be fair. Having settled on a punishment, which in truth was exactly the same punishment she would have given to any of the other children, she would then feel uneasy for hours, her thoughts in a tangle. Bill was probably quite unaware of this, and even if he was, he rarely let it bother him, for there was one crucial difference between Bill and Marie's father. Bill was anything but judgmental. He could be stubborn and exasperating in his insistence on doing things in his own way, but he never bothered about the way other people did things, except when it came to Carl.

Carl set his fork on the plate and pushed it forward as if to announce that he was not only done with the meal but, for reasons mysterious to everyone at the table but Bill, irritated to be there. Leaning back, he reached in his coat pocket for a small leather cigar case, removed a thin cigar, and lit it. The first puff hung over the table like gunsmoke. Bill stopped eating and looked at Carl, who was now checking his pocket watch. The two brothers had had several altercations during the week, and Carl had even threatened to fire Bill. Bill had then declared that he would quit and start his own dry cleaning business, that he knew more about the machines and the business and the people than Carl would ever know. Carl had laughed contemptuously and asked Bill where he would find the money to start the business and, more importantly, where he would find customers. "I'm the only one bringing in any money to this business," he sneered. "Even Papa knows that. If it weren't for me, you'd still be at Sangamo Electric."

It was true. Carl did bring in a large percentage of the business. Dedicated to securing every banker and every hotel in Springfield as a customer, Carl understood how to market Paris Cleaners and how to treat his customers, taking them out to lunch and always sending gifts for the holidays. He was amazingly successful; his customers were loyal and consistently recommended Paris Cleaners to others. But when it came to his employees and the rest of his family, Carl's ambition often blinded him to the rules of decorum he had mastered in his business negotiations, with the result that he seldom praised others who worked at Paris Cleaners. Convinced that his skills were irreplaceable, Carl thought his family should accord him greater recognition. For Helen, Elizabeth, and Otto, Carl's attitude was merely something to be endured or ignored. Bill, on the other hand, saw it as an offense to all the hard work he and the rest of the family put into the business. So he chafed at Carl's orders. And without the intervening authority of the father, during Frank and Marie's trip to Germany, this chafing soon had become an open sore.

Carl had hardly touched the meat on his plate. The rest of the family was still eating. Holding Marjorie, whom Helen had just brought into the dining room, Dorothy struggled with her other hand to free a piece of meat from the thigh of the goose. She looked to Carl for help, but he seemed lost in his own clouds of smoke. Marie, not knowing what had taken place at the cleaning shop earlier that week and oblivious to the tensions that had been rising during the trip, puzzled over Carl's apparent dissatisfaction.

"Is the goose not to your liking?"

Carl puffed at his cigar, not realizing that the question was directed to him. Disturbed at what she took as Carl's ingratitude, Mayme asked Carl very curtly: "Carl, is there something wrong with the goose?"

Carl started. "No, not at all." Taking another draw on his cigar, Carl then tapped it on the edge of the plate with ash falling on the untouched meat.[5] "I'm not hungry," he added.

"Well, the least you could do is put your cigar out until the rest of us finish our dinner!" Mayme scolded. As the eldest sibling and as his twin, Mayme took it as her birthright to criticize Carl.

Otto, still working on his portion of goose and potatoes, chimed in, "I'd be happy to take that breast off your hands."

Carl drew another puff on his cigar, shoved the plate in Otto's direction and stood up from the table.

"Just where in the heck do you think you're going?" Bill asked, jumping up from the table so as to block Carl from leaving the room, his long frame looming over Carl's. Helen, holding little Frances Marie, stood with Milton at the kitchen door to see what the commotion was about.

"Who is asking?" Carl said loudly and defiantly.

"I am," Bill said, doing his best to keep his voice down.

Carl walked around the table so that he could enter the living room unhindered. As he made his way through the doorway, he announced calmly, "I don't think I need to answer you."

Bill leaped toward Carl, grabbing him by the collar. Otto intervened quickly, and with his strong arms was able to separate the two.

Now Bill was shouting. "That's just it, Carl! That's just it! You do need to answer your family. You can't get up in the middle of Christmas dinner. It's Christmas for God's sake!" He was on the verge of losing control. Shoving Otto to the side, he approached Carl, fists clenched.

"Go ahead, Bill! Hit me! It's about all you can do."

Carl leaned his chin forward with the cigar pointing up from his mouth, inviting Bill to knock it out. Charles sprang from the table to assist Otto, who had managed to sandwich himself between the two antagonists.

"Animals!" was all that Marie could utter before she ran into the kitchen, tears pouring from her eyes.

Frank looked at his sons with his lips parted as if he were going to speak. But he could neither speak, nor even think. He was completely at a loss.

II

Weeks passed and no one in the family said anything about the fight between Bill and Carl. Marie was almost in mourning. She barely spoke, and when she did, it was in a low monotone. A mood of gloom settled on the house, which Frank moved through like a specter, making himself known mostly by his absence. This only made matters worse for Marie, for she desperately needed his help to make things right between Carl and Bill, but when she appealed to him, Frank simply asked that they not speak about it. She was angry and confused. Although generally reticent, Frank had never been slow to wield his authority over the children, especially when they were younger. As he and Marie lay in bed some three weeks after Christmas, Marie asked him again if the fight between Bill and Carl had been resolved or whether the tensions had at least slackened a bit. Frank did not acknowledge her inquiry. A minute passed and she asked him again. She could see him staring at the shadows on the wall of their room. Not a word came from his lips.

"Fine," she said, rising up from the bed. "We won't discuss it. I'll be sleeping in the living room."

Frank groaned and rolled away from her. Marie walked out, slamming the door.

The following morning Frank woke up later than usual. Marie and some of the family were downstairs finishing breakfast. Milton had his coat on to go to school. Helen had already left for work, Carl having asked her the night before to come in early in order to go over a delinquent account. Frank's eggs sat cooling on the breakfast table when he came into the kitchen.

"Why didn't you wake me up?"

Without answering him, Marie proceeded to wash the dishes.

"Where's Bill?" Frank asked. Marie's eyes were fixed on the frying pan she was scrubbing.

Volunteering to speak on her mother's behalf, Elizabeth said, "He had to leave early to pick up some drapes."

"Where?"

"I think it's at one of the new hotels downtown, but I'm not sure. Ask Carl. He'll know."

Frank walked up to the kitchen counter where Marie was working. She could see him but refused to face him. Making every attempt to get her attention without words, Frank finally pulled Marie around by her shoulders. She still didn't look at him. "Isn't it clear from what Elizabeth said? Everything's fine."

"We'll talk about it later," whispered Marie.

Frank shrugged his shoulders; the problem certainly would not be solved that morning, so he set about finding some bread in the cupboard. When he saw Elizabeth waiting in the doorway of the kitchen with her coat over her arm, he asked, "Are you ready to go? I have an appointment downtown at 8:30." She hunched the arm holding the coat to indicate that she'd been ready for some time. Visibly annoyed by this gesture, Frank quickly drank his cold cup of coffee without sitting down. Bidding Marie a good day, Frank and Elizabeth hurried out.

It was a warm day for January. There was still snow on the ground, but occasional patches of brownish yellow grass interrupted the neat squares of snow in the front yards of the houses along Adams Street. The sky was low and gray, recalling a winter's day in Derz, but something about the perfect flatness of the Midwest made the cloud cover seem more oppressive. When they reached the end of the street, Frank asked Elizabeth about the situation between Bill and Carl.

"They're still not talking to each other," Elizabeth replied, looking more closely at her father's face. "They generally communicate through me or Helen."

Turning toward the traffic, Frank averted his eyes from his daughter so that she could only make out a slight twitch at the corner of his eye. He adjusted his black bowler nervously before they crossed the street. Elizabeth was surprised by his inquiry. While her father did have the final say on all business matters, including any management decisions, he usually left that work to Carl or, if there was trouble with a floor worker, to Otto. Elizabeth wanted to ask him what he was thinking about, but considering his sometimes explosive anger, she thought better of it. So they continued down the street in silence.

When Frank asked Bill to leave Sangamo Electric and join the family business in 1913,[6] Paris Cleaners was expanding rapidly. All the other children had willingly accepted the invitation to work for the business, but Frank knew that it would more difficult with Bill, who was satisfied with his job at Sangamo. Within a year of his son's employment there, Bill had become a supervisor, and Frank learned from one of the managers at the plant that Bill was one of the most highly valued employees. His ability to earn the respect and trust of his coworkers made him especially suited for a management position. Frank, however, wanted a family business like the one Marie had grown up in, one at which the whole family worked. Deep in his heart, he felt that such a business would serve as a correction to the mistakes of his own past or, to put it more accurately, the mistakes of the past that had been given to him. He had watched his brothers and sisters leave home, one by one, for another town in search of work or marriage. After he moved to Berlin, he couldn't afford trips home to Derz, so his contact with his family was exclusively through letters. He believed America would provide the opportunity to change that. With the advantages of industrialization and a seemingly unlimited supply of land and resources, there was no reason his children should ever have to leave Springfield.

Since Carl was the eldest son and had come up with the idea for the cleaning business it was only natural that he should become president of the company. But Bill was more independent-minded than his brothers and sisters. "Too many cowboy stories," Frank would say to Marie whenever Bill got into trouble as a boy. And Bill and Carl never had got along. So Frank waited for the right opportunity to approach Bill.

Financially, 1912 was Paris Cleaners' best year since they started. Carl had made an agreement with two hotels to handle all their dry cleaning and had anticipated several similar opportunities, but the plant was already operating at full capacity. Agreeing that it was time for the business to expand, Frank presented the idea that they should open a second plant on the north side of Springfield, thus positioning the firm to serve a new group of customers with a full-service plant in their neighborhood. After some consideration, and several discussions with the bank, Frank confirmed that it was a sound investment. He also saw it as an opportunity to bring Bill into the fold by having him manage the North End plant. By the time Frank spoke to Bill about it, Bill had already been thinking along similar lines. Not only did he wish to show his loyalty to his father and his family; he also saw it as an excellent opportunity. He could manage, help build the business, and invest in something that had already proved itself. By the fall of 1913, the North End plant was up and running with Bill acting as manager.[7]

Friction between Bill and Carl began almost immediately. Bill refused to take orders from Carl, citing both Carl's arrogance and his lack of knowledge about the actual work of dry cleaning. For his part, Carl could not tolerate what he perceived as Bill's insolence, and he feared that Bill might take on more authority in the business. As the eldest son, Carl felt entitled to supervise and direct the North Side Plant. At first, Frank was able to keep Bill and Carl in line by his mere presence at one of the plants. But when he and Marie left for Germany, the patch that held the family together was ripped off, leaving a tear worse than before.

IV

Frank walked home with Elizabeth in silence as earlier. Helen had gone to the library after work, and Marie had picked up Milton from school. The day had grown brighter since the morning, and now that evening was settling across the city, the air was colder. Naked elm boughs framed the wintry blue of twilight. Gazing up at the stars, Frank tried to orient himself by Orion but was unable to locate it. The lamps along the street flickered awake. People shouldered the cold in cars and on foot. Reaching a quiet section of Adams, Frank asked Elizabeth again about Bill and Carl.

"How were they when your mother and I were away?" he began.

"Carl and Bill?" asked Elizabeth, still surprised by the inquiry earlier that morning.

When her father nodded, she made her best effort to answer accurately. "It was fine at first, just after you left. The business was running smoothly and everyone was in good spirits. Sometime just before Independence Day, the cleaning machine broke down at the main plant. After working on the machine all afternoon, Otto said that we needed to replace a bearing, but we would have to wait until after the holiday to fix it. It seemed reasonable to everyone. We were only planning on doing one more load that afternoon anyway. Besides, it was Independence Day, and no one would pick up their cleaning until the Monday after the holiday. So Otto and the rest of them finished the pressing, and Otto told them to go home early for the holiday. Carl came back to the office from a late lunch with a client. Actually I think he was with someone from the Elks' club; maybe they were planning something for the parade. Anyway, when he came back he seemed to be in good spirits. Then he decided to walk to the plant. Of course, it was empty, and he started shouting for Otto." At this point, Elizabeth did her best impression of Carl; her "Where's Otto?" captured Carl's tone so well that even Frank couldn't hold back a smile.

"Otto came out from the back," she resumed. "I think he'd been looking at the cleaning machine at the time. Carl asked him where all the workers were, and when Otto told him that he'd sent all of them home early because of the holiday, Carl exploded. It was so bad that I decided to close the store temporarily. I thought it was better for our customers not to see this side of the business. And of course, when Carl found out that I'd closed the store, he started shouting at *me*, telling me that I was ruining the business, that you have to always keep your posted hours so as to earn the customer's trust and respect."

By Frank's fierce breathing, Elizabeth could tell that her father was losing patience and that he was in agreement with Carl. In an attempt to deflect his anger, she added, "But that's neither here nor there. The real problem came when Carl ordered Otto to fix the machine before he left that night. Otto tried to explain that he needed a new part, but Carl just said he didn't care whether Otto had to make the part out of dirt, but that he wanted Otto to stay until he'd fixed the machine. And you know Otto. He's not going to let you down. So he went over to the machine shop and consulted with his friend over there. Apparently Otto had to come in on Independence Day. He spent all day trying to jerry-rig that part into the machine. He didn't get done until some time after dinner."

They drew closer to their house. The light in the front room had already been lit. Deliberately slowing their pace to a crawl, Frank twirled his finger to suggest that Elizabeth hurry her story, to which Elizabeth tried to oblige.

"So Otto worked all day, and that's where the real trouble began. Bill was supposed to meet Otto at church in the morning to help assemble a float. Of course, Otto never made it because he was at work. I saw Bill later that day at the parade downtown, and he asked me where Otto was. I told him I didn't know but that I thought he might be at work. And then I told him the story about the broken bearing. When he heard that Otto was at the plant, he came apart at the seams. He told me he was going to find Carl and wasn't going to let Carl do this again. I didn't know it at the time, but Carl had gone fishing for the weekend on the Illinois River. Bill was waiting for Carl in his office when Carl got back on Monday afternoon. I overheard Bill and Otto arguing before Carl got back to the office. Otto was telling Bill not to say anything to Carl about the broken bearing, that everything was fine, but Bill just wouldn't listen to him. He said Carl shouldn't be allowed to take advantage of his brother that way; if Carl was going to make Otto come to work on a holiday, Carl should come in too, even if he couldn't help fix the machine. When Carl got back, he went straight to his office and found Bill waiting there. Bill closed the door behind Carl. I heard voices raised, but I couldn't make out what either of them was saying. Bill came out about twenty minutes later and went back to the North End plant. He didn't say a word to any of us, nor did Carl. But after that, they hardly talked to each other. I mean, there were occasions when they were cordial, but they never liked to be around each other for long. Carl would ask *me* to tell Bill to do something, and Bill did pretty much the same. Honestly, they hardly exchanged a word until Christmas dinner. And we all know what happened then."

Frank came to a full stop in the middle of the block. Elizabeth waited with him patiently.

"Are you OK?" she inquired.

Frank resumed walking.

"Thank you very much," was all he said and he put his hand on her shoulder as they climbed the steps to their house.

Once inside, they were greeted by Bill, Frances, Milton, and Marie, who were sitting in the living room drinking tea and eating gingerbread. Before he could recall the trouble from the morning, Frank asked rather gruffly, "What's the occasion?"

Marie looked at him coldly.

William Franke, 1915.   Frances Brennan, 1915.

"Bill and Frances have an announcement to make."

Removing his coat and hat, Frank adopted a warmer attitude and asked Marie if he could have some tea. She nodded, and Milton sprang to his feet, eager to bring his father hot tea and a cookie. Under normal circumstances Frank would demand that Bill give up his chair, as it was the chair that Frank favored, but considering the strain with Marie, he decided to sit on the couch next to her. Milton returned dutifully with the hot tea. After taking a first sip, Frank looked up and asked, "Well, you have something to tell us?"

Bill cleared his throat. His pants and shirt were freshly pressed, and his bow tie sat squarely on his starched collar.

"Yes. We have something to say."

At that moment, Frances moved her hand toward Bill. She was sitting in a chair next to his, wearing a modest dress with a laydown collar. Clearing his throat again, Bill said, "I have spoken to Frances's father to ask his permission to marry Frances. He agreed, and we are getting married in April." Before Marie could get up to embrace them both, Bill continued more confidently. "We will be married at Frances's church, Saint Peter and Paul's, on April 26, and after our honeymoon we'll move into 407 Keys Avenue. As you've always insisted, I've saved enough money to build a home for my bride. Frances is the bride I've had in mind for the past year, and now she's said yes to my proposal. We're really excited about starting our life together in that dream house. It's only about a thirty-minute walk from the North End plant."

Frank could sense that Marie was a little disappointed by the announcement, or by some aspect of it. But he himself jumped to his feet to congratulate Bill and to welcome Frances into the family. Marie followed, kissing them both, although her hesitation was evident.

After they had shared dinner in celebration of the engagement, and everyone else was asleep, Frank and Marie lay awake in their bedroom.

"I'm tired, Marie. We'll talk about this later."

"I don't think that's wise," warned Marie.

Frank sighed heavily, got up from the bed and sat down in a chair in the corner of the room. He recounted the story that Elizabeth had related to him earlier in the evening. It was a windy night with the temperature dropping off sharply. A streetlight stood like a sentinel outside of the window. A row of maple trees formed a line between the light and the house, casting their shadows onto the bedroom walls. As she listened to Frank, Marie tried to discern a pattern to the shadows. Failing to do so, she thought perhaps she simply couldn't see enough of the pattern to make sense of it. Nor was there any apparent solution to the problem between Carl and Bill, which was exactly what she had been lamenting in the weeks following the annual Christmas dinner.

"What are you going to do?" she asked Frank pointedly.

"There's nothing *I* can do about it," he replied, suggesting that there might be something *she* could do about it. They sat together in silence for a moment. Frank changed the subject. "Is there something wrong with Bill and Frances's engagement? It didn't come as a surprise, did it?"

Marie replied rather defensively, "No, there's nothing wrong . . ." And then she confessed, "No, it's true. I was disappointed—not by their engagement, heavens no—but because it will be a Catholic wedding . . . Did I show it too much?"

Frank shook his head, but her comment smarted a little. "What's wrong with a Catholic wedding?" he asked calmly, as if he had no idea why it bothered her.

"Oh, there's nothing wrong with it, really, and that's why I didn't say anything, because I know there's nothing wrong. It's just that, well, we are German Methodists, and when we came here I thought we were starting over again. I suppose I assumed that all of our grandchildren would be German Methodists . . . and it was a happy thought to me. I realize what an impossibility that is here, but it did take me by surprise this evening . . . at least a little bit."

Marie was proud of her association with their church and grateful for it. She often thought it was one of the best decisions she and Frank had made together. It provided precisely the right balance between familiar forms of devotion and freedom from the very pressures which they had fled in Germany. It was both earnest and open to anyone, and they always felt welcome there, especially Marie. What she was beginning to understand was an aspect of her own parents' rejection of her marriage to Frank. Until the return trip Germany, that disapproval had been a forbidden topic. Marie now added, by way of explanation, "I just know so little about how Catholics do things."

Frank smiled. "You've known me for thirty-three years and you know how I do things."

"But you're not Catholic anymore. You were hardly Catholic when we met," she responded inquisitively.

"Well that's true," he admitted. "But we know more now than we knew then."

"What do you mean?"

Frank opened his hands and turned them slowly as he spoke. "I just mean that things stick with us. Things are more a part of us than we ever thought."

She was surprised to hear this coming from Frank, not so much because it represented a new attitude—he was German to a fault, she would sometimes explain to the children—but because he could be particularly critical of the Catholic church, especially when they were first married. She wondered if he had had a change of heart. She let it go, however, in the interest of resuming the conversation about Bill and Carl.

"It breaks my heart," she burst out, "when I think about our children fighting with each other. It comes to me as a great weight that presses down on me and almost suffocates me. And when I think about it at all, my only thought is, 'How did it come to this?'"

Frank moved closer to her and held her hand as she began to cry.

"What did we do, Frank? Where did we go wrong?"

"Shhh," whispered Frank, "let's not wake them up."

Marie tried to contain her tears, but resistance only increased her distress. Frank recognized that this weight she referred to was a palpable thing settling over the house. The shadows ceased scurrying across the walls; there were no patterns, no signs. It just grew colder in the room. Frank got back into bed and tried to comfort Marie. It was a feeble effort, for he was distracted by his own failure to mend the rift between his sons.

"I don't know," he finally whispered in response to her question, "I don't know."

But these words, uttered so mechanically, haunted him. He realized their numbing effect: through their repetition he had come to believe that he had done all that he could do. But, of course, he had done nothing. The tension remained between Bill and Carl, and he worried that it was beginning to affect the business. He couldn't get around the fact that Carl, if not in name then in fact, was the son in charge and the head of the cleaning business. Of course, it was his business; he had lent Carl the money, and the firm was called, after all, F. Franke and Son. But Carl was driven to make the business succeed, and Frank knew well that without Carl's promotional talent and energy, the business might never have gotten off the ground. Besides, he had spent countless hours preparing Carl to take over as head of the business and, in consequence, as head of the family. So he was responsible to Carl. Even if Carl's leadership could be rather severe, Frank couldn't, in good conscience, reprimand him for managing the business successfully.

With Bill, things were more complicated. Frank had had his difficulties with Bill who, of all the children, was the least obedient. In general, Frank believed that he had done a good job of correcting this, but Bill nevertheless retained some of his youthful rebelliousness, especially in matters of justice. Frank respected, indeed, even empathized with this characteristic. He had fought his own battles and had known the sting of exclusion. In retrospect he sometimes wished he had had the courage of Bill's convictions. But as he grew older, he came to value the virtue of obedience, which he understood to be at the heart of harmony and order. And order was the principal goal in this life. So much of Frank's passage into adulthood had been spent sorting out the chaos of his youth. Carl could be unfair—Frank had seen it with his own eyes—but wasn't order worth the price of a minor injustice?

"I don't know," he whispered again, this time to himself; "I don't know."

v

Several weeks passed without further discussion of the rift between Carl and Bill. Life had resumed its usual pace, and now there was additional responsibility of preparing for another wedding. Further, both Frank and Marie believed, for different reasons, that there was nothing to be done, at least not yet. Marie still grieved about it. She imagined that she had somehow failed her two sons and, as a consequence, her whole family. She could not teach them to get along—that was her failure—and during her prayers she often wondered if there weren't something else, some other sin, for which she was now paying dearly.

Since the fight at Christmas, Carl and Bill had not spoken to each other. They behaved almost as if the other did not exist. Bill pretended he was receiving all his orders from his father, and Carl, when dictating the orders to Elizabeth, referred to Bill only as "the manager" at the North End plant. It was easier for both of them this way. They saw how it grieved their mother, and Elizabeth made it very clear over a series of private conversations with each of them—often after she had relayed a message or an order from the other—just how devastated their mother was. "I'm the last person on earth who would willingly hurt mother," Carl concluded every time Elizabeth mentioned the problem, but he couldn't bring himself to apologize to Bill because he firmly believed that Bill had initiated the fight. So he settled on the awkward truce of silence. Bill was even more adamant. "Why should I apologize?" he would begin, and then intone a litany of complaints. "You were there. You saw how he sat there smoking at the table before everyone was finished. As far as I'm concerned, that's not just an offense to Mom, but to the whole family. And that was just the tip of the iceberg. When has he ever said thank you? And since he always refuses when someone asks for time off, why doesn't anyone question him when he goes on one of his fishing trips? Why are we always stuck fixing the machines when he gets to go home to a nice hot meal? Carl may come up with the flashy slogans, but if it weren't for us, there'd be no business to back them up."

Elizabeth tried to be diplomatic. "You don't know how hard Carl works. And even though he has a hard time showing it, you don't know how proud he is of the business."

To which Bill replied, "Yeah, but that's because he thinks it's *his* business and nobody else's."

"That's not true and you know it, Bill."

"Oh come on. We know he thinks this is all his doing," said Bill, indicating the whole shop. Then he added, "I mean, I know that I had very little to do with it. But what about Otto? What about *you* and Helen? And most of all, what about Dad? It took him twenty-five years of hard work at the store before he could open Paris Cleaners. Before any of us were born, Dad was working day and night just so we could be in the position we're in today. If this is a family business— and it most definitely is— and if it's successful because the whole family has worked hard to make it a success, then the business belongs to all of us, and not solely to Carl. Of course we need a leader, and Dad is that leader; he keeps the family working together. Without the sacrifice and work of all seven of us children and the investment of Dad's money this shop would never have gotten off the ground. We're working here because Dad called us back to the family business. It's not fair for all the rewards to go to Carl. We're not here for a weekly pittance. We're not here so Carl can take the profit and go out to long lunches, take big fishing trips, and go to Florida while the rest of us keep the shop running. He's rude to the workers and he takes advantage of his position as the oldest in the family. Each of us should be sharing in the success of this business, not just working for wages."

Elizabeth grew more defensive at this remark: "You think Carl doesn't know that? Don't you remember when he went to school? How hard he worked when he came home? Of all of us, I think Carl is probably the most grateful for Dad's hard work."

"Well, he sure has a funny way of showing it," Bill harrumphed.

"Besides," Elizabeth said, changing tactics, "you've seen Mom lately. She's really upset by the two of you. For her sake, you've got to try to get along." And then, appealing to his sense of duty, she added, "We are a family, after all."

This cut to the heart of the matter. Bill agreed to maintain silence between himself and Carl. "I just can't talk to him anymore. I'll see him. I hope he attends my wedding, but I just don't want to talk to him anymore."

VI

At the end of February 1915, Marie received another letter from her sister Anna. It told of worsening conditions in Germany and a somber mood in Berlin, where many believed the war might last another year. Anna described the enthusiasm of soldiers marching off to the Potsdammer Bahnhof from where they were ferried across Prussia to Belgium. She concluded by stating that another of her sons had been wounded at the front.

Marie moaned at the news, and spent the rest of the afternoon in a daze of grief. After dinner that evening, she announced the news to the rest of the family. Frank shook his head in dismay. At a certain point after learning of Martin's death, Frank had ceased reading accounts of the war in the papers. Descriptions of the trenches sounded as though the world had reverted to sheer barbarism. When he was soldier, he had learned how to march, fire a rifle, aim a cannon, and take a position. In all the scenarios he had trained for, not one of them anticipated the mustard gas, grenades, and trench warfare described in the papers. It all seemed apocalyptic.

Before Helen and Elizabeth began clearing the table, Marie asked if they would pray for their distant cousins in Germany tonight. "Pray for peace," she said, "and let us give thanks for what we have been given here in America."

Once the dishes were cleared, Marie sat down with Bill at the dining room table to talk about the wedding. Without hesitation, she asked him if he would be attending the German Methodist church after they were married.

"I hadn't really thought about it," Bill answered.

"You haven't thought about it? But what about the children? Where will you take them?"

"I assume we'll take the children to Saint Joseph's, the neighborhood parish school," Bill offered.

"You mean this is an issue you haven't discussed with Frances yet?"

Bill, who was never very devout about his Methodist faith to begin with, didn't consider it an issue. All Christians were basically the same to him, and since Frances had asked that they raise their children Catholic—it was required that they agree to this in order get married at Saint Peter and Paul's—he had no objection. His primary concern was to be with Frances.

"Yes. We have discussed it," he returned more formally, "and we've decided to raise the children Catholic."

Marie was distraught. She and Frank had spent months agonizing over this same issue as they were beginning their married life in the autumn of 1884. They had attended a different church every Sunday for their first several months in Springfield until they decided on the German Methodist church. They both agreed not to attend a Catholic church. At that time, Frank, fresh from his religious battles with his family in Berlin, was thoroughly disillusioned with the church and agreed that it was better to start anew in their new home. As much as she was devoted to Frank and sympathized with his circumstances in Berlin, Marie had no stomach for what she considered the festoons and baubles of the Catholic Church. As a child in Swinemünde, she had been a devout Lutheran and had become even more so during her Berlin adolescence. Her disillusionment with the Lutheranism of her parents, however, could not shake her inherent disapproval of the abundance of images in the Catholic Church. The life of the spirit was an austere endeavor and the place of worship should reflect that. Because the German Methodist Church was neither Lutheran nor Catholic, and because the services were conducted in German, they agreed to join it. The decision was difficult but, for Marie especially, liberating. As she now listened to her son casually mentioning his drift toward the Catholic Church, she was distressed by the memory of what she and Frank had gone through in Germany—his parents had refused even to meet her!

"Don't worry, Mom," Bill tried to comfort her, adding, "Frances is a good woman. She will be a wonderful mother to our children."

She smiled. "I know, Bill. It's not that. It's not that at all."

"What is it, then?"

Bill was always one for asking the most direct questions, a trait Marie usually appreciated. Here, however, she was confronted by something she had never fully understood, and yet it was a major tension in her life that had caused hours of indecision, hours of grief, and the manner in which she had dealt with it had altered the very fabric of her life. She fumbled for words. She could only conclude, "It was just very different for your father and me."

Only twenty-three years old at the time of his engagement, Bill had a great deal of experience for a man his age. But his experience was limited to the world of work. Like Carl and Otto before him, Bill had spent his boyhood afternoons after school at his father's business. He had performed an assortment of odd jobs until he secured full-time work at Sangamo Electric at the age of seventeen.[8] Although he was only an average student in the classroom, Bill's habit of questioning the way things are done led to his success in the workplace.[9] His questioning the status quo resulted in more efficient plant floor procedures. For Bill, and indeed, for any young man growing up in Springfield, work defined who you were and served as a badge of adulthood. It didn't matter if the work itself was drudgery; the mere fact that you had a job was what mattered. Just as a bow tie and shirtsleeves signified respectability regardless of class or education, a job meant that you had a purpose, a sense of worth in the world. Bill not only possessed this sense, but he loved the actual work. He loved working hard, and he loved the camaraderie he shared with his coworkers. Customers, even competitors—anyone he encountered along the way—were as enjoyable as the work itself. He liked, and was liked by, those from all walks of life. People often said that Bill "never met a stranger."[10] It was through work, then, that Bill found himself and managed to direct his energy and his talents.

"But what does he understand," Marie thought to herself, "of the sacrifices of his parents, or his grandparents, and the decisions they had to make, which led to where he stands now. He goes about his business as if he were solely responsible for his success. It's better that he doesn't know. Otherwise he wouldn't be able to make a decision."

But somehow these thoughts didn't add up. It wasn't just that things were different for Marie and Frank. There was something else. Addressing Bill again, Marie tried to clarify for him and, for that matter, for herself just what she meant.

"I'm sorry. It's just that things change when you get older. You have a much better understanding of what battles to fight, and you also know how much damage can be done. I don't think I quite understood this until your father and I went back to Germany. It struck me how much courage and innocence it took for us to come here. At the time, we just *had* to do it. There was no other choice than to move to America. But I guess I see now how much pride and stubbornness it took to do it. We left *everything* behind."

Bill's curiosity was peaked by this sudden disclosure, and he listened carefully as his mother recalled the immigration.

"And when we came," she continued, "we had to start all over again. I didn't know how hard that would be. It was exciting, to be sure. But we didn't have a church, we didn't know the language, we couldn't rely on our traditions to guide our decisions, and we hardly knew anything about America. It was all new to us. So when I said that it was different for your father and me, it really was different. We had to know exactly how we were going to raise you children; we had to know what kind of church we were going to. We had so many mistakes to make."

"But Frances and I do know, Mom," Bill interrupted.

She took him up immediately, "I know, I know . . ." and then she stopped. Bill wondered what the matter was. "I have to admit, Bill," she resumed, "that when you first mentioned you were getting married, I was, as much as I tried to deny it, a little disappointed that you were getting married in a Catholic church. I thought we'd left that behind. And besides, Carl, Otto, and Mayme all were married in Protestant churches."

Bill started in again at this, particularly sensitive at the mention of Carl, but before he could object, Marie cut him off. "I know. I know. Your brothers and sisters are different. But we are a family. As hard as it is to believe, Carl cares a great deal about you. He always looked after you when you were little."

"Otto looked after me when I was little. I can't remember a time when Carl liked me," insisted Bill.

"Oh, I remember a time," Marie responded. "When you and Otto were little, Carl was very protective of you, and when he came back from playing in the neighbor's yard, he would always ask me, 'How's baby Bill, how's baby Bill?' It was very sweet."

"I know what you are trying to do, Mom, but don't worry about it too much. Carl and I have settled our differences since Christmas."

"Settled your differences?" she raised her voice incredulously. "When was the last time you spoke to Carl?"

"You mean actually spoke to Carl?" He had to think about it for a moment. "Two weeks ago," he finally concluded. "Yes. It was early in the morning. I went to the plant to pick up some cleaning before I went to the North End plant. I assumed I would be the only one there, but I found Carl working in his office. We were civil."

"What did you say to him?"

"I don't remember the details, but it was brief. I think I said 'Hi,' and he may have nodded at me." Bill smiled and then admitted, "It might have been the other way around."

Marie chuckled, not so much at the story but at Bill's good humor. After a few moments passed she became serious again. "You and Carl have to resolve your differences. It tears your father apart, you know. As I said, we are a family. He is your brother. Flesh and blood."

"But we *have* resolved our differences."

"What, by not talking to each other?"

Bill tried to lighten the conversation again. "Yes. We discussed it and resolved that it was best to not speak to each other anymore."

With tears in her eyes, Marie pleaded, "You've got to try, Bill. You've got to find a way, both of you. I don't care how long it takes, but promise me that you will try."

"I can't guarantee anything, because, you know . . ." he began. But as he saw the tears streaming down his mother's face, he paused and said, "I'll try, Mom."

Marie left the room so as to regain her composure. Feeling that she had broken a long silence, she was genuinely relieved, but the fear of repeating the mistake her parents had made kept the tears flowing. As she stood in the kitchen, she could hear the train from Chicago blowing its horn. "All the way from Berlin," she sighed as she unclenched her jaw and began to breathe again. Bells rang when the train pulled into Springfield station. She needed to finish her conversation with Bill.

Returning from the kitchen with a warm cup of tea, Marie began again. "As I was saying before, everyone else was married in the Methodist church. Not that I mind the Catholic church. It's just that everyone else was married in our church."

"But Otto was married in a Lutheran church and I don't remember you being upset by that."[11]

Marie flushed with embarrassment. He was right; Otto had been married in a Lutheran church at the request of his wife, Anna, and until now Marie hadn't given it a second thought. "You're right," she admitted, "you're right."

After an awkward silence, Marie explained. "You probably don't know this, but your father and I were founding members of the Nast Memorial German Methodist Episcopal Church twenty years ago when you were just a little boy. I guess I thought that with the founding of that church we had a solid foundation of our own. I never thought we'd have to go through this again."

"But there's nothing to go through with again," Bill said, uncertain what she was referring to.

"That's what you don't understand. That's what you *can't* understand. You don't know how hard it was to change our lives in that way. You don't know how hard it is to start all over again. And when you do start again, you want to preserve some of what you've done," she insisted as if she had finally discovered something. "You can't understand that. Not now. Not yet."

At that moment Bill stumbled into a thought, and before fully working it out, he let it go: "And what I don't understand *now* you didn't understand *then* either."

Marie was stunned by what her son had just said. She felt as if she were floating in a fishing boat off the Baltic Coast in the deepest part of the bay, with the water calm and the sun shining. Looking down into the clear waters, she realized just how much water was underneath the boat, how much of it was unknown to her, how much of it could never be known to her. She recalled the first time her father told her that she must not see Frank because he was a Catholic, how unfathomable his cruelty seemed then. She remembered the bittersweetness of her parents' farewell the night before she left Berlin. It had haunted her all her life, that trace of regret on their faces as she left.

Her thoughts filled the silence. Without understanding the full effect of his comment, Bill waited patiently for his mother to come around.

"That's right, Bill." Her smile was wistful and her eyes were glassy. "That's what I meant to say."

Bill sat at the dining room table trying to follow the thread of what his mother was saying. But there was no thread, at least not for him. For her, on the other hand, the words her son had just uttered were like sighting land after months at sea. She wanted to explain this, but couldn't.

"And that's why your father and I wish only the best for you and Frances." She kissed her son tenderly on the forehead and returned to the kitchen to finish the dishes.

VII

On the way upstairs that night, Marie began to count her blessings. The conversation with Bill filled her with a sense of gratitude. The hallway was cold, but she knew there was a warm bed waiting for her. The house stood in the center of the city where she had lived for the last thirty years, the very place where they had forged a new life. She recalled the day when she and Frank got married and how they walked over to the state capitol and looked at the statue of a young and pensive Abraham Lincoln. Who was this peculiar, gangly man? He was no Bismarck, that's for sure.

At the top of the stairs hung a family portrait taken six years before. Marie traced the faces of her six children in the dark and recalled, a little mortified, the incredible fuss she had made on the day the picture was taken. Since it was their first family portrait, she wanted to make sure that everyone looked their best. She and Frank had spent weeks preparing the children's clothes; Frank tailored all the boy's suits while she fretted over the girl's dresses. When it was over, she vowed never to do it again. But it was a fine portrait and came to represent their full arrival in America; they had made it and her beautiful children stood around her as evidence of their blessing.

Marie now entered the bedroom. Frank had been reading there and had turned off the lamp before going to the bathroom to get ready for bed. Marie stood by the window and felt the cold air coming through the cracks. "Soon it will be spring," she sighed, looking at the bare branches and clear night sky beyond.

Remembering Anna and thinking of her sons on the front, in freezing weather somewhere in Belgium, Marie fell to her knees. She prayed for their safety and wondered when the war would end.

Just then Frank returned to the bedroom; noticing Marie in prayer,

Franke family portrait, 1909. *Back row:* Helen aged 13, Otto aged 18, Bill aged 16, Elizabeth aged 20. *Front row:* Carl aged 22, Marie aged 49, Milton aged 6, Frank aged 49, Mayme aged 22.

he walked quietly around her and got into bed. Marie felt good with Frank in the room, her children asleep or going to sleep, and tomorrow another day. Yes, it would be cold, and if it weren't cold tomorrow, she knew it would be cold again before the warmth of spring. But that didn't bother her now, as there was no greater feeling of security than a warm bed on a cold night. She stood up and went again toward the window. The street was quiet. All of Springfield was going to sleep. She thought back to the conversation with Bill, and thought back further to those conversations with her father and mother. It *was* necessary to begin again. Leaves turn red and fall from the trees, and the birds fly south for the winter. The crows stay, cawing to remind us that spring is resurrection, albeit earth's fallen version. So what's left for us but to live through this cycle of growth and decay? And the most bittersweet aspect of life is that wisdom is not wisdom until it's your own. Begin again then. That's what life is. Again and again and again. It's what makes the heart skip a beat at the sight of the first crocus pushing through the snow; it's why a dead tree makes us feel uneasy.

As Marie climbed into bed with her thoughts, she tugged at Frank's beard. Pretending that she had woken him, he gave her a grumpy look. She laughed and tugged again as he turned on his side. Before he could say anything, she kissed him and told him how dear he was.

VIII

A warm spell in March lasted several weeks, and Marie took advantage of it. The trouble with Bill and Carl was subsiding. Elizabeth brought back reports almost every day about how they were speaking to each other again and how both seemed to be making a real effort to get along. "Of course, Bill and Carl getting along is very different from normal people getting along," Elizabeth informed her mother. "But it's better. Carl says hello. Bill says hello. It's definitely better."

For the first time in her life, Marie began to relax. Helen and Elizabeth were quite independent at this point and had relieved her of many of the household duties. There was Milton to take care of, but he was still in school, and after school he usually went over to the cleaning shop and helped out his father. While Bill and Frances's wedding was coming in April, Frances's mother was handling most of the preparations, which left the days wide open for Marie. Feeling a general lightness, she went out to lunch, had tea with her friends, and bragged about her grandchildren. She was in the best of spirits and she seemed to raise the spirits of those around her, something she wasn't often able to do.

On Wednesday morning, March 24, 1915, Marie woke up earlier than usual. She sat in the kitchen by herself and sipped a cup of tea. Light streamed in through the window above the kitchen sink as she studied the steam drifting up from her cup. In the unusually warm March weather, friends from church said they had already planted cabbage in their yards. At the time, Marie dismissed this as a form of wishful thinking, but as she sat contemplating the sunlight in the silence of her kitchen, she wondered if spring had indeed come early to Springfield. Still in her slippers and her robe, she went down the back stairs and opened the door to the yard. The air felt warm, although the sun had been up only twenty minutes. Streetcars rumbled in the distance. A flock of sparrows took cover in a nearby yew and piped loudly. Marie looked at the small rectangle of earth at the back of the yard and thought, "Today might be a good day to start." By the time she came back into the house, Frank was in the kitchen asking whether she had made coffee. "Not yet. Do you want any eggs?" And soon she found herself cooking eggs for the family. By nine o'clock everyone was out of the house. "Peace at last," she sighed, but at once found several friends at her door with coffeecake. The morning went by like that, with jokes and laughter, interspersed with reports of the distant war in Europe. And when things finally settled down, Marie had the afternoon to her garden.

She began by weeding the small lot. The weather had turned windy since morning. Marie knew well that this meant winter would be back soon, if not by nightfall, then by the next day for sure. So she decided to turn the earth, even though she was sure she'd have to do it again. When strong gusts of wind blew, she stopped tilling the black soil for a moment and faced the raw wind. It was just like summers in Swinemünde when a storm blew in from the northeast and she would stand with Anna and Stefan while listening to the waves grind the sand on the Baltic shore. But she stood now on the edge of a thousand miles of bare, black earth about to be planted with corn.

That evening, as Marie made preparations for dinner, she felt a deep fatigue. Wondering if she wasn't coming down with a cold she decided to rest in the living room until Helen and Elizabeth came home. When they returned they insisted that their mother not lift a finger; they would take care of dinner. Arriving home with Milton, Frank saw Marie lying on the couch and asked her what was the matter.

"I am very, very tired," she said hesitatingly. "I think I'm thirsty."

"Can I get you some tea?"

When she nodded, Frank told Milton to have Helen bring out some tea with honey. Exhausted himself, he took off his coat and black bowler and sat in the chair next to the couch where Marie lay. He sighed and stroked his beard. She smiled faintly at him. As he was about to tell her about new troubles brewing between Bill and Carl, she sat up to take the tea. But just as she put out her hand to take the cup, she collapsed and rolled to the floor.

"What's wrong? What's wrong?" Frank cried.

She was unable to respond.

With profound panic in his voice, Frank kept asking, "What's wrong? What's wrong?"

Elizabeth, Helen, and Milton came running out of the kitchen. "What is it? Is it Mother? Mother!"

Frank was completely in shock. He was paralyzed by the sight of his wife lying on the floor. Her eyes were open and able to follow the movement of her children in front of her, but she was unable to speak. The left side of her mouth curled up as if she were trying to smile. But it was not a smile. There was a deep look of anguish on her face, not of pain, but of frustration in not being able to express herself. Elizabeth called the doctor.

Within an hour, all of Marie's children were home with the exception of Mayme, who lived in Champaign with her husband and daughter. Bill arrived about a half-hour after his mother was stricken. He had been working late at the plant and had known nothing of his mother's condition. He sat next to his father on a chair near the couch, onto which Marie had been lifted. Her eyes, unblinking, moved slowly from one person to another. Her face was sagging and her breathing was labored. Sitting opposite the couch, Helen gently stroked Milton's hair. The child appeared confused by his mother's blank stare. "Does she want something?" he would ask Helen periodically, received no answer.

Carl and Otto came from the plant at the same time. Their wives, Dorothy and Anna, remained at their homes with the children. Elizabeth had called them after she spoke to the doctor. "Something happened. Mom can't move. I think she's had a stroke or something like that." Both Carl and Otto left for their parents' home within minutes of receiving the call. Before entering the living room, Carl asked Elizabeth for an assessment of the situation. "I'm not exactly sure," she answered. "Dad hasn't spoken to us since she was stricken. Apparently he asked Milton to get some tea for Mom, and the next minute she was on the floor. She hasn't moved since."

When Carl took off his hat and coat and came into the room, he looked at no one, not even at his father.

Elizabeth stood opposite the coffee table before the couch where her mother lay. There was no response from Marie. Her eyes continued to stare into a mysterious middle distance imperceptible to her family. Stepping over the coffee table, Elizabeth knelt at her mother's side and held her left hand. It was limp and utterly lifeless, unlike any human flesh she'd felt before. Elizabeth broke down weeping. It was the first moment since the stroke that she had had an opportunity to be with her mother.

After Elizabeth's grief had slowed to a steady sobbing, everyone in the room felt a little more at ease, as if they could begin to reckon with what was taking place before their eyes. Helen began talking to her mother again, asking her if she was comfortable.

"Can we get you anything?" she continued, and when her mother said nothing, Helen looked to Elizabeth, who promptly went into the kitchen. She returned with cookies for everyone and asked if anybody needed something to drink. As the children began to move closer to their mother, Frank made way for them and stood next to Otto, who appeared equally incapable of expressing any emotion.

By ten o'clock in the evening, the doctor had yet to arrive, and Elizabeth had no luck reaching Mayme by phone. She had sent a telegram but was sure that Mayme would not receive it before morning. Mayme had planned weeks ago to come to Springfield that weekend in any case, and would be arriving on Friday.

Elizabeth continued to bring out food and drinks, although no one was hungry or thirsty. She knew that her mother was going to die, but she also knew that her mother would have wanted people to be comfortable.

After his initial inquiries into his mother's condition, Carl too withdrew into himself and sat now in the chair opposite the couch, smoking a cigar. A distinct chill had settled on the house. The outside temperature had plummeted since the afternoon, and Carl wondered whether it would snow. The only notable change on his mother's face was that her eyes had ceased moving. The bottom corner of her left eye drooped severely. It was clearly a stroke. One of the hotel managers had suffered a minor stroke only the year before. Carl distinctly recalled now how slowly the man's mouth moved when he spoke. Cigar smoke rose to the ceiling in nervous bursts. Anticipating the doctor's arrival, Carl planned to ask whether his mother was going to survive this stroke and, if she did, would she be able to recover her speech and coordination enough to enjoy the rest of her days? While gazing into his mother's dull stare, Carl realized that he wasn't at all prepared for his mother to die, that he had assumed she would live another thirty years. He would have to entirely reconfigure his sense of the world. He loved his mother deeply, but it was the fragility of life that shook him. He watched his mother carefully for any movement, for any sign of improvement.

The doctor arrived at about a quarter past ten, accompanied by a younger physician. Helen answered the door, with Carl right behind her. The first flakes of snow were falling. The doctor apologized for taking so long, but he was on another call when Elizabeth notified the hospital of her mother's condition.

Entering the living room, the doctor was greeted by Frank, who had been standing in the same spot for over an hour, gazing at his wife. It was the first time Frank had spoken since Marie had collapsed. He recounted to the doctor in some detail the general condition of her health over the past several weeks and informed him of what had taken place since he had arrived home that evening. The doctor approached the couch and checked Marie's vital signs, observed by the young doctor. After a few moments he asked Frank if there was a bed downstairs.

"No. But we can put her upstairs."

The doctor nodded. He glanced at the young physician and asked, "Can you give me a hand?" To which Otto and Bill responded by lifting their mother's oddly limp body from the couch and carefully carrying her upstairs. Emerging from the bedroom, the doctor told Frank, who had followed them up the stairs, "Your wife has had a stroke, probably two strokes over the past six hours. On account of the escalating seriousness of the symptoms, I'd say the first stroke was mild and the second was more severe."

Frank gestured his acknowledgment, and the doctor continued, "People can regain consciousness from such incidents and after some time are able to acquire their motor skills again. I've seen some remarkable recoveries."

With genuine concern, the doctor looked at Frank, who was now gazing at the ceiling, apparently thinking of the various scenarios he might face in the next several months. The doctor recognized a glimmer of hope in Frank and worried that it was too much hope. "Now I don't want you to lose hope, Mr. Franke, but I will say that your wife's condition is rather severe. She has suffered an extreme shock. I don't want to mislead you."

Again Frank nodded, but this time it was evident that he either didn't understand or that he didn't want to understand. The doctor had opened the door to hope, and Frank had entered and had no intention of turning back. It was agreed that the younger physician would remain at the house to monitor Marie's condition. It was past eleven o'clock, and Carl saw the doctor to the door.

"Thank you so much for coming here so quickly," Carl said as the doctor put on his frock coat and hat.

"She's had quite a shock. She may recover," he said gravely. "She's in good hands, though." And then, as he went out the door, the doctor turned back to Carl and advised, "Keep an eye on your father."

Carl took this warning earnestly and watched the doctor walk down the street. With his hand now on the doorknob, he looked back into the room and his eyes met Bill's. No sound came from either brother, and a shadow of pain crossed each of their faces. Finally, Carl turned and went out into the cold. There were black clouds on the horizon and the first buds of spring were dusted with snow. "How do they survive this weather," wondered Carl with respect to those tender buds, and closed the door gently.

IX

Marie Franke died in the early hours of Thursday, March 25. The young physician pronounced her dead at four in the morning. Frank had watched at her bedside while the rest of the house had retired to their rooms. Marie's eyes remained open in a fixed stare; he had wanted so much to talk with her. As he accompanied Marie on her final journey, he watched the snow gather on the windowsill of their bedroom. Quite suddenly he noticed that the steady rising and falling of her breast's shadow on the wall had stopped. In turning quickly to see whether Marie had stopped breathing, he knocked aside the lamp by their bed, thus waking the young physician, who was sleeping on the couch downstairs.

After the doctor had confirmed the death, Frank asked to be alone with his wife for a moment before the children were informed. Her eyes were closed. He touched them gently and could feel her body cooling rapidly. He wanted so badly to look at her eyes again even if only to see the soul fading from them. Whispering the secret words of their love, Frank fell gasping at the bedside. He held her hands; he stroked her hair. It was, quite simply, Marie's face that convulsed him with sobbing.

Even in the darkness of the room he could see that she'd already grown pale. He re-lit the lamp and looked at her face. It was relaxed, and the sagging on the right side seemed to have lessened, so that she was more like herself in death than a few hours earlier when fighting for life. Frank's eyes followed every line, every curve: the way her lower lip met her upper lip, the precise angle at which her lower lip extended from her chin, the lovely roundness of her eyes, and the way her eyebrows echoed that roundness. He had studied her face for over thirty years. He had watched lines of worry and grief, of joy and laughter, etch themselves there.

In the early hours of the morning, long before sunrise, Frank recognized those lines as defining the very shape of his life. They formed the thread of his hopes and sorrows and joys. What was he to do without them? He touched Marie's cheek; he kissed her forehead and detected something sweet in the air around her. But again it was her face that made him give way. He had felt homeless, like an orphan, when he met her in Berlin so many years ago, and that same loneliness had engulfed him before she joined him in Springfield. It was like sunlight when he saw her again at Sherman House. If her eyes were the watchmen of his soul, then her face was its very dwelling, a home wherever he went.

His body groaned. He felt as though the fabric of his soul had been torn from top to bottom and all that remained were its tatters.

He covered Marie's face with the sheet.

The snow, it seemed, had stopped for the time being.

FABRIC RENT

Perhaps the most surprising document I discovered was the marriage agreement entered into by Frank and his second wife, Ottilie Sutter, in 1920. I was impressed with its attention to detail and its anticipation of the problems of inheritance, especially for two widowers.

ARTICLES OF AGREEMENT made and entered into this 5th day of May, A.D., 1920, by and between F. Franke, of the City of Springfield, County of Sangamon and State of Illinois, party of the first part, and Ottilie Sutter, of the City of Springfield, County of Sangamon and State of Illinois, party of the second part:

WITNESSSETH, that Whereas a marriage is shortly intended to be solemnized between the said parties in view of which they each desire to settle and provide for their respective property interests, and to provide that the entire Estate, real, personal or mixed, including all property of every kind and character and wherever situated, now belonging to, or which may hereafter be acquired by either of said parties, shall be used, possessed, enjoyed, conveyed and disposed of by each respectively, the same as if each were sole and unmarried and without the help, aid, joinder or hindrance of the other;

And Whereas the party of the first part has made unto the party of the second part, and the party of the second part, and the party of the second part has made unto the party of the first part a full, fair and complete statement and disclosure of their present property and Estate, respectively, and each party with full knowledge of the respective property and Estate of the other, and with full knowledge of the terms and provisions, intent and purpose of this agreement, now desires to enter into, and does enter into the same, and each party hereby waives and forever binds himself and herself and their respective heirs, executors, administrators and assigns to waive any claim or contention that such full, fair and complete disclosure was not made by the parties respectively prior to entering this agreement, and each party having made an investigation satisfactory to himself and herself of the property and Estate of the other prior to entering into this agreement;

NOW THEREFORE, in consideration of the sum of One Dollar paid by each party to the other, the receipt and sufficiency thereof being here [noted...], convey and dispose of the same, absolutely or conditionally, by Deed, Will or otherwise, notwithstanding such marriage, without the help, aid, joinder or hindrance of the party of the second part, the same as if the party of the first part were sole and unmarried and without any right in the party of the second party by way of Dower, Inheritance, survivorship, Homestead or award, or any claim, demand or interest, statutory or otherwise, at law or in equity.

It is further covenanted and agreed for the consideration aforesaid that the party of the second part shall continue to possess, control and enjoy her entire Estate, now in possession or hereafter acquired, with full and complete power to control, manage, encumber, convey and dispose of the same, absolutely or conditionally, by Deed, Will or otherwise, notwithstanding such marriage, without the help, aid, joinder or hindrance of the party of the first part, the same as if the party of the second part were sole and unmarried, and without any right in the party of the first party, by way of

Dower, Inheritance, survivorship, Homestead or award, or any claim, demand or interest, statutory or otherwise, at law or in equity.

And each party for himself, herself, and his and her heirs, executors, administrators and assigns, for the consideration aforesaid, covenants with the other, and his or her heirs, executors, administrators, and assigns, that neither party hereto, shall or will in any manner disturb the other in the possession, enjoyment, disposition, control and power herein provided for.

And each party for himself and herself, and his and her heirs, executors, administrators and assigns, covenant and agree with the other, and that others heirs, executors, administrators and assigns, that neither party shall or will at any time claim or assert any right in any of the property or Estate of the other, as husband or wife, widower or widow heir or next of kin, and each agrees to execute upon request any Deed or conveyance, which may, by counsel, be deemed necessary or expedient more marriage relations are consummated.

IN WITNESS WHEREOF, the parties hereto have hereunto set their hands and seals, at Springfield, Illinois, on the day and year above written.

(Seal) _Ottilie Sutter_

(Seal) _F. Franke_

State of Illinois:

Sangamon County:

I, John S. Schnepp, a Notary Public in and for said County in the State aforesaid, Do Hereby Certify that F. Franke and Ottilie Sutter, personally known to me to be the same persons whose names are subscribed to the foregoing Instrument as having executed the same, appeared before me this day in person, and acknowledged that they signed, sealed and delivered the foregoing Instrument as their free and voluntary act for the uses and purposes therein set forth, including the release and waiver of the right of Homestead and Dower.

Given under my hand and Official Seal this 5th day of May, a.d., 1920.

_____
                                Notary Public

I

In addition to the establishment of trench warfare on the western front by the spring of 1915, Germany added to the growing list of the world's industrial aberrations a new weapon. It was the latest in naval technology: powered by petroleum and nearly undetectable by air or by sea, the U-boat probably did more damage to Germany's western foes, and ironically to Germany itself, than any other weapon or diplomatic bungle since the assassination of the archduke in the summer of 1914. General Admiral Alfred von Tirpitz announced in December 1914 that Germany would close all British waters to shipping—that is to say, all ships would be subject to attack without warning. Britain's merchant shipping losses during 1915 totaled over one million tons.[1] This element of random surprise and universal fear gave unparalleled power to U-boats patrolling the waters from the Baltic Sea to the Atlantic Ocean. But the perceived affront to humanity by the random slaughter of civilian populations proved to be an incentive to unite the allies and, ultimately, caused Germany's undoing.

On May 7, 1915, a German U-boat sank the Lusitania, taking the lives of 1,198 passengers and crewmembers, 128 of whom were United States citizens.[2] President Woodrow Wilson responded sternly through diplomatic channels to avoid entering the war in Europe. German diplomats argued that they had had evidence of espionage aboard the Lusitania that justified sinking it, but they nevertheless agreed to suspend attacks on passenger ships.[3]

As the war in Europe was drawing the rest of the world into the fray, matters between Bill and Carl had become more intractable, with the result that every member of the family was torn by their loyalties. Since the death of their mother, Bill and Carl barely maintained a modicum of civility with one another. Whether some new element was fueling their conflict, no one really knew. Elizabeth wondered if it didn't have something to do with their mother's funeral, but there was no comment and no argument that she could recall. It was almost as if the brother's reason for civility had died with Marie. "Like oil and water," Otto often said to Elizabeth, "they weren't made to mix."

To Frank, the latest silence between Bill and Carl was merely another indication of a life that had been tapped of all its sweetness. With the news of the war in Europe added to his personal sorrow, he began to lose faith in almost everything. While his daily routine had changed very little since Marie's death—he got up, ate breakfast, went to work, sometimes went to the tavern for a beer after work, and then came home to dinner, which was usually prepared by Helen—life had lost its savor. Springfield seemed sad and unfamiliar. The daily administration of Paris Cleaners had become such a chore that he relinquished most business decisions to Carl. All that remained for him was a kind of rigid authority, which he dealt out resentfully. And to make matters worse, he was beginning to lose his sight. Like a cloud of gloom that hung over his every move, a small, hazy disk appeared in the center of his field of vision. He was suffering from a cataract. As a result, work became progressively more difficult for him. And work, he often cried out to himself, was all that was left for him in this life.

By the summer of 1916, Frank had even stopped going to church. When the minister came into the cleaning shop and saw Frank working at his table, he asked Frank where he had been over the past several months. At first Frank replied rather coldly that he'd "been fishing." It was partially true. He had been fishing with Milton, but only on a few occasions and certainly never on Sunday morning. And then, in a rare moment of sarcasm, Frank added, "I've found that the Lord does work in mysterious ways."

Frank was not suffering from a crisis of faith. He lacked the mental energy to question the meaning of God's intentions. Quite simply, he was in mourning, and he felt sad, vulnerable, and brittle in a world that had become increasingly harsh. He was ashamed by the audacity and callousness of his former countrymen. The gas, the U-boats, the trench warfare—all of it seemed atrocious beyond belief: the German Empire, which had once ascended so surely to the heights of order and civility, was now plummeting to chaos and barbarism. Frank was losing his bearing in the world. And to make matters worse, while America remained reluctant to enter the war, the Franke sons were fighting their own battle—Bill and Carl in particular—marking and claiming their own territory and further entrenching themselves in their attitudes by impugning the others' behavior.

Frank tried to distance himself from all of it—the war, Germany, the family feud, and his family back in Germany. The rest of Vinegar Hill was in a similar mood. No one spoke German on the street any more, but many were desperately worried about their relatives back home. Frank received a letter from his sister Rosa that contained a litany of dead cousins, nephews, and family friends. Many had died on the front, the younger ones especially, and many others died of illness from lack of proper medical attention or because they had no access to clean water. Meanwhile, Frank's eyesight worsened. Cataracts now hovered over both pupils, so that when he was working he could see what he was working on only by looking askance. This world that had shown him so much favor was crumbling, almost literally, before his eyes.

II

Carl prospered during the war, not only personally. As his father became less directly involved in decisions at Paris Cleaners, the business grew. Not that his father ever showed poor judgment, but Carl was able to effect decisions more quickly. The cleaning business was very different from the tailoring business, and because he understood it so well, Carl thought he could better take care of his father by exercising control.

Although Frank never complained of his eyesight—in fact, he made every effort to conceal his condition—it was clear to everyone that something was wrong. He often strained his eyes, especially in the afternoon. He had Helen write up all of his orders. He made mistakes that he had never made before. On one occasion, he even began to sew a sleeve on backwards. Quite simply, he was going blind. The only thing worse for a tailor was to lose the use of his hands.

While seizing the opportunity for Paris Cleaners to grow, Carl felt genuine pity for his father. Just by virtue of working with him the longest of all the children, Carl had perhaps the deepest sense of how devastating the loss of eyesight was for his father. He had grown up

watching his father make suits. As a result, he had a sense of the ennobling aspect of the tailoring business. And given his Prussian sense
of filial piety, Carl wanted to ensure that his father was secure in his
old age. The best way to do this, as was always Carl's way, was through
the business.

His first thought was to reorganize Paris Cleaners into a clear
chain of command in order to streamline the decision-making process.
As he mused over the reorganization plan near the end of 1916, it was
evident to Carl that his father, while still critical to the business as a
investor, should no longer be involved in its day-to-day decisions.
Carl's solution was simple, but not without controversy; he himself
would remain president and general manager of the business; Otto
would become the foreman of the whole operation; and Bill, who
would cease to operate semi-independently at the North End plant,
would instead act as a department manager. In effect, nothing would
change for any of them in terms of the daily work—Otto had always
been more a foreman than a chemist, Bill had always reported to Carl
(even if it was through Elizabeth), and Carl, in turn, reported to their
father. Carl's idea was to clarify their respective roles.

It was on this point that Bill objected to the reorganization. "Why
do we have to change our titles if our jobs haven't changed?" he asked
Carl a week after Thanksgiving in 1916. Carl had approached him cautiously that afternoon. On the way to the North End plant, Carl realized he could count the times he had actually spoken to his brother
since the death of their mother a year and a half before. He had discussed his reorganization plan extensively with his father, for he
wanted to make sure that he had his blessing. Frank offered no other
suggestions, nor did he seem too concerned with the changes; he was
barely speaking to anyone at the time. "Fine, fine," he had said to
Carl, almost dismissively. Otto had taken the change of title in stride:
"Chemist, foreman, it doesn't matter to me. Either way it means
cleaning and pressing." But with Bill, Carl feared resistance.

Carl began by explaining that their father was obviously losing his
sight and that it was the family's responsibility to ensure a comfortable retirement for him.

"Of course," Bill said matter-of-factly. "We all know that."

Somewhat surprised by his brother's approval, Carl continued his
presentation. "I've been talking to Dad about decreasing the amount

that he works. In his absence we'll need a clear structure to avoid any confusion. In essence your duties won't change, but we've decided to change your title to department manager."

Ever suspicious of Carl's motives, Bill asked, "What will you do?"

"I'm still president and general manager."

"So how is this going to help Dad to retire?" Bill continued.

"Well," Carl tried to put it tactfully. "I think it will make him feel better about the future of the business."

"In what way?" Bill asked suspiciously.

"Just so he knows the business is well organized and in good hands."

"Fine," Bill agreed. "What's my title again?"

"Department manager."[4]

And with that, Carl returned to the main office.

III

To Bill, the reorganization represented Carl's feeble efforts to consolidate his control over the business and to confirm his position as the leader of the family. It was just another of the silly business ideas that Carl got from one of the innumerable clubs he belonged to. As with the "13, Unlucky for Spots" advertising campaign, Bill had always been amused at the business inspirations of his older brother. "The savvy businessman," he would sometimes joke with Otto about Carl's schemes.

But Carl's advertising campaigns did have an effect on the success of the business, and he worked at his campaigns tirelessly. As competition in the dry cleaning business increased in Springfield, Carl understood that quality alone would not distinguish Paris Cleaners from its competitors. "After all," he argued with Otto and Elizabeth, "if there's another cleaning business down the street and there's nothing to distinguish the service that they provide other than a name, what's going to bring a customer to us rather than to them? We know how to dry clean, and we always aim to provide the best service, but new customers really don't know how to distinguish service. So you give them a little story to remember us by. Anything to get them in the door."

In the early days of the business, Carl tried to build an ad campaign around the name of Paris Cleaners. The ads explained that modern dry cleaning was discovered in Paris and that Paris Cleaners continued in that tradition of sophistication and service. The idea worked for a time until new cleaners began to appear. Carl then learned from other successful businessmen that for an ad to work well, it needed a story that was curious enough to grab customers' attention and simple ehough so that they could recall the basic idea when recommending a particular business. So he came up with the "13, Unlucky for Spots" story.[5]

A few months after his mother died, Carl had attended a party held at the Elks' Lodge at which there was a raffle for a set of steak knives. Carl bought a ticket, which happened to be number 13. When he won the raffle, the idea for an ad occurred to him. If somehow he could associate 13 with Paris Cleaners as a lucky number, that might do the trick. Carl spent weeks trying out various stories and writing out ad copy. He sounded out his ideas on Helen and Elizabeth. While some of the schemes were hilarious, both sisters were patient with Carl, understanding how rare it was for him to share anything of importance. So they took his enthusiasm as an opportunity to connect with him. After several weeks, however, they had to admit that the idea wasn't working. Carl appreciated their help and told them so. Frustrated, he stayed late at work that night staring at the wall of his office. Everyone was long gone, and the store was dark except for a lamp by his desk. Carl thought about his little daughter Marjorie. He imagined her as a adult looking at him now with his face in his hands, stooped over a desk, trying to come with some childlike ad. He stood up and turned off the lamp. The streetlights shone through the windows. He paced back and forth behind the counter and thought of the difficulties that his mother and father had faced in coming to this country. He knew his ad needed a story. He wasn't going to come up with it that night, however, so he decided to go home.

As he was making his way around the counter, he heard a noise coming from the back of the cleaners where the pressing machines stood. He turned on the lights and looked around. When he realized it must have been a noise in back of the building, he stood for a moment looking at the machines and the pipes. He laughed at himself for not coming back here before. After all, it was a cleaning business, and where better to find inspiration than by the pressing machines? He walked around the plant floor muttering, "Just one thing, that's all I need. Just one idea, that's all I'm asking for." It was a game he played with himself. By telling himself how pathetic was his inability to solve a problem, Carl goaded himself toward a solution. It was from the military school of inspiration, but it had always worked. Focusing on his fear of failure and his hatred of humiliation, Carl could summon his creative powers. But he was too tired, tonight, and he knew that Dorothy and little Marjorie were waiting at home. Walking to the front of store past four rows of machines, he noticed that there were four machines in the last row, but only three machines in the previous three rows. He turned around to count the machines again. Sure enough, there were thirteen. He laughed at himself. "Thirteen machines," he said, and turned out the lights.

On the way home, the irony was not lost on him. "Thirteen machines: lucky for me, unlucky for spots." That was it. He'd found his idea.

He could hardly sleep that night and kept turning over slogans in his mind. Each time, however, he returned to "13, Unlucky for Spots." It was perfect. It was just strange enough to be memorable. He pitched the idea the next morning to Helen and Elizabeth. They were hesitant about associating an unlucky number with Paris Cleaners.

"Don't you see?" Carl tried to explain. "It's a lucky number for me. I won a set of steak knives a couple of weeks ago with 13. We have thirteen pressing machines in back. What's lucky for me is unlucky for dirty clothes—that is, if they want to stay dirty."

Elizabeth and Helen looked at each other and tried to resist smiling. Carl looked tired and haggard, even in his crisp serge suit.

"Is it that hard to understand?"

Helen tried to put it tactfully: "No, it's not that hard to understand, but it is a little strange, don't you think?"

"Exactly," said Carl as if he finally got his point across. "You want it to be a little strange. That's what grabs people's attention."

Helen waited a moment and then added, "But why don't you emphasize how beautiful the clothes will look. You know, something like, 'Paris Cleaners, the place where the most fashionable people meet.'"

Elizabeth burst out laughing.

"What's wrong with that?" Helen asked, her eyes flashing at her sister.

Carl jumped back in. "What's wrong with it is that the people of Springfield don't care about fashion. Oh sure, they want to look good and clean, but in general people here are too modest to want to be associated with fashion. Springfield is a practical place. People want good service and a little laugh. '13, Unlucky for Spots.' That's what they want."

Neither Helen nor Elizabeth was convinced, but Carl persisted: "Think about the products you remember from when you were young. Take Ivory Soap, for example. 'So pure it floats.' Who cares if it floats? As long as it cleans your hands, you're happy. But somehow the slogan sticks in your mind, even if it's not a particularly good slogan. I haven't used Ivory soap in probably fifteen years, but I remember the slogan even though it has nothing to do with cleaning your hands."

"So what is your point, Carl?" Helen asked impatiently.

"My point is nostalgia," he proclaimed. "You buy Ivory soap in part because you like the soap. It cleans your hands. But you also buy it because you remember the box of soap sitting on the kitchen counter when you were young. You want to be reminded of that. Everyone does. We are all nostalgic for our childhood."

And then, as if he'd almost forgotten his point, he resumed: "And what reminds us? You see 'Ivory' embossed in the soap and you remember the slogan, 'So pure it floats.' And that keeps you buying Ivory Soap."

"So what does that have to do with Paris Cleaners?" asked Helen somewhat carelessly now. Carl looked to Elizabeth for some support, but Elizabeth remained silent.

"You have to start somewhere," said Carl with an air of importance and purpose. "The people at Proctor and Gamble had to start somewhere with Ivory. It hasn't been there forever. So that's where we are going to start. '13, Unlucky for Spots.' I guarantee you that people will remember it fondly, as silly as it sounds to you right now."

Over the years Carl cultivated an entire mythology around himself and the number 13. Despite his being born on September 12, he now claimed that he was born on September 13. He also mentioned in interviews and promotional material that he came from a family of thirteen children. Every one of the Paris delivery trucks had the "13, Unlucky for Spots" slogan emblazoned on its side. There were endless variations, but they all reinforced the same basic concept: 13 is a lucky

"13" Has No Terror For Franke Family!

Today is Friday the 13th!

But the day has no terrors for the Carl D. Franke family.

As a matter of fact, Carl Franke, Jr., is thirteen years old today, and he's the son of Carl D. Franke, Sr., owner of the Paris Cleaning company who is one of thirteen children, born on the thirteenth of September, has thirteen letters in his full name and even went so far as to get Capitol 13 for his telephone number. Not content with stopping at the 13 there, Mr. Franke's various trucks have 13 in all their license tags.

So aside from the fact that today is the birthday of Carl D. Franke, Jr.,

Carl Franke's marketing program: delivery truck decked out in festive decorations — "Everything back 'cept the dirt."

"13, Unlucky for spots."

Illinois Journal article with a bit of hyperbole.

number for Carl Franke, and since he runs a dry cleaning business, 13 is unlucky for spots.

IV

Bill wasn't the only person to have problems with Carl. As Carl had always endured the burden of being the eldest son, he considered it his birthright to order his siblings around. When growing up, he had been especially insistent on asserting his authority over Otto, the brother closest to him in age. Bill was just a pesky annoyance then, but Otto presented real competition. He was a better fisherman, a better mechanic, and a better hunter; manually, Otto was more skilled than Carl was. Since their father made his living with his hands, and Carl was his presumed successor, Otto's mechanical skills made Carl a bit nervous. To compensate for this inequality in natural skills, Carl took advantage of his authority as the eldest. He emulated his father's strict manner, and in doing so was able to intimidate the rest of the children. When all else failed, Carl would verbally proclaim his title as the eldest, thereby reestablishing any authority he may have lost in a skirmish.

As the family grew older, Carl fulfilled the role of the bossy older brother, Bill that of the mouthy younger brother, and Milton that of the darling youngster of the family. Otto felt uncertain of his own position, and when still working in his father's tailoring shop, he determined that it was best to make his own way in the world. The first thing to do was learn a trade. In 1908, the year before Paris Cleaners opened for business, Otto began work at the Illinois Watch Company as an apprentice. His early success at that company gave him reason to believe that he would become an exceptional watchmaker. He found the trade much to his liking: so many details, so many parts, and always the demand for harmonious precision. It was work that afforded him both a sense of accomplishment and the solitude he craved from years of growing up in a cramped household. Because of the delicacy of the parts and the concentration required to put them together, there was no obligation—and no time—to speak to one's coworkers except on breaks, and even then the talk was almost always focused on the task at hand. It wasn't that Otto didn't like conversation, but he possessed little patience for idle talk, unless it was about fishing, which wasn't idle talk for him. He moved swiftly through his apprenticeship, and by 1910 he learned of an opportunity as a watchmaker in Albuquerque, New Mexico.

It was a long journey there from Springfield, but Otto had nothing to keep him in Springfield and no regrets about leaving. Indeed, one of his purposes in joining the Illinois Watch Company was to learn a trade that he could take with him wherever he went. He loved his family, but he longed for the wide-open spaces of the west. Like almost every boy at that time, Otto was fascinated by stories of cowboys and cattle rustling and all that land. His father saw him off at the station; though seemingly distracted by something at the cleaning plant, he wished Otto well. Otto boarded the train and waved goodbye. "I'll send you a postcard when I get there," he called.

The almost week-long trip west was exhausting. The train arrived in Albuquerque at two in the morning. With nowhere to go, Otto wandered into a saloon next to the train station and waited out the desert night there before finding a boardinghouse. From the bartender's easy manner, Otto decided that he liked New Mexico.

Otto lived and worked in Albuquerque for nearly a year, refining his skills as a watchmaker. The standards weren't as high as at the Illinois Watch Company, but this allowed him to quickly gain respect and authority on the job. And while Albuquerque certainly wasn't at all what he had expected—it was not as wild as he had imagined although it lacked many of the conveniences of Springfield—Otto loved the mountains and the dry heat. On Sundays, his only day off, he used to walk past the outskirts of town and into the desert mountains south of the city. Sometimes he would spend all day pulling rainbow trout from the little streams up there. He gazed at spires of cloud formations and upended slabs of granite the shape of ancient temples, fantastic in their architecture and even more improbable in their structural integrity. Across all that great frieze of rock and bracken, nothing moved save the quivering leaves of the desert cottonwood.

Loneliness was beginning to set in, however, and his few acquaintances from the tavern could hardly stave off his isolation. As if his father knew that Otto needed to reconnect with his family, he wrote to his son, requesting that he come back home and work for Paris Cleaners. Otto was sipping water from a tin dipper when he read the letter. He snorted at his father's demand, as if he had forgotten how to communicate in his isolation and was reduced to crude gestures of scorn. He returned the letter to its envelope and waited for his father's message to burrow into his soul. The message's very brevity haunted him at the oddest moments during the day and kept him awake at night. He grew so agitated by the request, that he was only relieved by gazing again at his father's cursive handwriting. He read the letter over and over. It seemed to exert a magnetic force so that he couldn't set it down. Otto was by inclination an obedient person; he respected authority and above all, that of his father. But while he respected Carl's authority, as his father had taught him to, he did not respect Carl. There was too much rivalry between them, and Carl had abused his authority growing up. Aside from being brothers, they had virtually nothing in common. Otto was torn. He could stay in Albuquerque. After all, what would his father do? Take a train out to New Mexico and drag him home? For a moment Otto could picture his father coming into the Albuquerque station, beard flowing like old Moses down from the mountain of the Law, eyes ablaze, raising hell in pursuit of his prodigal son.

In the end he decided to return to Springfield. Stopping by the local tavern for a drink later on that week, he told his story to the bartender. After explaining how his parents had come to America, he found the answer to his own question: it was impossible for him to turn his back on them after they had sacrificed so much for him and for the rest of his family. So he left his job, his trade, and the little window of his boardinghouse room that looked west into the red evenings of the desert, in order to show respect to his parents and perhaps to return to them a fraction of what they had given him. By 1912, Otto was a full-time employee as a chemist at Paris Cleaners. He rarely talked about his time in New Mexico.[6]

v

Elizabeth maintained her position as negotiator and go-between in both the business and the family after her mother died, but it was a position that taxed her. It was essentially the same story: Bill and Carl didn't get along; Carl and Otto didn't get along a whole lot better, but at least Otto made an effort at diplomacy; and her father was as withdrawn as ever.

While Elizabeth had always acted as an extension of her mother's love and consideration for the family, in the absence of her mother's fortitude she found it difficult, if not impossible, to maintain the former family stability. She began to resent her father and brothers. It started slowly at first—she wouldn't allow herself to give in so easily—but eventually their blunt silence started to chip away at her patience. Frank was in such a deep state of mourning that there was nothing to do but wait. But she had always had the ability to approach her brothers at odd moments in the day in order to prod them toward some form of communication. Now that all three were married, however, Carl, Bill, and Otto had settled into their own routines, and except for the most mundane business matters they all found it easier not to talk. "They're not even trying," Elizabeth finally confided to Helen.

In the spring of 1916, Elizabeth had confronted Carl directly about what she feared was the deterioration of the family. She asked Carl if she could have lunch with him one Friday afternoon. It was a cold April day. It had drizzled since morning, and aside from a few crocuses, Springfield looked gray and muddy. The two siblings made their way over to the Angel Family Restaurant and sat down to a hot bowl of chicken soup and sandwiches. When they had finished their soup, Elizabeth put down her spoon.

"Carl, how do you think Dad is doing?"

Carl's eyes darted around the restaurant in search of an object on which to fix his gaze, finally settling on Elizabeth's napkin. "I don't know," he admitted; "he seems OK to me."

Elizabeth looked at her brother incredulously. She rolled her eyes—in some ways she expected such an answer from him—and tears began to form. Carl looked at her uncomfortably and then rather tenderly asked if she was all right.

"No. I don't think so." The tears were now flowing; Carl discretely handed her his handkerchief. Taking a deep breath, Elizabeth asked, "Do you know when the last time we were together as a family? Do you?"

Carl shook his head. "It was at Mayme's picnic last summer—which is almost a year ago."

Carl requested two cups of coffee from the waiter.

"I just can't take it anymore—you and Bill and Otto. What's happened to us?" Elizabeth was close to sobbing. Carl rubbed her shoulder and said, "Don't worry. Things will turn around."

Things did turn around, but in none of the ways Elizabeth had imagined. She fell in love with Frank Long, a regular customer at Paris Cleaners. Everyone called him Hop—he had a severe limp from a hip injury in his youth—but Elizabeth always called him by his real name. He worked as an accountant at Wabash and had grown up on a farm near Springfield. He kept his hair closely cropped at the sides and always wore a short necktie and white shirt. Helen, Bill, Otto, and Carl all knew him and liked him. One afternoon when he was in the store alone with Elizabeth, after an awkward pause in the conversation, he asked her whether she would like to go out to dinner with him that evening.

Love had the dual effect of freeing Elizabeth from the constant worries of family and allowing her to cast a more critical glance at her own role in the family. She came to see that her job as treasurer at Paris Cleaners would destroy her emotionally, and that the reason she'd had the strength to endure it for as long as she had was her devotion to her mother. With Marie gone, she had no reserves to draw from. So when they were planning their wedding, Elizabeth told Hop that she would like to quit working as soon as they were married. After six and half years as bookkeeper and treasurer it was now time. Hop was delighted; he insisted on it, in fact, and with that it was decided.

When Elizabeth and Hop told the rest of her family of their plans, they were met with mixed emotions. Of course, everyone was happy for Elizabeth and pleased to welcome Hop into the family, but each in his or her own way was nervous about her leaving Paris Cleaners. Carl was the first to try to convince her to stay; he knew, perhaps better than anyone else, how important she was to the success of the business. Although he had rarely praised her for her work, he now assured her that "we wouldn't have made it this far without you." Elizabeth was genuinely touched by his appeal. Although she considered it seriously for a few days, she concluded that it was "time to move on, to start a family of our own." Carl agreed and left it at that, but Elizabeth never forgot Carl's kindness before she was married.

Otto too knew there would be trouble without Elizabeth running the office and acting as a buffer between Carl and the rest of the employees. But he thought it was best for her to go and told her as much. "It's for your own good," he said pensively, as if trying to convince himself of something altogether different.

Bill made it clear to Elizabeth that she could always reverse her decision. "I won't lie to you, Elizabeth," he confessed. "I want you to continue working here. You've not only made my life easier, but you've made everyone's easier. It's selfish to want you to stay, I know, but it's not just for me. I'm just saying that you can always come back to work here. Just because you're leaving now doesn't mean you can't come back."

Elizabeth smiled at her younger brother, but before she could say anything in response, Bill backed up. "But you've been working here longer than anyone else, almost seven years isn't it? You deserve a break."

VI

On January 9, 1917, American intelligence officials intercepted the Zimmerman telegram, in which German officials secretly swore to the Mexican government that if Mexico assisted in the German war effort, the German government would guarantee Mexico its former territories of Texas, New Mexico, and Arizona. This prospect, combined with the recent sinking of the Laconia, another passenger ship with U.S. citizens aboard, made it impossible for President Wilson to resist entry into the war. On April 2, 1917, he went before the Congress to propose a declaration of war on Germany. By April 6, both the House and Senate had overwhelmingly approved the declaration.[7]

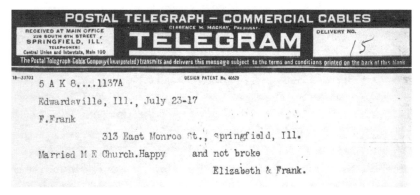

A solemn mood hung over Springfield in the spring of 1917, especially in the German-American community. Suspicions about their loyalties abounded, and there were rumors that the leaders of the community acted as spies for the Reich. Even the school board decided to cancel German classes. Amid concern for troops being sent off to war, it was difficult to plan a wedding. As a result, Elizabeth and Frank Long's wedding ceremony on July 23, 1917, was decidedly more modest than that of her older sister Mayme: they eloped. They drove down to Edwardsville, Illinois, where they were married, with Helen and her boyfriend Julius Kinney as witnesses. It was Elizabeth's decision; with little help other than Helen to put on a traditional wed-

Frank Long and Elizabeth Franke, July 1915.

Back row, left to right: Two unknown persons, Charles Creighton,
Elizabeth, Julius Kinney holding Marjorie, Frank, Bill. *Middle row, left to right:* Unknown person,
Dorothy, Frances, Otto, Anna holding Frances Marie, Mayme, Carl.
Front row, left to right: Helen and Milton.

---

ding, Elizabeth opted to save the money for a house. The muted celebration of Bill and Frances's wedding had persuaded her that it would
be best to avoid a public event altogether. While it had been over two
years since the death of her mother, the family, especially her father,
was still grieving. Besides, she didn't want to give Bill and Carl further
cause for dispute.

Since her marriage to Charles in 1914, Mayme had kept her distance from the family. She loved her family and was devastated not to
have been with her mother the night she died, but she found it was
better to limit her visits to Springfield to once every two months at
the most. Carl and Dorothy visited her in Champaign once or twice a
year. When Mayme found out that Elizabeth and Hop were going to
elope, she felt a lingering obligation to her sister for all the work Eliz-

abeth had done at Mayme's own wedding. As a result, Mayme insisted that they have a family celebration the weekend after the wedding. "Nothing fancy," she explained to Elizabeth. "Just our family." And then, to justify her proposal, she concluded, "It's been too long." The last time the whole family had gotten together—and the first since Marie's death—was at Charles and Mayme's yard in the summer of 1915. Everyone had seemed to gather strength from that occasion. Now, two years later, Mayme was the only one who could have called for another reunion at the family home in Springfield. Only she had enough distance from the current state of affairs—the crumbling truces and the pervasive silence—to see how important it was to honor Elizabeth and celebrate her marriage. They all gathered together on the last day of July 1917. Mayme arrived at the house on Adams Street two days early with her daughter Dorothy, in order to prepare the food. While she made potato salad, spaetzle, sauerkraut, and desserts, Helen and Milton watched little Dorothy and helped with setting up the table in the back yard. Otto assisted by cooking the bratwurst over open coals, Carl brought beer, and Bill did his best to keep everyone in good spirits. It was a German picnic, more or less, and Elizabeth was touched by her sister's efforts.

Mayme and Dorothy Creighton, circa 1916.

The event, however, was haunted by the ghost of Marie. Frank seemed at once distracted, agitated, and tired. Hardly touching his food, he stared distantly at his grandchildren playing on a blanket in the backyard, puffing intermittently on his cigar. Mayme had her problems as well. No one, not even Elizabeth, had said anything about her cooking. When she finally asked Carl and Otto what they thought of the food, Carl merely gave her a vague look, and Otto only admitted that it was good. This lack of recognition only added to Mayme's sense of being the odd one out. But it was more than that. Mayme had stayed away from Springfield for so long, in part, because her mother's criticism was so hard to bear. The family business was difficult too, but she had made it very clear years before that she had no interest in working at Paris Cleaners. After her mother's death, Mayme had dreaded going home, remorseful about not seeing her mother before she died. It was also fear that kept her away, a fear of confronting so much that had made her unhappy, both her lingering feelings of inadequacy to live up to her mother's standards and a nagging sense of having abandoned the family. In throwing this party for Elizabeth and Frank Long, she was doing her best to confront that fear. Her inability to measure up to her mother's cooking further shook her fragile confidence.

After the family had eaten, after the desserts had been passed and—too late—praised, Carl and Charles started to discuss the recent events in Europe and the American war effort, which was now in full swing. Except for Helen and Milton, the table grew quiet to listen to their conversation. While Carl's report was generally patriotic, he was not insensitive to what he thought must be his father's mixed feelings about the relatives in Germany. Carl understood the war almost entirely in terms of trade. The Germans had effectively stopped all American trade with Europe. There was nothing the president could do but declare war, or so his argument went. "Besides," he said, "the German government was trying to make war on us with Mexico." Charles modestly agreed, being also in favor of the war effort—his parents were British by birth—but he too was less than hearty in his approval, frequently mentioning what "a terrible thing" the war was. No one else added to the conversation, leaving the burden of diplomacy to Carl alone. When it became clear that the discussion was stifled, Frank broke in—it was practically the first time he'd spoken all day—"Just so you know, I never really considered myself a German, but rather an East Prussian."[8] And then he added, as if to explain, "What did Germany ever do for me except force me to leave?"

The bitterness of his comment had a seismic effect on those gathered at the table. "How could he say this?" wondered Carl, and felt that everyone else was thinking the same thing, particularly Bill and Otto, their eyes wide in disbelief. His father had shown nothing but pride about his Prussian roots since as far back as he could remember. Since the unification of Germany, the word "Prussian" had almost become synonymous with "German," and Frank almost never made the distinction. Indeed, Carl recalled that his father had often cited his very Germanness to justify the way he did things, especially when it came to matters of discipline. "It's the German way," his father would say, and leave it at that. While Carl rarely used this justification verbally, he had internalized the idea, and when he searched for an answer to a questionable decision, whether in business or at home, he would often repeat his father's explanation as if he were destined by blood to uphold a particularly German identity.

Before the shock had passed into a quiet series of nods and recognition of what had taken place, a photographer showed up in the backyard. He could sense the mood at the table and began rather awkwardly, "I'm here to take a family portrait." Mayme appeared confused and was looking to Carl for help when their father stood up in a deliberately lighter mood and said, "Yes, we've been waiting for you."

Elizabeth was touched and struggled to hold back the lump in her throat. It was the first time since their mother's death that Frank had shown any interest in the family as a family rather than as merely a collection of individuals. Pride, it seemed, had returned, but this time apparently it was not a German pride.

The whole family walked to the front of the house and crossed the street to the high school, where they gathered on the front lawn. The men dutifully took their position in back, flanking the proud patriarch, who stared out into the distance of posterity. The mothers sat in front with their little ones while Milton laughed at the photographer's effort to get the family to smile. Helen sat close to her newly married sister; she couldn't have been happier for her. Elizabeth wore a serene expression; perhaps the family had passed through a period of mourning, perhaps they could return to a time less burdened by

Franke family photo, July 1917. *Standing, left to right:* Frank Long, Carl, Frank, Charles Creighton, Otto, William. *Seated, left to right:* Elizabeth (Long), Helen (Kinney), Dorothy and daughter Marjorie, Milton, Mayme Creighton and daughter Dorothy, Anna and daughter Frances Marie, Frances and son Robert.

worry. Mayme, sitting with her daughter Dorothy, betrayed a mood fraught with uncertainty. She was, in the end, satisfied with the picnic; it had clearly pleased Elizabeth, which was its main purpose. But although happy to see everyone, to spend a little time with the family, she could not shake the feeling, with her father standing over her shoulder, that this might be the last time the family got together under such good auspices.

VII

Matters at Paris Cleaners reached a crisis just as the war in Europe was ending in the autumn of 1918. The celebrations were soon tempered by the devastation from the Spanish influenza that was sweeping over the entire world, particularly the hospitals of Europe. The flu came rather quickly to the United States, and it seemed that no one was safe, especially the elderly and young children. With the gradual deterioration of his eyesight and the reports of people dying by the tens of thousands, Frank began to entertain the notion that this really was the end of the world, that the wicked were being punished, and that his cataracts were some form of retribution, some kind of penance to suffer before the final tribulation. Such thoughts were paranoid, of course, and Frank knew it; yet he was gripped by the fear that "if God does intervene in history, then this surely is some kind of punishment."

Because of his very limited eyesight, Frank was in semi-retirement. He went in to work most days but rarely did anything but sit silently behind the counter and greet customers whose voices he recognized. He was still able to do minor repairs on items brought in for dry cleaning, and he was pleased to receive these chores, but he could no longer do what he had done for his entire adult life, which was to tailor a suit of clothes. His role at the shop had diminished slowly but steadily since Carl's reorganization the year before. Initially the reorganization had simply involved new titles. As time went on, however, Bill grew more suspicious. He thought that Carl was taking greater liberties in the business and consulting the rest of family less frequently. And Otto, privately consulting with Bill, wondered if Carl wasn't manipulating their father's funds.

Bill wasn't afraid to make his opinion known. He spoke at length to Helen, citing the history of the business as justification for his dissatisfaction. "Didn't Dad call us all back to the business one by one? It was never Carl I worked for; it was Dad. I'm sure that's true for Otto too."

Helen, who was always a confidant of Bill's, and candid like him, asked her brother, "What does it matter anyway?"

"What does it matter? It matters a lot!" Bill paused to organize his argument. "It matters because when Dad asked me to work for him; it was for him that I intended to work." He started again. "What I mean to say is that I always thought of this business as a family business, a democracy. And a democracy has a president, so we have a president. I realize that Carl has the title of president, but we all know that it's only in name. Dad has always been in charge. We make decisions together, as a family. Each of us has a stake in the business. I'm certainly not here to be one of Carl's employees. We are partners. I wouldn't have come to work here if that weren't the case. And now that Dad is losing his sight, Carl comes along and decides to reorganize the business. Fine. It doesn't mean anything to me. But now I hear that Carl is buying more toppers, and I find this out from the sales rep! I even heard from a neighbor of mine that Carl was looking to buy land for another plant on the north side of town. So when are we supposed to find out about these decisions?"

Helen cut him off before he could grow even angrier. "Come on, Bill. That's what Carl does. He manages the finances. He looks into those decisions. And as for the toppers, the only reason you didn't know about them is because Elizabeth isn't working here anymore. She would have told you." And then, adding insult to injury, she concluded, "This sounds to me like your own problem with Carl."

Bill was genuinely offended. "It's not my problem. It's *our* problem. With Dad acting as the head of the business, it was run more in the family's interest. Now that Dad's no longer active, Carl's starting to run it like a dictator. I won't stand for it."

Helen shook her head and left it at that. For as long as she could remember, Bill and Carl had been fighting, so Bill's latest complaint was nothing unusual. Besides, the business had never been a democracy to her, as she had no part of the decision-making process. It might have been more democratic for Elizabeth or Carl's wife Dorothy, who kept the books, but Helen was often the last to learn of any decision. It didn't bother her, though. She was biding her time there and she knew it. Julius Kinney would be returning from the war any day now, and although he had not proposed to her yet, she hoped that they would be married soon and go live on his parents' farm outside Springfield. She was just waiting for the opportunity to leave Paris Cleaners. She liked the work well enough, but it was time to leave her father's care to someone else in the family and make a life of her own.

But Bill's complaint this time, at least to his mind, was based on more than sibling rivalry. He truly believed that Carl had crossed the line, that in effect he had taken over the business and made his family *his* employees, and that his lifestyle was evidence of his betrayal: Carl had joined the country club, lived in a luxurious house, employed a maid, and threw dinner parties serving fine wines and gourmet meals. Meanwhile, the rest of the family lived from one paycheck to the next, and the fanciest meals they had were potluck dinners on Sunday. That just wasn't how it was supposed to be. So Bill went to talk to his father. While he couldn't accuse Carl of living off the backs of his siblings, Bill wanted his father to know that something was seriously wrong. He tried to persuade his father that Carl should share the business decisions with the rest of the family. Frank did not entirely agree with him but promised he would talk to Carl about running the business more appropriately.

Carl respected his father's word, but when he found out that Bill was behind it, he was livid. He went to the North End plant late in the afternoon and waited until the workers had left for the day. Then he went inside to confront Bill.

"You've done a lot of things," Carl began, "a lot of things. And I've always looked away. 'He's my younger brother,' I'd say to myself. 'He doesn't really understand what he's doing.' But now you go and pull this stunt. Just what in God's name do you think you're trying to do?"

Bill, of course, knew what he was talking about and had prepared himself for some kind of confrontation, but he didn't understand what Carl was specifically referring to. "What do you mean, Carl?"

"What do I mean! What do *I* mean! What do *you* mean!" Carl bellowed. He moved away from his brother, and when he turned around, the tone of his voice betrayed his disgust. "You're so wrapped up in your own concerns you don't even see it. You don't even understand."

But Bill had heard enough, and he walked away.

"Don't you dare walk away from me." When Bill refused to acknowledge him, Carl came storming from behind. "Did you hear what I said?" Carl grabbed his brother by the shoulder and turned him around. Bill shrugged him off angrily and warned, "The next time you touch me, there will be trouble."

Carl got right up in Bill's face. "Do you know who you are talking to? Do you?"

Bill slowly raised his eyes to meet Carl's. "Yes, I do," he said.

"I don't think you do," Carl snapped. He moved in even closer. Through clenched teeth, he declared, "I'm your brother—your *older* brother. You *will* listen to me. You'll listen to me because you are supposed to. I don't make the rules, but I do obey them. You *will* obey them too."

Carl was trembling. He stood back from his brother in order to give him room to respond, but Bill simply walked into the office and closed the door behind him. When Carl tried to open the locked door, he raised his voice. "You're killing Dad, you know. You're killing him. He's worked his entire life for us, *for you,* and what do you do to repay him? He doesn't need this, not right now. Not ever. I won't have his blood on my hands. I won't let you!"

The door never opened. It was well past nightfall before Carl left the building. Soon after, Bill left too. Both of them headed in different directions, back to their separate homes.

VIII

By the fall of 1919 the situation between the brothers had grown so intolerable that Helen was forced to step in. Much like Elizabeth before her, Helen had become indispensable to the business. Of course, Elizabeth had plenty of insights to offer her, but the secret to Helen's success at Paris was humor. Instead of the discretion that Elizabeth favored, Helen made light of Bill, Carl, and Otto and all their problems. Humor was natural to her and paid off; it was impossible to be angry with her. But as Bill and Carl grew more hostile toward one another, her ability to lighten the mood became less effective. At first she wanted nothing to do with her brothers' squabbling and did everything in her powers to avoid direct confrontation; it was an absolute bother, and she never fully understood why Bill and Carl got along so badly. Besides, she was in love with Julius Kinney, who was now home from the war. Having been gassed in France, Julius suffered permanent lung damage,[9] and with his injury came a new sense of purpose: he wanted to get married and return to the farm he grew up on, and for him there was no other woman than Helen. Grateful that Julius had escaped worse injury or death, Helen gladly accepted his proposal of marriage and was counting the days when she could leave all the troubles of the family behind her and live in the country, close to cornstalks and sunflowers. But before she could retire to her conjugal paradise, she had to perform one last duty for her father, her brothers, and Paris Cleaners. Because Carl and Bill had ceased all communications since their fight, a number of missing garments were not being accounted for. Helen first consulted Otto, but he was barely able to acknowledge the problem to begin with, let alone offer a solution. "Otto doesn't want anything to do with his brothers' quarrel," Helen told Elizabeth. "He didn't say anything except that it would eventually blow over and that the main thing was to try not to be too distracted by it."

Elizabeth was happy to be of some help. It was the first time since she left Paris Cleaners that her negotiating skills were called upon.

There were, of course, many routine details that Helen or Carl's wife Dorothy needed to ask Elizabeth about. This was different. When Elizabeth revealed that she had to manage the relationship between Bill and Carl in the past, Helen just shook her head. "How did you do it?"

Elizabeth laughed. "I'm not really sure. Necessity made me do it, I suppose. I mean, what would have happened if I hadn't? Do you think Dad would have stepped in?"

"I don't know about this," said Helen warily. "Julius and I are going to be married in the spring, and there's still a lot of planning to do. In fact, I know I don't want this."

"But it doesn't matter what you want, Helen," said Elizabeth rather abruptly. Then she modified her comment. "I mean, it matters, of course. But the family also matters."

"Of course it does," Helen began wondering aloud to herself. "But I do question sometimes if this is really about the family. It's about business, it's about money, isn't it?"

"It is to some degree about business, but in a family like ours it is sometimes difficult to distinguish between the two."

"I suppose it is." And Helen left it at that.

Elizabeth, assuming she had put out yet another fire in the Franke family, was surprised when Helen proceeded to do something that she herself would never have done, which was to go directly to their father and explain everything. Elizabeth came over the following Saturday morning, in part to find out what had happened.

"Where are Dad and Milton?"

"They went driving somewhere," Helen said, handing Elizabeth a hot cup of coffee. "I'm not sure, but they may have gone fishing."

Elizabeth looked out the living room window. It was one of those gorgeous autumn mornings that grace Springfield in October—a crisp refreshing chill in the air and an immaculate blue sky that vivified the colors of the leaves. A victory parade was scheduled that day in downtown Springfield at which Elizabeth had planned to join Bill and Frances with their older son, Robert, and their new baby, Allyn. She sipped her coffee gingerly and watched her sister sit down on the couch. Helen looked tired and annoyed.

"Are you all right?" Elizabeth asked.

Helen smiled. "So you must have heard."

Elizabeth nodded. "I ran into Otto at the bakery."

"What did he say?"

"Oh, you know Otto. Not much, really. He just told me that you spoke to Dad."

"You think it was a bad idea, don't you?"

"No," Elizabeth responded tentatively in an effort toward diplomacy. Elizabeth then tried to justify her reluctant tone. "Well, *I* wouldn't have done it that way." And before Helen could object, Elizabeth added more emphatically, "but *you* could and you *should* have done it that way."

"I don't understand." Helen was feeling defensive, and the last thing she wanted from her sister, her strongest ally, was subtleties and equivocations. It was a difficult challenge for Elizabeth to meet, because of all the siblings, she could see the most, could feel so many sides of what felt like an infinitely sided thing—the family. But it was this very affliction of sympathy from which she was trying to distance herself. She had to be especially careful to avoid the temptation of being, like her mother, the hub of the wheel.

"All that I mean to say is that you have a way. You can be very direct, especially with Dad. I couldn't do that. I can't do that."

Elizabeth's acknowledgment gave Helen felt a sense of her own power. She had wanted that acknowledgment, from Elizabeth especially, for a very long time, but now that she had it, an unexpected bashfulness overcame her. "What are you talking about? I've never been able to talk to Dad. I've always been scared of him."

Elizabeth gasped, half laughing. "*You've* been scared of him?" No, you and Bill have always had that ability—to just say whatever is on your mind, even to Mom and Dad. I admire that, Helen."

With that further acknowledgment and with the confidence her sister inspired, Helen began again. "I just told him what happened. I didn't know what else to do, and I knew I couldn't do what you do. I mean, I couldn't just go between them like that—Bill and Carl. Where you may be afraid to talk to Dad, I'm afraid to talk to Carl. He's *scary*."

They both laughed together, thinking of Carl. Helen resumed: "I knew it was better for me to talk to Dad than talk to Carl. So I told him about the fight, about what I knew of the fight, and that Carl and Bill weren't talking to each other, and that Carl was threatening to fire Bill—did you know that?"

Elizabeth sighed, "Bill told me all about it." She began to chuckle: "Bill even said he was thinking about firing Carl, but that Otto wouldn't have anything to do with it."

"I hadn't heard that," Helen said through her laughter. "Well, anyway, I told Dad about all of this, and then, in a manner of speaking, I told him he had to do something about it, that the fight was beginning to be embarrassing for the business."

"And what did Dad say?"

"Nothing."

Elizabeth nodded, as if something she suspected had been confirmed.

"He just muttered something in German when I finished, and that was all," Helen continued.

"He didn't say anything else?" Elizabeth asked.

"No. He went to bed early, and he left the house before Milton or I even got up."

Elizabeth was looking for clues as to what could have led to her father's actions earlier that week. "So you didn't see him or talk to him?"

"No. By the time I got to work, he had already talked to Bill, and he was in the office with Carl. When Dad came out of the office, no one said a word, and he just sat down in his chair and looked out the window for the rest of the day. No one at the shop said a word. I felt bad. I didn't know what had happened. Carl wasn't talking to me then, and I wasn't sure if Otto knew."

"So when did you find out what happened?"

"I didn't find out until yesterday," said Helen. "Nobody blamed me. I mean, Carl was actually very nice about it. But Otto told me first. He said that Dad was angry with all of us; that he felt that none of us could handle the responsibility of the business and that none of us were loyal sons and daughters to our mother. If I didn't know better, I would have sworn that there were tears in Otto's eyes when he told me about this. Anyway, Otto said that Dad decided the only thing to do was to remain at the store and make sure everything was getting done. He even took back the title of vice president and told Carl that every decision he makes has to go through him."[10]

Helen stood up and picked up both coffee cups. She offered a refill, and Elizabeth nodded. When Helen came back into the living room with the second cup of coffee, she looked upset.

"It was horrible. I feel horrible," she started. "You know what you were talking about earlier. About saying whatever is on my mind. Well, you're right about that, but I'm not so sure it's something to admire."

Helen had always thought it *was* something to admire, and she had spent her youth trying to prove it, not only to her brothers and sisters, but to nearly everyone she met. This quality was part of Helen's charm, and people liked her for it. When she met the poet Vachel Lindsay, she found in him validation for that frankness. Lindsay also admired her exuberance and sweetness and fun, her enjoyment of life and of simple pleasures such as an afternoon by the river. All of these qualities or attitudes, as the poet called them, were not just a part of her but rather constituted her way of seeing and of being. So when she began to doubt the wisdom of her approach to people, she was shaken.

Elizabeth tried to be very gentle. "Of course it's admirable, Helen. Honestly I think it's better this way. What would have happened otherwise? This might have dragged on for years. He needed to know. Mom, I'm sure, would have done the same."

Helen, distracted by the golden crown of one of the oak trees across the street, replied rather absent-mindedly, "Maybe . . . but what about Dad?" She came back suddenly. "I'm starting to think he's right: we are selfish. He's old. He's almost blind in his right eye, and his left eye gets worse everyday. After all that's happened, do you think he wants to deal with a family fight?"

IX

Helen was right; dissension in the family was the last thing Frank wanted to deal with. It was something he had been avoiding for the latter part of his adult life. By reclaiming his stake in the business, he managed to call a modest truce among his sons. It was, after all, his business; he had put the money down in the first place, and it was his savings that built the North End plant. The whole experience was exhausting; he no longer had the strength, the eyesight, or the desire to be at work in this capacity. He calculated that he had worked for nearly fifty-five of the fifty-nine years of his life. He wanted, more than anything, to spend his days fishing for which he needed only his hands and a companion. And he had a willing companion in Milton.

But it was not to be—not yet, at least. The current situation did buy him some time for a much larger decision. For perhaps the first time in his life, the entire situation was in his hands, yet he felt completely indecisive about what to do, about how to arrange the business so that it would survive him. And, more than that, he was resentful at having to make a decision. Why should it come to this? Why couldn't they manage to get along? Why couldn't Carl just be a little more agreeable? Why couldn't Bill just listen to his older brother? These questions plagued him as he sat at the table at which he had shown so much industry for over thirty years.

Despite the hostilities of his sons, and despite the prospect of losing most of his eyesight—he was sure to lose everything except his peripheral vision—Frank nevertheless found small pleasures. It was in these pleasures that he began to discover hope again. For the past four years since the death of his wife, it was not merely his eyesight that had dimmed but all the little things that make up a day—the satisfaction of accomplishment, the sharing of a meal, the taste of coffee in the morning, the incidental conversation on the street with an old acquaintance, the smell of wood smoke on a cold autumn evening. Frank had been entirely unprepared for his wife's death and had had no close friends with whom he could pour out his heart. The pleasures, the reminders of the sweetness of life, returned slowly. Of all the children, Frank was most able to connect with Milton. Because he was still young, Milton carried none of the expectations or grudges of the other children. His mild disposition made him neither eagerly obedient nor unwilling to take orders. Milton's stutter and the silence that resulted from his frustration with stuttering was a mirror for the silence of Frank's solitude and mourning. Together, they filled their long walks, their fishing trips, and evenings at home with this silent companionship. Frank developed a tenderness for Milton that he had never known with any of his other children. He realized that it might seem unfair to the others, but he was getting too old to let another opportunity slip away. So the pleasures of fatherhood, as opposed to the stresses and pressures with which he was so familiar, came to him late, but their coming was like the visitation of grace and reminded him of what and how much he had been given.

There were other pleasures too. Ottilie Sutter, with whom he was on first-name terms by the spring of 1919, was the widow of an old acquaintance, Henry Sutter. When Henry died quite suddenly in 1910 at the age of 50, Marie had been a source of comfort to Ottilie and her family, cooking meals for them, and paying visits and even inviting them to Christmas dinner that year. Ottilie was able to repay that neighborly kindness when Marie died by providing the Franke family with baked goods and friendship. Because she lived not far away in a modest house on Carpenter Street,[11] Frank occasionally ran into her when he was out walking or coming home from work. She would always ask him gently how he was doing, how the health of his family was, and in particular how Milton and Helen were getting along. During the blackest days of his mourning, Ottilie's inquiries were a source of comfort to Frank. "Really," he recalled to her in the fall of 1919, "your kindness was one of the few bright spots at the time."

Frank continued to run into Ottilie once every few months after Marie's death. One afternoon in the fall of 1917, when Frank was already battling his cataracts, he was able to recognize Ottilie near Paris Cleaners. He found himself running across the street to get her attention. She, in her typical manner, was all smiles and sweetness. He asked her where she was going. "Can you believe it?" she laughed, "A baker's wife is going to the bakery."

After asking her if she didn't mind his company on the way to the baker's, Frank felt comfortable enough to tell her about his cataracts and his fear of going blind. Offering him no direct words of encouragement, Ottilie extended her hand to his forearm and held it tightly. That simple gesture of condolence was what he needed most at the time.

There were more meetings such as this, and as time went on, Frank began to desire Ottilie's company. Fearing that it was somehow a betrayal of Marie, he fought this desire at first. But as things grew worse at Paris Cleaners, he felt more isolated from his family. There was always Milton, but Frank longed for adult companionship and specifically German companionship. With Ottilie he not only shared memories of Berlin—she too went to Berlin before coming to Springfield with her husband—but he could also talk to her about the particular circumstance of being a German Catholic. After several months of resisting the temptation of her company, Frank sought his minister's advice. The minister reminded him of the story of the Saducees' asking Jesus which of several wives a man will join in heaven. The Saducees, not believing in the resurrection, wanted to trick Jesus into a theological controversy. Jesus quickly dismissed the question and the Saducees for their attempt to undermine the spirit of the law and the truth of the resurrection, incomprehensible as it may be to ordinary people. "With all due respect, I don't understand how this relates to my question," said Frank after the minister had concluded the synopsis.

"All I meant to demonstrate by this story is that we can sometimes get so caught up in the letter of the law that we forget the spirit behind the law. If you've begun to see this woman, and let's say that you decide to marry her, would you then have sacrificed the thirty years of your marriage to Marie just because you seek a little companionship in your old age? That's ridiculous, and that's exactly what Jesus was trying to say to the Saducees."

Frank, dressed in his usual coat, vest, and tie, considered the minister's advice. Stroking his beard nervously, he got to the heart of the matter: "But do you think that this would somehow be a betrayal of my wife?"

The minister smiled. "Do you think that your friendship with this woman could ever diminish the years of devotion to your wife, the years of raising a family together?"

"No, I don't think so," Frank ventured.

The minister, sensing that Frank needed more encouragement, continued. "Did you love your wife?"

"Yes."

"Can you ever imagine not loving your wife?"

"Of course not."

"Then I don't see the problem with two people coming together in a time of need. Nothing could change the sanctity of your love for Marie. You can take that with you wherever you go."

After thanking the minister for his time, Frank took the long way home. He was comforted by the minister's advice, but was still uncertain what to do. It had been almost four years since Marie's death. Spring had come early to Springfield, but he knew too well not to trust it. Although the trees were still bare, the crocus in the front yards had crowned and some were already in bloom. The air had a rich and fecund odor to it. Frank walked over to the Gulf, Mobile and Ohio Station and watched a train come in from Chicago and leave for St. Louis. It made him wistful.

He sat for a while on the station bench staring at the loose gravel between the railroad tracks and ties. It was strange to think how important this otherwise modest train station had been in his life. The sun was reflecting on the windows of the station house. Members of a family stood inside embracing one another. Coming from or going to this place had marked almost every major event in his life. He remembered the time he saw Carl off to Chicago, the time he watched Otto heading to New Mexico. Most of all he remembered the days waiting at the station for Marie. He remembered how wildly his heart would pump at the approaching train and how it would plummet when her face did not appear among the crowds. Oh, but it was worth waiting to see her face framed by the long shadows of Sherman House, to feel her in his arms again.

Frank rose and walked the neighborhood where he had spent his first five months in America. That was an even lonelier time than his first weeks in Berlin, where there had been at least distractions. Springfield only offered scenes of what he might never get if Marie were somehow forced to stay in Germany. Frank recalled with a chuckle those walks he took around the quiet, darkened streets of Springfield in the summer of 1884. There were trees and fields everywhere. He'd find a road going out of town and then he'd take the first trail off the road he saw. He'd follow the trail to a cornfield or a meadow where he would lie down and look at the moon. He often wondered then if Marie too was looking at the moon through the haze and smoke of Berlin. After an hour or two he would head back to Sherman House weaving his way through the streets and stopping at houses where he might like to live. They all looked inviting with their beautiful front steps and porches. He would imagine what it would be like to come home from work to Marie. He would show her all the little places he had gone to alleviate the suffering of her absence and then they would discover all their own new places of shared joy together.

By the time he came home that spring afternoon in 1919 after his conversation with the minister, Frank was lonely. Evening was coming on, and there would be hours of loneliness before he felt tired enough to go to sleep. When he thought of Ottilie, it was not as a replacement for Marie—nothing could replace her—but it was rather as a companion to his solitude. Besides, she needed his companionship too, a way to pass her days in dignity. That evening he decided to seek her out the next day.

They went for a short walk that Sunday afternoon, and they continued to take walks together in the following weeks. Soon Ottilie was inviting Frank into her house for tea, for a game of cards, or sometimes for a meal. By the fall of that year they were spending much time together. Frank was still going to work everyday. Helen continued to live at home and take care of most of the meals, though busy with her own wedding preparations. Milton was old enough to hold down a regular job by now; Frank had secured an apprenticeship for him with Romie Field, repairing automobile engines.[12] Like his older brother Otto, Milton was an excellent mechanic. Frank still went on regular fishing trips with him, but he filled most of his spare time with Ottilie.

There were pleasures and discoveries to their friendship, but mostly Frank and Ottilie knew each other's rhythms, the comforting pattern of sitting quietly on the porch, sharing dinner, and talking about how much things had changed. She was a devout Catholic and attended Mass daily. In the process of sharing stories about their German Catholic upbringing, Ottilie asked Frank one Saturday if he wouldn't like to join her at Mass the next morning. Frank was so pleased to revisit the Roman liturgy of his youth that he accepted her invitation without considering what it meant in the larger scheme of his life. In the short term, however, it brought him closer to Ottilie. By Christmas of that year, Frank had proposed to Ottilie. She gladly accepted his proposal, and they made plans to be married in the spring.

X

Shortly after proposing to Ottilie, Frank asked the family to return home for dinner, a family reunion. Surprised and delighted by the idea, Elizabeth and Helen agreed to handle the goose and all the trimmings. It was decided that they would eat together on the Saturday after New Year's day.

Everyone except Milton was surprised to see Mrs. Sutter at the family gathering. Only he knew just how much time his father had been spending with her. There were more people to feed than there were the last time the family had gotten together like this. It had been five years since their last Christmas dinner, and cooking didn't go as smoothly as it had then. They couldn't fit all the geese in the oven, so Elizabeth had to go home and cook two of them at her house and then bring them back. There was also a minor problem with the potatoes. Since neither Elizabeth nor Helen remembered exactly what their mother had done to prepare them they way they all enjoyed, the men in the family were unhappy with the results. But all made polite comments and seemed glad to be together again.

"Look at Dad," Helen said to Elizabeth. "Can you believe it?"

"I know, I know. I couldn't believe it when I walked in the door. I mean, just the fact that she's here at all. Incredible."

Frank and Ottilie joked with each other quietly at one end of the table. Frank was dressed even more formally than usual. He wore a dark wool coat, which he kept buttoned over his high waistcoat, and dark gray pinstriped trousers; the ensemble was accentuated by a black tie, which suggested an impending announcement. Ottilie was no less elegant in her navy blue dress of wool poplin with its embroidered collar and pretty slash pockets. Frank proudly introduced her to all his grandchildren—Carl and Dorothy's Marjorie and Carl David Jr., Mayme and Charles's Dorothy, Elizabeth and Frank Long's Drusilla, Otto and Anna's Frances, and Bill and Frances's Robert and Allyn. He then bounced each in turn on his knees. He was positively buoyant this evening.

After the traditional holiday pudding was served, and the diners were beginning to lean back in their chairs, Otto and Carl lit cigars. Second only to his father in elegance, Carl wore a double-breasted navy blue serge suit adorned with a silk scarf in his breast pocket. Otto, as if he had just returned from work, was in shirtsleeves, vest, and tie. He blew smoke rings to the amusement of the children, while Bill and Milton, also in shirtsleeves and tie, talked across the table about engine parts. At this point, Frank cleared his throat and stood up, a lit cigar in hand. He began ceremoniously. "It's wonderful to be with everyone again." After that overture, he paused. Elizabeth and Helen exchanged glances in surprise. The men straightened in their chairs, eager to hear what prompted this enthusiasm on the part of their father. The infants stirred in their mothers' arms, while the toddlers tried their best to remain seated.

"I can't see the little ones as well I would want, but the sound of their voices is music enough."

Elizabeth and Helen had tears in their eyes.

"When I was a boy back in East Prussia, the winters were very difficult," Frank continued, now more solemn. "They were cold. There was very little daylight. It was generally not the best time of the year. But oftentimes someone in the village would take one of their animals—usually it was a pig—and would invite all the neighbors into their house. Other times we'd take a sleigh ride out to one of the nearby estates, where a feast would be waiting for us. Winter was the time when couples announced their engagement. Usually they celebrated their engagement with a modest but wonderful meal. They would end the meal with their announcement, and there was always dancing afterwards. I don't know that any of you can really know what it was like, but I remember those feasts so well. They got you through the darkest part of winter."

Discreetly dabbing at her eyes, Elizabeth leaned forward to listen more intently. Mayme, at the opposite end of the table, in her newly made turban wreathed with silk-centered velvet pansies, made eye contact with Helen and shared her sister's anticipation of what was about to be said.

After another pause and a deep breath, Frank resumed, his hands tugging the dark lapels of his coat: "So I decided to get the family together for an announcement of my own." He looked briefly toward Ottilie, who was smiling bashfully, her eyes moist with delight. "Mrs. Sutter and I will be married this spring."

Elizabeth was the first to stand up and congratulate the couple; Helen soon followed. They were not only surprised but genuinely delighted at the news. To them it was positive proof that their father was moving on from his crippling grief. The announcement also came as a relief to both of them, for it would allow them to relinquish, in part, their caregiving duties. Of course they would continue to visit, but they would no longer have to see to his needs every evening.

Mayme took the news in more slowly, and after thinking about it for a moment she too felt relief. Although she didn't know Ottilie well—remembering her only slightly from earlier years—she seemed like a nice lady. But, more to the point, even the announcement began to ease Mayme's sense of guilt over leaving Springfield, so she boldly walked around the table and embraced the couple.

As for the men in the family, Otto was glad that his father wouldn't be so lonely in his old age, but otherwise little had changed; Bill and Carl, however, had their own reservations. For Bill it was a question of respect for his mother and one that he did not feel free to discuss. As his father had done earlier, Bill wondered whether this second marriage somehow dishonored his mother. So he couldn't express unreserved happiness as his sisters had done.

A flood of questions came to Carl: what did this mean for Paris Cleaners, and how would Ottilie Sutter fit into the picture? When his father rather casually mentioned that they were to be married at Saint Peter and Paul's, Carl could barely conceal his dismay. He couldn't imagine why his father would remarry in a Catholic Church. He felt, in a strange way, betrayed. As an active Freemason,[13] he had acquired a general distaste for Catholicism; he regarded Catholics as lazy and uneducated. Along with the other Masons, he also held deep suspicions about the intentions and legitimacy of the papacy.

Bill, however, had no such distaste. He smiled at the irony of it: just five years ago his mother had fretted over her misgivings about his own marriage at St. Peter and Paul's. Learning of his father's plan to marry there, he was able to connect with his father in a way he was rarely capable of. The connection was simple, Bill thought. It wasn't Catholicism per se, but rather his father's easy relation with religion, an attitude Bill shared. It was all basically the same. The important thing was to treat people right. It was in this manner, as the evening drew on, that Bill too came to enjoy the news.

A Mason like Carl,[14] Otto too was confused by his father's willingness to be wedded in a Catholic church. Moreover, his father's decision struck him as a betrayal not so much of his marriage to Marie but of his whole life and livelihood. Milton was a Mason also, but would never comment on the subject at a time like this.[15] Hadn't Frank come all the way to this country to get away from the constraints of religion? Yet Otto was certainly not one to question his father, especially at this stage in his life. It'll be all right, he told himself, and continued puffing at his cigar.

The evening came to a close, and the family gathered in the living room. Frank thanked everyone again for coming and then made an amendment to his original announcement: "As you all know by now, I am slowly losing my sight. The doctor has told me that in some cases there is every possibility that the cataracts will not get any worse. He also said that in many other cases it's most likely that they will get worse. So in the light of this news and in the light of new prospects, I want you to all know that I plan to retire from an active role at Paris Cleaners after our wedding."

XI

At first Carl was ambivalent about his father's retirement. Of course he had been anticipating it for years and a part of him had been even looking forward to it. But given the uncertainty of the past year and his father's return to full-time duty at Paris Cleaners, Carl had no idea what was going to happen to the business. Having little patience for such uncertainties, Carl met with his father for lunch the following week.

"So that was very exciting news on Sunday," Carl began. "I assume you've worked out the ceremony and where you will have the reception."

"No, but I'm sure it will just involve the immediate families," his father replied.

Carl hesitated a moment. Such pauses were common in conversations with his father. As their soup and sandwiches arrived, Carl asked casually, "So what are your plans when you retire?"

Frank could feel what his son was driving at; he had expected it. Mildly annoyed by Carl's attempt at a subtle introduction, Frank played along. "I'm planning on fishing more often."

"Really? Where do you plan on going?"

Frank leaned back. "You know, the usual places: Illinois River, Sangamon River."

"The fishing in Florida is wonderful, Dad. Maybe you should take a trip down to Miami and do some fishing down there. You know, fishing in the ocean is the big leagues compared to our local fishing in the Illinois River."

"I like my little lakes and rivers," Frank concluded smartly.

Carl was looking for some way to broach the real subject. "Anything else?" he asked at last.

Frank looked up from his bowl of soup and simply shook his head.

He *had* changed. Carl had been noticing it over the past several months but this conversation confirmed it. Yes, his father was happier, there was ample evidence of that: just by the way he walked it was clear that there was hope in those limbs again. While glad about his father's happiness, Carl now perceived something more. It was as if he detected in his father's mood that the impending retirement was not merely a retirement from Paris Cleaners but a retirement from the family altogether. It was a strange thought, but a nagging one, as Carl watched his father so carelessly consuming his soup and sandwich.

So without further ado, Carl raised the question: "What are we going to do about Paris Cleaners?"

Appreciating his son's honesty, Frank smiled. "Well, I don't see why we should make any changes. I just won't be coming in anymore."

Frank looked out at the wet, chilly street to indicate that he was through talking about the subject, which left Carl no closer to understanding whether the retirement or the marriage would have any legal bearing on the business. As they made their way back to the cleaners through the clammy January air, Carl recalled to his father the first day they opened the store together in 1909.

"You didn't think it would work, did you?"

Frank stopped in his tracks. "Of course I knew it would work," he declared. "I wouldn't have done it if I hadn't thought it would work."

Carl seemed taken aback by this response, so Frank explained, "I did my research and I had faith in you—what more did I need to know?"

Carl laughed at his own need for reassurance and then quickly grew more serious. "Dad, now that you and Mrs. Sutter[16] are to be married"—it was the question he had wanted to ask all afternoon—"Where does the business stand with her as a member of the family? If something happens to you, does she control the ownership?"

Frank looked in Carl's direction as if he could see Carl's eyes clearly. With the hint of a smile, he said; "Now I see what's behind your questions. Your father is a bit more farsighted than you thought. Mrs. Sutter and I have signed a marriage agreement, a prenuptial agreement they call it. Neither of us will participate in the estate of the other when we pass on. Should I die first, Mrs. Sutter will stay in the family house for the rest of her life, and then it will become the property of my heirs. Don't worry, Carl," he urged his son as they continued on their way back to Paris Cleaners. "Your father still has a head for business and an eye out for his children."

XII

From his conversation with his father, Carl assumed with relief and gratitude that there would be no change, that things would remain as they always had at Paris Cleaners, that he would remain president. No change meant that the eldest son, the next male in line in the Franke family, would take over. After all, it was only fair. His father had been preparing him for this all his life. Besides, Carl felt that he knew the business better than anyone else did; he understood how to manage money and investments better than Bill or Otto, and most especially he understood how to generate business. No argument was necessary, however. It was, by birthright, Carl's business.

The feeling was one of tremendous satisfaction. He would have the control to guide the business properly, and with this authority he was confident that he could provide for his father and for his brothers. In effect, it had been this way for a long time now. He was following in his father's footsteps and was at last beginning to assume the position of the patriarch.

But it was precisely this assumption of patriarchy that riled his brothers. Otto had grown so impatient with Carl and what he perceived as Carl's arrogance that he could hardly stand being in the same room with him, let alone take orders from him. While Bill was now on speaking terms with Carl, their truce was, as always, tenuous. A few months after their father's last day at work, Otto paid a visit to Bill at the North End plant. He started first by making casual jokes about Carl, which were soon followed by serious complaints.

"I don't know what's gotten into Carl," Otto said as he stood in the doorframe of Bill's office. "I mean, it's always been difficult dealing with Carl,. But nowadays you wouldn't believe it. The suits, the fancy lunches, the long weekends, the hunting trips. I feel like all we're doing is working and all he's doing is fishing. And try talking to him these days. It's impossible."

Bill studied his brother's face. "Really," he began with a tone of mock surprise. "What has he been doing?" And seeing the puzzled look on Otto's face, he explained, "I've hardly spoken to him since Dad's last day of work."

"Yeah, that's the day it started," Otto jumped in. "Actually it was the day after. I got to work early that morning—there was a problem with the pump again. Anyway, Carl comes strolling in at 3:00 p.m. so I ask him where he's been. He says, 'None of your business.' 'None of my business?' I said. And then he just walked off into his office. OK. Fine, I can live with that. He wants to let things cool down. So I see him later around six o'clock—apparently he had a meeting. And then I said more calmly that I didn't mean to accuse him of anything earlier and that I was just wondering where he was. And he reacted the same way as before: 'Do I have to tell you where I'm going?' And I said, 'Of course not, but it is a workday and we do have a business to run.' And then he just blew his top and said he would take care of everything and that he always had to do everything."

"Sounds like the Carl I know and love," Bill interrupted. "So what happened after that?"

"Nothing really. Nothing out of the ordinary, I mean. But there is something. It's nothing that he's done; it's just the way he walks around the place. It's driving me nuts."

Bill didn't quite follow. "What do you mean? Hasn't Carl always walked around in that way?"

"I don't know. It's different," Otto couldn't put words to it. "You'll know what I mean the next time you see him."

There was bitterness to Bill's laughter when he said, "Maybe it's just that you're seeing what I've seen all along."

Otto didn't take this remark kindly. "Oh no, Bill. I know what you've seen all along. But instead of making all your noise, I keep my mouth shut and my head down. Sometimes I wonder where your fussing gets you."

Bill stood silent. He didn't know how to respond. Clearly Otto was bothered by something, but Bill couldn't say anything further as he watched his brother walk out the back door of the plant. Going home on foot that evening—it was a beautiful summer evening—Bill decided to go by Otto's house. He wanted to talk to Otto again. Ashamed by his brother's accusations, Bill wondered if he hadn't made too much noise. He was suddenly embarrassed. He had not recognized the extent to which Otto and he were on the same side, and now he worried that he was losing a silent ally.

Bill had started down Otto's street when he realized that he had no idea what he was going to say. What was he going to apologize for? Otto had criticized *him*. Otto should be the one to apologize. If he had seen how unfair and how bossy Carl had been over the years, why hadn't he ever spoken up?

About half a block before Otto's house, Bill stopped and turned around. Lifting his boater, he wiped his brow with a handkerchief. The neat, symmetrical lawns were littered with bicycles and children whirling around their yards. Concluding that it was best not to further aggravate the situation tonight, Bill turned back and made his way home.

XIII

Otto was right. Something had changed in Carl's behavior. Still disturbed by his conversation with Otto, Bill decided to visit the main plant of Paris Cleaners the following morning. After opening up the North End plant, he drove one of the delivery trucks over to the main store. When he walked in the door, he was met by Carl's usual sharpness. "What are you doing here? Did I tell you to come over here?"

"It's good to see you too, Carl."

Suddenly Carl's aspect changed. He chuckled. His shoulders loosened. He took out a cigar from his breast pocket and lit it.

"Seriously. What are you doing here?"

Bill was confused. This was neither the Carl he knew nor the Carl that he was expecting from Otto's description. He was more relaxed and more affable. He even offered Bill a cigar.

"No," Bill replied. "No thanks." And then he got to the point of his visit. "Is Otto around?"

"He's doing a delivery right now. He should be back in an hour or so."

"Well, I can't wait that long. Do you have anything for me?"

"Not that I can think of."

"OK."

"OK. I'll tell Otto you stopped by."

As Bill was starting the delivery truck, he watched his brother through the front windows of Paris incredulously. Carl closed the door of his office and Bill shook his head. "What's going on?" he asked aloud.

When Bill returned late that afternoon, Carl was gone. All the employees had left for the day and Otto was working on the tumbler motor in back. Bill approached him somewhat cautiously. "Hi."

Otto looked up from what he was doing. "I'll be with you in a minute."

"OK. I'll be waiting up front."

Bill walked to the front of the store and removed his jacket. The late afternoon sun streamed in through the big panes of glass, striking the dark countertops and filling the room with heat. People were walking past the storefront, going home for the day. Eventually, Bill wandered into Carl's office to check his calendar. Other than a legal document placed precisely on the center of its surface, Carl's desk was completely bare. Curious, Bill picked up the document. It was their father's prenuptial agreement with Ottilie Sutter. Just then Otto approached.

"So what can I do for you?"

Bill was clearly distracted. He kept flipping back and forth between pages of the document.

"What are you looking at?" Otto inquired. But Bill only seemed to become more absorbed by what he held in his hands.

"What? Is it an account?"

Finally Bill looked up. "No. Come here for a minute. Take a look at this," he said walking out into the front room of the store. "Why would Dad have a prenuptial agreement, and why would Carl have a copy of the agreement on his desk?" he asked Otto.

"I've no idea," said Otto.

They read the document together.

"I've no idea why they're doing it," Otto repeated, wiping his greasy hands on a fresh towel. "This is the first time I've heard anything about it."

"It's his business," Bill replied bluntly. "Which means that we're his employees."

Otto stood back from the counter. "I don't follow you at all," he said. "Nothing's changed. What does a prenuptial agreement have to do with anything anyway?"

"Think about it," Bill started. "Dad gets married, and before he gets married he decides to have a prenuptial agreement with Mrs. Sutter basically stating that they each retain their assets in case of the other's death."

"Yeah, I know what a prenuptial agreement is. But what's that got to do with Carl?"

"Well, nothing necessarily, except that the agreement is sitting on Carl's desk."

"I still don't follow."

"Why would Dad give Carl a copy of his prenuptial agreement unless it was to indicate that, in the case of Dad's death, Carl would control the assets of the business?"

Otto looked at the document again and warned, "Whoa, let's not jump to any conclusions."

"What do you mean, let's not jump to any conclusions? You were the one who told me Carl was acting funny. This is why."

Otto questioned Bill's logic: "First of all, Dad has always kept Carl up on these kinds of things. So what's different about this? Dad gives Carl a copy of his prenuptial agreement. That doesn't mean the world's turned upside down."

"That's right," Bill agreed. "Carl doesn't want us to think anything has changed, but everything has."

"What *has* changed?"

"It's now Carl's business. Before, we were working for Dad; now we'll be working for Carl." Bill was emphatic now, shaking his hands in front of his face in a gesture that suggested that some terrible wrong had been committed.

Stiffening his resolve, Otto folded his arms and said, "I don't see anything in what I just read that says that."

Bill sat down and sighed. "I don't know how you could say that, Otto. How could you say that after what you told me last night?"

"All I said last night is that Carl was being a pain in the neck," explained Otto.

Bill jumped up from his seat. "Oh no, Otto. You said a lot more than that."

"Well, if I did say more, I didn't mean more."

Bill was pacing now around the room with his shirttails coming untucked from his trousers. "Don't you see that this is what Carl has wanted all along."

"What's that?"

"He wants to control everything. He wants to reap the harvest of our labor."

Otto stepped back and looked at his brother coldly. "Sounds to me like you've got an axe to grind, brother."

Bill felt as if he were bursting at the seams, it was all so obvious now. "This is no axe, Otto. The only person here with an axe is Carl. Better get used to it."

XIV

In a sense, Bill did have an axe to grind. Since childhood he had little patience with unfairness. Not only had he often complained that Carl was unfair, but he himself had always stood up for those working for him. When he thought they were being treated badly or underpaid, he made sure that they were duly compensated. He was not a crusader, however; he simply kept his eye out for those around him, for those he cared about. When it came to Carl, though, Bill was zealous about keeping things fair. After the most recent conversation with Otto, he began to question everything about the family. To him, it was as plain as day: Carl was getting the business, which was alarming because he was too stern and too selfish to run the business fairly. But when Otto accused him of casting aspersions on Carl, Bill again found himself wondering which way was up. What was Otto doing, and why had Carl been so cordial to Bill a few days before?

Bill went home that evening and talked things over with Frances. By the end of their conversation, Bill was quite unsure of himself; so he resolved to discuss matters with his father in order to clarify his own position at Paris Cleaners.

On a Saturday in mid-July, Bill and his father drove together to Beardstown to go fishing on the Illinois River. Since it was a muggy morning on the water, they decided to fish from the shore rather than rent a boat. Low clouds hung over the bluffs and the fields beyond them, but there was no immediate threat of rain.

"It'd be nice if it did rain," Bill began. His father nodded in response. Frank wore his big straw hat, and the bugs swirling around it tapped on its sun-bleached fibers. The river was still and quiet. Having looped a nightcrawler in three places on his hook, Bill threw it out as far as he could into the water and then sat down next to his father on a grassy knob. Frank, however, moved up the river a few yards. Mosquitoes made tiny ripples on the surface of the water close to the banks. He cast into the shallow water and then turned to Bill and asked, "Can you see any grass in the water where I'm fishing?"

Bill stood up and followed his father's line to where it entered the water. "No, it looks OK."

Within five minutes, the old man had a fish.

"Pretty good, huh?" Frank was laughing. "Maybe you should reconsider where you cast."

"No, I'm OK where I am."

"Fine. Suit yourself." And then Frank was quiet again.

They barely spoke for the rest of the morning. Frank had caught eight fish already and couldn't resist a little friendly bragging. "I don't even need my eyes. The fish just come to me."

But Bill was too busy going over what he wanted to say to his father to pay attention to the fish. He had felt so sure of himself when he picked Frank up in the morning, but now he could no longer locate his confidence. Why had he come here? Was he going to ask his father what would happen to the business after he died? It was, after all, Carl whom he was thinking about, and while his father may have had some perspective on Carl's management style, Carl was—there was no doubt—the favorite son. So what was he thinking? Perhaps Otto was right. Perhaps Bill did have an axe to grind. But the more Bill thought about the situation at work, the more he realized that he couldn't continue like this without knowing where he stood. Something would have to give. As he stood on the banks of the Illinois, mosquitoes biting his neck, Bill wondered what that something was.

"Let's go get some lunch." With that, Bill broke the nearly perfect silence that had descended on the river. His father looked at him disapprovingly. "There's still five more fish out there with my name on them that need to be caught."

Bill adjusted his collar and removed his bow tie. A small cloud of mosquitoes swarmed around his head. "I'm getting eaten alive," he declared, slapping his neck.

"Keep still. They won't bother you."

Amazingly, the mosquitoes bedecked his father's great hat, but they did not appear to be biting its wearer. Bill waited another five minutes, trying to clear his mind. And then a mosquito bit him in the ear. He flailed his arms wildly.

"That's it. Too many bugs out here. I'm waiting in the car."

Frank gazed in his direction with impatience. Bill packed up his gear and walked to the car. Half an hour later, when he saw his father packing up, Bill went back to the river to help him. As his son approached, Frank pulled out a long string of fish from an old turpentine bucket.

"I told you they wanted to be caught," he taunted. "Where's your catch?"

"In the car."

As they were loading up, Bill pointed to the bucket in the back seat where he kept his catch. Frank lifted up the six rock bass Bill had caught and looked at them askance. "It looks like you've got enough here for lunch."

"Bill turned the car around in a little meadow overgrown with cornflowers. As they pulled into Beardstown, Frank said, "It's still early yet. Why don't we head home and pan fry these instead of going out to eat."

"That sounds good."

The two men drove east to Springfield along a smooth gravel road, past miles of cornfields. The tall stalks threatened to drown the little farmhouses in a sea of green leaves. Every time Bill slowed down at a crossing, the noise of the crickets in the fields overwhelmed even the sound of the engine. Bill was still thinking about what he had come out here for, and he was tempted to reserve his question for another time. When they got back to Adams Street, Frank immediately began filleting the fish.

"Do you need any help with that, Dad?"

"You *feel* the bones; you don't see them."

Ottilie, now Frank's wife, stood next to them in the kitchen in her slippers and a light blue dress, similar to the housedresses Marie used to wear around the home. As Frank finished filleting each fish, he handed it to Ottilie, who dipped it first into some egg yolk and then into a large bowl of flour mixed with a little salt and pepper. She then gently laid the fillets in a frying pan with butter, which filled the kitchen with such a familiar smell that Bill found it almost disturbing that it was Ottilie tending the fillets and not his own mother. When the fish was done, the three of them carried their plates piled high with fish, boiled potatoes, and wedges of lemon to the dining room. A pleasant breeze blew in through the windows as they enjoyed the meal.

After they had eaten, Ottilie stood up and asked Bill if he would like some lemonade.

"That would be wonderful," said Bill.

Ottilie returned from the kitchen with two tall glasses. Frank rose and motioned Bill into the living room. Ottilie returned to the kitchen to do the dishes while father and son sat down on the couch. It was warmer in the living room and much stuffier. Bill asked if he could open a window.

"It stays cooler in here if you don't," Frank advised.

"But there's a nice breeze outside."

"And then it gets hot outside and then the living room gets hot. Believe me. I know. Keep the windows closed and the shades drawn. That's the best way to stay cool."

So they stayed, sipping their lemonade in the darkened room. From where he sat, Bill could see the framed family portrait that hung at the top of the stairs.[17] He walked up the stairs to look at it more closely. They all looked so young! Bill remembered the day very well. Carl and their father had just opened Paris Cleaners, Otto was still working at the watch factory, and Milton was still a boy. "We were all children then," Bill thought to himself. "This is a great portrait," he said aloud, examining his own face and trying to recall what he was thinking then. He thought that his younger self looked sad in the picture. As he descended the stairs, that sad look prompted him to ask the question that he had been waiting to ask all day.

"Dad, who owns Paris Cleaners?"

Frank couldn't conceal his shock and embarrassment at the question. It was like being reminded of an unpaid debt, that one considered long settled. After fumbling for words, he asked defiantly, "What do you mean?"

"I'm not sure," Bill replied tentatively. "I guess I mean legally."

Frank paused to consider the situation. What made him so uncomfortable? He then said, "It's mine, of course."

Here was Bill's window. "So even though you're retired, you still own the business?"

"Yes." Frank was growing impatient, and he had suspicions about where Bill was going with these questions. He was tired of taking care of problems at Paris Cleaners. Setting his lemonade down on the coffee table, he leaned forward. "When I die though, it will be Carl's business. I want to make that very clear to you. It will be Carl's business."

It was like a body blow. The reiteration of "Carl's business" felt cruel. "What about us?" Bill asked meekly. "What about Otto and me?"

"Yes, what about you and Otto?" Frank tried to be gentler.

Then Bill let himself go. "We've worked harder and spent more time building that business than Carl ever has. You've seen the way he goes off to his 'business lunches' and then never comes back. Why does he get to take the long vacations when we only get the long weekends? Why does he . . ."

"Enough!" His father scolded him. "I don't want to hear about it any longer. You have not worked harder than Carl has! Otto has not worked harder than Carl has! Before you were old enough to work, Carl spent all his evenings cleaning clothes. He was up to his elbows in naphtha. Besides, even if he didn't work as hard as you, it wouldn't make any difference. I decided a long time ago it would be this way."

Bill rose and walked into the dining room. Standing by the open window, looking toward the state capitol and the pale gray sky behind it, he took a deep breath.

"But you told me it would be different," Bill said calmly. "When I came to work for you, you assured me that I was working for you and not for Carl. When you came back to work full time a couple of years ago, wasn't that what you were doing? Weren't you saying that it was *your* business?"

"Absolutely not," Frank insisted. "I came back full time because I didn't think that Carl was ready to run the business by himself."

Bill turned around, raising his voice. "How could you say that? You said it was a *family* business. You know I would have never worked there if I were working for Carl. I don't think Otto would have either."

"Lower your voice!" Frank said as he raised his own. They were both silent for a moment. Frank picked up the thread again. "I did say

it was a family business, you're right. But how does that change anything? Just because it's a family business doesn't mean someone doesn't
run it. Remember, a business is not a democracy." He paused a moment to find a metaphor. "Imagine a company of soldiers. Where
would they be without a leader? They would argue and argue while
their enemy planned an ambush. Without a leader they would be
dead. It's the same principle here. Someone has to be finally account-
able for what happens to the business. I've been that person all these
years and you've never objected to that. So it really won't be any different when I die. Carl will simply pick up where I left off. It's the
only way it can work."

Bill tried to object. "But you didn't tell us that before."

"I never told you otherwise," Frank concluded sternly.

Bill lowered his head. When he left that afternoon, his glass of
lemonade remained on the coffee table in the stuffy living room.

XV

The following week, when Bill came over to the main plant at the end
of the day, Carl had somehow found out about the conversation on
Saturday.

"Did Dad say something to you?" Bill asked.

Carl removed his linen coat abruptly. It was clear that he was extremely agitated. "That's absolutely none of your business. None of
this is your business! But you've always got to stick your nose in
everything, make sure that you're getting your fair share." Pacing behind the counter, Carl turned back toward his brother. "Take my advice, Bill. Don't worry so much about everyone else. Mind yourself.
And another thing: If you have a problem, come to me with your
problem. Stop putting the burden on Dad. He doesn't need this. He
doesn't want this. He's *retired*, for crying out loud!"

But Carl wasn't finished. "And one last thing," he said in a low and
threatening tone. "If you ever go snooping around my office again,
there'll be hell to pay."

Bill had been stewing all week over the conversation with his father. He felt ashamed of his actions. At the same time, he couldn't
help but feel betrayed. He had gone through the history of the business in his mind, recalling the time when his father asked him to join
Paris Cleaners. The implication was that he would be a partner. Why

would his father have bothered to invest in the North End plant if not as an enticement for Bill to come back to work? But that wasn't the way things had turned out. As a result, Bill found his brother's threats chafing, to say the least. He felt confused and betrayed by his father's dictates, and now his victorious brother was rubbing his nose in it. What was Carl so angry about anyway? Without thinking, Bill aired his frustration: "Then hell I'll pay."

Carl considered his brother's response for a moment and said, "What are you doing here anyway? Get out of here. Get back to work."

"Don't tell me what to do."

"I'll tell you exactly what to do. Go. Leave. There's work to do."

"Why don't you do it yourself? Can't get your hands dirty? Or is it that you don't know how?"

For a split second, Bill thought that Carl was lunging at him.

"Leave, Bill. Just leave," Carl demanded calmly as he put on his coat again.

Bill opened the front door abruptly, clanging the bells. As he walked out, he felt immediate relief. His senses seemed to be sharpened. Walking down the street, he took it all in: the barber shop, the bakery, the tavern, the coffee shop, the millinery, the drug store, the movie theater. All over downtown, people were walking or driving cars and honking their horns. Bill talked to the policeman on the corner for a few minutes before moving on. When he saw two kids trying to haul a mattress up a flight of stairs, he stopped, took off his jacket and dragged the mattress up himself. The sidewalks seemed more alive than ever before: children with ice cream, men and women out for a stroll, some of them shopping. The air was clear. A few clouds veiled the sinking sun. As he drove back toward the North End plant, Bill could see the first stars on the rise.

XVI

Otto regretted being the bearer of bad news, but after days of listening to his brothers complain about each other, he feared a much more serious problem was brewing. His father might see a way to make peace. Perhaps he could insist that his sons work together civilly. So he came over on the first Sunday afternoon of September, dressed neatly in a high collar and church clothes.

"Well, that's just fine," Frank said calmly after listening to Otto's account of the most recent trouble between Bill and Carl. "You work your whole life. And for what? For your children to reject everything you've given them."

Otto was silent.

"Ingratitude!" Frank erupted. "Simple ingratitude. What kind of sons have I raised? Thankless ones, utterly thankless."

Otto wanted to defend himself. He wanted to explain that *he* had not been thankless, but as he opened his mouth, the words would not come. Otto had become what he dreaded: the man in the middle. Of all the family members, he felt least qualified for this role and least interested in it. Where was Elizabeth, he wondered, though he recognized there was only so much she could do. She had her own life now anyway. Better to leave her out of it. As for Helen, she never wanted any part of the quarrel, and Otto had always tried to shield his little sister from these intractable conflicts. Besides, she too had a new life on a farm with Julius Kinney. At last, Otto decided, "I guess it must be up to me."

Having failed—or so he believed—his first attempt to persuade his father how bad things had gotten at Paris Cleaners, Otto tried again the following week. He informed Frank that Bill had gone so far as to apply for a loan at the bank in order to start a new dry cleaning business. When his father scoffed and began muttering "thankless!" again, Otto worried that he had caused more trouble. He went home that evening with the enormous weight of his family and the family business on his shoulders; he had never felt more alone in his life.

But Otto's efforts were not in vain. His plea had somehow made its way into a chamber of his father's heart. The following Sunday, after his second conversation with Otto, Frank attended Mass with Ottilie as he had done from time to time since their marriage. She had made it clear that she wanted to go to Saint Peter and Paul's with Frank but would gladly accompany him to the German Methodist church on Sundays as well. Unwilling to go to church twice on Sundays, Frank usually ended up going to Mass with his wife.

The Gospel reading that morning was from Matthew. It was the parable of the prodigal son. By the time the father brought out the fatted calf for his long lost son, Frank had a tear in his eye. He found himself, much to his surprise, engrossed by the parable. When the priest finished his sermon on the nature of forgiveness, Frank stood up and loudly proclaimed, along with his wife and the rest of the congregation, the Apostle's Creed. He hadn't said the creed in thirty years or more. Much to Ottilie's surprise, Frank even received Holy Communion. After Mass, Ottilie asked him if he'd had a change of heart. Muttering something, he avoided answering her question.

When they returned from church, Ottilie prepared eggs, bacon, and toast for Frank, Milton, and herself. Although his father was often quiet, Milton could sense that something wasn't quite right. "Are you OK, Dad?" he asked tentatively after his stepmother had cleared the table.

"I'm fine," said Frank, and then added, as if he assumed Milton already understood him, "Will you drive me to the river this afternoon?"

"I thought we were going to take a walk this afternoon," Ottilie said as she came back into the dining room. She was clearly disappointed.

"I'm sorry. It will have to wait. I have some business to attend to," Frank explained nervously.

"Since when is fishing business?" Ottilie joked.

"Please," said Frank simply.

Milton, for his part, now knew something was up. So he drove as fast as he could down the gravel road out of town. His father sat in the back seat of the car in his black bowler and black topcoat; he wasn't going fishing, but Milton asked no more questions, and for this Frank was grateful. Although he couldn't see much, he could smell everything and from the corners of his eyes he could see the corn growing. When they arrived at their familiar spot on the Illinois River, Milton assisted his father out of the car.

"Thank you," Frank said, brushing cottonwood seed from the sleeves of his coat. He then set off down the dirt road by himself and turned into the meadow next to it.

"Where are you going?" Milton asked, following his father into the meadow.

"Walk with me," his father requested, and so they walked together among the undulating prairie grass. The rustling of the grasses as the wind passed through it was soothing and mysterious. It reminded Frank of that part of life that could be neither grasped by the hand nor comprehended by logic. Which way would the grass bend? He loved to look at the grass in the evening after a full day of fishing. Sometimes he imagined the first settlers coming to this territory on horseback. The sun would be blazing and the huge stands of grass dotted with Indian paintbrush and tiny daisies would lead inevitably to others where different flowers unfolded and little clouds of pattering butterflies rose over the prairie. Although now interrupted by cornfields, the grass had represented everything that was new and strange and beautiful about coming to America. Frank held Milton's shoulder and took it in.

"Beautiful, isn't it?" Milton stuttered.

Frank shook his head yes and said, "There was a field like this where I grew up. It was outside the village. I used to go there sometimes, but it wasn't nearly as pretty as this." Frank paused for a moment. "Do you know the story of the Prodigal Son?"

Milton looked at his father to see if he was all right. "Sure I do."

Frank realized how strange all of this must have sounded to his son, but he was as lucid as ever. "It's a good story."

"Yeah, but I always felt sad about the oldest son, the one who worked the farm and then had to watch his brother get to eat the fatted calf. I suppose it's wrong of me to think that, but I always felt sorry for him."

Frank smiled as he and his youngest son walked back toward the road. "Me too, Milton."

XVII

That late September afternoon was crisp. The leaves would be turning soon. Frank had left for breakfast downtown followed by a meeting at the bank. He stopped in Paris Cleaners for an hour to talk to Carl and Otto, and then he met Bill for lunch. They each ordered a bowl of chili, Bill's favorite.

"I've come here this afternoon to discuss a business proposal," Frank began ceremoniously after they had finished their chili and were sitting over apple pie and coffee. Bill looked up to his father nervously.

"Otto tells me there's trouble with you and Carl again."

Bill looked surprised and somewhat embarrassed. Straightening his back, he replied, "No. Not really. Nothing out of the ordinary."

Frank moved to the point. "Otto told me it's nearly impossible for you two to work together." And before Bill could object, Frank said, "I'm tired of dealing with these problems. I'm retired. I don't want to put out fires for the rest of my life."

Bill was ashamed. It was true and he knew it. "I'm sorry, Dad. But I'm trying. We're trying."

"I'm tired of your trying. You've been trying your whole life."

It was difficult to hear it directly from his father. "I'm sorry, Dad."

"Well, I have a solution," said Frank decisively. "You know that Paris needs to expand."

"Probably the past two years it's needed to expand. Maybe more," Bill concurred.

"Here is my solution: you take the North End plant and make it into your own business. You really have developed the business in that end of town. I'll give it to you in the same way Carl got Paris. Then Paris can build a bigger plant elsewhere. You sign a loan agreement to me in the amount of the money that I invested to get the plant built. You make monthly payments to me and over the years you will finally own it outright. It's a great disappointment to me to split up the business, but this looks like the only solution that will work with you and Carl." Frank withheld any additional comments for a minute or two, before asking, "Well, what do you think?"

Quite simply, Bill was overwhelmed. He had fought so many years with his brother Carl. He realized, in part, that he had been fighting his father through Carl all along. Or, rather, it was his father's way of doing things that Bill had fought. This, however, was the last outcome he expected. And, in some respects, it wasn't at all what he wanted; Bill wanted Paris Cleaners to be a family business with equal partners among all those involved. If everyone had a stake in the business, everyone would work that much harder to ensure its success. That would be simple and fair. He was sure that the absence of such a shared organization was the reason why Elizabeth and Helen had left and why Mayme never wanted to be a part of it. But his father's new offer was completely unexpected. What could possibly account for this change of heart?

"Have you discussed this with Carl?" Bill finally asked.

"What do I need to ask Carl for?"

"Well, I'm pretty sure at this point that he would feel that I was cutting into his business by taking over one of his plants."

Frank waited a moment to consider and then said, "Carl doesn't always know what's best for the business. He may think he does, but he doesn't always know."

Bill was pondering his father's proposal. The North End plant *would* be the perfect place to start a business. He knew everything about that building and all the machines in it. In some ways, it was the perfect solution to his dilemma. But there was still the question of Carl and Otto. Bill assumed that Carl would never speak to him again if he took this offer, but with Otto it was different. A sense of duty and friendship remained.

"I suppose you need some time to think it over," said Frank.

"Yes, I think I need a couple of days to think it over," Bill echoed and then added, as if he'd forgotten about the extraordinary event that taken place that afternoon, "But thank you, Dad. Thank you so much for the offer. It means a lot to me."

Frank left the lunch counter feeling as spotless as a lamb. It was as if a burden had been lifted, a burden so old that it was like a familiar ache in his bones. Returning home that afternoon, he kissed Ottilie happily on the cheek.

"What's that for?" she asked him kindly.

"That's because."

XVIII

After a week of deliberation, Bill decided to accept his father's offer. Despite Otto's suspicions, Bill hadn't seriously considered opening a business on his own. After talking with a loan officer at the bank, he realized it would be a long time before he could qualify for a bank loan to open his own business. His father's proposal was the only real opportunity he was likely to see for years.

Just before the matter was sealed, Bill ran into a man who used to work for Bill at the North End Plant but now worked for Carl at the main plant. As they were talking, this man started to complain about Carl as a boss. In a moment of carelessness, he told Bill that he had overheard Carl laughing about Bill's attempt to establish a dry cleaning business.

"He said you couldn't run a business if it was handed to you," the man said. "But if you do open a new business, let me know. I'd be the first to sign up for a new job." With a smile of assurance he added, "Even if it meant taking a pay cut."

All the old resentment came flooding back to Bill. It was poison and Bill knew it, but it had to run through him before he could be rid of it. Yet some of the poison remained, festering into a genuine hatred by the end of the day. He took a long walk home to clear his thoughts; by the time he opened the front door of his house, he'd made up his mind. The little reminder from his former employee was all he needed to strengthen his resolve. He would show Carl that he knew how to run a business.

The following morning, Bill drove over to his father's house and told him he would like to take him up on the loan offer. Frank stroked his beard and smiled in approval. He stood up, patted Bill's shoulder, and embraced his son. "Blessings to you and your new business," he declared warmly.

It was as if Bill had been living underground his whole life and for the first time was seeing the light of day. Overwhelmed by this new world that lay before him, ripe with possibilities, Bill wept in his father's arms, saying, "Thank you, thank you."

XIX

Curiously, in all of these negotiations Bill and Carl never saw each other. As usual, they communicated with each other through other members of the family. The first battle came over the name of the new business. Bill wanted to call it Franke Cleaners, but Carl adamantly refused.

"F. Franke and Son is on the original loan that set up Paris Cleaners. It's still the official name of the business," Carl explained to Otto one afternoon in mid-October. "Bill can't use our name. I won't let him. It's our name."

Carl was deeply disturbed by his father's latest resolution. Why was Bill, who had always been a troublemaker, suddenly being rewarded for quitting the family business? Furthermore, Carl questioned whether it was his father's decision to make anymore. "It's *my* business," he confided to Dorothy that night. "And not just in fact, but in deed. *I* built that business. Dad would never have invested in it if it hadn't been for me."

Carl paced around the bedroom in his silk robe and slippers. He lit a cigar and took a few short puffs before stubbing it out in an ashtray. Dorothy had never seen him so upset. After staring out the window a moment, Carl buried his hands in his face and fell onto the bed.

"What's wrong, Carl?" his wife asked. When he rolled over, there were tears in his eyes. He looked exhausted.

"You work hard and you play by the rules and for what? So your little brother who's never played by the rules gets his way. Where is the justice in that? I don't understand. Where is the justice in that?"

Carl never asked his father why he suddenly made the decision to give Bill the North End plant. "That's no way to conduct yourself," he told himself, but the question often kept him up at night. He humbly accepted the new arrangement and poured himself into making Paris Cleaners the biggest and the best dry cleaning business in Springfield.

X

The final, irreparable tear in the family fabric came later in that fall of 1920. It was a cold and rainy November. Bill had been working day and night to get his business up and running. After a series of angry threats and accusations between Bill and Carl concerning the name of the new business, Bill finally conceded. "Fine," he said to Otto over lunch, "I'll call it Avenue Cleaners. I just want to be done with it."

Then Bill made Otto an offer. "You know, if things ever become unbearable there with Carl, you always have a job. I know you're the best at what you do, Otto, and I know how much you would bring to Avenue Cleaners.[18] I'm not asking you to quit right now. I'm just saying that whatever happens, you're sure of a job at my place."

Otto was flattered and, for a moment, intrigued, but his commitment to Paris Cleaners and his father kept him from considering it further. "I appreciate the offer, Bill, but no. I've spent too many years there to give up on it now."

Bill gave the offer no further thought, but for Otto it came as a bargaining chip that he could use when he felt that Carl was abusing his authority. And that time wasn't long in coming. On January 2, 1921, Otto's wife Anna had just given birth to their second child, Otto

Jr. Next day, Otto asked Carl if he could use some of his vacation days; things were rather hectic at home with the new baby and there were several things he needed to do around the house.

"You *just had* a holiday," was Carl's response. "Besides, there's way too much work to do."

"But you took the whole week off," Otto came back angrily.

"Yeah, but I let everyone know well in advance."

"You never let me know."

Carl remained calm. "If you wanted to know, all you had to do was ask."

Otto took another tack. "Come on, Carl. I just need two days. The work will get done, and if there are any problems I'll be right over here."

"I'm sorry, Otto. Next time, let me know in advance."

"Next time I'll be working at Bill's," Otto shot back.

"You'll what?"

"That's right. I said I'd be working at Bill's."

"Are you threatening me? Because you can walk out that door right now." Carl glowered at him, pointing to the door.

Otto looked at the little bell hanging from the top of the door and for a moment imagined the sound it would make as he crossed that threshold. But he knew himself and his own situation, and he knew his brother Carl. It just wasn't his way. If he walked out that door then and there, Carl would never have him back. Carl was too proud to be insulted like that, and Otto was too invested in Paris Cleaners to quit over a little squabble. He was going on nine years with the business. Despite the loss of some customers to Bill's new business, Paris Cleaners was doing better than ever. And with the new plant under construction, it appeared that more business was coming their way. Besides, Otto had two children now, and working with Bill was risky at best. So reason subdued his anger, and he managed to resist a dramatic exit.

By the following day, things had returned to a normal level of civility between Carl and Otto, but Carl could not get over the audacity of Bill's invitation to Otto. "So first he steals my plant, and now he wants to steal my brother!" Carl had confided to Dorothy the night before. "What kind of a man is he?"

It was the ultimate insult, for which Carl would never forgive Bill. It was also the final nail in the coffin of their relationship. There had been so many insults, so many slights, so many attempts to undermine Carl's legitimate claim to Paris Cleaners, but it was this last attempt to get Otto to work for him that Carl clung to in cultivating his disgust for his brother Bill. In his mind, Carl accused his brother of pettiness and maliciousness and total disrespect for the sanctity of family and brotherhood. He rehearsed a kind of trial scenario in which he served as the prosecutor to his brother's litany of crimes. This fantasy flashed through his mind in moments of frustration, yet he never divulged the depth of his sense of betrayal.

At work, things had returned to normal between Carl and Otto, but an unease lurked beneath their cordiality. Carl now was forever worried that Otto was scheming behind his back for better offers. This loss of trust in Otto was more devastating to Carl than was Bill's new business or his offer to Otto. With his father's retirement and the nature of the decision about the North End plant still veiled in mystery, Carl had the nagging sense that he could no longer rely on his father for insights or advice. The encroaching sense of loneliness and isolation was impossible for Carl to avoid. There were no more roadmaps to where he was going, and now he no longer had a brother with whom he could share the worries or savor the victories.

The unease weighed even more heavily on Otto. After the scrap with Carl, Otto realized that he had bet everything on Paris Cleaners. What would he do if they went under? Or, even worse, what would he do if Carl fired him? "He'd never actually do that," Otto repeated to himself hours into the night, reflecting on the possible trajectories of his life without Paris Cleaners.

And so all three brothers kept a close watch on one another, making sure to keep their distance, however, while their father did his best to avoid watching them at all. He had done his work, and now it was time to enjoy the twilight of his life.

Sonneberg 16 Mai 1923.

Lieber Vetter, Vögere, Onkel!
Es ist schon lange her, wo wir uns nicht
geschrieben haben. Gott sei Dank sind
wir noch alle gesund u. munter, was wir
auch von euch hoffe und wünschen.
Es herrschen hier schreckliche Zeiten.
Nichts als Elend und Not. Es ist fast
unmöglich noch etwas zu kaufen.
Butter 6–8000 Mark. Milch 1 Liter 740.
1 Ei 3–400 M. Roggen 60 aus Bayern
70,000 M. die Centner. 1000 Fuß 80.000
M.? bleibt da noch einer Mann?
Die Saat steht nicht zum besten, ob ist
noch immer kalt hier. Die Bäume fangen
an zu blühn. Lieber August ist im
Kriege gefallen, Grundstück in fremde Hände
deine schreckst Frau Wade und sterb sie
auch vor 2 Jahren gestorben. (deine Prostes).
Nun lieber Onkel habe ich eine Bitte.
Ich möchte gerne auch mal annähen kommen,
aber mit unserm Papier geht wohl
man 2 Millionen M. brauchen.

STITCHES

By 1922 Frank had become almost completely blind from cataracts and a letter was sent to him from his relatives in Germany. Frank Long found this letter from Wonneberg, dated May 15, 1923, among the papers that his mother, Elizabeth, had saved. I was given the letter to have translated as part of my research. Frank Long remembers his mother saying that she doubted that her father ever answered this appeal from his siblings.

I

By 1922, a general truce pervaded in the Franke family, but not one that had been settled by negotiation and debate. Rather, it came about as a result of resentment, disappointment, a sense of futility, and, above all, silence. Elizabeth had resumed her central role in the family—she was the only one to maintain regular contact with everyone else—but she refused to act as messenger any longer. She and her daughter Drusilla had suffered from tuberculosis in 1921 and had spent half the year recovering in the sanatorium outside of Springfield,[1] after which Elizabeth promised herself that she would no longer advise anyone on family matters. As a result, with no one to communicate or act to diffuse perceived slights among the various family members, each of them settled into his or her own version of the truth. And once that truth was settled, there was little to change it.

The truth for Frank was, above all else, ingratitude. Days would go by when he'd sit in his living room, the shades drawn, listening to the radio that Carl had bought him.[2] He'd sit back and wonder where all his children had gone and why they never visited any more. "Sure, they visit," he'd say to Ottilie, growing agitated, "but how often? Once every two months! I had to visit them once a day. The least they can do is drop by once a month."

But life, for each of his children, was pressing on. With the exception of Milton, who was still living at home and working at Romie Fields, all of Frank's children had children of their own. Helen and Julius Kinney, who had just had a baby boy, were now living on the family farm in Loami.

"I know they have children to take care of," Frank would argue. "I'm not asking them to cook me my meals. I'm just asking that they pay me a visit." To which Ottilie would gently reply, "How often were you able to visit your parents?"

This usually kept him quiet, but it stung more than he ever let on. During those years of full retirement, Frank often found himself thinking of his childhood in Derz. His eyesight was so poor that he had little else to distract him other than the radio and his imagination. He found himself returning, in his mind, to the long winters of Derz. It was a strange comfort to him, the simple act of remembrance. One day he might recall something totally unusual, such as the time he found three dead crows in the field behind his house; they formed an equilateral triangle although it appeared that no one had arranged them as such—or was it his brother August, who had woken up before him and done that? On other days, he might recall the contents of a room, or the corner of a room of his childhood, and eventually settle on an object of fascination and mystery: what exactly was that brown rubber disk in the hayloft? What was it used for? Did anyone ever use it? Such were the questions and memories that consumed the hours before the evening radio programs began.

There was, of course, always fishing with Milton. And since Milton was older now and often worked on Saturdays, either doing odd jobs or working on a neighbor's car, they couldn't go as often as Frank liked. On occasion, less than once a month, he would go fishing with one of the other sons. They were simply too busy and in their own way had grown resentful of some of the decisions their father had made. Carl still chafed that Frank had given the North End plant to Bill. His wife Dorothy would explain, "He didn't give the plant to Bill. You heard Elizabeth. It's a *loan*." But the mystery for Carl was why his father would deliberately encourage the breaking up of the family business. They all knew the German code; the eldest son has to lead the family business. He refused to dwell on this question for more than a moment, however, and he always performed the solemn duty of both delivering the monthly stipend from Frank's savings account and informing his father of what was happening at Paris Cleaners. Nevertheless, their relationship had grown colder and stiffer. Whenever Ottilie reminded Frank how often he saw Carl, Frank would immediately note that "he was really here on business. Besides . . ." He never managed to complete his thought, as if the sudden ellipsis marked the limit of his relationship with Carl.

Bill, too, visited his father and sometimes brought his son Robert with him, but generally he preferred to deal with his father on his own. With him there was also the nagging question: why did his father give him only a loan, and why was he so insistent about regular payments? Of course, Bill was firmly committed to paying off the loan, but it was still a small business. In 1922 he only had four employees, and sometimes there was no money left at the end of the week after making the payroll. There were times when he could have used a little time to make his monthly loan payments. On one occasion, Bill did ask his father for an extension, explaining, "Money is very tight; we have several outstanding bills that we will collect next week. I will be sure to have the money for you by then." But Frank would have none of it. "Absolutely not. When I gave you the loan, you gave me your word. If your word isn't worth anything, then you are not worth anything."

Never had he been as harsh as this to Carl, or so Bill concluded. In some respects he was right; Frank was never as rigid and demanding about loan payments from Carl. In fact Carl still had a large loan to repay by 1922, but in effect it had been all but forgiven. On the other hand, Frank was demanding about many other things with regard to Carl, as he always had been.

To complicate matters further, only a few months after offering Bill a loan, Frank had questioned the wisdom of his own decision. It had felt right at the time, but he began to regret his decision for the

Frank Franke and Ottilie Sutter Franke

very same reasons that Carl did. Although Carl would continue to ensure the success of Paris Cleaners, the dream of a family business was
finally dashed with Bill's departure. So Frank compensated for his regret by insisting that Bill pay back every cent of the loan and that he
do so on time.

As for Otto, he continued to work at Paris Cleaners with the same
dedication as always. The business had expanded enormously in the
early 1920s; Carl's ad campaign "13, Unlucky for Spots" seemed to be
holding the public's attention. Otto often worked past suppertime
and regularly worked Saturdays. It was a grueling schedule, but it was
one in which, in an almost militaristic manner, Otto took particular
pride. The result, however, was fewer opportunities to see his father.

Much to Frank's surprise, the child who visited him most often in
these later years was his eldest daughter, Mayme. Every summer,
Charles, Mayme, and their daughter Dorothy would spend a two-week
vacation at the old house on Adams Street. Charles loved the history
of Springfield, particularly the Lincoln history. When they came to
town, he would often find another Lincoln site to explore. Mayme, for
her part, found it easier to see her family this way; she preferred to

concentrate her visits rather than string them out over the course of a year. She could prepare herself emotionally, and if the visit ever became unbearable, she knew that she could take the next Inter Urban back to Champaign. When all the old family ghosts came back to haunt her, she simply told herself the visit would soon be over. Living a distance from the family gave Mayme a broader perspective, which made her visits more bearable. She wanted to see her brothers and sisters as well as her father, and she wanted Dorothy to get to know her grandfather. Frank, however, in his isolation, had become more distant with Mayme, so their conversation had its awkward moments. Charles or Ottilie would step in to defuse the tension.

II

Bill and Carl had not spoken to each other since the partition of Paris Cleaners, and it was presumed by all that the silence would be permanent. "It's best this way," Carl assured Elizabeth as she was dropping off her cleaning at Paris. "We bring out the worst in one another."

Carl was right, but it was hard for Elizabeth not to feel some guilt, since she had refused to act as an intermediary between her brothers. Ever since their mother died, Elizabeth felt that it was her duty to make sure the family stuck together. While working at Paris Cleaners, she had often wondered whether her father made this task more difficult, but now that he had isolated himself, she realized that he was the last thread holding the family together. She could visit her brothers as often as possible, making sure that they were informed of one another's activities, but such efforts were like trying to mend a tear with too small a patch. With her cheerfulness, Helen had always supported Elizabeth's efforts, but with her new baby boy, she barely came back to Springfield anymore. Helen was finally free of the headache and the heartache of the family, and Elizabeth, far from resenting her sister's good fortune, only wished for a similar release. The six months in the sanatorium with Drusilla had been exhausting and, at times, harrowing. There had been many days when she was on the brink of losing hope. After they were fully recovered, Elizabeth felt that she had been given a second chance and wanted to honor that feeling with some tangible reminder of the new life and health she felt surging within her. Returning to her home in Springfield, she discovered a genuine pleasure in the old routines that filled her days.

Frank Long family, 1923. *Left to right:* Frank, Tootie, Drusilla, and Elizabeth.

But this pleasure quickly wore thin as she found herself drawn into the family fabric again. It was then that she decided that she would no longer advise Carl or Bill on family matters. A sense of obligation still lingering, she looked at Helen's situation with envy. If only she could clarify her relationship to the family like that; if only she could honor her health and fill her days with the goodness of things that she so clearly saw now.

Expressing her frustration one evening in the fall of 1922., Elizabeth said to Hop, "There'd be no Franke family left, if it weren't for me. It's the honest truth. Bill would have no idea what was happening to his brothers if it weren't for me. The same goes for Carl. And Mayme might as well have left the family seven years ago after Mom died. Now with Helen off on the farm, I really don't know what's keeping us here."

Hop straightened his tie, tapped his cigarette into the ashtray on the kitchen table, and said, "Well, let's go then."

"What do you mean?"

"Do you remember that post office job out in Long Beach my sister mentioned a few months back?"

"Yes, I think I do." Elizabeth vaguely remembered when he had spoken of the job in the summer, but she had been absorbed with her father's health at the time. Now she was curious.

"Well, I just heard from Drusa again, and she tells me the job's mine if I want it," Hop explained.

"It's not a delivery job, is it?"

"No, no. It would be a desk job, but the pay is right and you can't beat the job security. Somebody has to deliver the mail, no matter what."

Out of habit, Elizabeth was skeptical. It was too good to be true. Better pay and no more winter! "How sure are you, Frank?"

Hop lit another cigarette and calmly explained that his sister's letter had not arrived. "The job's mine if I want it," he repeated. "What do you say?"

As she pictured the palm trees of Long Beach, Elizabeth could also see her father walking down Adams Street with his cane. "I don't know, Frank. It's a long way to California…"

She paused, thinking of a reason why the move would be impossible. Hop seized the opportunity. "But you just said that you didn't know what was keeping us here. Think about it. What's the worst that could happen to us in California? All that terrible sunny weather?"

Indeed, Elizabeth sensed that fate was handing her a chance that would be foolish to ignore. She smiled at her husband. "Oh, I don't know, Frank. Do you really think we can do it? Do you really think we can leave?"

So it was decided. Hop and Elizabeth sold their home on Fourth Street and started to pack their belongings.[3] When Elizabeth told Bill of their plans to move, he assured her that "there was no reason to stay in Springfield."

Together, Hop and Elizabeth made their rounds to each member of the Franke family and explained that the job was too good to resist. Much to her surprise, Elizabeth discovered that her brother Otto was the only one of her siblings to express regret at her leaving for California. Otto had invited her and Hop into the living room, and immediately began talking about a recent fishing trip.

"Well, we won't be fishing on the Sangamon River anymore, or the Illinois River, for that matter," Elizabeth announced.

"Why's that?" Otto asked.

"Because we're moving to California."

"California? How's that?"

After Hop had explained, and had invited Otto and the family out to California, Otto said reluctantly, "Well . . . that's wonderful."

The three of them sat uncomfortably while Anna made coffee. They talked about how they would drive to Los Angeles. When they were finished with the coffee, Otto saw them to the door.

"I'll be sorry to see you go," he said with his eyes averted. And then he added, "I just hate to see the family go."

Elizabeth was haunted by the faint crack in her brother's voice as he said this. As much as she had grown to resent her siblings' tacit expectation that she would hold the family together, she also felt the responsibility as a need. She needed the family to be harmonious because she believed in it. To hear her younger brother echo that conviction was enough to call the whole move off.

"But we can't stay now," Hop argued with her that night. "We've already sold the house. We have to be out of here next week regardless." He then tried to assure her that it was fine to have second thoughts, but that in the end the move really was best for the future of their family. She agreed that Hop was right. It was best to leave Springfield. It was, after all, her father's family that she was worrying about. "At some point," she told herself, "it's time for my own family."

Just as Elizabeth found herself emotionally prepared to say farewell to her life in Springfield and even excited about her new life in California, a telegram arrived from Drusa. Elizabeth was preparing dinner at the time and she sat down on the steps of the porch in her apron to read the message. The job in Long Beach had fallen through.

Elizabeth smiled at the news. Of course the job fell through. She scolded herself for feeling guilty about leaving. "I couldn't leave here if I tried," she sighed.

At the end of the following week, the Longs finished packing and moved into a rented house on Dial Court, near Butler School.[4] It was a chore to move and to turn the family upside down like that, but the whole decision to move only to have the job taken away had confirmed for Elizabeth that her purpose required her to remain in Springfield, sunny or otherwise.

"Well, at least I've still got a job," Hop declared, scanning their new kitchen.

Elizabeth nodded silently.

III

Things had not been easy at Avenue Cleaners, and Bill feared he would have to close before the end of the year. Just at that point, perhaps the most important force toward the success of his new business—besides his own determination—walked through the front door wearing knickers. A tough-looking kid walked straight up to the counter. Bill could see from the dirt on his neck that he probably hadn't bathed in a week.

"Can I help you, young man?"

The boy scratched his head. His blue eyes and prominent chin had a distinctly Irish quality about them. He took a deep breath and said, "I'd like to see the owner." He spoke loudly to compensate for his nervousness, and Bill thought he could hear an Irish lilt.

"That's me," Bill said.

"Oh. Hi."

"Do you need some cleaning done?"

The boy stood back from the counter and explained, "I've been watching your store all day, and I thought you might be able to use some help."

"From you?"

"Yes, sir. From me. I can do lots of things."

Bill looked at him carefully. "Shouldn't you be in school?"

The boy lowered his head and mumbled into his sleeve. "Yeah, they kicked me out."

"Kicked you out? What did they go and do that for?"

The boy looked up at Bill. "They said I was fighting, but I wasn't fighting. Those boys were the ones who were fighting. I was just defending myself."

"And they threw you out just for that?"

"Well," the boy returned bashfully. "They said I was fighting another time before that, but it was the same thing. I wasn't fighting. It was those boys."

Bill walked around the counter and stood next to the boy. "How old are you?"

"Fourteen, sir."

"Fourteen! Are you sure you're fourteen?"

"I swear on the Bible, I'm fourteen. I'm not very tall, but I'm fourteen. I've been taking care of myself since I was nine."

"Yeah and it looks like it. How did it come to that?"

The boy reached into his pockets as he began to explain: "Me and my sisters were at the orphanage at Alton, and then when my sister turned twelve they sent us back to my Dad's house. But my dad's never home, so it's just me and my sisters."

"Where's your dad?"

"He's a rail-driving man, so he's got to go away and build the railroads, but he comes home every three weeks or so."

"What about your mom?"

"Oh, she died I don't know how long ago. She died when I was still a baby."

Bill looked at the boy and tried to imagine what he would have done if his mother had died when he was young. It was bad enough that she died when he was twenty-two.

"What's your name, boy?"

At this the boy straightened his back and said, "Eddie. Eddie Ryan."

"Well, Eddie, you can call me Mr. Franke," Bill said as he extended his hand toward the boy. "Why don't you follow me." Eddie followed, and soon they were in the back of the plant where Bill's four employees were pressing. After introducing Eddie, Bill informed them that he was going out for a few minutes and that someone should go up front while he was out.

Eddie continued to follow Bill outside Avenue Cleaners and down the street. "Where are we going, Mr. Franke?"

Bill said nothing but led Eddie into a clothing store across the street. When the salesman inquired what he was looking for, Bill replied, "We need some pants for this boy." And then he turned to Eddie and said, "I can't have a boy working for me, and if you wear those knickers that's just what you'll be, a boy."

The salesman returned with a neat pair of khakis.

"Try those on," Bill instructed. "Men wear long pants."

Eddie smiled somewhat bashfully as he took the pants from the salesman. "Thanks, Mr. Franke."

Bill's bet paid off. As early as the New Year, Eddie had become a decent presser. With time, he would certainly improve. And Bill knew there would be plenty of time for Eddie Ryan. After a few meals at home and two months of long Saturdays at the Avenue Cleaners, the two of them became like father and son.

IV

Frank first heard about cataract surgery that same autumn. Milton had taken him to a regular appointment with his physician. After examining the cataracts, the doctor mentioned that there was a hospital in St. Louis that was having some success removing cataracts.

"Really?" Frank asked eagerly. "How do they do it?"

"They cut them out very carefully," the doctor came back matter-of-factly.

"How do the incisions heal?"

"It's basically just like any surgery, as far as I understand it. They remove the cataracts surgically, close the wound with sutures, and then your eyes heal within a couple of weeks of bed rest."

"That sounds dangerous, awful."

"Yes, the recovery can be difficult, but I think the results are well worth the temporary discomfort."

"What are the results?" Frank was skeptical.

"I was just reading in a medical journal last week that one patient's vision was restored to over 90 percent of what it had been originally."

By the following weekend, Milton was speeding down the main road to St. Louis with his father riding in back. Although it sounded too good to be true, Frank had to go down to St. Louis to see for himself. They arrived in town late Sunday afternoon and spent the night in a hotel. Without an appointment, Frank and Milton went over to Barnes Hospital to inquire about cataract surgery. After they had waited most of the day in the hallway of the hospital for one of the doctors to appear, a nurse came by and explained that the doctor who performed the cataract surgery was still in the operating room but would be in tomorrow. They made an appointment for the following morning.

Frank met the doctor early the next day and was then led into the examination room where a light the size of a searchlight was suspended from the ceiling. After several minutes of tests and questions,

Milton chauffeurs his father around town, circa 1920.

the doctor informed Frank that he would be a prime candidate for the surgery. "I have to warn you, however, that the recovery can be very demanding on patients," the doctor explained. "And the procedure is not without risks."

"What kind of risks?" Frank inquired. He stood up and brushed the sleeve of his gray coat.

"Well, specifically, during the recovery period the patient is not allowed to move. Even the slightest disturbance such as a bump on the arm, or turning the head too quickly could result in a rupture of the sutures."

"And what would that mean?" Frank asked more cautiously, pulling on his beard somewhat nervously.

"In some cases, the hemorrhaging can be stopped, but any disturbance can result in total blindness in that eye."

Frank scanned the room, which, except for the great light above him, was occluded by the cataracts that covered his eyes. "Well, I hardly see the difference," Frank concluded. And to prove his point, Frank held out his hand in front of his face and said, "I can't see my own hand in front of my face. I couldn't tell you how many fingers you were holding up."

But the doctor warned him further. "I can assure you, Mr. Franke, there is quite a difference between your condition and total blindness. Your eyes are still sensitive to light, and with your peripheral vision you can see colors and shapes. If you were totally blind, you would see nothing at all. It would be a permanent black curtain in front of you. There would be no looking around it or past it."

Frank quickly responded, "On the other hand, if the surgery were successful, I would be able to see and I would be free to walk around without any assistance."

"Again, removing the cataract is not the difficulty in this procedure. It's the recovery period that is most critical. The patient is confined to a hospital bed for two weeks with sandbags placed around his head to ensure that he doesn't make any sudden movements. After the initial recovery period, the patient is on bed rest at home for another six weeks. As I said, this is the most difficult aspect of the procedure."

The doctor also encouraged doing one eye at a time, just in case of a bad outcome. Despite the warnings and risks outlined by the doctor, Frank had identified his holy grail. "How bad could it be?" he asked Milton on the road back to Springfield. "Just eight weeks, and I have the rest of my life." He could picture each blade of prairie grass by the Illinois River waving in a gentle breeze. He could see the pink blossoms climbing the branch of the redbud in his front yard in the first blush of spring. It was decided; he was going to have the surgery.

The St. Louis doctor recommended that the surgery be performed in Springfield at St. John's Hospital, where Frank's friends and family would be nearby. It turned out that the eye surgeon in Springfield, Dr. Bullard, was trained at Barnes. Almost a month after his journey to St. Louis, Frank had a routine appointment with Dr. Bullard, who informed Frank how much the operation would cost. Surgery on both eyes, anesthesia, and the hospital stay, would total just over fifteen hundred dollars. It was a worrisome figure.[5] As an older person, Frank was living on his savings. With expenses like this he was concerned that he might outlive what he had in the bank. Having always been a provider, Frank hated the thought that his children might have to take care of him.

"I'm retired, Dr. Bullard, I don't know if I can come up with that kind of money right now."

"I understand, Mr. Franke. It is a very expensive procedure. But there are a few ways around it. For one, you could have the procedure done on both eyes at once in order to save on recovery costs, although I would not recommend that route. And we can always come up with a monthly payment plan."

"How much would I save by doing both eyes at once?" asked Frank.

"You might save as much as half," the doctor admitted. "But again, Mr. Franke, I don't recommend it."

"Why not?"

"Because," the doctor proceeded slowly, "if we perform the surgery on only one eye and the surgery is unsuccessful, then you will still be able to see out of the other eye."

"But I can't see out of either of my eyes right now," Frank said impatiently.

"Well then, that's something to think about," the doctor offered cautiously. "But do consider all of your options. You'll have plenty of time to do that, because I won't perform this surgery until next summer."

"That seems like a long time to think about it," Frank said, trying to look directly at the doctor.

"No it isn't," Dr. Bullard insisted. "I prefer this surgery in the summer for valid reasons. Recovery is easier and safer in the summer, if only because there is less opportunity for colds and respiratory diseases. I know that may sound a little strange, but the eyes are so sensitive after the surgery that even a coughing spell could be disastrous. Besides, if we did it now, you might slip on the ice on the way home from the hospital."

V

By the time Frank left the doctor's office, he had made up his mind. He was going to have both eyes operated on as soon as possible. He met with Carl the following afternoon to discuss the costs. He always discussed his financial decisions with Carl. Recognizing how important it was to his father, Carl assured him that there would be enough money and encouraged him to go ahead. It was agreed that Frank would have the surgery in July of 1923.

At the end of June 1923, as Frank was mentally preparing for the surgery, a letter arrived from East Prussia. Excited by a message from home, Ottilie woke Frank from his afternoon nap. "Who is it from?" Frank asked, still sleepy.

"It doesn't say," Ottilie replied impatiently. "It just says it's from Wonneberg."[6]

"Wonneberg?" Frank immediately came to life and quickly rose from the bed. Ottilie reached for him, as he was about to knock over a lamp. "Well, open it, open it."

After fetching a letter opener from the living room, Ottilie carefully broke the seal, pulled out the letter, and handed it to Frank. He was incensed. "I can't read that. Not yet at any rate."

"Would you like me to read it?" she calmly asked.

"Of course, of course."

She stepped back from the bed, unfolded the letter and ceremoniously began: "Wonneberg, May 15, 1923. Dear Brother . . ."

"Who is it from?" Frank interrupted.

"I'm not sure yet," she said thumbing through the pages.

"See who signed it."

Ottilie came to the end of the letter. "Here we are. Your brother Joseph Frank, your nephew Franz Frank, your sister Magdalena, and your sister-in-law Mathilde."

The mere mention of those names filled Frank with dread, guilt, and remorse. He had almost forgotten his family after the war had ended. So confused and disillusioned had he become with Germany during the war, he all but erased the memory of his relatives back home. He had never been actively in contact with any of them, even after the reconciliation in 1914, but the war and his grief over the death of Marie had made it impossible for him to maintain any correspondence. And when his spirits returned, there were the tensions between Carl and Otto and Bill and the whole problem of the business to solve. In short, he simply had not had the time to write to his brothers and sisters. With his worsening eyesight and the subsequent reminiscence of his childhood in Derz, however, he had felt a twinge of guilt at his negligence, and when he let himself think about it, he felt genuine remorse. After such instances he would resolve to write his sister to inquire after her health, but invariably something else would come up to keep him from writing. As he thought about all that now, he could only see his negligence and laziness. The thought was painful.

With some dread, Frank nodded to his wife to continue reading the letter from the beginning. "Dear Brother, Brother-in-Law, and

Uncle. It has been a very long time that we haven't written. Thank God we are all still hale and hearty, and we hope and wish that you are too. These are terrible times in our country. Nothing but misery and poverty. It is almost impossible to buy anything any more. Butter costs 6,000 to 8,000 marks, milk 740 a liter, one egg 300 to 400, rye 60,000 a hundredweight, wheat 70,000, a thousand kilos of peat 80,000. What is a poor person to do under such conditions? The crop does not look very promising; it is still cold here; the trees are beginning to bloom. Brother August was killed in action; his farm is no longer in the family. Your sister Mrs. Rode who lived in Derz also died two years ago."

Ottilie stopped there to look at her husband. He held his face in his hands and appeared to be weeping. Approaching him gingerly, she held out her hand and stroked his hair. "Would you like me to continue?" Frank leaned back on the bedpost and looked at her. There were no tears, but the color was gone from his face. "Yes, yes," he said matter-of-factly, "continue. Please."

Before she began again, Ottilie explained, "This next section is from your nephew presumably." She then continued reading from the letter: "Well, dear uncle, I have a favor to ask. I'd like to come to America too, but it would take two million marks of our paper money. I am an experienced shoemaker, and I do good work. Do please write and tell me if there might be a chance for me to find work over there. I could also do other work or help you out in your business. If you were willing to help me out and might send me a little money or a free ticket, I'd pay everything back with my thanks. I'd really like to get out of this misery. Many young people are now going to America. I think I'd be better able to help my parents from over there than I can from here. Please do write and tell me what you think. The trip from Hamburg to Springfield would cost about 150 to 160 dollars, I believe. One dollar at present is worth 20,000 to 25,000 marks. I'm not exactly sure, but one needs to have some cash—how much?—upon arrival. But if a United States citizen vouches for an immigrant, he is in a much better position. So, dear Uncle, please write to me and let me know what I must do to get over there. The necessary papers required by the authorities over here I could get together without much trouble. So I'm asking you to answer soon and tell me what you think. There's an American saying, 'Where there is a will, there is a way also.'[7]

Let me close for today and send you all my best regards. The others too send their regards. Farewell, till the day of our happy reunion. Your brother, Joseph Frank, your nephew, Franz Frank, your sister Magdalena, your sister-in-law Mathilde Frank. Well then, good-bye."

Ottilie looked again at her husband; he seemed to be staring out the window, but she knew that he was not looking at anything. "I'm sorry," she tried to console him, but he wouldn't answer. As she left to go prepare dinner, he said, "Don't worry. I'll be all right."

But he wasn't all right. It was too much to consider all at once. August was dead and Anna was dead. Everyone was dying. Could it have been any other way? What would I have said to them, even if I had written before they were gone? What would I have told them? He thought of Marie; he could picture her face, he could see the cold creeping over her eyes. He tried to recall his last words to her when she still understood him, and was horrified to think that it may have been something about work. "But what would I have said to her that could possibly have expressed what I wanted to say?" he asked himself. "Words fail . . . how could they say anything? Death doesn't listen anyway."

He sat quietly in his bedroom for the rest of the day, and when Ottilie called him for supper, he told her that he wasn't hungry. The evening light came in through the redbud at the side of house, but it gave him no peace. "Though I know the fruit will fall come autumn, it's not enough," he mourned. "Though I've tried to make it right, it's not enough. Though I've raised my children and have seen them raise their own children, it's not enough. Though I've prayed and followed the law as best as I know how, it's not enough. Though I've worked and prayed and tried to make it right, it's never enough."

Frank fell into a fitful sleep filled with regret. Of course, he knew that his brother and sister were of an age that their death might not be a surprise; however, he couldn't believe he hadn't made a greater effort to say his last good-bye. But, perhaps more poignantly, their uncelebrated deaths served to remind him of the way he had left his father almost forty years before. All those feelings of rejection returned. "How dare they ask me to pay for my nephew Franz Frank's journey to Springfield?" he wondered. "With nothing more than my hands and the clothes on my back I managed to save enough to make it here? Why shouldn't he do the same? Don't they know that I'm an old man too now? They know nothing of the problems that I face in my family."

It was a cruel coincidence that of all his nephews, it was Franz Frank who wanted to come over. The fact that his brother Joseph had bothered to write on behalf of his son was like reopening an old wound. It was a wound that he had assumed was healed by the trip back to Germany, but once again it hurt, even more sharply now because the opportunity to change things, to correct things, was long gone. Only now could he understand how good it would have been to have made peace with his father. All his father had to do was to say good-bye and good luck. It would have saved Frank twenty years of guilt and heartache. But his father didn't say good-bye and neither did Frank. He couldn't say goodbye to August or to Anna either. When he had thought of them, imagining the grim things they were seeing during the war and after, he had just sat there. "All I needed to do was write a note and let them know I was thinking of them," he reproached himself. "Is it my time now? Will I be the next one to go?"

The next morning Frank woke up early. Ottilie brewed him a pot of coffee. He was grateful for her company in the early morning hours, when the evaporating dew still cooled the summer air. He sat at the kitchen table, staring in the direction of the light across the backyard. He thumbed his beard as she placed a bowl of fresh strawberries and milk before him.

"Strawberries and milk," he observed. "I remember strawberries and milk." Their conversations often began this way. Frank leaned over the bowl to take in their lovely, fleeting scent. "But we never had this kind of strawberries. We only had those small, sweet, wild strawberries." Ottilie nodded. "We too."

Frank went on, "If we were lucky, my mother would let us go out strawberry picking. There was a meadow only about a mile away where they came back every year. August and I would eat our fill and then smear them on each other's faces until my mother threatened us with none for dinner."

Frank stopped. He ate a single strawberry and said, "I have to go talk to Carl today. Would you take me over there this afternoon?"

In the midst of his confusion and regret, Frank wanted to find out whether he could pay for his nephew's way to Springfield. He wasn't entirely sure why—perhaps it was the mere fact of his nephew being his namesake. After explaining the situation to Carl, Frank asked if there was enough money to bring his nephew over and provide him with a job at the cleaners. Carl took a puff of his cigar and leaned closer to his father. "I'm not sure of the exact figures, but from what I can tell right now, your surgery costs will make that impossible."

"That can't be," Frank objected. "How can that possibly be?"

Carl patiently explained. "There are two things to consider. First is how much money you are spending each month, and second for how long you will need that money. Assuming that you will live at least another five years, there's simply no way that you can afford both the surgery and the cost of your nephew's ticket."

"Are you sure?" Frank seemed a little desperate.

"I'll double-check over at the bank tomorrow morning," said Carl.

As Frank left the office, his broad hat between his hands, Carl followed him. "You know, one thing you might consider is postponing your surgery," he suggested. "Your nephew wrote that he would pay you back for the price of the ticket, right?"

Frank nodded.

"Well, just wait until he's paid you back, and then have the surgery done."

Frank chuckled. "It might be five years before he can pay me back."

"That's a long time."

"I could be dead by then."

"Come on, now, Dad. Don't say that."

"I'm an old man, Carl. I just want to watch the vapor rising above the river again."

And with that, Frank and Ottilie opened the door of Paris Cleaners and stepped out into the pungent haze—the heat of July mixed with humidity from the Gulf of Mexico coming up the Mississippi River valley into the cornfields of central Illinois. Frank could feel, taste, and smell that humidity like a curtain separating him from the rest of life.

VI

Frank had to make a quick decision: Would he sacrifice his savings and his sight to help a nephew that he had met briefly only once before? Or would he ignore the desperation in that letter and save his sight instead? He had Ottilie read the letter to him again, and when

Milton came home, Frank asked him to read it as well. When Milton came to the part written by the nephew, Frank asked him to stop. "I've heard enough."

Milton was twenty years old, roughly the same age as Frank had been when he first went to Berlin. From what he gathered when meeting him back in Germany nine years ago, his nephew was now about twenty. The hunger described in the letter was clearly the same hunger that had driven Frank to leave home. At that time, he would have done anything that might move him toward self-sufficiency. How desperately he had sought a little help: he recalled going to Heider and Jean-Jacques for an apprenticeship. How much it would have helped if someone had encouraged him a bit, had told him that although he had a long way to go before owning his own business, he was farther along than most men his age and would eventually find himself enjoying the fruits of his labor. But not even his father could tell him that he was doing a good job. He had to do everything on his own. There was no map to his destination, not even a pointer. Work was the beginning, the means, and the end. In those days, when he wasn't working, he was looking for ways to work more and to make more money. Yet there was never enough. It was a miracle that he ever made it to Springfield.

Milton sat down on the couch next to his father and asked rather abruptly, "So what are you going to do? Are you going to send Franz Frank the money?"

Setting his feet on the nearby footrest, Frank replied, "Well, it's either that or the cataract surgery."

Evidently disappointed, Milton asked, "You mean that you're not going to have the surgery?"

"No, it means that I have to make a choice."

They both let the burden of that decision fill the room momentarily. "So who are these people?" Milton stuttered.

"They are your aunts and uncles and cousins."

After that plain statement of fact, the burden no longer appeared voluminous or unmanageable. Before Frank could finish his thought, Milton interrupted. "Well, whatever you decide, Dad, we can go fishing either way. And we can always go on the roller coaster again."[8]

But Frank had decided; he was going to have the surgery. Neither Milton nor any of his children knew their aunts and uncles and cousins. It was up to Frank. It had always been up to him. His siblings had never helped him, so why should he help them now? But what really mattered was that his own son Milton didn't even know them, his own son who had been taking him fishing for the past seven years, who had dutifully led him around town for appointments and on errands. It wasn't so much that he owed his German family nothing—but that he owed Milton something; that he owed Ottilie something for love and dedication; and, most of all, since he had been doing for himself all along, that he owed himself something.

VII

Two weeks later, Frank entered the hospital for surgery as scheduled. The operation lasted an hour longer than the doctor had anticipated, but it was no matter to Frank; he had been fully etherized and hadn't felt a thing. When he came out of the operating room, his eyes were covered by thick layers of bandages. Milton and Ottilie accompanied him to his recovery room in silence. They were encouraged by the doctor not to talk to Frank for the first three days after surgery, so as not to over-stimulate him. He was under sedation.

The room itself was located at the end of the hallway. It was windowless and very small. Of course, Frank didn't mind, but for his visitors it was a depressing place to sit for hours on end with nothing to look at but the institutional white paint on the cinderblock walls. Ottilie and Milton took turns watching Frank, with Ottilie taking the longer shifts. Frank could hear them enter the room as quietly as they tried. He played a game with himself during those first days of recovery. He would guess who was in the room. He was sure he was right. He was sure he could distinguish Ottilie's light shuffle across the floor. He was certain he could feel Milton's heavier footfall.

But there was no way to confirm anything. It was dark. On all sides of him he felt the dead weight of the sandbags. He could feel their even granulation through the thick weave of the bags. He even tried to count the grains of sand to pass the time. But time was at a standstill, or it simply ceased to mean anything to him lying there in the dark. Footfalls came in from the halls. The vibrations came up through the bedposts. Then came the sweet smell of corn and the feel of the corn in his mouth, but no one was allowed to speak, nor was he allowed to speak to anyone. Not, at least, in those first three days, which seemed interminable. He spent his days wondering whether there were birds just beyond the walls and what the light would look like when they removed the bandages from his eyes.

With the darkness of his recovery came a surprising lucidity. Never before had his memories been so sharp, so clear in their details. It was as if, until then, he had only recalled half of his experience, but now he could recall all the visual details that accompanied the emotionally defining moments of his life. If only he could see the silhouette of the migrating stork again. If only he could consider the grain along the handle of his father's spade again.

His dreams were hardly different from his waking life, and so it all began to seem like one of those dreams in which the dreamer wakes up only to discover that he is in yet another dream. He was on a train in Germany. Was it west or east that he was traveling? He could not be certain. A conductor stood on the opposite end of the car where he was sitting. The car was teeming with people; children and animals were sleeping in the luggage compartment. An infant had been left to its own devices on the seat next to his. The baby was crying and cried louder each time the train crossed another crossing. He was trying to find which direction they were headed and who would leave a baby alone on a train with an unknown destination. He tried to speak up, to ask, "Whose child is this?" But when he moved his lips, no words would come. The bang of another crossing came, and the child moaned as if it were old and sick. Frank stood up abruptly to ask, "Who would leave a baby to such a fate?" But again the words didn't come. The train came to a screeching halt. Just before the crash, Frank saw the conductor smile. His body was hurled forward by the impact. He tried to cover his eyes before he hit the seat in front of him, but it was too late.

When he woke up he was screaming and sitting upright. There was no pain and the scream came out effortlessly, almost joyfully, for now he knew that he had been dreaming. That was when he sensed warm blood on his cheeks. "Oh my God," he wailed. "Oh my God."

VIII

Frank Franke became permanently blind when one of the hospital orderlies who was moving a large surgical light in the room next door dropped the awkward piece of equipment against the wall behind Frank's bed.[9] Milton had been with his father and had noticed a noise coming from the neighboring room. It sounded as though someone were hammering a nail into the ceiling. Fearing that the noise might upset his father, Milton got up to see what they were doing and to tell them to stop. He had just opened the door when the light came crashing against the wall. When he saw his father bolt upright in the bed, knocking several of the sandbags on the floor, Milton ran back toward the bed. His worst fears were confirmed when dark circles of blood oozed through the bandages. Milton stood frozen, staring at the blood as his father screamed.

"What did I do? What could I have done?" his father shouted.

One of the orderlies from the other room came in to check on the noise. When he saw the blood and heard Frank wailing, he said, "Oh my God. I'll go get a doctor right away."

Milton turned to speak, but the orderly was already gone. Frank was wringing his hands. "Wickedness! Wickedness? Whose wickedness? Not mine." Milton broke down in tears and ran to his father's side. "I'm here, Dad. I'm here. Don't worry. It's going to be OK. The doctor is on his way. The doctor is coming right now."

"A doctor? What can a doctor do for me?" Frank was delirious. He burst out laughing. "I need a priest. Get me a priest. That's what I need."

Just then the doctor entered the room. He asked Milton to step away from the bed and he had the two orderlies remove the sandbags from the bed. "Mr. Franke, I need to check your stitches, so you will need to lean back and relax while I remove the bandages."

"What do I need to see anyway?" Frank went on. "For that matter, what do I need to hear either? Take away my ears! What's there left to see or hear?"

"OK, Mr. Franke. This will take just a moment." The doctor lifted Frank's head and quickly unwrapped the bandages.

"Why should I see when there's nothing left that's sweet to see?" Frank was calmer now. It was unclear whether his eyes were opened or closed, such was the profusion of blood.

After the doctor cleaned up the blood, he examined the stitches in Frank's eyes. Milton watched him closely and moved in for a closer

Frank Franke after failed eye surgery, circa 1923.

look, but the doctor betrayed neither emotion nor judgment before standing back from the bed. Without making a sound, he then motioned to Milton to meet him outside of the room.

Once they were in the hallway, the doctor informed him that "it doesn't look good."

"How bad is it?" Milton came back.

"Well, there was still too much blood to see whether the sutures ruptured or how many of them ruptured, but with that amount of bleeding there is real concern that he has permanently lost his sight."

Milton had already assumed his father was blind. "When will we know for certain?"

"We'll proceed with the usual recovery period with special attention to the hemorrhaging. After two weeks we'll check his sight." And then the doctor added, "but don't get your hopes up. The signs thus far are not promising. It's important, however, to keep his hopes up."

"Well, I'm not going to lie to him."

"No, no," the doctor came back. "You don't have to deceive him. Just let him know that there is a chance that he may see something— a streak of light, red or blue or purple—again."

Ottilie prayed to God to restore her husband's sight. But it was all over; Milton knew it and Frank knew it. "Take me away, Milton. Take me away." Frank no longer looked in the direction of his son but instead to the ceiling. "To a place out of the way!"

"Shhh," Milton tried to calm him. "You're not supposed to be talking for another day."

"My son, you are the only one steadfast." He held out his hands. "Come here. Let me touch you." He put his hand on Milton's shoulder. "You are the only one who has stayed with me and here you are nursing a blind man." His body heaved slightly in short sobs and Milton moved quickly to calm him. "You're not supposed to move, Dad."

"I know, I know." He lay there defeated. Holding out his hand again, he felt his son's hands hold him. "Your love is not unnoticed, Milton." His beard was quivering. His lips were trembling. "Talk to me, Milton. Tell me a story. Let me listen to your voice. It's all I have."

Ottilie watched as father and son drew on each other for strength. She knew her great test still lay ahead.

THE LAST THREAD

The issue of inheritance was an important matter in the Frank Franke family. The drama created around the reading of the will helped define the events that unfolded over the next several decades. The will was dated March 23, 1925, and was read to the family immediately after Frank's death on January 21, 1930.

THE LAST WILL AND TESTAMENT OF FRANK FRANKE.

I, Frank Franke, of the City of Springfield, County of Sangamon and State of Illinois, being of sound and disposing mind and memory, do make, ordain, publish and declare this my Last Will and Testament in manner and form following:

Item 1, It is my will that my funeral expenses and all of my just debts be paid in full.

Item 2, I give and devise to my beloved son Carl D. Franke all of the notes which I may hold against him at the time of my death.

Item 3, I give, devise and bequeath any interest that I may have at the time of my death in and to Lot Three (3) of E.Illes' Subdivision of Lot Four (4) in his Addition of Out Lots to the City of Springfield, Illinois, to my beloved son Milton Franke.

Item 4, I give, devise and bequeath Lot Seven (7) of W.O. Converse's Subdivision of the Southwest part of the West Half

(1/2) of the South East Quarter (1/4) of Section Twenty-two
(22), Township Sixteen (16) North, Range Five (5) West of
the Third Principal Meridian, to my beloved son William
George Franke, but I charge the said William George Franke
and the property herein devised to him with the payment to
my Executors hereinafter named of the sum of Fifteen Hundred
Dollars ($1,500.00) within one year from the date of my
death.

Item 5, I give, devise and bequeath three-tenths (3/10)
of all of the rest, residue and remainder of my property,
whether real, personal or mixed, of every kind and character and wherever situated to my beloved son Otto F. Franke.

Item 6, I give, devise and bequeath two-tenths (2/10) of
all of said rest, residue and remainder of my property,
whether real, personal or mixed, of every kind and character and wherever situated to my beloved daughter Helen K.
Kinney.

Item 7, I give, devise and bequeath nine-fiftieths (9/50)
of all of said rest, residue and remainder of my property,
whether real, personal or mixed, of every kind and character and wherever situated to my beloved daughter Mamie K.
Creighton.

Item 8, I give, devise and bequeath eleven-fiftieths
(11/50) of all of said rest, residue and remainder of my
property, whether real, personal or mixed, of every kind and
character and wherever situated to my beloved daughter Elizabeth M. Long.

Item 9, I give, devise and bequeath one-twenty-fifth
(1/25) of all said rest, residue and remainder of my property, whether real, personal or mixed, of every kind and
character and wherever situated to my beloved son Milton
Franke.

Item 10, I give, devise and bequeath one-fiftieth (1/50)
of all of said rest, residue and remainder of my property,
whether real, personal or mixed, of every kind and character and wherever situated to my beloved son Carl D. Franke.

Item 11, I give, devise and bequeath one-fiftieth (1/50)
of all of said rest, residue and remainder of my property,

whether real, personal or mixed, of every kind and character and wherever situated to my beloved son William George Franke.

Item 12, Having an Ante-nuptial agreement with my beloved wife Ottilie Sutter Franke in which she waives all interest in my Estate I nevertheless give, devise and bequeath to her the remaining one-fiftieth (1/50) part of all of said rest, residue and remainder of my property, whether real, personal or mixed, of every kind and character and wherever situated.

Lastly, I hereby name, constitute and appoint my said beloved son Otto F. Franke and my friend John S. Schnepp as joint Executors of this my Last Will and Testament, Hereby revoking all former Wills and Codicils by me made.

IN WITNESS WHEREOF I have hereunto set my hand and affixed my SEAL the 23rd day of March, A.D., 1925.

Frank Franke_____(SEAL)

This is to certify that the foregoing Instrument was at the date thereof signed, sealed, ordained, published and declared by Frank Franke, the Tes-tator, as and for his Last Will and Testament, in the presence of William A. Young and J. E. Francis, who in his presence and at his request and in the presence of each other have subscribed their names as witnesses.

STATE OF ILLINOIS, } ss. TO THE JUDGE OF THE PROBATE COURT SANGAMON COUNTY }

of Sangamon County May Term, A. D. 1931 The undersigned Otto Franke and John S. Schnepp, Executors of the Estate of Frank Franke, deceased, would respectfully submit to the Court the following report of their acts and doings as such Executors from _____appointment _____

to May 14, A. D. 1931 they charges themselves with the following, to-wit:

DATE	ITEMS OF RECEIPTS	AMOUNT
Feb. 18 1930	Received from the Springfield Marine Bank	$ 214.41
Feb. 24 1930	Received from the Mid Park Building Corporation	516.25
July 1 1930	Received from the Smith E. Foutch and wife, notes	1545.00
Oct. 10 1930	Received from the Kenrose Hotel Building Corporation	548.75
Mar. 23 1931	Received from the Home Building and Loan Association	1869.70
Apr. 10 1931	Received from the Henry J. Schaffer and wife, notes	2157.66
Mar. 20 1931	Received from Sale of Goldblatt Bros, Inc. Bonds & Int.	380.00
Mar. 20 1931	Received from Monticella Building Corporation Bonds & Int.	382.50
Apr. 15 1931	Received from the R. K. Hilton Loan and Interest	2203.00
May 9 1931	Received from the William George Franke Loan, & Int.	2520.00
May 9 1931	Received from Carl D. Franke, note, bequeathed to him	00.00
	Total amount received	$ 12,337.27

CONTRA

ask to be credited with the following payments to creditors
of deceased as per vouchers herewith submitted.

DATE	ITEMS PAID OUT	AMOUNT
Feb. 18 1930	Paid W. A. Pavey, costs	$ 39.70
Apr. 9 1930	Paid St. John's Hospital, claim	154.75
Apr. 9 1930	Paid Ellinger & Kunz, claim	298.00
Apr. 9 1930	Paid Rev. Albert J. Wolf, burial services	15.00
Apr. 9 1930	Paid Rev. L. Riesen, burial services	10.00
Apr. 9 1930	Paid Will G. Franke, claim	91.91
Sept. 10 1930	Paid Dr. C. W. Compton, claim	36.00
Sept. 10 1930	Paid 20TH Century Monument Co, claim	85.00
May 5 1930	Paid Springfield Marine Bank, box	5.00
Apr. 9 1930	Paid Basil W. Ogg, Co Treasurer, Taxes	94.52
Apr. 9 1930	Paid Basil W. Ogg, Co Treasurer, Taxes	2.60
Mar. 20 1931	Paid Charles F. Koehn, Co Treasurer, Taxes	287.00
May 8 1931	Paid, Gave, Carl D. Franke, Legacy of note	
May 8 1931	Paid L. E. Bird, final costs	10.35

May 8 1931	Paid, Executors Compensation	740.00
May 8 1931	Paid Otto F. Franke, Legacy	3140.23
May 8 1931	Paid Helen K. Kinney, Legacy	2093.49
May 8 1931	Paid Mamie K. Creighton, Legacy	1884.14
May 8 1931	Paid Elizabeth M. Long, Legacy	2302.84
May 8 1931	Paid Milton Franke, Legacy	418.69
May 8 1931	Paid Carl D. Franke, Legacy	209.35
May 8 1931	Paid William George Franke, Legacy	209.35
May 8 1931	Paid Ottilie Sutter Franke, Legacy	209.35

Frank Franke's obituary was printed in the Illinois Journal *on January 21, 1930*

OBITUARY OF
Frank Franke (Springfield, January 21,1930)

FRANKE FRANKE, 69, DIES AT HOSPITAL Plans for the funeral services for Frank Franke, 69, of 312 1-2 West Adams street, who died yesterday morning at St. John's hospital, had not been completed at a late hour last night.

Mr. Franke was born in Germany, April 14, 1860, and came to this city when a young boy. Shortly after arriving Mr. Franke was married to Miss Maria Weighbrot, also a native of Germany, who preceded him in death a number of years ago. For over thirty-five years Mr. Franke was engaged in the merchant tailor business, retiring about 10 years ago.

Mr. Franke later married Miss Matilda Sutter, who survives with the following children: William G., Otto F., Milton F., and Carl D. Franke, all of this city: Mrs. Frank Long, city: Mrs Julius Kinney, Farmersville: Mrs. Charles Z. Creighton, Champaign. Twelve grandchildren also survive.

I

Ottilie led Frank down the steps to the sidewalk. It was the summer of 1929. From there she took him around the back of the house to Radke's garage. Frank knew every step to get there: two steps from the front door, another step forward and down another eight steps to the sidewalk, then left for twenty-seven steps, and so on. She'd leave him there every morning at the end of the garage with a pencil in his hand.[1] In his mind he could see her waving good-bye, her hat perched on her head, floating down the street in her long dress. He could follow her past the redbud by the side of the house, down the sidewalk vaulted by elms, all the way to church. In his mind he could see himself waving too, the morning sunlight glancing across his hand.

Frank Franke had been blind since cataract surgery had failed him six years before. Every morning he dragged the erasure end of a pencil along the side of Radke's garage. Back and forth, back and forth; this was his constitutional morning walk. All along the garage, for the full hour that Ottilie was attending morning Mass, Frank walked with a plain pencil to guide him. At times he attended Mass with her, but during the summer months he preferred the meditation of his ambulatory routine to that of going to church. Of course, he attended church—whether Methodist or Catholic—every Sunday. It was only during the week that he sometimes let his wife go her own way. She often persuaded him to go to Mass with her, but she could tell how much a sense of independence did for his spirit, and as a result she rarely pushed him too much. Ottilie accepted Frank's Methodism; she understood it and considered it largely a family matter. On occasion, particularly at Easter and Christmas, Frank would go to church with Carl's family or Elizabeth's, and Ottilie gladly went along with them. In general, however, mindful of transubstantiation and the Holy Eucharist, she would argue that Frank was "missing the most important part: the greatest grace and gift of Christ." At this point in his life, Frank had no energy for theological debate; all such matters lacked color or texture and instead bled into one another. There was only one thing that really mattered, and that was forgiveness.

Frank began to count his steps early on, shortly after the surgery, whether it was from the chair in the living room to the bathroom or from the front door to Radke's garage. He counted his steps not simply out of a habitual fastidiousness but to remember what space was like.

Ever since Frank had become blind, he had the uneasy feeling that he was always outside. Not just outside, but in outer space, drifting in an infinite blackness. The feeling was worst when he couldn't locate himself in his memory of the grid of Springfield. Even when Ottilie, Milton, or Elizabeth was leading him across the street, if he suddenly lost his count, he felt he was teetering on the edge of a precipice.

Frank often wondered whether it was better to be born blind. If you were born blind, the pleasure of color would never have graced your eyes. What you don't know, you can't miss. And then there would be no regret. Or would it be like always hearing about a new country, a country of vision? A country that everyone talks about, but one to which the blind are not admitted.

Frank thought of his brother Joseph and his nephew Franz back in Germany, enduring another meager harvest and always hearing about American prosperity. When he and Ottilie reminisced about Germany together, invariably the topic would turn to his family, to his brothers and sisters, prompting Frank to conclude that "even if they are still alive I don't deserve their forgiveness." But in the innermost privacy of his solitude, Frank most wanted their forgiveness. He wanted, above all, that they might know why he made his decision. He knew now that it was the wrong decision—but it was a decision based both on the possibility of seeing and, he realized, a resentment of which he hadn't been able to let go. He was still angry that not one of his siblings had stood up for him when he left Derz. They just watched him walk out into the cold and the snow. One of them could have walked with him to Lemkendorf or at least part of the way. Why should he help them when they never helped him? It was a poisonous logic and one for which he now suffered blindness as a punishment or, he hoped, as a penance. But it was a logic that his brothers and sisters could surely understand. He battled with this thought. Should they even know what led him to make his decision? Could he even explain it? In the end, it didn't matter; after the letter in 1923, he never heard from anyone in his family back in Germany again, and out of shame and embarrassment he refused to write to them. The last thread tying him to Germany was broken.

Frank drew further into himself than ever before. Days went by when he spoke to no one, not even to Ottilie. He just listened to the radio all day and all night. He listened to music, to variety shows, and to baseball games. Sometimes he would sit in the living room listening to the bells of the grand clock at the school across the street, and

when they didn't chime, he'd find his way to the school to tell someone to fix the clock.[2]

To the end of the garage in Frank's regular summer routine, there
were fifteen steps to walk. It had been thirteen steps just after he lost
his sight, but he was much frailer now and he had to take shorter
steps. The heat and the tender brush of honeysuckle vines at the end
of the garage stimulated his memory of Springfield summers to such
a degree that he could picture each leaf of the vine spilling onto the
next leaf and the bees wobbling there among the morning glory and
other slender, tube-shaped flowers. From the distant whiff of truck
exhaust, he could imagine the din of downtown Springfield. On
humid, windy days especially, he could smell the miles of corn growing beyond the city limits. But the most evocative perception was listening to the horn of a freight train in the distance. Often he would
cease his exercises and cling to the sound; he would let it fill him with
the consciousness of that flat, rolling, and raw land. He would recall
riding the train down the Appalachians at night, the wind from an
open window blowing on his beard, looking out to the dark silhou-
ettes of towns and houses. Yes, everything was terrifying and fresh
then.

II

Except to go to church and the occasional walk around the block,
Frank rarely left the house, especially in the winter. As a result, he
rarely saw anyone. Elizabeth still came by with some regularity, and
Mayme still visited once a year in the summer, but he almost never
heard from Helen. After moving out to Julius's farm in Loami, Helen
usually came back to Springfield once a month. Being somewhat careless about their money—Mayme often complained how Helen used
to walk around the mud in her fancy shoes[3]—the Kinneys had to sell
the farm in 1927. Julius got a job building roads in southern Illinois. It
was an itinerant life, moving from job site to job site, and money was
always tight, so Helen and Julius and their little boy Billy rarely got
back to Springfield anymore.[4] Milton still came around and would try
to persuade his father to go fishing with him, but even that was with
less frequency.

In 1925, Carl introduced his maid, Dorothy Greer, to Milton. After
an awkward start, and with a little help from Carl's matchmaking

Milton Franke garage, circa 1927.

skills, their relationship blossomed.[5] They were married on June 16, 1926, at a modest ceremony in Springfield. In 1927, as a delayed wedding present and to his mind as a reward for his loyalty, Frank gave Milton a piece of land and a loan of some money to start his own garage. Milton had worked for Carl at Paris Cleaners fixing delivery trucks, but early on both brothers knew that they could not get along. Frank had hoped Milton might be part of the "family business" dream, but when he saw the dark clouds begin to form between Milton and Carl, he decided to give his youngest son an opportunity to be his own boss.[6] With the loan money Milton bought a garage, named it the Milton Franke Garage,[7] and built a modest home immediately behind it. Since most people knew he lived so close, Milton was busy at all hours, especially on the weekends. He was happy—he was a well-respected mechanic who ran his own shop —but he was not able to see his father as often now.

With Otto, life was more of the same. Throughout the 1920s, Paris Cleaners had been expanding every year. The new plant brought with it a greater volume and, hence, more workers. It was an enormous task to manage the workers and to make sure that orders were delivered on time, but Otto was totally committed to it. Almost all of his time was devoted to work and to his immediate family. When he went fishing, he usually drove over to Milton's place, and they would go to Beardstown together. As a result, Thanksgiving and Christmas were the only times Otto saw his father.

Frank seldom saw Bill anymore and almost never saw Bill's children

Robert, Allyn, and Helen except at the annual Christmas party, when he would pull out his velvet pouch and give each grandchild a silver dollar.[8] Bill took the name of his brother's garage as a sign that it was now acceptable to use the Franke name in his own business. As a result, he changed "Avenue Cleaners" to "Will Franke Cleaners," the very name he had wanted to give it all along. Soon after this change, Bill was at his downtown branch filling in for Vera, the manager, who was on a lunch break. Unannounced, Carl stormed into the store. "You have no right to use the Franke name in your business," he fumed. "And I want you to get our name off your trucks. There is only one Franke cleaners in Springfield—Paris Cleaners, Carl D. Franke, Owner." Bill was just as angry: "Get out of my store! You have no right to tell me what I can or can't do. *Franke* is my name and I will use it if I want to!"[9] The only way to settle the dispute was to defer to the wisdom of their father. It was a task Frank loathed and for which he had almost no strength. At first he ordered Bill to resume the name "Avenue," but Bill cited Milton's new business as justification. "If it's only an issue of the name, why should Milton be allowed to use it and not me?" Frank tried to defend Carl's position and right to the name, but he acquiesced when Bill blurted out, "I'm a Franke too." There was no doubt he was a Franke, and it wasn't worth a fight. Frank explained his decision to Carl. "But we're in the same business," Carl protested. Frank, however, insisted, arguing that the name would certainly do no injury to Paris Cleaners.

At that point Frank had given up hope on any reconciliation between these two sons. "Get it over with," was his motto, and the less he learned of their feuds the better. But he still stood behind Carl, since Paris Cleaners was, after all, his legacy. Besides, he had made his peace with Bill. He had done all he could do for him when he allowed him to open his own business; any more would have been a betrayal, or so he believed. Nevertheless, the whole experience was a painful reminder to Bill of the wall that separated him from his father, and aside from the requisite holiday gatherings, he found it difficult to visit more frequently.

III

Mayme, Charles, and Dorothy came to see Frank again in the summer of 1927. He found their company a welcome relief from the lonely routine of his days. Charles was always pleasant company, and of all the grandchildren, Dorothy was the one closest to Frank because she at least would go for walks with him and sit on the porch swing at his side. He wasn't able to entice the Springfield grandchildren over to his house even with the promise of cookies. And, of course, Mayme's presence in the house was reassuring; she had a special relationship with her father, particularly now that he was blind. In temperament, Elizabeth was more like her mother, but Mayme had Marie's voice, at least in terms of intonation. While Elizabeth had assumed her mother's duty as the peacekeeper in the family, Mayme's intensity and dedication reminded Frank of Marie. In sharing stories with Mayme about her mother in his own rather reserved manner, Frank was lifted from his isolation.

Because she had stayed away during the times of the greatest crisis and bitterness in the family, Mayme, in many respects, had the most balanced outlook on the family. She loved Bill's easygoing manners and certainly sympathized with his predicament, but she remained loyal to her twin brother. And while the other members of the family had no definite alignment with either Bill or Carl, Mayme found that she saw less and less of Otto, and when she did, she worried about him. As he grew older, Otto seemed harsher and more hardened to the world. Mayme saw him growing more isolated like their father, but because they were not close when they were growing up, and now lived in different cities, she felt it was difficult to forge a closer connection. After visiting briefly with Otto and his family that summer, Mayme told Elizabeth "he wasn't doing so well."

"What do you mean?" Elizabeth asked.

Elizabeth's surprise struck Mayme as unusual. Elizabeth was normally very observant, and Otto's bitterness seemed so obvious. "You don't think he seems troubled?" Mayme wondered. "That he seems somehow beyond reach?"

Elizabeth reflected for a moment and concluded, "No, not at all." She continued, "Hop and I play cards with Otto and Anna about once a month, and he doesn't seem any different. You know Otto. He's a lot like Dad. He works hard—nobody works as hard as Otto—and he keeps to himself. Yes, he can be a little gruff, but that's always struck me as part of who he is."

"I suppose," Mayme conceded uneasily. "I guess I just haven't spent enough time with him recently."

"You should," Elizabeth urged her sister. Taking this as a criticism, Mayme replied, "Well, there's only so much time. And we already spend our summer vacations in Springfield."

"Well, I will say that he and Carl seem to be getting along."

"More so than usual?" Mayme asked.

"Yes. I suppose. They go up to Willow Dell cottage all the time. Otto comes back and drops us off a dozen or more fish every time. It's nice to see. You know the focus was always on Bill and Carl, but I can tell you firsthand from working at Paris that things weren't always so great between Otto and Carl. But, like I said, Otto keeps to himself and keeps working away."

While in Springfield, Mayme also visited Carl and Dorothy and their children. Otto's family came over to their father's house for dinner. Milton and Dorothy came as well. Mayme even had dinner with Bill's family, but it was during the week and somewhat rushed, as Bill always closed up his plant himself and came home late.

IV

One morning during Mayme's visit, when there was nothing planned for the day, Ottilie woke up early to make pancakes and eggs. When she'd finishing cooking, she quietly opened the door to the guest bedroom—it was Mayme and Elizabeth's old room—and crossed the bare wooden floor to the bed where ten-year-old Dorothy was sleeping. She gently rocked Dorothy awake, all the while singing "Good Morning Mary Sunshine."[10] The sun was already coming in through the split in the drapes. Ottilie told the child that breakfast was ready and that everyone was waiting.

After they had all eaten, Papa Franke asked Dorothy if she would like to go for a walk with him that morning. Dorothy looked nervous and made no response. Her mother eyed her disapprovingly, motioning her to speak up. Dorothy wanted to say that she didn't like her grandfather's rough prickly beard, but she knew better. "Yes, Papa," she ventured tentatively.

"Good. Ottilie, will you get my hat and walking stick."

It was the same old straw hat that he always wore, but with the addition of the knobby walking stick, Papa looked like a scarecrow come to life.

"Do I have to go?" Dorothy whispered to her mother.

"Yes. You have to go. And that's the last I'll hear of it."

Dorothy liked her grandfather, but he did strike her as odd and, more to the point, rough. His movement was deliberate and his hands felt like worn pieces of leather. The truth was that Dorothy was scared of her grandfather, and the responsibility of acting as his eyes made her more nervous than ever. But what could she do, she was just a ten-year-old girl? So she walked out the door reluctantly, waving to her father.

"Three steps down," her grandfather began abruptly.

"Not too fast!" he scolded her down the steps.

Dorothy turned back to the front door to look for her mother. She wanted to cry.

As they got to the bottom of the steps, Papa Franke held out his frail wrinkled hands to her. "Twenty-seven steps to the end of the block," he announced in a strict tone.

He was so slow! How would they ever make it around the block? To make matters worse, Papa Franke uttered not another word on their walk.

What seemed like an eternity to Dorothy turned out to be forty-five minutes around the block. Papa Franke was slow and old and his breathing was labored. After she guided him back up the front steps, they sat down together in the living room. Mayme greeted them and asked if either of them wanted something to drink.

Frank appeared to have forgotten something. His hands fumbled around his coat pocket. After a moment, he settled and told Mayme, "I'm fine. In fact, we were both just about to go out to the porch."

Dorothy looked surprised. She looked to her mother, who again, this time silently, insisted that she follow her grandfather out to the porch. So they went back out together, and Frank sat down on the porch swing.

"I don't want your mother to hear. That's why I asked you out here," he began in a low whisper. "Now you sit here," he said indicating a spot on the swing next to him. "I want to tell you something and I don't want you to tell your mother." He fumbled again in his pocket for a moment and pulled out a handkerchief that was wrapped around something.

"I have something for you." He slowly unwrapped the handkerchief, which revealed a crushed box. He continued in still hushed tones: "I don't want you to tell any of the other cousins. Don't tell any of them. You are the one who comes and you walk with me and you talk to me and the rest of the kids are too busy. They live right here within a mile or two of this house and they are too busy to see me."

He handed the mangled box to Dorothy, who promptly opened it. It was a Gruen wristwatch.[11]

"Papa, it's a Gruen!"

Her grandfather nodded. Through his long, thick beard Dorothy thought she detected a smile.

"How did you get this watch?"

Her grandfather began gently rocking the porch swing. "I have an old friend in town. He is a jeweler. He was a customer of mine for many years. In fact, I purchased your mother's diamond from him. Do you know the diamond? I gave it to her when she was eighteen."

"Yes. Mother wears it whenever there's a fancy occasion."

"Well, anyway, I called up my friend and said, 'I've got this grand-daughter and I want to get her something really nice. She's very sweet. I want to give her a watch, the nicest one you can find.' So he picked me up the day before you came. We drove out in the country and we sat out in his car and he showed all these different watches. He handed them to me and I felt them in my hands and decided on this one."

"Well, I love it. Thank you very much, Papa." She stood up from the swing and put her arms around his frail frame and kissed him. While he tried to maintain his usual austerity, even his heavy beard could not hide his delight.

V

To a certain degree, Mayme was right about Otto. There had been a change, but the change had taken place so gradually that no one in Springfield noticed it happening. It really began in 1927, when Milton opened up his garage. During the war, when kids at school picked on Milton for being German or for his stutter, Otto had always pro-tected him.[12] But as Milton grew older, he and Otto discovered a con-nection. Otto would come by the garage on his way home from work and they would talk about various techniques for fixing engines. It was a rewarding friendship for Otto; he had always felt that he had neglected his duties as an older brother to Milton, and this was an op-

portunity to make up for lost time. There was a twelve-year difference between them, and when Paris Cleaners opened, Otto was simply too busy to really get to know his younger brother as he grew into
manhood.

But there was another reason he became closer to Milton, which
had something to do with the bitterness Mayme had detected. When
their father had given Milton the garage, Otto suffered a crisis of
confidence. As much as he had understood and accepted the complications between Bill and Carl that had led to his father giving the
North End plant to Bill, it stung a bit nevertheless. Why should Bill
be rewarded for his disobedience? The question had haunted Otto.
Although he tried to banish it from his mind, in moments of frustration over the years, he lingered over it. Being perseverant by nature,
however, Otto invariably found the strength to quell the treacherous
question and continue working. "After all," he would tell himself,
"what else could my father have done in that situation?"

Milton's receiving the garage, however, further tested Otto's faith.
Why had all his brothers received gifts except him? When he examined his behavior over the years, he could only conclude that he, of all
the children, had unfailingly obeyed his father's orders. He had had
no desire to come home from New Mexico, but when his father
asked, he came without question. And while he certainly would have
liked to run his own business—he had always wanted to get back to
making watches again—he never complained to his father as Bill had.
He stuck to the family business with the very sense of honor and duty
that his father insisted upon. So why was he the only one of the sons
to go unrewarded? Whenever he contemplated asking his father why
Milton got the garage, why Elizabeth and Mayme and Helen all received beautiful diamonds when they were young, he would tell himself that he was above such pettiness and was not looking or asking
for any special rewards.

Yet his not asking began to burn like an ulcer. By springtime, what
was once a minor annoyance had become a constant, severe irritant.
All at once, however, Otto recognized that he had been secretly directing his anger toward Milton, blaming his youngest brother for his
own bitterness, so he attempted to confront the problem directly by
becoming closer to Milton. After all, it wasn't Milton's fault. If he had
received a similar gift, he would not have refused. Besides, Milton re-

ally was the one who cared for their father both before and after the surgery; he deserved something for his dedicated service. It was with this thought that Otto sought the companionship of Milton.

Milton, of course, was not in the least bit suspicious about his brother's motives and was only too happy to discuss the finer details of machines with someone who could appreciate the challenges. The relationship—Otto usually managed to stop by Milton's place once every other week—helped Otto to overcome his anger and thus to maintain the consistency of his character. This consistency, this solidity, this obedience and silence had become the source of Otto's pride. He rarely compared himself to his brothers in any direct way, and he certainly would never speak of it to anyone, but on occasion, when he was having a few drinks perhaps, he would let himself go. He might say something to his wife when he got home, or, more likely, he would entertain thoughts of his moral superiority over his brothers. It was never about Milton, however; he had come to believe in Milton's sincerity and, indeed, what he considered to be his brother's purity. It was primarily about Bill and Carl. He liked Bill and even respected him, but he wondered whether Bill had his fortitude. "He just doesn't have the strength," he would say. "He just couldn't take it." As for Carl, it was always his arrogance that Otto questioned. "Sure Carl can make up these fancy advertisements. He can add all his numbers up, but the bottom line is that there wouldn't be any numbers without me." But he would often scold himself for allowing himself to think such thoughts. "It doesn't matter what they do," he would tell himself. "It only matters what I do. What I do. How does the Bible saying go? Remove the beam in your own eye before plucking the mote from the eye of your brother."

While the friendship with Milton was important and certainly offered its own reward, it did not cure Otto's malaise or root out the cause. Eventually the malaise evolved into the bitterness that worried Mayme. It was in subtle ways; Otto was only slightly more irritable than usual, only a bit less patient. He found it more difficult to sleep at night, and this made him bristle sometimes at the sheer volume of work he had to do the following day. On occasion, when he felt that he couldn't relax, he would pour himself a nightcap. When that didn't work, he plunged into his work with greater determination than ever. Coming home exhausted, he would collapse into sleep.

VI

On the afternoon of January 2, 1930, Frank Franke felt something strange in his throat. Ottilie, who was preparing lunch, came into the living room to ask him what he would like to drink. Frank tried to tell her that he wanted a glass of water, but when he tried to speak, his words slurred together.

"I'm sorry, I couldn't hear you Frank."

Frank began again, this time more slowly. When he failed to utter anything comprehensible, Ottilie looked at him with concern and asked him yet again to repeat what he had said. Frank leaned back in the couch and sighed deeply.

"I . . . wald . . ."

He was clearly struggling, but as she began to interrupt him, he held out his hand to indicate that he had more to say. He suddenly understood what Milton must have felt like when people tried to complete his stuttering sentences. "I . . . waald . . . kkhh . . . waaaa . . . rrr." He was exhausted by the time he finished.

Clearly something was wrong. "Water? Is that what you want? Water?" She raised her voice as if to compensate for Frank's slurred speech. He nodded his head in response. When she returned, she handed him a glass. His hands were trembling. He lifted the glass to his mouth and drank.

"Kh . . . kh . . . kaa . . ."

Frank let his glass drop in frustration; it shattered on the hardwood floor. He was as lucid as ever, he just couldn't speak. He tried to indicate this to Ottilie with his hands, but when he heard no response he wondered if she was still in the room. She was still there but was in a state of shock. As soon as he began to wave his hands around, she assumed he was having some kind of convulsions. Then, thinking that Ottilie had left the living room, Frank stamped his foot in an effort to get her attention. When she didn't respond, he let out a slurry shout.

She was sure he was suffering from convulsions now, so she called Milton at his garage.

"Milton, your father has fallen ill. Come over right away."

"Wha . . . what happened?" Milton too was struggling to get it out.

She lost her patience. "I don't know what happened. I came into the room and he was having convulsions. Can you come over?"

Milton arrived within fifteen minutes. "Dad, are you OK?"

Frank slurred something incomprehensible.

"You can't talk?"

Frank nodded his head emphatically.

"You feel OK otherwise?"

Frank raised his hand to indicate "so so."

"I'm going to take you to the doctor's office right now."

Milton drove his father straight to the emergency room at St. John's Hospital. After the doctor had examined Frank, he invited Milton and Ottilie into the room where Frank was resting.

"Mr. Franke has suffered a minor stroke. Certain arteries are probably blocked. As a result he has lost his ability to speak. This is most likely temporary, but we would like to keep him here."

Ottilie cut in: "So there were no convulsions?"

"There may have been something that looked like convulsions, but no, he had a minor stroke, and his prognosis is positive."

"Why," Milton stuttered. "Why does he have to stay here then?"

"It's a precaution. Sometimes one stroke follows after another. We'll give him some medication to prevent that from happening."

"Does he know what has happened to him?" Milton asked. And before the doctor could respond, Frank made a sound and moved his head to indicate that he indeed understood what had happened to him.

It was a strange and somehow fitting affliction, Frank thought to himself. He felt strange; something was wrong beyond just his inability to speak, yet he was relatively clear-headed. He could comprehend everything, he could remember most things, and he was certain that he was going to die. He wanted to say this, above all else. He wanted to tell Milton and Ottilie that he was going to die and that they should contact all his children, especially Mayme and Helen, and tell them to come home to their dying father, that he had something to tell them. But he couldn't say it.

After the doctor had left, Frank began stirring, trying to get Milton's attention.

"Yes, Dad. I'm right here."

Frank waved Milton to sit next to him by the bedside. With great effort, he tried to begin.

"You want water? Something to drink?" Milton tried to anticipate his father. Frank shook his head.

"Are you uncomfortable? Do you want another pillow?" Milton asked, at which Ottilie came over with a pillow in hand. Milton gingerly lifted his father's thin body, and Ottilie quickly placed the pillow behind Frank's back.

"Is that better?"

For nearly an hour, Milton tried to understand what Frank wanted, and Ottilie did everything she could to help. Finally Frank gave up in exhaustion and fell asleep.

When he awoke from the brief nap, he was filled with anxiety. "This is exactly how it was with Marie," he thought. He resumed his effort to communicate, but although he was able to get his mouth around certain words, none of them made sense to his hearer. In frustration, Frank began striking his left palm with his right fist.

"What's wrong?" asked Ottilie, but he only hit his palm harder in response. Eventually Milton understood that his father wanted a pad of paper and a pencil. After acquiring these from a nurse, Milton carefully placed the pad in one of Frank's hands and the pencil in the other. Frank began to write furiously, but all that came out was scribbles.

"Go slower," Milton advised. Frank went more slowly but still made only scribbles.

"No, sorry Dad. I still can't make out the letters."

In addition to losing the ability to speak, it appeared that Frank had lost his fine motor skills. He sighed heavily and dropped the pencil and pad in disgust. At that moment, Carl entered the room.

"Dad? Are you all right?" He was flustered. "Is he all right?" he turned to Milton. "Dad, I came down here right away. As soon as I heard from Mrs. Sutter, I came here as fast as I could."

Frank made a groaning noise. He was smiling and nodding. Carl stepped over to the side of the bed and embraced his father.

"I told Otto what happened. He had a few things to take care of before he could leave, but he'll be over here right away."

Frank nodded again; he was getting exactly what he wanted without being able to say what he wanted. When Otto came, the first thing he explained, before asking his father how he was, was that he had called Bill and Elizabeth and they too were on their way over. Silence fell upon the room. No one could remember the last time Bill and Carl had stood in the same room together without there being a fight. Bill, however, accepted his position in the family and came to the hospital with no intention of challenging Carl or offering him the slightest disrespect; he was only looking to show his concern for his father. And Carl for his part was too worried about Frank to worry about Bill. The rest of them, knowing those two, *were* worried.

Propped up in his bed, Frank had so much to say to all of them. Why had he waited until then? But he smiled happily as he listened to his children, together again, discussing who should try to get ahold of Helen and what time Mayme would arrive. It was what he had wanted for so long. He felt like old Jacob calling all his children together to announce his blessings. His hand moved slowly and awkwardly in an effort to tug his white beard.

VII

The doctor sent Frank home as there was little more they could do for him at the hospital. Just as the doctor had feared, he had several additional minor strokes. Alas, nothing could be done. He could neither speak nor see nor write. His ability to communicate was reduced to a simple yes or no.

Ottilie cared for him lovingly. She talked to him. She prayed the rosary with him. She stayed with him when no one else could. She was there so that he was never left alone. She was his companion to the end.

In the evenings, one of the children usually came to sit with their father. They rotated nights, Elizabeth scheduling the visits. On Friday night, Bill was there.

"Can I do anything for you, Dad?"

Frank's face was gaunt. With a slow turn of his head he indicated no.

"Do you mind if I talk?" Bill asked.

A little more quickly this time, Frank nodded. Satisfied that he may have found a way for his father to pass the time, Bill began by telling him how the children were. And when he had finished, he talked about Will Franke Cleaners.

"Times are pretty tough, Dad. Since the stock market crash, people are starting to worry. It wasn't immediate, but business has definitely slowed down. It may have been the holidays, but we had a terrible November and an even worse December. People are worried about money. I don't want to lose my best employees. Especially the ones that have been there since the beginning. As much as I'd like to be able to give them a raise, we really can't afford it. It's a difficult decision. I've got men who left and now have come back. I always hire them back for what they were making before they left. Experience counts. It makes a big difference. On the other hand, I want to be fair to the ones who have stayed. I mean, I want them to know that I appreciate them, especially at a time like this."

His father sat in bed unmoved, but he appeared to be thinking. "Do you want me to stop talking?" Bill asked. His father then indicated that he wanted the pad of paper and pencil. Knowing that his father couldn't write, Bill nevertheless placed the pencil carefully in his father's hands. After a few frustrating scribbles, Frank gave up and then waved Bill closer to him. Bill had his ear right next to his father's mouth.

"Aaaww . . . tow."

"I'm sorry. Say again, Dad."

He wound up this time. "Au . . . tow."

"Otto?" Bill asked. "Are trying to say Otto?"

Frank nodded emphatically.

Bill was perplexed. "What about Otto?"

Frank began moving his hands in a circling motion, bringing his hands in toward his body.

"You want Otto to come here?"

Even more emphatically, Frank nodded again and let out a high groan.

"You want him here now? Tonight?" And when Frank had so indicated, Bill assured him, "OK. I'll go get him right now."

Not perceiving the connection between what he had said and what his father had requested, Bill assumed that his father was losing, in addition to his speech, his ability to reason. At this point, however, he wasn't interested in questioning his father; he only wanted to see him die peacefully. So he drove over to Otto's house and gave him a lift back. "I think he has something he wants to say to you, if he can," Bill said as Otto opened the car door.

Otto found his father asleep. Noticing a rosary wrapped around his hands, Otto frowned and gently removed the string of tiny black beads from his father's hands, muttering, "Mrs. Sutter." As he did so, Frank woke up with a startle.

"Dad? It's me. Sorry about that. I didn't mean to wake you up."

Frank threw his hand forward to suggest that it was nothing.

"Bill said that you wanted me to come here."

His father held out his open palm. Otto took it into his own rough callused hand. His father's hand was cold and clammy; Otto rubbed it, trying to warm it up. Frank muttered something unintelligible. He appeared so frustrated that Otto expected him to cry. He held Frank's hand tighter and waited with him into the night.

It was getting late, however, and Otto had to work the next day. "I've got to get up early tomorrow, Dad. Work to do."

Frank lightly squeezed his son's arm and brought him closer. He then said to Otto in a voice as clear as he had had since the first stroke, "Some . . . day."

"Sunday?" Otto asked, but his father indicated no. "Someday?" Otto said, emphasizing the "some." Frank slowly nodded in approbation.

"Someday what?"

But Frank continued as before: "Some . . . day."

It was a mystery to Otto. "Well, at any rate, I probably will see you on Sunday," Otto said as he was leaving. He paused at the door to look at his father, who *was* crying.

VIII

By the next week, Frank's condition had worsened so that Milton and Ottilie had to take him back to the hospital. He was barely conscious anymore. The doctors could do little; they didn't know if he was continuing to have small strokes or if there was a new problem. By this time, Frank was essentially immobile. Without the movement of his hands, he could no longer communicate. He could still hear, however. He could hear his children talk about him as if he were already dead. They knew he wasn't going to recover; he knew he wasn't going to recover. It was all just waiting at this point.

Early one morning, or so Frank surmised by Ottilie's presence, days and nights having lost distinction for him, the whiff of incense and unction hung in the air. The scent reminded him of his childhood in Derz when he was an altar boy. Frank then recognized the voice of Father Lubertus Risen from Saint Peter and Paul's. Father Risen had been a good friend to him and Ottilie over the past few years. Frank felt a crucifix pressed against his lips and then the low whispers of the

Misereatur and the Indulgentiam. Listening intently, he tried to pick out a few words he remembered from church Latin. *Misere.* Yes. Mercy. Have mercy.

Frank felt the priest's thumb rub oil gently on the lids of his eyes, eyes that had seen a new world rise up in the tall grass swaying along the banks of the Sangamon River, eyes that had watched the old world descending into war, and eyes that had finally plunged him into darkness. Next the priest touched his nostrils with the oil, then his mouth, and finally his hands and his feet.

"You must blend your sufferings with those of your savior Jesus Christ," Father Risen exhorted in a gentle whisper. "Abandon yourself to his divine mercy."

Frank felt Ottilie's frail hands upon his own. She wrapped her cherished wooden rosary around his hands.

"There are times when the Lord finds it necessary to prolong the life of the sick and the suffering. It may be for the purpose of their salvation or it may be for others' salvation. Regardless, we must freely and gladly accept his divine mercy."

Frank remained motionless. He felt his hands getting warmer. Was it Ottilie's tears or the unction?

"Corpus Christi," Father Risen said, at which Frank instinctively tried to say, "Amen." He opened his mouth to receive Communion.

Frank listened as Ottilie led Father Risen out of the room. He heard her say, "Now that the Extreme Unction has been administered, the children will be coming by shortly to see their father."

More footfalls in the hallway. Carl was the first to approach his father's bed. Noticing the rosary wrapped around his father's hands, Carl immediately removed it and set it on the nightstand.[13]

"What are you doing, Carl?" Ottilie inquired.

Losing his patience, Carl replied, "I haven't said much until now, but I'm sorry, Mrs. Sutter. You've crossed the line. My father was not a Catholic. It's disrespectful to him to force it on him."

"I never forced anything on him!" None of them had ever heard Ottilie raise her voice before.

"What's this?" Carl said, holding up the rosary.

"Come on now Carl. Put that down. She didn't mean anything by it," Bill tried to intervene.

"What do you know about her or Dad?"

Before Bill could reply, Mayme scolded both of them: "Have you no respect? Our father is on his deathbed. And you go on like that. Our own father!"

Suddenly both Bill and Carl straightened their backs. It was as if the spirit of their father had entered Mayme momentarily.

Both Elizabeth and Otto took exception to the presence of the rosary and were very uncomfortable about anything papist. Helen had yet to arrive; she was due anytime. Milton refused to join in the discussion, embarrassed that an outbreak like this should take place.

Having regained her composure, Ottilie reminded them that they were there to pay their final respects to their father, who did not have much time left with them. Each paused and said a silent prayer as they said farewell to him. With heavy hearts and frayed emotions, the family went to their respective homes, knowing that the next day held another set of challenges.

As he heard his children leaving the room, there was nothing Frank wanted more than to be able to speak. He would have reminded his children that the reason he and Marie had left Germany was to leave behind precisely the religious intolerance that they had just expressed. He would have asked one of them to bring him some pudding, to soothe his throat. But he couldn't speak, and there was no one left in the room. Because of the deep sense of dislocation his blindness caused him, Frank liked least of all to be left alone in his bed while he was still awake. He listened desperately for the cold January wind outside or the noise of feet in the hallway—anything to remind him of the dimensions of his room. Frank held on to a single image to reach sleep.

He was young, practically a boy. His father was away with his older brother harvesting potatoes just north of Fleming late into the evening. They had to spend the night in Fleming with one of his uncles. He was at home with his mother and the rest of his siblings after a long day of harvesting. It was unusually warm that night, and the air was completely still. Normally, winds from the Baltic swept down on their part of East Prussia and cooled the house down to an agreeable sleeping temperature. But not on this night. Franz and his brother August had arranged a few potato sacks in back of the house as bedding, much to the consternation of their mother. Considering how hard the family worked for their home, she had explained, it was unseemly for her boys to sleep outside when they had a proper roof over their heads. But with the heat and the oppressive air surrounding them, even she had to look past her pride and concede.

This minor victory had been for naught; the air was no better outside. The only movement noticeable was that of the mosquitoes buzzing up from the damp haystack nearby. Any wink of sleep young Franz might have gotten was immediately disturbed by the periodic buzzing around his ears.

Incredibly, August fell asleep after an hour of counting stars under his breath. Franz stirred even more with the noise of locusts growing louder by the hour. Or was it frogs? Someone once told him it was frogs, but he never could decide. August was now snoring. Hours, backward and forward, going nowhere: the heat was simply unbearable. If only the air would *move*! Franz finally rose, shooed the mosquitoes from his face, and stumbled past their small plot. He jogged down the main road of Derz, careful not to wake any neighbors, and careful to avoid the eye of those still scratching themselves to sleep. The whole town smelled of damp earth and newly mown hay. He slid behind his nearby uncle's garden plot and ran across a fallow field and beyond, where he was sure no one would follow. The moon and the stars were bright enough so that he could see his way into the woods, but he needed no light for where he was going. He and his father had walked this way so many times before; it was as sure to him as the arrival of the first storks in spring. As he entered the woods, he picked up a tall oak staff with its patina of lichen and moss. Parting a few low-lying branches, Franz peered beyond the leaves to his favorite fishing hole. The noise of frogs and bugs settled into an almost rhythmic drone. He stepped through the branches as if approaching hallowed ground. His oak staff suddenly sprouted fresh buds. The pond was motionless and bible-black. Two steps into the reeds and he laid his body down in a bath of black ivory littered with stars.

IX

The following day, January 21, 1930, Ottilie sat by Frank's body, praying for his departed soul. Milton was the first to arrive. Soon all the other children came. Helen had come on the late train the night before and was staying with Elizabeth; they were the last to show up. Each, in his or her own manner, was relieved that their father had finally gone to his rest. For Ottilie, however, it was harder. After all, she faced life alone for a second time, and she was twenty years older now than when Henry Sutter had died in 1910.

There was a knock on the door of the hospital room. Father Risen quietly opened the door and entered, dressed in a black suit and clerical collar.

"Hello, Father." Bill was the first to notice.

Ottilie stood up and embraced the priest. "Thank you for coming over so quickly."

After the introductions, Father Risen began to ask about funeral arrangements: "Shall we have a requiem Mass for Mr. Franke?"

"Absolutely not," Carl said, deliberately placing himself between his father's body and the priest.

Father Risen looked to Ottilie for guidance. She was flustered. "Excuse me," she said and then turned to Carl. "You don't want your father to have a proper funeral?" she asked in her usual sweet tone.

"Of course I do. And he will have a proper funeral."

As if oblivious to what had been said, Ottilie declared, "Well, all the arrangements have been made. The Kerlin and Egan funeral home will provide the casket. The funeral will take place at Saint Peter and Paul's."

"Like hell it will!" Carl erupted.

"Mind your tongue," Mayme came back.

"Like hell it will," said Otto, stepping forward and looking directly at the priest.

Ottilie covered her ears and began singing to herself. Helen whispered in Bill's ear, "It wouldn't be a family gathering without some fireworks."

But Carl wasn't taking any of this lightly. He pursued Ottilie around his father's bed. Singing more loudly now, she shuffled faster as he turned the corner. Finally Carl caught up to her. He was determined to see that there would be no more Catholic rituals.

"This is a man's life we're talking about," Carl began slowly. "Just because in his delirium he agreed to clutch onto a string of beads doesn't mean that he's Catholic. You've got to take the whole life together. This is a man who was so disgusted with the corruption of the Catholic Church that he fled his native Germany in pursuit of religious freedom. Now why would you want to take that choice away from him?"

Nast Memorial German M. E. Church

Ottilie was listening to him now. Father Risen tried to add something to the conversation, but Carl cut him off. "You've said enough already, I'm sure. My father was a German Methodist. My parents were charter members of the Nast German Methodist Church. They helped build that church on the southwest corner of Second and Adams, just three blocks from their house. Dad and Mother came to this country, among other things, to be German Methodists. The least we can do is to respect that difficult decision. The least we can do is bury him with his faith," Carl concluded very solemnly.

"But you don't understand, Carl. Your father changed," Ottilie objected.

Otto stepped in. "I saw you putting those beads in his hands. And now you're trying to tell us that he changed?"

Ottilie was weeping. "You don't understand. Please show me the courtesy of listening to my explanation of the funeral plans," she said. "Over the ten years of our marriage, your father and I have been attending each other's churches. I grew comfortable with the Methodist minister and Frank reacquainted himself with the Catholic Church, which no longer carried any of the distasteful aspects of his memories of Germany. Over the past year, as his health started to fail, Frank and Father Risen spent many hours together talking about life and its problems. Frank decided that he would be buried by his personal friend Father Risen, but was worried that it would be a shock to his children. He still fondly remembered his days as a Methodist but felt comfortable again in the Roman Catholic Church of his youth. I, of course, agreed with him. He also decided that he should be buried in Oak Ridge, the Protestant cemetery, next to your mother and the twins, Willie and Mary. Father Risen will go out to Oak Ridge Cemetery and bless the gravesite this afternoon. I know it's odd, but it's the way both Frank and I planned his funeral. When I pass on, I will be buried at Calvary Cemetery with my first husband, Henry. Frank wanted to be reunited with his wife and didn't want to be separated by religion. We were all friends in life and I know we will all be friends in heaven."

Carl was visibly moved by her strength and her words. "Don't worry, Mrs. Sutter," he said, taking up a conciliatory tone. "We will take care of the funeral arrangements. We are all very upset."

The wake took place that evening at the family home at 314 West Adams, the casket placed in the corner of the living room. The funeral Mass was held two days later, on January 23 at Saint Peter and Paul's.[14] For the majority of the Franke family it was the first Catholic Mass that they had attended. Since most of Frank's friends had already died, the gathering was small, and the ceremony was brief. Carl and Otto bore the front end of their father's casket, Bill and Milton the back end. They loaded the casket into a horse-drawn carriage and made a slow procession through the city and out to the cemetery. It was bitterly cold, and with the thick, low cloud cover it was nearly dark by the time they arrived at the cemetery. Bill and Otto removed their gloves and warmed the hands and the feet of each of the shivering children.[15] After the casket was removed from the caisson, the Methodist minister, the Reverend Albert J. Wolf, offered a final prayer. "Lord, receive your humble servant Frank Franke, who, by coming to this bountiful land, was able to provide for his family and his community and by doing so with love and honor and charity through your grace was able to serve you. We offer a song at his departure from this life and separation from us, for we understand there is a communion and a reunion. For even in death, we are not forever separated from one another, because we all run the same course and we will find one another again in heaven. We shall never be separated, for we live for Christ, and now we are united with Christ as we go toward him."

Because the ground was frozen solid and no graves could be dug until the spring thaw, a temporary mausoleum sheltered the casket.

X

By the spring of 1930, the economy had worsened. Newspapers were filled with dire reports. Fortunes had been lost in the stock market and bank loans used by individuals to purchase equities were called as the stock market went into a free fall. A full-scale economic depression was in the making, and depositors throughout the country became concerned about their banks' ability to meet requests for withdrawals. As the spiral of deflation quickly took hold of the economy, business closings and bank failures were announced almost every day. Due to the widespread panic, businesses dealing in discretionary spending for such services as dry cleaning were quickly affected. Both Paris Cleaners and Will Franke Cleaners, along with other enterprises, had to reduce their number of employees in the face of a sharp decrease in business.

In the general panic, Frank Franke's estate was being settled. Within a week of the funeral, an attorney for the estate of Frank Franke walked into Paris Cleaners.

"I'm looking for Mr. Franke," he said to the cashier.

Carl, who had seen the man enter the store, stood up from his desk, but waited until the cashier informed him that someone had called.

"Carl Franke. Can I help you?" he said, extending his hand.

The attorney looked puzzled and a little embarrassed. "I'm sorry. I'm looking for Otto Franke."

"Oh . . . well, can I tell him what this is in regards to?"

The attorney replied rather awkwardly, "No, I'm afraid you can't."

Annoyed, Carl sent the cashier to find Otto and then waited in his office to see what this was all about.

Otto came up front and introduced himself. "What can I do for you?"

The attorney looked around and noticed that the door to Carl's office was still open. "Is there a place we can talk privately?"

"What's wrong with right here?" Otto asked defensively.

"Nothing, I suppose. I just thought it would be better. It's about your father's estate." And then he added, "I'm sorry for your loss."

"Who are you?" Otto asked abruptly.

"I am William Young, an attorney from Jacob Schnepp's law firm, and I'm here to talk about your father's estate."

Otto looked surprised and repeated, "What can I do for you?"

The attorney then said, lowering his voice. "You were named the executor of your father's will, so we need to set up a meeting to discuss the particulars."

"I *was*?" Otto interjected as a slight smile broke across his face.

"Yes, of course. You didn't know?"

Otto took a deep breath and stood a little taller. "I had no idea." He was smiling now.

After setting up the appointment, Otto walked back to his cleaning machine, Carl popped his head out of his office and asked, "What was that about?"

"It was about Dad's will."

"What about it?"

"I guess I'm not supposed to say."

"Come on, Otto. That's just some lawyer talking. We're family."

Otto could hardly hold back a smile. "Well I guess I was named the executor of Dad's will."

"What? Did Dad name you?" Carl couldn't believe it.

"I don't know. I guess so."

As it turned out, nobody in the family knew anything about the will. Everyone hoped that they would get something, but suspected that most was going to Carl and that perhaps Bill would get a share of the business. None of the women in the family expected much, and although Otto had hoped for some recognition, he expected nothing. So when he arrived at the attorney's office later that week, he was surprised about almost everything he learned.

The first surprise was meeting John Schnepp at the office as "the other executor." John Schnepp, former mayor of Springfield, prominent attorney, and savings and loan banker, was an old friend and customer of Frank's.[16] Back before he became mayor, they used to fish together. Frank had tailored all of Schnepp's clothing until the day he retired. He had been at Frank's funeral but never mentioned anything about the will. When he saw Otto, Schnepp stuck his pipe in his mouth and stood up. Although old enough to have known Frank for years, he hardly looked a day past forty. All the wrinkles on his face had been smoothed out by a healthy plumpness, and his neatly trimmed mustache was as black as it had been the day he first set foot in Paris Cleaners.

"That's twice in two weeks. I like that better than twice in two years," joked Schnepp as he shook Otto's hand. "Don't do much fishing anymore?"

Embarrassed by just how long it had been, Otto tried to explain, "Well, yes, you know how it is; raising a family, cleaning boilers. And to tell you the truth, I've been doing most of my fishing up at Carl's place at Quiver Beach near Havana."

"I didn't even know Carl had a place."

"Oh yeah, he's got a real nice place on the Illinois River. The fishing's great. The hunting's wonderful. We go up about once a month. At least once every other month."

"Well, it's been too long." And then, his tone mournful, Schnepp added, "and by the way I'm very sorry about your father."

Otto bowed his head. "I appreciate that, Mr. Schnepp."

"Call me Jake, please."

"That will be difficult," Otto admitted. "But I'll try."

A wistful smile stretched across Schnepp's whiskers. "For almost thirty years I tried to get your father to call me Jake. Never once could he do it. It was always 'Mr. Schnepp,' no matter how often I saw him and no matter how often I asked him."

"That sounds like my dad," Otto confirmed.

After a slight pause, Otto asked, "Did you know about this?"

"About what?"

Otto stepped back. "Oh, about the will, I suppose."

"Yes. I helped him draft the document. Your father called me . . . let's see, it was five years ago. It was a little strange. You know, ever since his surgery, I didn't see him much. Oh, on occasion Milton would come by and ask if he could use the boat, but that was only on occasion. Anyway, I hadn't heard from him in probably a year or more and he called me up and sounded urgent. He said, 'I want you to help me draw up my will and would be grateful if you would also be the executor. Can you do that?' He was insistent about doing it soon. And you know your father. What was I supposed to say? I said, 'Of course,' and he said, 'Good,' and that was it. That's all he said."

"That's all he said? He didn't say anything about me, didn't say anything about what he was doing or what he was trying to do?"

"No. He was just his usual person. He just told me what he wanted me to do and that he had made all the arrangements. I think he was only too glad. He came over the following day—his wife waited in the waiting room. Then he dictated the terms of the will to me. I didn't have to advise him on anything. He knew exactly what he wanted. I think he was only too glad that I didn't have any questions for him."

Otto had thought he might be able to get some sense of why his father had appointed him executor, so he couldn't hide his disappointment with Schnepp's answer. "Yeah. That sounds like my dad. He preferred it if you didn't ask any questions."

The young attorney from the Schnepp office invited both men into his office and began to explain to Otto his duties as co-executor of the estate. "Since everyone mentioned in the will is still alive, we will not need to call upon you to make judgments about the disbursement of property or assets. Your duties will likely be limited to signing documents of the court and overseeing sales of the estate. I'd also like to call a hearing of the will. Mr. Franke, can you set a time and date when your family can attend such a hearing?"

Otto called everyone in the family and told them that the hearing was scheduled for the following month. It was a simple obligation, but there was some speculation between Elizabeth and Helen about the outcome.

"Carl, of course, will get the Paris . . . the eldest son, you know. But what about Bill?" Helen asked.

"I'd be very surprised if he didn't get half of the business. They both knew how to build it up, and they were both successful," replied Elizabeth.

"To tell you the truth I was surprised that there would be a hearing at all. I had just assumed . . ."

Elizabeth completed the thought for her. "That it was already settled between them."

It was in mid-March when they gathered together again in William Young's office. Thin, gray sunlight shone through the grimy windows of the room. It had been raining all morning before they met, and the mud from the street spattered the curbside before draining in the sewer. Carl was the last to arrive. He stomped his feet and took off his galoshes at the door. Jealousy and resentment hung in the air, Carl thought, as he entered the room and sat down at one end of a long oak table, directly opposite to the attorney, who was now adjusting a podium on the table.

"Before we begin, I want to thank Otto Franke and Mr. Schnepp for gathering everyone for this meeting. I will read the will set forth and signed by your father, Frank Franke, on March 23, 1925," said Young, adjusting his glasses.

Otto wondered about the significance of that date five years earlier, but could draw no conclusion before the lawyer began reading their father's last words.

"I, Frank Franke, of the city of Springfield, County of Sangamon and State of Illinois, being of sound and disposing mind and memory, do make, ordain, publish and declare this my Last Will and Testament in manner and form following . . ."

Mr. Young continued to read each of the individual items. The second section established Carl as the major beneficiary of Frank's will. It was very brief but conveyed the most substantive assets to his eldest son.

"Item 2. I give and devise to my beloved son Carl D. Franke all of the notes which I may hold against him at the time of my death."

There were several surprises in the will, but most especially items 4 and 5.

"Item 4," the attorney continued in a monotone. "I give, devise and bequeath Lot Seven of W. O. Converse's Subdivision of the Southwest part of the West Half of the South East Quarter of Section twenty-two, township sixteen north, range five west of the third Principal Meridian, to my beloved son William George Franke..."

When Bill heard those words he felt tears in his eyes. How often he had sought his father's approval only to be met with scorn. How badly he needed the break from the initial loan. The words "beloved son" were like heavenly balm sent from beyond the grave. But as the attorney concluded item 4, that balm turned to salt.

"But I charge the said William George Franke and the property herein devised to him with the payment to my Executors hereinafter named of the sum of fifteen hundred dollars within one year from the date of my death."

"One year?" Panic came before pain, and so Bill let out his astonishment.

"Mr. Franke, please!" Young quieted him. "You will have ample opportunity for questions when I have finished reading the will."

Even the word "will" felt like a form of persecution, as if his father's will were meant for Will Franke Cleaners, as a punishment, or rather as a judgment, protected forever in the silence of the grave. Bill sat heavily in the upholstered chair. He could barely breathe. And what he hated most was what he perceived to be Carl's sense of victory and the unbelievable weight of his father's scorn pressing down on his shoulders. At that moment he felt a small warm hand on his. He turned to see his sister Elizabeth leaning toward him. She now placed her other hand on his. In an attempt to assure her that he was all right, Bill smiled briefly.

Young continued: "Item 5. I give, devise and bequeath three-tenths of all of the rest, residue and remainder of my property, whether real, personal or mixed, of every kind and character and wherever situated to my beloved son Otto F. Franke."

This announcement came as a tremendous surprise to the whole family. It was, in many respects, the vindication Otto had been seeking all his life, and everyone in the family felt a certain relief at this benediction. It made sense of his having returned to Springfield from New Mexico. And it was, finally, something he had resigned himself to never finding in his lifetime. Otto sat straight in his chair as if receiving a Medal of Honor or some nobler designation from a higher authority. He looked neither to the right nor to the left, but adjusted his tie and fixed his gaze on the lawyer, who continued reading from the will.

In the end, Carl received by far the largest inheritance: title to the family business Paris Cleaners and forgiveness of all debt he owed to his father, plus a token recognition of one-fiftieth of the cash remaining in the estate. Mayme, Elizabeth, and Helen each got approximately one-fifth of the estate, Elizabeth receiving a little more and Mayme a little less; Otto received three-tenths, which came to $3140, whereas Milton was deeded the property on which his garage was located and received one twenty-fifth of the estate. Only Bill was asked to pay his debt back to his father's estate plus interest from the time of the original loan, which amounted to $2520. To add insult to injury, Bill received a cash payment, as Carl did, of one-fiftieth of the estate, or $209.

As they were leaving the lawyer's office, Carl put his hand on Bill's shoulder. "Well, I guess we both got what we deserved—one-fiftieth!" He was chuckling when Bill knocked his arm away from his shoulder. It wasn't funny to be the only one in the family to have to pay his debt in full—where could he get $2520 in the midst of a depression and a financial panic?

"What's your problem?"

Bill waited until they were outside to answer. "Believe me, my one-fiftieth would be looking very good if you'd paid back all *your* debts to Dad."

Bill knew his father always asked for a note to be signed for any monies he provided for investment in the business. Carl had several notes outstanding to his father over the twenty years Paris had been in business, and now he had just been freed of all that debt.

Carl affected an air of disgust. "My debts. What do you know about my debts? What did you ever know about my debts? Believe me, all I really owed him was money for the brass bowl I used when I cleaned everything by hand."

"You know what, Carl? I'm sick of hearing about you cleaning out of that brass bowl. How long was it before you had an electric machine? Nine months? It was the least you could do for flunking out of tailoring school."

If it weren't for the fact that they were on the street in broad daylight, Carl would have hit Bill.

"What's the matter with you? You're mad because you have to pay a debt back when you stole the North End plant from me and got all my customers?"

Otto was standing next to Carl in order to ensure that his brothers didn't get into a fistfight. His presence there only added to Bill's sense of outrage. "*Your* customers? *Your* plant? Where do you get your nerve? *Your* business! Where would you be without us? Where were you on Sunday? Hunting? Fishing in Florida? Do you know where your brother was? He was on his knees, not praying, but cleaning out the boilers. You want to know why I know that? Because I used to do it every Sunday with him, when *we* built that business *together*. I don't know if you know this, Carl, but advertisements don't press clothes, and fancy lunches don't either. Steam from boilers does. You need boilers to generate the steam and you need steam to press the clothes. But you wouldn't know that. You're above that. You never got your hands dirty because you couldn't stand to have your hands dirty, not for your fancy lunch appointments."

Before Carl could respond, Otto pulled him away and started walking with him back to the store. Milton and Schnepp had already left, and Elizabeth and Mayme remained with Bill on the sidewalk. Bill watched Otto and Carl walking away and noted Otto glancing back on occasion.

"Dad never liked to talk much," Mayme sighed. "I suppose this is his last statement. This is how he wanted us to know how he felt."

Bill, who had cooled off a bit, raised his eyebrows.

"I didn't mean it like that," Mayme tried to catch herself.

"But you're right," said Bill. "That's exactly what Dad wanted to do. He wanted to tell me that he didn't approve of me or my business at all."

Bill said this with a certain bravado, which Elizabeth admired. "If he really was trying to say something, why didn't he tell you himself? I mean, what happened in 1925 when he wrote the will? Why did he write this in 1925 and then never tell anyone about it?"

"And for that matter," Mayme added, "what was he trying to tell us by giving you eleven-fiftieths of the estate while I only got nine-fiftieths? Why bother?"

Bill was quick to the punch: "He wanted to make sure that you knew he liked Elizabeth two-fiftieths better than you."

They laughed together for a few minutes, hoping the humor would ease the pain a little before it started to rain again.

XI

As bad as hearing his father's will was to Bill, it was good news for Otto. In one unexpected moment, Otto received more than a year's salary. And with the prices of durable goods and services plummeting from the stock market crash, the money suddenly meant that much more. For the first time in his life, and at a time when it really mattered, Otto was rich, relatively speaking. It was now possible for him to send both Frances Marie and Otto Jr. to college.

On May 8, 1931, Otto received his legacy of $3140.23. On May 9, Bill paid to his father's estate the sum of $2520, satisfying the loan agreement with interest. On the same day, the estate recorded the receipt of Carl's notes, which were promptly canceled. On May 14, Otto and William Schnepp appeared together at the Sangamon County Court to submit their report as executors of the estate of Frank Franke. Afterwards, Schnepp took Otto to lunch.

"What are you going to do with your money, Otto?" inquired Schnepp as they finished eating.

Otto took a puff of his cigar and said matter-of-factly, "I'm going to stuff it in my mattress, and when it comes time for Frances Marie to go to college, I'll pull it out."

Mr. Schnepp chuckled. "And when your house burns down, then what are you going to do?"

"No, I'm only kidding. I've already put the money in a savings account. Why do you ask?"

Straightening his vest, Schnepp said, "As you know, I'm currently the president of a savings and loan." He studied Otto's face over the rim of his beer mug. "Do you know what a savings and loan is?"

"Sure," Otto shrugged. "It's kind of like a bank."

"It *is* like a bank, only it's better. With a savings and loan, you receive shares of the association with each deposit. We then take that money and invest it in loans secured by first mortgages on homes. It's similar to what your father did to make all of his money."

Before Otto could reply, Schnepp added, "With one crucial difference. When your father was making those loans, there was no guarantee that he would get all of his money back. Fortunately, he did. But that doesn't always happen. Especially at times like these. With a savings and loan, you're guaranteed your money back whenever you want."

"It sounds good," Otto said, sipping his beer. "But I don't see how it's any different than a bank."

Schnepp smiled. "There really isn't any difference except that we offer better interest rates than the banks do."

And with that Otto was sold. The following week he transferred all of his savings to William Schnepp's Savings and Loan.[17] "We can rest

easy," he explained to his wife Anna. "It's safer and it's a better interest rate."

For the first time in his life, Otto did rest easy. Certainly, he
worked harder than ever at the cleaners, but he no longer felt the tug
and gnaw of something deep in his gut, which had kept him up at
night and had hardened him over the years. He felt his limbs slacken
with this newfound security. In fact, it was exactly the vindication he
felt at the hearing that had buoyed him since then. It wasn't revenge
so much as justification. There was an order to the world: if you follow the rules, if you remain patient and true to your word, you will be
rewarded.

XII

In May of that year, Otto decided to pay a visit to his parents' graves.
It was a Saturday afternoon. He had been working all morning. Seeing a stand of daffodils growing out back, he clipped them to lay them
on the graves. As he drove out to the cemetery alone, he couldn't help
but think of his fortune. "Some day," he said aloud, almost as if he
were addressing his father. "I'll be able to repay it. Some day, I'll be
able to give it back."

The words were enough to jog his memory of that evening at
home when Frank had requested his presence. What was his father
trying to say to him anyway? Some day: that was it! But what *was* it?

By the cemetery gate stood a stand of lilac bushes in full bloom.
Their perfume filled the cemetery with sweetness; there was a trace
of fermentation in the humid air. Almost rotten, Otto thought. But
not rotten. Sweet and heavy like death.

He came to the place where he had buried his father a year before
and his mother fifteen years before that. A few damp leaves clung to
the base of the headstones. After removing them, Otto placed the
bouquet of daffodils between the two graves, as if both of his parents
could enjoy their brightness together. He then got on his knees and
said a prayer for both of them. As he stood up, he whispered "thank
you" in the direction of his father's grave. Some of the last crab tree
blossoms had fallen onto his mother's grave. Removing them, he
noted the date of his mother's death: March 25, 1915.

"Why does that date ring a bell?" Otto wondered. Of course, he
well knew the date of his own mother's death—he could never forget

that night. But what more was there to it? Pondering the date, he wandered back to his car slowly. By the time he had turned the engine over, he had it. Otto recalled that his father had signed his last will and testament in secret, just two days before the tenth anniversary of his mother's death. During the settlement of the estate, he had puzzled over that date. Why, he had wondered with great interest, had his father chosen to do it at that time? But he could never recall what *he* was doing at that time, let alone what his father was doing. In truth, he saw his father very little then, and it was this coincidence of their absence of contact and his father's decision to show favor upon him, as it were, that was most mysterious. And why did his father not tell anyone about it?

Of course, his father couldn't have known that he would be mute when he was dying. Had he been waiting until the day he died to tell his son that he loved him? *Some day.* Those words had haunted Otto at the funeral and had continued to haunt him. *Some day.* Was his father betting his life that some day Otto would discover the truth, that he not only loved his second son but intended to show him favor? As Otto sat in the car, staring at the crab tree in front of his parents' graves, it struck him how careless his father had been to wait so long, to gamble so much in secret.

But it was the Prussian way. He could hear Carl saying that to him, and in hearing Carl he could see his father. He could see him standing there in his black coat and black bowler with his white beard spilling over the neatly pressed lapels of his coat, blind, silent as a sentinel.

What finally made Otto return to his parents' graves for a second time that day was imagining the moment that his father decided to write his last will and testament. Otto could picture him so clearly in his living room with the curtains drawn—"cuts down on the draft!" he would say—and the radio going. What do the days mean to a blind man? It is one endless night. So when he heard the date, it must have struck him: ten years! My God, ten years! Sometime after that point, Otto continued to imagine, the shade, or rather the voice, of his mother must have announced itself. Undoubtedly, his father first would have complained and protested to her about the lack of loyalty and above all about the lack of honor. Just picturing the conversation, Otto laughed to himself in the car. He would first have complained about Bill, then about Mayme and Helen, probably then about Elizabeth and Carl. He would have sung the praises of Milton to her. And finally, after all of his complaining, she would have gently reminded him, "What about Otto?"

There were tears in his eyes, just thinking of such a conversation, how those words must have touched the very generosity of his father's heart, how those words must have rung so true to a man who had himself been forgotten by his own father. Otto couldn't bear it anymore. He returned to his parents' graves with a sprig of lilac for each of them. He placed the sprigs on the ground in front of the headstones where he thought their hearts were. He wept. With the crab trees in bloom and May in the air, there was finally something to look forward to. "Thank you. Thank you. Thank you."

The Paris Cleaning plant in 1929. Lincoln Library, Sangamon Valley Collection.

CABBAGE AND
TATTERS

*After Frank Franke died, the Franke family began to scatter across the country.
In 1932, Helen left for Arizona with her husband, Julius Kinney, and son Bill.
Both Will Franke Cleaners and Paris Cleaners survived the Depression, but not
without severe austerity measures. Because the third generation of Frankes were
born by 1931 (Milton Jr. and I, the last of the third generation, were both born in
that year) the collective memory of the Franke family is richer in detail.*

*Prohibition started in 1919 and was repealed in 1934. Alcohol consumption
continued throughout the fifteen-year period, and bootleg whiskey became a part
of the folklore, even in conservative Springfield. Otto Jr. related the first story in
this chapter about the Beardstown river rats—which had been told to him by his
father. I was particularly drawn to the story because it suggests that, despite the
tensions, there were many good memories about Paris Cleaners. Our story continues in the summer of 1930.*

I

"Did you talk to them?" Otto asked.

"Yes, I talked to them Thursday night, and I saw them last weekend before I went hunting. Don't worry. They know we're coming."

Carl stood by one of the cleaning machines in a tan linen suit. It was evening and there were no lights on at the plant.

"How did you find out about it in the first place?" Otto, in shirtsleeves and suspenders, smoking a cigar, stood next to a huge stainless steel drum.

"You know them. The river rats down in Beardstown. I was hunting pheasant and I ran into one of them. He was wondering whether I was looking for any bass, said that he had all kinds of game fish in his deep well. I asked how much and he said, 'trade, not cash.' When I asked him what he was looking for, he didn't fool around. 'Hooch, moonshine, anything you got, as long as it's strong.'"

They both started laughing through their cigars. The smoke hung thickly in the rafters of the plant.

"Well, I'm not sure how this will taste, but it'll put hair on your chest," Otto admitted, leaning over the solvent drum and whiffing the recently distilled alcohol.

"Let's bottle this up and get going," Carl said as he began removing gallon jugs from a box.

"How much of it do they want?" asked Otto.

"I'm not sure, but there's a bunch of them over there, and they're sure to have some fish or duck or pheasant or whatever. We'll get as much as we can, and what we can't use we can store in the fur vault."

"Yeah," Otto laughed; "I don't suspect that too many folks will be storing their furs here this summer."

Carl sighed. "No. Not this year."

They measured out twelve gallons of liquor to take with them that night. There was a long discussion as to whether to bottle it in corkers, screw tops, or jugs, which were pints, fifths, or gallons respectively.[1] Otto thought that since these men would probably want a little nip while they were fishing, corkers would be handiest. Carl dissuaded his brother of the notion of such convenience, assuring him that "those boys are strictly interested in quantity." So it was decided; they filled twelve jugs, loaded them into the trunk of Otto's Studebaker, and drove off to Beardstown.

"We've got to be careful. When I talked to my friend, he told me there had been a lot of federal inspectors around . . . not for alcohol, mind you, but for game."

"For game?" Otto replied. "What for?"

"I really don't know. He said it was something about conservation. They want to make sure the geese have enough time to breed."[2]

Otto laughed. "Geese? I see geese in my backyard. If anything, they could use a little thinning."

"You don't have to convince me. We just have to be careful."

It was late when they finally pulled into the main square of Beardstown. Except for the lights above the filling station, the town was dark, further obscured by a river mist. Without a clear sense of where he was, Otto asked Carl where to go.

"Down by the river," Carl replied. "Like I said, we've got to be careful. We can't just go up to any one of these fellows and ask them for fish. We've got to find the fellow I met last week and talk to him."

"So where are we supposed to find him?"

"He lives in a houseboat right on the river."

Otto followed the narrow dirt road down to the river. When he spotted a few dim lights on the river, Carl told Otto to pull over. They quietly got out of the car. It was cool and damp by the water. As they walked through the tall grass by the banks, they felt the wetness soaking through their shoes.

"It's right over here," Carl whispered, indicating a clump of cattails.

The first few boards of a dock were visible. Otto parted some of the tall weeds and walked the rickety dock. As he passed through the stand of cattails, he was able to count twelve houseboats, their patchwork roofs canting over the darkness of the river.

Otto looked back at Carl. "A houseboat on the river—who would have thought he lived there?"

Carl waved his hand at his brother to move on, and when they came to the first boat he said, "Go ahead."

"Are you sure this is your friend's boat?" Otto whispered.

Carl shrugged his shoulders.

"I'm not going first," Otto said aloud.

"Shhhh!"

"I'm serious, Carl. You should have checked this out beforehand."

"What do you mean? How was I supposed to know there'd be twenty of them in this God-forsaken part of the river?"

"Fine."

Otto walked slowly toward the first boat, pulling up on his suspenders. It was a small houseboat with a ragged piece of canvas stretched across four broom handles for a roof. No one appeared to be out there. Otto kicked the side of the boat a few times and with a loud whisper called softly, "Hello? Hello?"

After waiting a minute in the dark for any sign of movement, Otto turned back to Carl and said, "There's nobody here."

And then, quite suddenly from behind them, an obscure figure approached. "What can I do for you?"

Carl was startled and dropped his straw boater in the tall grass.

Otto stepped forward. From the dim lanterns on the river, he could make out the shape of the stranger's beard. "Ah, yeah, we were looking for some fish," Otto said. He then felt Carl's hand tapping him anxiously in the back.

"No fish around here," the figure whispered, and disappeared.

After fetching his hat, Carl pulled on Otto's shoulder and led him back through the cattails. Near Otto's car, they met another man, holding a lantern. He was bearded, a few silver whiskers indicating his general age, though his beard could not cover the gauntness of his face, not even under the cover of darkness. The skeletal quality of his cheekbones gave his eyes a sunken appearance. Only his friendly, almost toothless, smile and funny-looking hat—it was like a felt sombrero—softened his hardened features. It was Carl's friend from the week before.

"They all think you're with the government." The man was laughing. "What have you got?"

"Twelve jugs," Carl told him.

And then assuming a businesslike manner, the man said, "Well, I'll have to inspect the quality before we can do any business."

Otto abruptly opened the trunk and pulled out one of the gallon jugs.

"Are you crazy? Not here!"

The man led the two brothers out to his boat, which was docked just off the bank in a thicket of tall grass. There he took the bottle out of Otto's hands and poured it into an empty tin can. He held his lantern over the cup and examined the curious brew. The greasy poteen looked and smelled as if it would take the varnish off a tabletop.

"Looks good," the man smiled. "What do you call it?"

"Ah . . . we call it Parisian Wine," Otto tossed back at him, elbowing Carl.

The man knocked the tin can back. After a brief wheezing fit, he joked, "Parisian Slime, huh?" A few coughs later, he added through his pinched face, "I like it. It goes down nicely. Why don't you bring the whole mess of it."

As Otto and Carl went bounding through the thicket of tall grass, they could hear the river rat make a strange cry that sounded somewhere between a whistle and the caw of a crow. They were able to carry all the liquor from the trunk in two trips. When they came back to the boat with the last of it, five more men appeared who looked as though they had just returned with Lewis and Clark from two years on the Missouri River. It was too dark to make out their faces, except for their whiskers and crumpled hats. The original river rat, Carl's friend, stood up and with a flamboyant formality asked all those gathered on his boat to sit down. An odd assortment of buckets and stumps and whatnot made up the seats on his boat. A thick cloud cover that had settled above the river made for a humid, moonless night.

"Come on. Let's have a sip." The river rat motioned to Carl to bring over a jug. Carl obliged and poured a tumblerful of the noxious concoction. The river rat began passing it around and so inaugurated a minor symphony of wheezes and snorts about the boat. Otto was growing impatient.

"All right, which one of you has the fish?"

The river rat looked up from his cup. "Hold your horses there fella. We'll get to your fish. But first we've got to sample the goods."

"You've been sampling ever since we got here. It's time for us to do some sampling."

The river rat stood up and with him, his five fellow anglers. Otto pushed up his sleeves and stepped right into the thick of them. Carl kept his distance on one of the old logs at the end of the boat; he watched his brother confront six men, each of them nearly a head taller than Otto. The youngest one threw down his cup, and before Otto knew it, the river rat dove straight for his midsection and took him to the deck. The boat canted sharply and all the men went tumbling along with the dozen jugs of hooch.

"Whoa! Whoa! Whoa! Look at what you've done!" Carl sprang up from his log and yelled to the anglers to turn the jars upright. "It's a good thing we corked those jars properly. Or else you'd be out of fish and hooch."

With the assistance of a compadre, the river rat got up off Otto and dusted himself. He had a grin on his face when he said, "No harm done."

Otto stood up warily and forced a smile.

Carl looked them all over and then said sharply, "Did you like our Parisian Wine? Because you all sure drank enough of it. Anyway, Otto and I are ready to go. We got someone waiting for us up at Crane Lake. Frankly, I'm tired of waiting around here until you fellas get drunk. It'll get light soon and we must be on our way."

Carl started to pick up two of the jugs.

"Hold it right there! Nobody said we weren't buying. Your friend here just got a little anxious and I don't like it when people get anxious." The river rat made a signal to one of the others on the boat. A bright lantern was lit and a hatch was flipped up. It was the "deep well." Otto followed Carl to the hatch, and they both stared into the dark waters.

"I don't see nothing," Otto said.

Before either of them could criticize the operation further, the river rat dipped a large net into the well. When he lifted it up into the lamplight, it was flipping with bass. Otto and Carl looked at each other wide-eyed.

"I can fillet 'em right now for you," the river rat offered, and before they knew it, he was cleaning a fish while one of his buddies put it on the camp stove.

"Taste this, you'll love it."

"You fellas like pheasant?" the river rat asked. "Got some fresh pheasant on the other boat. Just killed this morning. We've got duck, pheasant, geese, you name it."

"Bring it all," Carl said and within a few minutes, he was served a piece of fish. Carl tore the fillet in half and handed it to Otto. A breeze began to stir on the water bearing the faint trace of gas, which, mingled with the solvent origin of the hooch, made the boat smell distinctly like the back of the cleaning plant. Laughter drifted up over the cattails and watery weeds. A mauve-colored sliver of the moon was peeking through the night haze above the river when a tiny skiff appeared bearing more river rats. They pulled up alongside the boat with yards of fowl hanging from knobby poles.

"You want duck I heard," a voice called out to them.

"How much?" Carl called back into the dark.

"Oh, let's say five for one of your jugs."

"Five? I was thinking more like ten. It's good whiskey."

The original river rat chimed in; "I can vouch for that."

"How about eight?"

There was a slight pause for consideration. "I can live with that," Carl said at last.

Pretty soon there were more people on the boat, laughing, yelling, and drinking. Carl and Otto sat in the stern counting up their spoils, smoking cigars, laughing it up with the river rats, sipping the brew they had made. When they loaded up the trunk of Otto's Studebaker with all the game and the metal box full of live bass, they couldn't believe how much they got for twelve jugs. They drove out of there as fast as they could.

Once they were back at Paris Cleaners and had loaded everything into the fur vault, Otto said, "What are we going to do with all this fish? We can't just leave it here like this."

Carl looked at his watch. "It's already 2:00 a.m., Otto. What do you want to do? Do you want to fillet these right now?"

"I've got a knife and hammer in my toolbox," Otto said.

Carl pulled out two cigars from his coat pocket and handed one to Otto. "Go get them."

Within minutes they had a crude table set up. Carl had removed his coat and wore an old shop apron while he clubbed the fish that were still alive in the bucket. Otto remained in his shirtsleeves and suspenders and filleted the fish. When he was done, Carl wrapped them in newspaper and packed them into an ice chest in the fur vault.

"Good times, huh Otto?" Carl smiled through his cigar.

"Yeah. Good times."

II

After the reading of his father's will, Bill worked harder than ever. His business was struggling. All around Springfield, people were losing their jobs, especially at factories like Sangamo Electric, his old employer. Whenever Bill ran into any of his customers on the street, it was always the same story: "Lost my job. Got any work?" Whenever possible, he would give them an odd job, moving bricks, mowing the lawn, selling coats, whatever it took to give them a little work and a little dignity. But there were times when Will Franke Cleaners was completely stretched just trying to make payroll. In the week after learning that his debt had to be paid off so soon, Bill had been burdened by the knowledge that his father had publicly singled him out as the non-chosen son. There were so many things to think of then. First of all, there was the debt and the interest. It was a lot of money to pay off within a year. He could do it, of course, but it would mean making sacrifices at home. He had talked to Frances about it. They agreed that they would make ends meet one way or another. Second, there was the economy, which didn't show any signs of improvement. But neither the debt nor the economic outlook was the worst of his burden. It was rather the almost physical weight of his father's judgment; it was like a hard, dense lump in his esophagus. If his father was sending him a message, why hadn't he told him five years before that an accelerated payment on his loan would have to be made? He could have worked it off over a reasonable period of time, rather than all at once in a terrible market.

"What? So he felt that he didn't have enough to spread around after he died, and I have to make up for it. It's like a punishment. It's totally unfair. Just because he never took care of Otto and the girls, he forces me to pick up the tab?"

Such were the resentful thoughts that Bill expressed to his wife one night during that period, but they were hardly the darkest. Quite simply, he couldn't escape the sense of condemnation that came from the will. After all, he did love his father and he had believed that his father loved him. In some ways, what made the whole situation so much more unbearable was not Carl's lot or anyone else's, but the fact that, in addition to repaying his debt to his father, he was to receive a mere one-fiftieth of the estate.

"One-fiftieth! Can you believe it? Why not a slap in the face instead?" He remarked to Elizabeth over dinner later that week. "Why not a kick in the shin?"

In his typical manner, Bill kept up his humor, but anger was near the surface. When one of his oldest employees asked, "What's the matter with you these days?" Bill exploded. After his outburst, he apologized profusely. He went home that night with his head hanging low. When all of his children were asleep, he sat at the kitchen table with Frances.

"Of all my brothers and sisters, he had to pick me. He had to show them that I was his least favorite. It was his last cruel gesture." He slowly removed his coat and rolled up his sleeves. "It's not the money. We'll find a way . . . It's just that he never said anything near the end. Otto told me that Dad had signed the will in 1925 . . . 1925! That's five years before he died, and he never said a word about it, not even a peep. In fact, the more I think about it, the most he said to me in those five years was during the night I spent with him in the hospital, and that was when he couldn't even speak!"

Frances sat calmly at the table with him.

"Bill, it wasn't your father's intention to punish you. He was trying to be fair, I'm sure."

"Fair? That's an awfully strange way of being fair."

Frances came back with another explanation: "You know your father. It was a different world where he grew up. In his own way, yes, he was trying to be fair. He was trying to be even-handed with all of you."

"Then how do you explain how Carl got off so easily? Think about it. Dad gives the loan to Carl. We work for Dad to build up that business, and then when it's all said and done, Carl not only gets the business but he gets his debt forgiven. How do you explain that?"

"That's not the right way to look at it and you know it. Your father wanted that business for all of you. It just didn't work out. How was he supposed to know? Did you want him to turn his back on Carl then because it didn't work out? In some ways, he probably saw himself in you; he probably thought you didn't need the help."

Bill smiled. "That's a very generous way to put it. But I wasn't like him at all. I never was. I think it has more to do with the fact that I didn't do things exactly as he wanted me to do them."

"Like I said, Bill, he was from another country and from another time. You can't blame him for that."

Bill considered this for a moment. "I've known that for a while now. What little peace I ever made with my father while he was alive was due to that very thought. I told myself that he was different, that we would never see eye to eye on much of anything, that as long as I kept that in front of me it would be fine. For the most part it worked, or at least I thought it did. He was my father after all. I couldn't bear it if Bob or Allyn or Helen felt that way about me. But he didn't care. He didn't even know."

Bill put his elbows on the table and slumped forward. As he watched his wife clear away the last dish from the table, he understood what she had said: "You're right. I don't blame him. He had a deal with Carl and he stuck to it. And Otto deserves every penny he gets. If anyone deserves it, it's Otto. I can count on one hand the times I've heard him complain. He always did what Dad asked him to do."

Frances nodded her head as Bill continued. "No, I don't blame him. I always did wonder though. My father came to this country in 1884. He left Germany because he couldn't find any work, and he left because he couldn't live there with my mother. Neither family would approve or bless the marriage. If it was so bad over there that he had to leave, then why didn't he leave it all behind? Why did he have to act like that, to run his business like a good German family? It's not as if Germany was so good to him that he needed to keep it up."

"It's like I said before, Bill," Frances said, sitting down again at the table. "He's from a different time and a different country. I mean, there was only so far your father could go, even though he made it to Springfield. Think about it, Bill. What if we had gone to Germany just before we got married? How would we have done? Specifically, how German would we have been?"

"I see what you mean," replied Bill. "But it would have to be pretty bad here for us both to leave. No prospects for work. Or something terrible happened to us. All right. Let's say we were in that position. Let's say that our parents really disliked us or some other situation that was impossible. So we go to Germany because we hear about a nice little town in the center of the country where there's plenty of work and resources and the land is relatively cheap. How German would we be? Probably not much, you're right. But then again, how American would we be? I mean, would we always seek out other Americans there? Would we try to live like Americans?"

"No, we wouldn't try, but it would be inevitable," Frances was more insistent. "We just don't know what's it's like because we've never left. My father once told me that you can never overestimate how much your homeland and its customs are a part of you. You can leave home, but there's always something there that's pulling you back, something familiar. The comforts of home."

"You're right. You're right," said Bill. "I don't blame him. He was just a man like me. But he and I are different. No, I don't blame him. What good would it do me at this point anyway?"

Frances looked at him tenderly, as if her tenderness might assuage the sting of his recognition. What was causing Bill's grief, however, was the weight of shame that was bearing down on him.

"But I won't live like that, like he did, like he wanted us to do. I wouldn't and I won't. I don't have to. Not anymore."

III

The summer of 1931 was dry. By the beginning of August the tips of the cottonwoods and sycamores that dotted the sidestreets of Springfield had surrendered the last green of the season to the long scorching days of July. While conditions around Springfield produced significantly smaller yields than normal, many parts of the Midwest and the Great Plains fared far worse. It was the beginning of the Dust Bowl. No one knew at the time how devastating it would become, but people were already feeling its effects.

It was late afternoon on a Saturday in mid-August when Otto stopped by Milton's garage. As Otto pulled up, Milton noticed the fishing poles sticking out the back of his brother's car. Milton stepped out of the shade of the garage and told Otto that he would be with him in a minute.

Otto got out of his car and stood in the incredible heat on the blacktop. A few people could be seen at either end of the street, making a slow way through the sticky air. Otto removed his broad-brimmed straw hat, mopped his brow with a handkerchief, and fanned himself mechanically. Cracks on the blacktop appeared arterial in the afternoon heat, but lacked a heart to which the fissures returned. A honk came from the car in the garage. It was Milton. He was waving Otto to come in.

"I'll tell you," Otto declared over his shoulder. "Compared to the boiler room, this feels positively comfortable."

He was looking at the street and scanning the pale sky above Springfield when he began stepping backwards toward the garage. He turned around and saw Milton stooping over a hose, rinsing his hair with one hand and taking the water in great gulps. With his other hand Milton held his necktie close to his chest, so it wouldn't get wet. Both hands were streaked in black grease.

"Let me have a little bit of that," Otto said, and his brother handed him the hose. Carefully removing his hat again, Otto stooped over and sipped the water slowly. When he'd had enough, he let out a sigh and said, "Let's go fishing, Milt."

Milton squinted and stuttered, "Right now?"

"Fish can't hide under a rock all day. They'll be biting by the time we get there."

"It'll be dark by the time we get there."

Otto shook his head impatiently. "No, I'm not talking about going to Beardstown. I'm just talking about skipping over to the Sangamon River and catch a few bass."

"I don't know, Otto. I . . . I . . . I . . . gotta wash up, get my gear and everything."

"I've got two poles in the back of my car and a cup of nightcrawlers Junior and I dug up last night."

"Sangamon River?" Milton came back more forcibly.

"What? You're trying to tell me there aren't any fish in that river?"

"No. It's just been a while."

"Come on. Let's go. I'm hungry for a little pan-fry tonight."

Milton took one last sip from the hose and said, "OK. Give me a minute."

Otto returned to his former spot on the blacktop and watched steam rise from the water trickling out of the hose down into the gutters of the street. He rubbed his knees and walked gingerly toward his car; he was still sore from working all morning cleaning the boilers and repairing one of the pressing machines.

They drove north on Walnut Street until they reached the river north of town. Otto took a dirt road west from Walnut and followed the river through abject cornfields. Reaching a meadow by the river, he parked the car in the grass.

"It's probably been three years since I've been fishing here."

"Really?" Milton scanned the fields to the south of them. No swallow, no sparrow. Not a bird in sight. "I was here last fall with Dad."

Otto removed the long bamboo poles from the back of his car and handed one to Milton. As they trudged through the meadow of tall dry grass, they found to their amazement that it was hotter by the

(LEFT) Otto has a good day fishing, circa 1932.
(RIGHT) Sangamon River outside of Springfield, circa 1900.

river than it was in downtown Springfield. There was no breeze at the
edge of town, only the malarial stir of mosquito wings above the surface of the slow moving river.

When they were much younger, back when Otto was first married
and Bill was still working at Paris, the two brothers and their father
used to take the delivery truck up to this spot after work in the sum-
mertime, especially on weekday evenings. Sometimes Carl would join
them. Frank continued to go fishing with Milton here, even after his
other sons had stopped accompanying him. The meadow where they
parked was at a sharp bend in the river where the water pooled into a
marshy basin. As a result there were shallow, grassy areas to fish as
well as deeper spots in the middle of the stream. The fishing was
never great, but it was a short drive to the outskirts of Springfield and
it was always easy enough to catch a few fish before going home.

As Otto and Milton stood on the banks of the river, they could feel
the steamy heat rising from the shallow part of the water. In the
slough before them, blooms of moss and algae crowded near the
stiller shores of the river. Below this carpet were the feeding areas for
pan fish; they both knew that.

"There aren't going to be any fish in there, Otto. They're all dead from the heat," Milton said, looking around the shore, where bits of paper trash and rusted metal parts had recently been thrown. "Who leaves their junk here?"

Otto responded, "Just you watch." Otto was tying new hooks to the end of his line. He stood up, walked back to the car, and returned with an old mason jar full of dirt, the top of which was crudely perforated. He pulled out a long nightcrawler, stuccoed with clumps of black dirt and handed it to Milton, and then pulled out another for himself. In the dry meadow on the opposite shore stood a rusted oil drum and a half-moon of paint cans constellated about it.

"Since when has this place become the local dump?" Otto asked.

Milton doffed his boater and with a clean handkerchief mopped his forehead and then the back of his neck and his closely cropped hair. Algal debris marked the miniature eddies that stirred where the men were standing. "I noticed some tires out here with Dad last fall, but it looks like people have been hoboing out here since then."

"Yep. A couple of those poor fellas came into Paris last week looking for work."

"Where'd you think they went?" Milton asked, looking down the river as if he might see the squatters floating down the river on a little raft.

"Probably caught a freight train and headed west, just like Hop and Elizabeth were about to do."

"Me, I'd rather go south. Warmer, easier on the joints. Best fishing in the world, they say."

"Oh no. That's where you're wrong, Milton. There are rainbow and cutthroat trout everywhere out west. And that's good fishing. When I was out there, I used to go down to the river on my day off. I'd go out early. Bring a little pan with me and watch the sun come up over the mountains. I'd eat trout all day long until I couldn't stand it anymore, and then I'd walk home in the dark."

"That sounds pretty good."

"It was the best."

"But you know, down in Florida I read that you catch one tuna and you've got enough fish to last the whole winter."

Milton walked over to a muddy bank and descended it sideways. There were two large rocks by the shore where he and his father used to sit. Milton waved Otto over. The day wasn't as bright now, and a thousand crickets were chirping on the shore. Every so often a cricket would mistakenly hop into the water, and before long there was a movement below the surface and the cricket would disappear. Otto dipped his hand in the muddy water. It was warm. It felt warmer than the air. He drew his pole back and cast out into the water as far as he could, letting his line sink to the bottom.

"Too damn hot anywhere else," Otto muttered. "Do you think we ought to put a cricket or two on our hooks?"

"No, lets stay with the night crawlers; those crickets are harder to catch than you think," Milton said, and then motioned his brother to sit on the rock next to him.

"It's OK. I've been on my knees or sitting all day long."

"Boilers?"

"That and one of the pressing machines. I had the damnedest time with that thing."

"What was wrong?" Milton asked, his pole and line silhouetted against the setting sun.

"Well, first of all, the pedal for the steam release was broken. And then, for some reason, the nozzle wasn't distributing the steam evenly. Turned out that the valve was bent."

"Did you replace it?"

"No. I just bent it back. Works fine now," Otto said, indicating the fine crease parting the leg of his trousers.

Across the slow moving water and through a cleft in the wall of trees on the opposite bank, the tin roof of a barn glinted in the sun. Milton narrowed his eyes through his glasses in the direction of the barn, noting that the sky was unmottled by clouds and that the trees flanking the barn appeared to be stirring.

Otto mopped his brow and pulled out a cigar from his breast pocket. Setting his pole on the ground, he lit the cigar. The smoke lingered about his eyes and under the brim of his hat. As he pulled away from it, the smoke seemed to trail him, neither hotter nor cooler than the air surrounding him.

"Last time I was here must have been five years ago," he started, waving the smoke away from his eyes. "I remember I came here with Helen and Julius and their little Billy. He couldn't have been but four or five years old. I remember it was early summer and he was coughing and couldn't breathe, and then later on they found out it was asthma.[3] And you know Helen. She just sat right down in the tall grass and all. I watched her pull in ten or twelve bass as fast as I could get the worms on the hooks."

"Rock bass?"

"Yeah, rock bass. But still, I'll tell you, it was probably ten fish in twenty minutes."

"I just don't like the way it tastes."

"Doesn't bother me at all."

"I don't like it."

"It ain't pheasant, but it'll do in a pinch."

"Yeah. Not for me."

"Yeah. Anyway. Helen can fish."

Milton nodded in agreement and stood up next to his brother on the boulder where he sat.

It was quiet for half an hour or so before Otto pulled in a fish. He was chuckling as the little fish flipped back and forth over the tall grasses on the shore. It was a bluegill, no bigger than four inches.

Milton looked at the back of Otto's broad straw hat as he swiftly removed the hook and set the bluegill back into the murky water. For a moment, Milton could have sworn it was his father. The deftness of Otto's movements, like a cat after its prey, all cloaked in calm and confidence and quiet, was exactly as it had been with his father. Milton and his father had spent countless hours together like that, fishing, observing the weather over Springfield.

"Come on. Let's move up the river a ways," Otto said as he crouched down to screw the cap back on the jar of nightcrawlers.

"You think it's going to be any better up there?"

Otto smiled under the lid of his hat. "Well, we've got try something. Can't leave here without dinner."

Together the two brothers trudged along the banks of the Sangamon River, making their way past trees that leaned precariously over the water and through the thick underbrush. They came upon an opening that was familiar to both of them. A muddy bank sloped up sharply about five feet to a nice grassy ledge from which they had fished many times before. The river was relatively narrow at that point in the river, so the water moved more swiftly through the channel.

Otto scrambled up the side of the bank and cast his line out into the middle of the river. He looked directly north across the river and above the line of trees. He was looking for birds or clouds. As he turned to face northwest, Otto sniffed the air.

"I think it's going to rain. Eventually."

Milton was standing twenty yards down the bank from Otto with his line in the water. "That's what they've been saying all summer."

Just then Otto's line got caught in the weeds on the bottom of the river. He walked toward Milton with his pole high in the air and descended the bank gingerly.

"Snag," he acknowledged and continued to walk down river close to the shore. Having successfully freed his line, Otto noticed several crawdads coming out of their holes near the shore. He set his pole down on a nearby rock and walked toward the spot where the crawdads appeared.

"Ever eat these?" Otto asked, holding one up to Milton.

"Crawdads? Sure, I've had crawdads." As he said this, a smile broke over his lips. Otto was back on his knees looking for more crawdads.

"One time I remember coming down here with Dad," Milton began, scratching his lean jaw. "I don't know, I must have been twelve or so. I think it was the year after Mom died. Dad and I came to this same spot. Dad was standing over there where your pole is. It was just after the Fourth of July, so I had some firecrackers left in my pocket. Dad was eating lunch somewhere and I wandered over to the river just like you now and saw all them crawdads coming out of their holes. So I lit one of the firecrackers and sent it down the crawdad hole and boom! Muddy water all over the place. All over my shirt and pants. I lit a couple more before Dad came screaming at me with a big stick. You can just picture it. Boom! Boom! His beard streaming. He runs at me just as I'm lighting the last firecracker. Boy, did he give me the devil that day."[4]

"I'll bet he did."

"I'll tell you. I had the biggest time that afternoon blowing all them crawdads out of them holes."

They laughed together, and soon they were busy fishing again, taking in the incredible noise of bugs as the sun began to set. They remained quiet and could sense the boundary of each other's solitude. By the time they left, it was growing dark. Otto had caught his four fish and Milton insisted that his brother take his fish as well. It was enough for Otto's whole family, which is all that Otto wanted from the little excursion in the first place.

At a great distance, clouds were forming in the northwest. But the rain that Otto had predicted never fell. The night was hot, and lightning flickered along the horizon as they walked back through the tall dry grass to the little dirt road.

As they headed up the road toward Otto's car, Milton turned to his brother in the dark and said, "Gosh, I miss the old man. I really do."

But Milton couldn't see Otto's face as it was turned toward the ground.

"Yep," Otto said. "Wish I could still talk to him sometimes."

IV

The drought persisted through August, so that by the end of the month, Otto had all but given up on the Sangamon River. It was just too hard to catch anything in this heat. But whenever he went out close to dusk, he was sure to hear a hundred frogs croaking along the banks of the river. The only things he liked eating more than a fine fillet of bass were tender frog legs. When Otto came inside the house holding a canvas sack with Paris printed on its side one evening, Anna knew that he wasn't planning to take their cleaning to work the next day.

"How about I take Junior and Frances Marie out with me and we'll go jigging frogs," Otto announced.[5] "I drove by the lagoon in Washington Park just after work and I could already hear them croaking."

After dinner, Otto and the kids waited until just before dark before loading up the car with the requisite equipment: flashlight, canvas sack and jig. The jig was the proud handiwork of Otto. Taking a five-foot section of a two-by-four, Otto had pounded three very long nails through the end of the board, thereby creating a rakelike tool with which to "jig" the frogs.

By the time Otto and the kids arrived at the lagoon, it was dark. Whether they lay in the shallows of the lagoon or in the willow branches, the frogs could be heard in every direction. Junior held the flashlight above the murky surface of the water littered with fresh nimbuses of algae where a few slow carp shook their gray scales into the heavy night air. Otto remembered a good spot for jigging was just down from the band shell on the water's edge. So they went there directly, but the commotion of their arrival chased off the frogs.

Washington Park lagoon and band shell, Springfield. On Sunday afternoons during the summer, Homer Mourntz, conductor of the Springfield Band, presented many concerts to large crowds seated in lawn chairs around the gardens. The pond was full of frogs and had a healthy duck population in the 1930s and 1940s.

"Turn that light off, Junior!"

Otto then led his children around to the other side of the lagoon, Junior holding the flashlight, and Frances Marie the canvas sack. The water was absolutely still. A vegetal reek clung to the muddy shoreline. They reached the spot where children usually fed the ducks during the day and stopped. It was a low, sloping bank of dark, almost gray mud that was entirely free of vegetation. The frogs were croaking so loud that Otto had to raise his voice above a whisper for instruction. Pointing to the thin line where the black of the mud went a little glossy, Otto said, "When I say, 'now,' I want you to shine the light right there, Junior. You be ready with the bag, Frances Marie."

In preparation for the hunt, Otto rested the jig against his leg and wiped his hands on his pants. "A little muggy down here, isn't it?"

He picked up the jig and extended it into the nether dark, its three gruesome nails parallel vectors pointing to tomorrow night's gourmet meal. Frances Marie stood ready with the open sack. The frogs were croaking as fast as the hunters' hearts were racing. "Now!" Otto intoned.

The light shone on a mire of frog flesh, glistening and momentarily stunned in the bright light of the flashlight. The jig came down on them, barely inflicting a puncture and with a swift jerk Otto jigged them into the bag.

"Now!" Otto pointed just to the left.

Again Otto was able to hook several frogs at once and transfer them directly into the bag.

"This isn't even fair," he laughed as Junior moved the light along the shore.

Within half of an hour, they had about thirty frogs, which would be enough for dinner the following evening. "Don't want to get too greedy," Otto said as they headed back toward the car.

Anna was sitting in the living room in her apron reading the evening paper. It had been a long day and her feet needed a rest. Otto stood in the kitchen doorway flanked by Junior and Frances Marie holding a sack of frogs.

"Put them in the sink and I'll take care of them after I'm done with the paper." Anna said.

As soon as Otto opened the bag, two of the frogs leapt out. "I didn't think they'd have anything left in them after that," Otto said to himself as he returned them to the sack and placed the sack in the sink.

"I'm going to go wash up in back," Otto announced, walking toward the garden hose.

In less than a minute, he could hear Anna calling him from the living room.

"What is it?" His hair was still dripping.

"There are two frogs hopping around the living room. Are you going to do anything about it?"

"Junior! Come help me catch these frogs," Otto said, and Junior appeared from behind the couch with one in his hand.

Otto searched the living room for the missing frog, stooped over and muttering to himself, "I thought I whacked them pretty good, but I guess not enough."

"Otto!"

"I'm looking for him!"

Anna was standing up from her chair. "There's got to be at least ten of them in here now."

"Ten of them! You've got to be kidding me. I thought I whacked them pretty good, but . . . Frances Marie! Go get that sack again."

The living room had become an upholstered terrarium with frogs leaping off the couch onto the coffee table, seeking sanctuary by the fireplace. At one point there was a frog in every chair in the living room. It was an hour before the whole family could retrieve them all. But even as he was dozing that night, Otto swore he heard a solitary croaking somewhere in the front of the house. It wasn't until after several searches through the living room that he realized he was hearing the frogs outside. Perhaps it was an amphibian lament for their cousins, cut up and cleaned in the kitchen sink, ready to be eaten tomorrow. And with this happy thought, Otto slept.

V

Later on that fall, Otto turned his attention to rabbit hunting. He still preferred nocturnal hunting, and with the shortening days he had more nighttime to go after the rabbits. The plan was still the same—Junior held the flashlight while Frances Marie sat in the back of the car with the canvas sack—the only difference now being that Otto held a .22 instead of a jig. They drove through the outer neighborhoods of Springfield, Leland Grove, where the lawns were much wider and the garden flowers more abundant. Otto would slow down the Studebaker to a crawl, his gun at his side, and the three of them would scan the gardens for any movement. Sometimes Otto would stand on the running board of the car and use the roof to steady his aim, and when he was sure he had one of those furry creatures in his sights, he would fire. Then Junior or Frances Marie would hop out of the car and retrieve their prey.[6] One Saturday, Carl found Otto at the Paris packing up nearly a dozen rabbits in the fur vault.

"We had a big time the other night. I've got more than I can handle here, Carl. Want any?"

"Oh no. I've still got two dozen quail from Quiver Beach last weekend," Carl said, and then, teasing his younger brother, added, "Besides, that's not real hunting what you do on those poor people's lawns."

Otto smiled. "OK, OK. I'll admit it's not the most noble profession, but I'll tell you, Carl, it's a lot of fun. When I'm sitting down to dinner and I see Frances Marie and little Junior digging into the hasenpfeffer that Anna's whipped up,[7] the only thing I remember is the thrill of the chase and the joy of the taste. Besides, Carl, what you do

‹ 405 ›

Willemore Avenue, 2003. This Springfield garden provides nourishment
for rabbits today. Otto's hunting expedition in the 1930s was in this neighborhood.

on Quiver Beach I wouldn't call hunting either. It seems more like
buying to me." Otto couldn't hold back his laughter now.

"Come on, Otto. Those river rats wouldn't recognize a quail if it
flew right in their face, let alone shoot it on the wing."

"Oh yeah. I forgot. You've got to have a tweed jacket to hunt quail."
Otto made a move to stroke the lapels of Carl's jacket, but was
quickly brushed aside.

"Well, I guess you won't be getting invitations to Quiver Beach any
more."

"Oh, come on, Carl. You know I'm just messing with you."

Carl smiled. "I know, I know."

"Hey listen. I was just about to head over to Hop and Elizabeth's
to unload a few of these. Sure you don't want a few? All kidding
aside."

"Sure. I'll take a couple. Listen, while you're at it, take some quail
for yourself and for Elizabeth."

"That's awfully nice, Carl."

Otto picked out eight quail from the ice chest.

"You're not going to be in tomorrow?" asked Carl.

Otto shook his head.

"See you Monday then."

VI

Otto drove straight over from the cleaners to Hop and Elizabeth's new place on Dial Court. Elizabeth was hanging laundry in the side yard when Otto came up the walk with a loaded sack.

"I brought some fresh game for you. Rabbit. Got it last night, but we got more than we can handle. Carl also sends his regards and a few quail from Quiver Beach."

"For a minute there I thought you were coming back with our dry cleaning from yesterday. I thought, Gosh, that's awfully quick."[8]

"No. No dry cleaning. We'll have that for you on Tuesday. For now the rabbit will have to do," Otto said.

"Well, that's very nice. Let me just get Hop. Hop!"

Hop stepped out the back door in shirtsleeves and a short, dark tie. "Hello Otto. How are you doing?"

"Well, I was just telling Elizabeth I brought by some rabbit, and Carl asked me to bring some quail."

"Well, that's awfully nice. I've been meaning to break out my .22 again soon. Just haven't had a chance," Hop said as he lit a cigarette.

Otto pulled out a cigar from his breast pocket and asked Hop for a light before resuming. "I took the kids out with me last night. Good time."

"Where'd you go?"

"Oh, you know. Just over on the West Side of town."

"Lots of luck, huh?"

Otto chuckled. "Do you know those big houses out by the country club near Mr. Kreider's house with those huge yards full of flowers? That area is rabbit heaven."

"I don't know him, but I know the place you're talking about."

A devious smile stretched across Otto's lips. "Well, we were out there last night. I'd say it was getting close to nine o'clock and I'd already gotten a dozen or so rabbits, but I thought, 'Why not? It's the end of the night. Let's see if we can get some chickens. So we drive out Chatham Road to the first farm past the turnoff to the airport. I switch off the headlights as we pull up. Junior and I head around the side yard, and sure enough, there are chickens all over the yard. Then all of a sudden I see something stirring in the bushes, so I take aim and fire. Of all the chickens in that yard, I had to shoot the guard rooster.

So he lets out this blood-curdling cry and that gets all the chickens going and soon they're raising hell, clucking and squawking while that rooster just won't quit. In a minute, all the lights in the house are on, and Junior and I are running across the front yard. We jump in the car and I can hear the old man stumble out of his house, dogs barking all around him now. I'll tell you, we had the biggest time."[9]

Hop was bent over with laughter. "Sounds like you had it coming."

"O yeah. I got a little greedy there. Just took a little scare to bring me back to my senses."

Elizabeth looked askance at Hop and said, "Like you never had it coming."

At which Hop flushed instantly.

"You've got something for me, old Hop? How about a story?"

Hop lit another cigarette and blew a thin trail of smoke. The colors of autumn littered the lawn around him, while Otto leaned against the chain-link fence to take in his story.

"Well, it wasn't exactly a come-uppance or anything," Hop began bashfully. "I just got a little excited. It was a couple of weeks ago and I had an itch to do some hunting. Put a little food on the table. I took little Frank with me and we drove just north of Sangamon River. I like to hunt on the fly, you know. It's much too hard for me to get out of the car and sit and wait in the fields for the doves to come, so I like to drive around and have little Frank go fetch 'em after I shoot them. So we were having a pretty good day; I had my shotgun with me and I probably had four doves at the time. Little Frank and I were in the middle of nowhere on a dirt road. I couldn't even tell you the name of the road. We'd been waiting there for quite a while when I saw a whole flock of doves heading our way, and wouldn't you know it, they all lighted about a quarter of a mile down the road on a telephone line. So I turn the car around, we are moving about two miles per hour toward the birds—little Frank is in back, mind you—and by the time I get close enough to take a shot, they take off flying toward us. So I reach between the front seats for the gun with my finger on the trigger planning to shoot our the opposite window, all in one movement."

"What happened?"

"I'll show you," Hop said as he hobbled over to their car. There was a crude makeshift patch barely covering an odd protrusion in the roof of the car. Hop removed the patch to reveal a hole blown clean through the roof.

"You mean to tell me you shot through the roof of your car?" Otto hit the hood several times just trying to contain his laughter.

Hop cracked a smile. "I don't know what got ahold of me. I was going to get a clean line on those doves as they went over. But I must have been a little excited. Because I fired up at them while the gun was still in the car—it all happened so fast. You should have heard the noise in the car when it went off. Frank and I couldn't hear for half an hour."[10]

"I'll say, Hop."

"This is the first time Elizabeth's mentioned it since it happened. Boy, was she fuming when I came home!"

"I'll bet."

"Say, do you think Milton could fix this?"

Otto rubbed his fingers over the hole. "If he can't, I'm sure he knows someone that can, and for cheap. Anyway, Hop, I was about to go over and play cards with the dummies.[11] Any interest?"

"No. Not now. I should probably head over to Milt's shop and see if he can fix it."

"OK. Good luck."

"Thanks for the rabbit, Otto."

"Anytime."

VII

As Carl pulled up in his Packard, the bell in the garage rang loudly. Milton jumped to his feet, startled. It was just after lunch on a Monday afternoon in March of 1932 with the low cloud cover over Springfield threatening a cold rain. Carl stepped out of his car in suit, tie, and topcoat. He marched over to Milton, who was blowing his hands in the cold. Milton stood at attention in his dark tie and white shirtsleeves, as if awaiting his brother's instructions.

"I've got two more trucks that need to be repaired. I need them done by tomorrow."

"Tomorrow?" Milton stuttered and looked around at all the cars on his lot. "What . . . What's the matter with them?"

"I don't know, you're the mechanic. You tell me. Otto will be by with the both of them later on this afternoon." And then, as he was

Dorothy and Milton Jr. in front of their father's garage,
with their home behind, circa 1935. A reason for moving to sunny Florida.

getting back into his car, Carl warned, "Remember, I need them by tomorrow."

Milton watched Carl drive down the street back toward Paris Cleaners before he returned to work.

When Otto showed up a few hours later, Milton asked him if he knew what was wrong.

"I'm not sure," Otto admitted, "but it could be the radiators."

"The radiators?" Milton's voice was clear. "How am I supposed to get new radiators for those cars by tomorrow morning?"

Otto shrugged his shoulders as Milton continued, "This is exactly the reason I don't want to work on his cars anymore. And now he just waltzes in here, tells me he needs his cars fixed by tomorrow. I need money to buy the parts"

All too familiar with such demands, Otto advised, "If you can't do it, you can't do it. What else can you say?"

Milton lowered his eyelids and nodded. "Just bring 'em around to the side of the . . ."

"Garage?" Otto said, and waved two other men from the cleaners to do so.

The following afternoon, Otto returned in his Studebaker with two of the delivery drivers from Paris. The trucks had been carefully parked outside the garage, and Milton stood waiting for his brother in the cold, smoking a cigarette.

"Hi, Milt."

Just by the curtness of his nod, Otto could tell that his brother was angry.

"Trouble?"

Milton took a deep breath and said, "No. No . . . trouble. Radiators, just like you said."

The delivery drivers thanked Milton for fixing the trucks so quickly and got back to work. Otto studied his brother's long face carefully. Concluding that something was seriously wrong, he asked, "You OK?"

Milton gazed into the empty space in front of him. "I'm OK. Just . . . just make sure Carl . . ."

"Carl?"

"Carl. Just make sure Carl pays his bill."

At which point Milton walked into the office where he kept his files, and returned with an itemized list of parts, labor, and bills past due. Otto looked over the bill and commented, "Wow. That's a lot of money, Milt. He owes you big."

"He's gonna put me in the poor house if he doesn't pay. Some of these bills are three months old. You know, Sonny's almost one now[12] . . . I can't afford to let my bills go like this."

VIII

Later on that day, as Milton was closing the garage for the night, the bell rang twice, loudly. Milton hurried to the office to see who it was. Before he could make out the shape of the car in the dark, there was a loud knock on his door. It could only be Carl. Without saying a word, Milton let his older brother into the office. It had gotten even colder since the afternoon so Carl brought in with him a blast of cold, wet air. Milton could hear Carl's voice but couldn't make out what his brother was saying. Beneath his fedora, Carl's face was distorted in anger. He was shouting and waving the itemized bill in his hand. And then, suddenly, his voice became as clear as a bell. "Are you trying to cheat me, Milton? Because I have no idea where you are coming up with all of these expenses."

Milton turned as pale as his uniform. "Cheat? Are you calling me a . . . cheater?"

Carl removed his glasses as if to regain his composure. "I'm not saying you're a cheater. You just need to look at your bill again, because I won't pay it. Believe me, Milton. Times aren't hard just for you. Paris is just barely staying afloat, and all of the sudden Otto hands me this bill. I couldn't believe it. I thought, there's no way Milton would try to overcharge me. There must be a mistake. So I suggest you review your bill and come back to me tomorrow with a fair price."

At that Carl turned around and walked out the door.

IX

The following weekend, Helen and her son Billy were in town visiting Hop and Elizabeth. Julius had to work all weekend repairing a road in southern Illinois, so Helen took the chance to visit the family. It was lonely in those little towns down toward St. Louis, and Billy almost never had anyone to play with because they never stayed in one place long enough for him to make friends. Only a few years separated Billy from Hop and Elizabeth's daughters, Tootie and Drusilla. It was good to be around people they knew. Besides, Helen wanted Billy to know his cousins, so even with their budget stretched thin, they came up on weekends whenever they had saved enough money for the journey.

On Sunday, both families went to a luncheon at one of the rural churches in Sangamon County—all you can eat, and free admission for children.[13] Elizabeth had invited Milton and Dorothy and little Sonny to meet them at the church. Helen hadn't been able to see Milton at Christmas and requested that they get together this time around. The basement of the church was packed when they arrived. Normally the children were allowed to play in the churchyard, but because it was raining, the children remained with their parents in the basement. After filling their plates with fried chicken and mashed potatoes, the three families found a long table in the corner of the basement and sat down to eat. Milton was dressed in his Sunday best, which included a houndstooth jacket his father had given him. Helen sat next to him, and despite the slightly worn appearance of her dress she looked as radiant as ever. Elizabeth sat across the table from her siblings with a modest hat perched on her head.

"I talked to Carl yesterday," Elizabeth began. "He mentioned some trouble between the two of you last week."

Milton looked up briefly and muttered, "No troubles."

"Really? That's odd, because he gave me the impression . . ."

"It's all been ironed out," Milton came back more forcibly. "No troubles."

"Come on, Milt," Helen elbowed her brother. "You can tell us."

After a long pause, Milton pushed his plate forward and said, "No troubles. It's all been ironed out."

"Milton, you mean to tell me that you can't talk to your own sisters?" Helen inquired casually, so as to avoid upsetting her brother further.

"He's my brother, so I'm not going to say anything."

Elizabeth shifted in her chair uncomfortably. "What happened?"

At this point, Milton set his knife and fork on his plate, with the chicken almost untouched. "Nothing happened. I just realized it's best for me not to work on Paris's trucks anymore. I told Carl that, and I'm going to tell Bill that I can't work on any of his trucks. I'm sorry, but if you need help with your cars, you'll have to go elsewhere. I know it sounds selfish, but I realized that it's the only fair way to handle the situation."

"Well, what is the situation?" Elizabeth asked. "Carl just told me you had a little squabble over the bill."

"Yeah. A little squabble. That's all. I just realized that it was best if I didn't work on any of the family's cars. Gets too confusing."

"What did he say to you?" Helen asked now.

"Nothing. I just decided on my own."[14]

X

That same week Milton drove over to Will Franke Cleaners at lunchtime. When he stepped inside, no one was standing at the front counter. In a moment, however, Eddie Ryan appeared in gray trousers and a white shirt with his sleeves rolled up to his elbows.

"Hi, Mr. Franke. How are you doing?"

"Oh, not too bad, Eddie. Not too bad."

"Fishing much lately?"

"Not enough," Milton smiled.

"Is there something I can do for you, Mr. Franke?"

Milton stuck his hands deep into the pockets of his coat and said, "I was looking for my brother."

"Sure thing, Mr. Franke. I think he's in back right now. If you wait a moment, I'll go ask for him."

When Bill returned to the front, he was giving Eddie instructions for a delivery that had to be done immediately. Bill looked harried. His suit and tie seemed too tight. As Eddie was heading toward the back of the store, he turned to Milton and said, "It was nice to see you again, Mr. Franke."

Milton waved and looked at Bill. "Great kid."

"Who? Eddie?"

Milton nodded.

"I'll tell you what, I couldn't run the place without him. He knows the machines, he knows the business, and he knows the trucks. I can trust him with anything."

There was a sudden lull in the conversation. Milton was clearly uncomfortable. "Speaking of trucks, I wanted to . . . talk to you about that."

"What about?"

"Is there somewhere more . . . private we can . . . talk?"

Bill looked alarmed. "Private? No, I'm sorry, Milt. I've got to stay up front in case in customers come in. But don't worry. Nobody's going to bother us. Go ahead. Tell me what's on your mind."

Milton drew a cigarette from his breast pocket. As he began fumbling through his pockets, Bill produced a box of matches from a drawer that was packed with items left in the pockets of clothes brought in to be cleaned. "Thanks," said Milton, and lit his cigarette, sighing as he exhaled, looking through the glass panes to the street as if it were a jury box about to pronounce a verdict. "I can't work on your trucks anymore, Bill."

Bill pulled on his tie somewhat nervously. "Why not?"

"I just can't. It's my decision. I can't do it anymore."

Bill looked utterly bewildered.

"No more family cars," Milton said. "It's best that way. I'm not going to work on anybody else's cars."

At this Bill's face relaxed into its more familiar contours. "Let me guess. This has something to do with Carl, doesn't it?"

Milton shook his head firmly.

"You mean to tell me that I have to lose my best mechanic because Carl was bossing you around and is slow on paying?"

Milton put out his cigarette in an ashtray near the door and said, "I didn't say that, Bill. I've been working on everybody's cars since I was at Romie Field's and I just realized that it gets too confusing working for family, and there are too many sore feelings. Remember that time I fixed one of your trucks and you came back the next day and the brakes were shot? You were sore at me, but I swear it wasn't my fault. Your brakes just gave out on you and it happened the day after I fixed it up. Anyway, I got to thinking, and I realized that family and business just don't mix. So I decided I'm not going to work on anybody's cars anymore."

Bill studied his younger brother's face carefully and was sure he'd never seen such resolve there before. "OK. Fair enough. But I did mean what I said before about you being the best mechanic."

Milton lowered his eyes. "I appreciate that, Bill."

"In fact," Bill smiled. "I have one last request. It's not a truck, and I'm sure it will only take five minutes."

"What is it?" Milton sighed.

"It's the pump on the tumbler."

"All right. But this is it."

"I promise," Bill said as he led his brother to the back of the plant.

XI

Special care must be taken at any dry cleaning plant to avoid an explosion. Dry cleaning solvent, a petroleum-based product, is especially flammable. Whenever the clothes are dried, the drying generates static electricity. If that charge is large enough and is discharged near the tumbler, it can cause the solvent to burst into flames. Therefore, the dryers are kept as far away from the solvent tumbler as possible.

In the autumn of 1932, there was a loud explosion on the first floor of Paris Cleaners.[15] Otto was cleaning rugs on the third floor when he heard the boom. Uncertain where the explosion had occurred, he immediately got up from his work and ran to the window. He cranked open a large section of windows, poked his head out, and looked down. When he saw nothing other than the grass and the vines climbing the south wall, Otto turned his gaze toward downtown, momentarily taking in the magnificent colors of autumn. There was an odd neatness to the trees from up there, perfectly formed and rounded and distinct. And then suddenly, out of the corner of his eye he noticed one, then two, then five workers running out of the building.

"Oh my God! The plant's on fire."

Otto ran back to where he had been working. He took up the rug he had been cleaning, rolled it up and ran toward the window. Letting it drop to the ground, he resumed rolling up other rugs, until Bud Vanderwall, one of the recent employees who worked on rugs on the third floor, came up the stairway.

"Otto, what are you doing? The tumbler on the first floor caught fire and exploded. We've got to get out of here."

"Give me a hand with these, Bud." Otto pointed to several rugs rolled up on the floor.

"Mr. Franke, we've got to go before the stairs catch fire."

"I know, Bud. This will take less than thirty seconds, we don't want to lose these rugs."

Sure enough, with Bud's assistance Otto was able to send those rugs out the window quickly.

"Let's go, Bud."

They ran down to the second floor where Minnie Masterson and Mae Hostick cleaned hats, gloves, and furs. Otto yelled out their names: "Minnie, Mae, where are you?" After calling them a second time, he was convinced that they had left the floor. A thick, black smoke was creeping up into the second floor, so Otto and Bud descended the stairs to the first floor, where the dry cleaning was done. They could feel the heat coming from the back of the plant. Otto stood by the pressing machines while Bud urged him to come outside.

"We've got to put those flames out," Otto insisted.

"The fire fighters are on their way, Otto."

Just then there was another explosion in back followed by the dull tong of the steel tumbler hitting the ground.

"Let's go!"

As Otto and Bud made it out of the building, Carl pulled up in his Packard.

"What's going on? What's happening?" Carl asked, in a panic.

"Firemen are on their way. Looks like one of the tumblers caught fire," Otto replied defensively.

Carl gave an angry glance at Otto. "And whose fault is that?"

Otto led his brother back toward his car. "If you knew the first thing about dry cleaning, you would know that fires are always a hazard. We've been lucky. We haven't had a fire in over twenty years. So our time has come. Let's deal with it."

Bud came running to where Otto and Carl were standing. "Mr. Franke, Mr. Franke, we couldn't find Hazel anywhere." Hazel Labrier was the head spotter and one of the senior key employees at Paris Cleaners.[16]

"Where in hell are those firefighters you called?" let out Otto.

"I talked to Hazel just as I was getting ready to run upstairs to get you, Otto. She's the one who told me there was a fire. I talked to her less than ten minutes ago," said Bud.

Otto then asked Bud, "You checked with everyone else? Did anyone else see her? Did anyone see her leave the building?" There were approximately twenty employees on the three floors of the building when the fire broke out.

Bud shook his head quickly. "No. No one has seen her. I checked with Annie Siebert, who works with her in spotting, and she said the two of them were working together when the explosion blew out the window in front of them. Annie ran but she hasn't seen Hazel since. Everyone else is outside and accounted for."

"She's gotta be back there. Bud, you take a head count by department to see if everyone is accounted for. I'll go back to find Hazel."

And then Otto headed toward the front of the building.

Simultaneously Bud and Carl called out to him: "Otto. Don't go in there!"

Otto kept walking. Carl ran behind him and, before he reached the door, warned him, "Just wait until the firemen get here. I don't want anybody else getting hurt. There's nothing you can do."

"That's Hazel in there."

Carl saw the bottom of Otto's boot disappearing into the gray and black smoke that was billowing out of the building. The pressers—

Minnie Skevokos, Stella Shevokos, Edna Nation, Bill Halpin, and Lonnie Beard—were all accounted for. Because the tumblers and dryers were kept in the back of the plant, all the pressers were able to evacuate the building easily once they heard the explosion.

Once inside, Otto quickly made his way to the back. By now the smoke hung thickly in the pressing room, but Otto knew the floor better than the back of his hand. Crouching low, he made his way toward a wall of flames with a wet rag over his nose and mouth.

"Hazel!" he shouted.

It was much clearer where the solvent had already burned off. There appeared to be no smoke whatsoever. It was all fire. The runnels of flame formed a massive web, floor to ceiling. It was as if the air itself were afire.

"Hazel!"

Remaining then close to the wall and low to the ground—this time on his hands and knees—Otto entered the second room and frantically called out for Hazel. The heat was intense. He could discern the shape of the solvent drum near the opposite wall.

"Hazel!"

He heard a cough. "Hazel!"

"I can't see anything. Where are you?" It was Hazel's voice calling from behind the drum.

"Stay low Hazel and crawl to your right until you hit the wall."

"OK."

"Now when you hit the wall, go left."

Within seconds they were out of the room. "Stay low and go straight to the door. Move! Move! Move!"

Otto followed Hazel through the thick smoke on his hands and knees. Behind him he could discern a strange clicking sound. "Go! Go!"

An eerie silence precipitated the third explosion. They were halfway across the pressing floor when it happened. Otto looked up and the smoke had suddenly cleared as if the fire were drawing a deep breath. It was all bright and luminous and he felt a tremendous pressure at his back. He stood up in the midst of that web of flames in order to let his feet catch up with the force at his back, but soon his legs gave out and the blast knocked him back to the ground. He heard voices coming from the door. It was bright there too, but its candescence was different. When he tried to get himself up from the floor, he found that he couldn't. His head slumped to the ground. It was warm and soft where he lay. And then quite suddenly he felt the strange pull of something, almost as if he had been hooked and was now being reeled in. It pulled him through the doorway and out the door of the plant and into the brightening day. It gently landed his body on a bed of grass. He opened his eyes to look for the fire trucks and the din of men moving about the building. But he saw none of that. What he saw was more explosive than the flames that had engulfed him: it was the clear autumn sky above Springfield.

XII

When Otto awoke several hours later, the first person he saw was Bud Vanderwall. Bud was smiling. Otto reached his hand toward Bud abruptly and felt as if something was tearing. The pain was sharp and burning. Then he heard Hazel's voice. "Don't move, Mr. Franke. The doctors said for you not to move."

At the mention of the word "doctor," Otto sat upright. The pain was searing. Bud leaned over him and gently laid him back down on the bed.

"What in hell happened to me?"

Bud looked at him, his hat in hand. "You're a hero, Otto. You're a real, live hero."

"Bud, what are you talking about?"

Hazel stepped forward. "You saved my life, Mr. Franke. There's no way I was coming out of that building on my own. I didn't know where I was and I couldn't see a thing."

All of it came back to him first slowly, then in a rush. "What happened to the building? Did they put the fire out?"

Bud came on again. "By the time you left for the hospital in the ambulance, they pretty much had the fire under control. It never even reached the second floor."

"How much damage, then?"

"I'm not sure, but Mr. Franke should be coming over pretty soon. He'll be able to tell you much better than I can."

Otto looked toward the window. Between the curtain and the window frame he could discern a thin sliver of the perfect blue sky.

"Could you open the curtain?"

As Hazel did so, a golden light flooded the room. It was the end of the day, and its last light shone through the golden oak leaves outside the hospital window.

"How did I get out of that building?" Otto suddenly asked.

"Well, I was standing at the front door with Mr. Franke when Hazel came running out," Bud told him.

"The flames never touched me," Hazel explained.

"Actually, no. The explosion came first, then Hazel came running out."

"That's how I remember it," Otto confirmed.

"Anyway, after she came running out," Bud resumed. "We came looking for you. We opened the doors and an awful lot of fire came pouring out the doors. I stuck my head in and saw the flames all around you. You were lying on the floor."

"And then what happened?"

"Well, it was too hot to do anything about it right then. To tell you the truth, I was afraid you were dead."

"So who came in and got me?"

Bud looked at Hazel and then turned back to Otto. "Nobody got you. I watched it all happen. You just got up and ran right out the door."

"You're saying that no one picked me up?"

"Nobody but yourself."

Otto looked again toward the window. It was strange; he could have sworn that someone pulled him up. "But I guess not," he told himself and wondered for a moment at the strangeness of the situation. He could have died in the fire; he should have died. As he looked down at his body, mostly covered with a yellowish Vaseline and some bandages, he remembered that it was his first instinct to find the man who had pulled him out of the fire. His burns were limited to the upper part of his body. He wanted to thank that man for not only saving his life, but also for showing him how to see the miraculous blue sky that surrounds us. As he considered Bud's account of the fire, he had no doubt of its accuracy. But he realized it appeared different to him, different to everyone. Half of life is finding the right person to ask how they have seen something. And only then, when we see it for what it is, can we perceive what really matters.

"Thank you, Mr. Franke. You saved my life." Hazel was getting choked up. Otto held her hands and watched all of his employees file into the room. Some of them brought flowers and pie while others brought beer and sandwiches. It was quite cramped in there, but as Bud explained, "We just wanted to come by and let you know how much we appreciate you, Mr. Franke. You're always looking out for us. It doesn't take a fire to show us that."

And then Hazel added, "And we're looking out for you."

XIII

Otto spent the next several weeks in the hospital recovering from his burns. The major concern was a secondary infection coming before new skin covered the burned areas. Anna and the kids came by every day after school and stayed with him until visiting hours were closed. Carl had come by too on the day of the fire, but hadn't been able to return because the fire damage had created so much additional work along with the usual flow of dry cleaning. Elizabeth, on her visits, made it clear to Otto that Carl was taking care of things at the cleaners. "Yes, I saw him last weekend, on Sunday night, he had been at the plant all day." But such concerns now seemed remote, and even a little silly, from the simple confines of Otto's room. It was such a joy to spend time with his children. What had he been doing all those years in which they were growing up? Frances Marie was practically an adult now, and Otto Jr. was working summers as a "young Franke in training" at the Paris. He rode his bicycle to the plant each day and did various jobs like watering the vines on the west side of the building, earning $3.50 per week. It wouldn't be long before they could be working together at Paris Cleaners. In the light of his accident, Otto couldn't help wondering how much he had missed in those twenty years of hard work, how he could have spent time with his family in the evening, listening to what was going on at school. There was so much life left to live, so much to live for.

As Otto's condition improved, the doctor encouraged visitors to cheer up the patient. One Saturday afternoon the door to his room burst open and six musicians bearing instruments formed a circle around his bed. They were his coworkers from the Paris. The four delivery truck drivers—Dewey Blane, Guy Morris, Sandy Ahers, and Roland Bradley—were dressed in ersatz German costumes and sang a medley of drinking songs. They then produced a plate of sauerbraten, red cabbage, and boiled potatoes. It was the best meal Otto had had since coming into the hospital. With German chocolate cake as dessert, Herman Pousch, the maintenance man, and Louis Stolsech,[17] the dry cleaner whose exploding machine had started the fire, presented Otto with an enormous get-well card from the Paris employees. The goodwill group finally left Otto at the end of the day with the hospital staff in close pursuit.

Bill and his family came by regularly too, usually bringing a sandwich or cookies. Otto and Bill started talking one afternoon when Bill dropped by on his way back from a delivery.

"I'll tell you, Bill. I've seen a lot in these past few weeks."

"You look well. Well rested. Your burns are healing up nicely. You're almost ready to go."

Otto leaned back in his bed, "Yeah, it feels good. Makes me think I've been working too much."

"You have! You've always worked too much. You should tell Carl you're going to take a few days off here and there."

"Well, I'm definitely not going in on Sundays anymore. We can get those boilers cleaned on Saturday."

Bill nodded as Otto continued: "You work just as hard as I do, though. And Milton, too. Boy I'll tell you something, I don't think there's ever been a time I've been over to his shop when he wasn't fixing something. He must put in a hundred hours a week over there."

"I know, I was over there earlier this morning. He was working on two cars, and a third customer was waiting to talk with Milt."

Otto smiled. "It's good to see you, Bill. You should come by the house more often. You don't need a fire for an excuse to see me."

"I'll try, Otto. It's hard though. You know that. There are a lot of people to watch out for these days. When I'm not pressing, I'm beating the bushes for more work."

"Yeah, Elizabeth told me you found some work up in Chicago. Chicago! I thought, how in hell did he end up there?"

"It's a funny story, but basically the mob had infiltrated the cleaners' unions in Chicago and were extorting money from the dry cleaners up there, so the added costs were getting passed on to the customers. They can't compete with our prices. So I set up a network of contacts in Chicago where we line up customers who parcel-post their dirty clothing to us in those laundry boxes their kids used for sending their clothes back to Mom from college. You know the ones

I'm talking about. We dry clean the clothes, press them, fold them, and mail them back. Even with mail costs, they're saving 50 percent by sending the stuff to us. The Abraham Lincoln train arrives from Chicago around eleven in the morning, and we have the clean clothing back on the train the following evening. That's only a four-day turnaround from the time the customer first sends it. We are now one of the biggest shippers of parcels in Springfield. Our business is bigger than ever. I've even had to hire extra help just to handle the work. We're probably the only business in Springfield hiring right now."

"I'll tell you," Otto laughed.

"And get this," Bill went on. "The unions heard about our program, and so they put us on the list to be organized. They sent an organizer—one of their tough guys—down on the train a month ago to get our employees in the union. Sam Lapinski, a police officer I happen to know, got word from Chicago that they were coming and warned me what was happening. When the union man got off the train, three detectives met him there and advised him that it would be healthier for him if he turned around and went back to Chicago."[18]

"Sounds like years of cleaning police uniforms free of charge finally paid off," Otto concluded. "You know, Carl's got his new scheme going now. He tells me that it's going to keep Paris profitable. It's a quota system. Anyone we hire now has to bring in a certain amount of business in each week or else you're out of a job."

"That seems kind of rough."

"Yeah, it is, but it's working. That's why we're still doing it. You know Carl, he's always finding ways."

Bill concluded on a darker note. "It seems like everybody's doing that these days. I'm barely using cash anymore. I'll bet that I have over twenty customers who run a tab for their cleaning. Frances and I go to their store for payment in kind of what they owe us. We're swapping for groceries, milk, tires, and gas, even bricklaying and carpentry. We even swap cleaning for dentistry with Dr. O'Hara over at Second and South Grand. People just don't have any cash."[19]

"I know it. I know it. See it everyday." Otto was looking out his window now at the clear day above Springfield.

As Bill was going toward the door, Otto said, "It was good to talk, Bill. Thanks for coming by."

Bill shook his hand warmly. "Get some rest."

XIV

After a two-week stay, Otto returned home from the hospital. The following day he went into Paris Cleaners to talk to the workers and to Carl. He received a standing ovation from the workers.[20] Just as the applause was dying down, Carl tapped him on the shoulder. "We've got a lot of work to do."

"Actually, Carl, I came to talk to you about that. The doctors told me I should take at least a week before I come back."

"A week! I don't think we can do that, Otto."

"What do you mean, Carl? Doctor's orders, after all."

"Well, doctor's orders or not, we've got a business to run."

Otto became adamant. "I'm telling you, Carl. I can't. Not yet."

Carl stormed around his office. Otto was certain that he would start yelling, but instead Carl riffled through the papers on his desk. Once he found the sought-after sheet, Carl held it up in front of his brother's face. "Do you see that?" he said, pointing to a column of numbers. "That's the bottom line. I can't pay you if you take any more time off."

"Kick a man while he's down," Otto said through his clenched jaw.

"Don't tell me you've already spent your inheritance. It's there to be used for a rainy day. You're fine! Dip into some of that."

"I won't touch that. That's for Frances Marie and Otto Jr. That's for their education."

Carl backed off. They both looked at each other. Indicating the burn under his shirtsleeves, Otto said, "I can't work like this, Carl. Not yet."

Carl calmly set his papers down on the desk and removed his glasses. "Look, Otto. I've got men and women lining up for a job here, but there's no work, there's no money. What can I do?"

Otto looked at this brother directly in the eye and conceded, "All right, Carl. I'll be back next week."

Money, of course, was tight, as it was for everyone, but Otto had held a job continuously since the crash of 1929, whereas many people that he knew hadn't fared as well. While Carl didn't pay him much, he did pay him by the hour, and considering the number of hours Otto worked, his take-home pay would have made many of those men standing in line at the soup kitchen very happy. He went home that day preparing himself for a long week of work ahead of him. When he sat down with his family for dinner, he seemed distracted. He felt fortunate to have a job. Work was all that he could think of now. Work and money. He would just have to be satisfied with fewer hours for his family than he had planned. As Junior passed him a plate of rolls for his pot roast, Otto saw Frances Marie buttering her bread.

"Go easy on the butter. That's 75 cents a pound."[21]

XV

Just before Christmas 1932, Julius Kinney came home late one evening to his two-room rented cottage. Billy was sleeping up front when Julius entered through the back door into the kitchen, where Helen was waiting for him. Standing by the stove and trying to warm up, he tried to suppress his cough. It was cold and wet all over southern Illinois.

"What a terrible day," he muttered through coughing jags.

Helen stood up to stroke his back. Noticing that his coat was nearly soaked through, she said, "You'd better take this off. Let me get you a blanket."

The floorboards of the kitchen creaked as she disappeared into the other room. Julius hovered over the stove in his wet work clothes and broad-brimmed fedora. Helen returned with a wool blanket and a sweater.

"I can't believe they had you work through this weather."

"Well, they want the road opened before Christmas," Julius came back through another coughing fit.

"Let me make you some hot coffee. I've already got water on the stove."

Because they had run out of coffee, Helen had to pour the hot water through old grounds. "I would have gone out and got more coffee today, but I only had enough for bacon and beans, and I thought I should get that before coffee."

"That's all right," Julius said as took the piping hot cup of brown water from her hands. "I just need to warm up a bit."

Helen pulled up two chairs by the old stove, and they sat down together. With the wool blanket draped over his head, Julius took in the steam of the coffee. Before long, he started coughing again.

"Oh, it's awful," he said when he finally emerged from under the blanket. Just then they heard Billy coughing in front.

"Daddy's home," Helen called out. "Go back to sleep, honey."

Julius set his coffee on the stove, stood up, and looked out the kitchen window. It was so dark that he could hardly distinguish the road from the trees. Not a soul to be found and theirs seemed to be the only light that burned for miles. Julius turned to Helen with that light in his eyes and declared, "I lost my job today. We finished the work and that's it . . . Billy's sick with asthma. I'm sick. My body's breaking down . . . We have to go."

"What do you mean?"

"Let's go to Arizona. Sure, we'll be poor, but at least we'll be dry and warm."

"But Julius. We don't have that kind of money."

"We'll sell all we have and use that for gas money and food and we'll just go. I can't stay around much longer. I don't know if I'll make it."

It was settled. Besides, even in the worst circumstances, Helen was always up for an adventure. They loaded up all of their worldly belongings in their 1926 Chevrolet, and with Billy and their dog, Bob, in the back seat, they drove north to Springfield to spend Christmas with the relatives and to say goodbye to everyone for the last time.

As usual, Elizabeth went the extra mile in making special preparations for Christmas dinner and a proper adieu for the Kinneys. She invited all the families over to her house; even Mayme, Charles, and Dorothy came to see Helen off. It was an altogether strange affair. Family members didn't quite know what to say, being surprised by the sudden announcement. But Elizabeth and Hop gladly bought some of the Kinneys' furniture, and Otto took the rest. Just before Helen and Julius left town, they drove to Otto's house to drop off the dining room table and chairs.[22] After they had moved the table into the dining room, Otto saw his sister and her husband to the door. "We'll miss you, Helen Rose. You take care of yourself."

"Oh, Otto. You make it sound like we'll never be back. I'll send you a postcard."

In fact, the Kinneys were rarely able to make it back to Springfield. The journey to Arizona was long, and when they ran out of money along the way, Julius had to find temporary work before they could move on. In February they settled in Continental, a small town south of Tucson. They rented a modest two-room structure with an outhouse out back. Unemployed for months, Julius got his first real job under the Civilian Conservation Corps government program, building a state park facility in the mountains near Tucson. Times were very lean. Billy attended a three-room schoolhouse that had no running water; forty children drank out of a dipper from a bucket of water. But at night, when he was sleeping in the little screened-in porch of their cottage, Billy breathed in the dry desert air and, without so much as a cough, slept peacefully.[23]

Hunting and fishing—a family practice over the years

Bill Kenney teaching Frank Long Jr. to shoot, circa 1938.

Will Franke fishing in Miami, Florida, circa 1940. Figure 10.9 Milton Franke Jr., a two-fisted fisherman, circa 1932.

Milton Franke Jr., a two-fisted fisherman, circa 1932.

Frank Long Jr. with the big one that didn't get away, circa 1932.

(TOP, LEFT) Milton Franke Jr., circa 1935. Another good day fishing, but hard on business at the garage.

(TOP, RIGHT) Elizabeth and Milton in the mid-1930s.

(BOTTOM, LEFT) Frank and Elizabeth after a long day of fishing.

(BOTTOM, RIGHT) Milton in the Everglades in the 1940s.

UNRAVELED

The day Otto died, my father took me to visit Otto's wife, Anna. Otto's death was the worst thing that had happened in my father's life and remained a black hole of guilt and pain for the entire family. I wrote this chapter in an effort to bring some understanding to this tragic event.

OBITUARY OF
Otto F. Franke , April 15,1942
Illinois State Journal
OTTO F. FRANKE ENDS HIS LIFE

Coroner W. E. Dragoo today was to hold an inquest into the death of Otto F. Franke, 51, 419 Adelia street, who died at 11:55 p.m., Tuesday, from a gunshot wound which police said was self-inflicted. Dragoo said the man was despondent because of ill health.

Franke had been associated in the cleaning business in Springfield for more than thirty years.

The victim's wife, Anna, told Detective Charles Walker and John Keegan she, her husband and son, Otto, Jr., spent the evening at home. At 11:20 p.m. Franke left the house, and a few seconds later, the wife and son heard the shot. They ran to the garage to find Franke slumped to the floor, a small caliber shotgun at his side. He was shot in the left side of his neck.

Otto Franke, circa 1935.

A native and lifelong resident of this city, Franke recently had been employed by a brother, Will Franke, who operates a cleaning establishment.

In addition to his wife and son, he is survived by a daughter, Mrs. Frances Buerket of this city; three brothers, Will and Carl of Springfield, and Milton, Miami, Fla.; three sisters, Mrs. Mayme Creighton, Champaign; Mrs. Helen Kinney, Tucson, Ariz., and Mrs. Elizabeth Long, city.

The body was removed to the Vancil funeral home.

I

"Did you read about Jake Schnepp this morning?" Bud Vanderwall asked Otto as they unrolled a large living room rug onto the floor. "It's a terrible thing," he added as he stooped over and began scrubbing.

Distracted by a buckle in the rug, Otto straightened his back and adjusted his glasses. "No, I didn't hear anything. What happened?"

"It was all over the *Journal* this morning."

"Yeah, I didn't get a chance to read the paper. I was running late."

Otto had stopped working and stood in the thin winter light coming through the large factory windows on the third floor of Paris Cleaners. The floorboards led his eye to a dozen or so rugs rolled up at the end of the room. It was the beginning of February 1933. Bud glanced up at Otto and said, "He went under."

"Went under? What do you mean?"

It was impossible not to notice the twitch beneath Otto's jawbone. Bud came back more softly, "Bankrupt. All those poor people lost their money."

Otto let a scrub brush fall to the ground. His jaw slackened and he held his mouth agape as if all the air had been pressed out of his lungs quite suddenly. Was he one of "those poor people?"

"Do you mean that *he* went under or that his *Savings and Loan* went under?"

Bud did not reply.

Removing his glasses slowly, Otto stared off at the low, mottled, almost granular sky that hung over Springfield. His eyes were dry and half-closed and he rubbed them calmly as if to peel this veil of a dream from them. But it was happening. It was actually happening to him. His heart beat like a funeral drum in his ribcage. "I'm ruined," he groaned.

In the shock of disbelief, Otto rotated his body mechanically and began to walk toward the staircase. When Bud asked him where he was going, Otto mumbled that he had some things to take care of and that he would be back soon. He drove downtown in his car to Schnepp's office where a crowd of people was gathered outside. A sign on the door of the office read "Closed," with no further explanation.

"That bastard stole us blind!"

There were shouts coming from the crowd, calling for Jake Schnepp's head. Otto stepped out of his car to join the fracas. Several policemen threatened the people with billy clubs, periodically calling out "Order!" But what were they to do? These people had just lost all of their money. There was no order left in the world, not when a family couldn't entrust its money to a Savings and Loan. Otto stood back now and watched the police struggle to corral the crowd away from

Schnepp's office. A particularly forlorn-looking man dressed in a business suit and topcoat was approaching. His face was ruddy, as if he'd been drinking since early in the morning.

"You can forget about that box of chocolates for your wife," he slurred.

"What do you mean?" Otto asked the stranger.

"Gone. It's all gone. Every last penny. And there's nothing you can do about it . . . Did you have any money in there?"

"My children's college tuition," Otto admitted.

The stranger's eyes sobered a bit and he looked at Otto with compassion. "I'm sorry."

Otto, however, could not accept his condolences. As the crowd thinned out, he convinced himself that there had to be some money left. He waited until the end of the day for Mr. Schnepp to show up. There was no way that good old Jake Schnepp could have lost all of Otto's money. Jake Schnepp wouldn't do that.

Someone did eventually show up by the end of the day, but it wasn't the person Otto was hoping to see. It was Carl. He knocked on the window of Otto's car.

"Can I come in?"

Otto motioned Carl over to the other side of the car and swung the door open for his brother. Carl kicked the slush off his galoshes into the street, climbed in, and closed the door firmly. Putting forward a gloved hand, he said, "I'm sorry, Otto."

There it was again. Those two words. What did they mean? What was Carl sorry about anyway? And what could *his* apology do?

"I'll talk to Mr. Schnepp tomorrow morning," said Carl.

There was genuine pity in Carl's eyes, but it was a pity Otto found despicable. "I know Jake Schnepp," said Otto. "He and I worked together on Dad's will."

Carl tried to put it gently: "I know you know him, but it makes no difference. I read about it in the paper this morning. His was just one of many Savings and Loans that have gone under. There just isn't enough cash to meet everyone's demand for cash at the same time. It's not just here, Otto. It's happening everywhere across the country. These are terrible times, Otto. The banks can't be trusted. The stock market can't be trusted. The only safe place for your money is cash at home under the mattress or property you own debt-free."

Carl D. Franke, circa 1932. Illinois State Historical Library.

"That's exactly what Mr. Schnepp told me about the property he invested in!" Otto objected.

"I'm sorry."

They sat together in the car while Otto mulled over Carl's condolence. Of all the possible twists of fate, this struck him as the most damning. To lose all that he had, to lose all that his father had given him, was like losing the benediction itself. And to have it torn from him by some money-grubbing friend was unbearable.

Carl offered him a cigar, but Otto couldn't look at his brother right now. He waved his hand in refusal and stared ahead at the door of Schnepp's office.

"Listen, why don't you bring Anna and the kids over for dinner on Sunday? I'll take out some pheasant from the freezer. What do you say?"

Otto nodded.

"See you tomorrow then," Carl said, patting Otto on the shoulder.

"Tomorrow . . ." Otto let the word roll off his tongue as if it were a question. What was tomorrow? Tomorrow had always been Frances and Junior. Tomorrow had always been the possibility of a little cottage north of Beardstown.

"Oh my God, what am I going to do?" Otto asked as if Carl was still sitting in the car next to him. Sleet was falling. Covering his head with a copy of the *State Register*, Otto got out of his car and ran down the block to a corner tavern. He ordered a beer and tried to warm himself.

By nine o'clock he was drunk. Stumbling out of the bar and back onto the street, Otto clung to a street lamp. The street was empty save for one other sorry soul shambling down the block and into a distant alley. Some ragpicker, Otto thought. Since he had entered the tavern, everything had frozen over, so that the sidewalk and the awnings of the nearby shops twinkled in the moon's eerie candescence. It was time to move on. On his way down the block, Otto lost his footing and fell in front of Jake Schnepp's building. As he looked up from the cement walk, the "Closed" sign that hung on the door filled his blurred eyes. Lying there in a stupor on the icy street, with not a soul coming to offer him a hand, Otto imagined that someone was behind that door, that he could discern a moving shadow behind the curtains of Schnepp's office. He lay there for what seemed like hours, following the shadow's every move. Convinced that it was Schnepp hiding in there, or one of his surrogates, Otto sat up, prepared to bang on the door, to insist that the shadow answer the knock in order to hear his grievance. "I have been unjustly robbed of all of my earthly riches," he wanted to say. "Where is my remuneration?" he would ask. "Even a man like me has recourse to the law."

Otto stood up on the ice at Schnepp's door, but before he could knock, he had to admire the incredible woodwork on Schnepp's door. In the very grains of the wood, he could discern the most exquisite, minute carvings. As he followed the grains of wood down the door, it was as if he were seeing a perfect reproduction of Springfield. The closer he looked, the more he could see. He found the house he grew up in on Adams Street, including the redbud in the front yard. There was even a carving of a factory on fire with people fleeing all sides of it. Until he read the sign on the factory, "Paris Cleaners," he had not considered that this masterly piece of woodwork was the image of his life.

But the very precision of the detail disturbed him. Otto knocked at the door with all his strength. There came only a vibration, a dull thud, as if the door were made of stone. Otto backed up so as to kick the door. "I know you're in there," he slurred. As he started toward the door, he slipped on the ice, fell on his face, and flew toward the door headfirst.

When his head hit the door, he heard a loud splitting sound. "At last," he thought. "I've made it through."

But he hadn't made it at all. The door hadn't budged. Instead, his head was bleeding profusely and he wondered if he was dying.

Finally, there was a low rumbling sound from within the office, and miraculously the door opened. A dull light shone from somewhere behind the wall, but it was impossible to locate its source. What little of it that reached the sidewalk where Otto lay was warm and inviting. Like a great infant, Otto then raised his wobbling head and made a gesture toward the door, at which a bearded figure appeared to bar the way. It was the shadow. Otto wiped the blood from his eyes and craned his head past the shadow's legs to see thousands of people waiting in line.

"Where do you think you are looking?" the figure upbraided him.

Otto tried to speak, but the shadow interrupted: "Don't even think about talking. It's not yours to ask questions. You've done enough already, staining the door with your blood and tears. Haven't you learned by now that there are proper ways to enter? What makes you any different from all these other people?"

And with that, the figure firmly closed the door. There was a lot of blood coming from his head now. What were once intricate carvings appeared as so many grains of wood. He looked up at the sign on the door: "Closed," it still read in bold letters.

Otto ran his hand through his bloody hair and looked at his hand. There was no blood. His hand was wet and very cold. He felt the top of his head and he looked at his hand again and again; there was no blood.

"Thank God, it was a dream."

Struggling to get on his feet, Otto held on to a stop sign for balance. His body trembled and heaved.

"I've got to get warm, " he said aloud, looking about the street. Everything was closed. Even the lights had gone off in the tavern. His head was pounding as the nearby streetlights flickered on the "Closed" sign above the door to Schnepp's office. The electric company seemed in on a cosmic conspiracy to shut Otto out of the civilized world. He started cackling at the terrible coincidence of it all, slapping his wet knees and heaving his shoulders. "Closed!" he shouted defiantly as staggered over to his car. "Closed!"

He drove home slowly. His wife had waited up for him.

"Where have you been?" Anna was exasperated. "I've been worried sick!"

"Shhh!" Otto whispered. The rhythm of her voice synchronized with the dull hammer in his head.

"Don't shush me."

"But the children," Otto whispered.

"What about them? Where were you when we all sat down to dinner tonight? Don't you dare shush me because of the children."

"O my," Otto teetered.

"Wonderful. You're drunk. You were out getting drunk. That's just wonderful."

She was sobbing now, and Otto was trembling all over. The warmth of their home hadn't yet penetrated his cold body. Anna could see him shaking in the mirror that hung above their dresser.

"What's wrong with you?"

"Cold," he chattered.

She stood up to feel his hands. "You're freezing."

She led him over to the bed and warmed his shoulders and hands. "Where have you been? I'm drawing you a bath."

Otto leaned forward and ran his hands through his hair. "Oh, it was awful. I went down to Schnepp's office after I heard the news—"

"What news?"

Otto looked up at his wife. He heard the pounding in his head again. His eyes felt as though they were sinking into the back of his skull.

"What news?" She was much more urgent.

He didn't have the heart to tell her. As the warmth finally reached his bones, he felt his body slacken. He rolled over to his side. "I just need to lie down. Please just let me lie down."

She asked him again, but it was too late; he was fast asleep.

The smell of sizzling bacon woke him the next morning. Indeed, it had all been a terrible nightmare, a nightmare waking up into a nightmare. But as he stirred in his warm bed, Otto noticed that his pant legs were still damp. Just as the savor of the bacon was making its way to his consciousness, Otto bolted upright in bed. "Bacon! What are we doing with bacon!" He ran down the hall and into the kitchen. Before he could register how badly his head was pounding, he saw the platter of bacon on the breakfast table.

"Do you want some eggs?" Anna asked.

Otto was still dazed. His skin looked sallow. "Do we really need all that bacon?"

Anna inspected her husband skeptically. "You look terrible."

Otto looked up at the clock; it was 7:45! "Why didn't you wake me up?"

"I tried, but you wouldn't get up."

"Great. That's just great."

Otto ran back into the bedroom. As he was struggling to get dressed, there was nothing he wanted more than to return to his bed. He could stay there all day under the warm sheets and not have to look at another boiler as long as he lived. Just then he heard his children calling good-bye to him from the kitchen.

"Oh, but I have to go."

Anna entered the bedroom in her apron. "Just where do you think you're going?"

"I'm late for work, honey."

"You're not going into work. Not after last night."

"I have to go. I really, really have to go."

But Anna wouldn't let him. She threw herself on the bed and started crying.

Closing his eyes, perhaps to avoid the look in his wife's eyes, perhaps in the hope that it was still a dream from which he would soon awaken, Otto told her, "Schnepp went bankrupt. We lost everything. We lost Frances Marie's college money. We lost Otto's college money. We lost that little bit we set aside. It's all gone." The tears that poured from his eyes felt like blood.

Anna sat upright on the bed and tried to say something, but words wouldn't come.

"Yes. It's done," Otto assured her through his tears. "It's all over. We're broke. We've got nothing, and if we're going to have something for dinner tonight I had better get going to work."

He left her in the bedroom. Without even a cup of coffee he drove to work. The noise of the pressing machines was defeaning and the

William G. Franke, circa 1935. Illinois State Historical Library.

earful he got from Carl an hour after he arrived at work was enough to make him throw in the towel. It was obvious that Carl had no money on deposit with Schnepp. Carl's financial security was as solid as the concrete floor of his cleaning plant. Otto let that resentment burn in him all morning; by lunchtime it was hatred. The only way to cool it down was to have a drink. During the lunch break he headed over to the tavern for a beer. It was the first time that day that he felt he had the strength to open his own eyes.[1]

II

A long-standing customer, Judge William Conway walked into Will Franke Cleaners with an armful of clothes on a Friday afternoon in September 1935. Bill was up front bagging clothes in his shirtsleeves and bow tie. "Hello, Judge Conway, what can I do for you this afternoon?"

The judge wore a heavy, distant expression on his face. "The usual, Mr. Franke. The usual."

Noticing the judge's distraction, Bill prodded gently, "How are things over in the county court?"

The judge had known Bill since shortly after Bill opened his own store, then still called Avenue Cleaners. He looked at Bill with a weary smile. "Well, I'll tell you something: too many criminals and not enough places to put them. It always makes my job interesting."

"Jails are filling up, huh?"

"Filling up? No. I'd say full. Have been filled up for a long time. No money to build new ones either."

"So what do you do with them?" Bill asked.

"Well, that's the trouble. Most of these boys aren't criminals; they are usually men in need and just got into a little trouble trying to make ends meet. I can't incarcerate them because there's no room in the jails, and we need the space for real criminals anyhow. So what I usually do with first-time offenders is put them on parole and send them back into a world where they can't find any meaningful work. Unfortunately, they'll come back to me a few months later for a petty crime committed in order to support their families. If I had a penny for every repeat offender, I'd be a rich man by now."

"That bad, is it?"

The judge explained further, "Particularly because the Peabody and Panther Creek coal mines are closed.[2] That's all those boys have known. They've been mining their entire lives. They don't have any savings. They lose their jobs. Pretty soon they're caught breaking into a bakery, stealing bread so their children can eat something for breakfast. What do you say to something like that? How can you blame a man for feeding his children? But if I don't punish them in some fashion, then the whole social structure breaks down."

Bill turned his eyes toward the street. He could see half a dozen men walking up and down the block with tattered hats and safety pins holding up their dignity. "Terrible, just terrible."

"Just today I had an interesting case involving two coal miners, Ike and Possum were their names. Friendly fellows caught trying to blow up a safe at a small company on the edge of town. It sounds bad, I know, but these fellows had no idea what they were doing. They had a little dynamite from the mines, and they thought they'd find a little easy money for their next meal. They aren't hardened criminals; I know they are good men, but there's nothing I can do for them."

"I'll tell you what, Judge," Bill announced, straightening his shoulders. "Bring them over here. I'll put them to work. I'll keep them off the streets, and we can give them some dignity."

The judge smiled at Bill's gesture. "That's very generous, Mr. Franke, but I know how badly we are all feeling it these days."

Bill stood firm. "I've got the work for them and I'd like to help them out. Send them over here if they could use the work."

The judge leaned over the counter and said, "They're coal miners, Mr. Franke, not cleaners."

"Send them over. It's fine. I've got the work."

"Well, as long as you're hiring, can I interest you in one more man? Now I say this only because he's such a decent man. His name's Gene Tomlin. Lithuanian. Coal miner. He got caught up in one of the recent brawls at the strike, so I had to put him on parole, but the worst part of it is that he's a family man and he's got no way to put food on the table. They have to wait in line at the soup kitchen all day. Anyway, I guarantee you that Gene Tomlin will be a real asset. Can I send him over too?"

Gene Tomlin arrived that very afternoon along with Ike and Possum. Before they knew it, all three were out back of the plant, cleaning up the garbage bins and washing the walls. All were coal miners, strong and used to work. Just by the disproportionate bulk of his forearms, it was evident that Gene had spent years chipping away at the earth's crust. While Ike and Possum were smaller than Gene, evidence of their time in the mines could be found in the wiry lines of muscle that ran up and down their arms.

"I'll pay by the hour as I long as I have work. But don't worry, I'll have plenty of work for you," Bill told them.

The very word "work" sounded unfamiliar to them. Ever since John L. Lewis had organized the mineworkers,[3] the owners used the lockout to squeeze the unions into lower hourly wages. Gene, Ike, and Possum had been among those who were often out of work. And for nearly a year they had stood in line at employment offices to no avail. The promise of work, even if only part-time, was like manna from heaven.

That Saturday morning, Bill met Ike and Possum in front of the plant at seven in the morning. Gene had been cleaning up in back and came around the corner where they stood.

Bill, in his suit and fedora, greeted them. "Let's get some coffee."

They stood at the counter of a little coffee shop on the other side of the street. "Do you want breakfast?" Bill asked Ike as he ordered some eggs.

Ike looked at him awkwardly, his brown hair falling over his eyes. Bill assured him, "Don't worry. It's my treat."

At which Possum promptly removed his cap, scratched his head and said, "Two? Over easy?"

Gene claimed to have eaten earlier, but took Bill up on his offer of coffee. As the four of them sat at the counter, Bill announced that they had to drive up to Chicago that day to pick up some coats. "Gene, can you drive a delivery truck?"

Gene nodded.

"OK. Possum, you will go with me, and Gene and Ike can follow us in the delivery truck. If you need to stop for any reason, honk or pull up alongside of us."

Taking two of the Will Franke Cleaners delivery trucks, they made their way to Chicago. It was a five-hour trip, and they stopped off for lunch before finding their destination.

"What do you need all them coats for anyway, Mr. Franke?" Possum asked him on the way to the warehouse on the southwest side of Chicago.

"They're good for trade," Bill began matter-of-factly. "Do you have a winter coat?"

"No."

"Exactly. Nor do a lot of people. But you're not going to go out and buy a coat. Too expensive, right? You'll never have the money. But you need a coat. These are fine winter coats but no one wants to buy them. An old friend called me and said they are mine if I take them off his racks—they have newer inventory due in tomorrow. The price is right, and I'll see that they get used. I can always trade them for a little work."

"What kind of work?"

"Oh, I've got all sorts of plans for work."

When they arrived at the warehouse, they loaded two trucks with what the proprietor generously called "last fall's winter wardrobe." Odd sized and itchy, the greatcoats looked as if they were punched by a machine from a bolt of wool made for army blankets. No cold could penetrate those woolly shields. They came in navy blue and army green and were utterly shapeless. "My dad's probably turning over in his grave right now at the very idea of these things," Bill said to Gene as they were loading them up. "But people don't need tailoring right now, they need coats." And then, as if declaring it a good day's work, Bill proclaimed, "These will do just fine."

When they got back to Springfield, Bill had them store the coats in the fur vault alongside the raccoon and fox coats that had been in storage in this unlikely tomb since the 1920s, relics of a golden age. Bill told the men each to pick out a coat for himself, explaining that "it will be getting cold soon." After a few minutes, Ike and Possum came out of the fur vault empty-handed.

"What's the matter?" Bill asked. "Couldn't find one that fit?"

Removing his crumpled driving cap, Possum rubbed the back of his head and bashfully admitted, "They fit just fine, Mr. Franke."

"You don't like the way they look?" Bill said holding up one of the shapeless pieces of wool.

"No, we like 'em, Mr. Franke," Ike joined in. "We like 'em fine. It's just that, well, we've been staying in the church basement lately and we don't exactly have a place to put our things."

"Just pick your coats out and tag them. And when it comes time that you need the coats, pick them up."

"That's awfully generous of you, Mr. Franke."

"Don't mention it. Now, listen. I'll need your help next week. Come by on Wednesday morning. We're going to take another trip. This time down to southern Illinois."

They nodded in agreement.

"Until then, here's your pay." Bill handed them five dollars each. "Get yourselves a nice dinner tonight."

The following Wednesday, all three men met Bill again in front of Will Franke Cleaners. A steady drizzle came down as they stood under the awning. "Did you get any breakfast?" Bill asked.

"We got some at the church," Ike replied as Bill handed him a raincoat and a pair of gloves.

"You'll need these today."

"Where are we going today, Mr. Franke?"

"To a brickyard downstate. Gene, why don't you and Ike drive down together. Possum and I will lead the way."

Ike and Gene looked at each other and hopped into a borrowed flatbed truck. When both trucks reached the brickyard, Bill adjusted his tie in the mirror of the delivery truck and asked the first man he saw where the manager was. They were led to a crude-looking shack in the middle of the brickyard. Inside, the floorboards seemed swollen with moisture. Water mixed with pitch dripped from the ceiling beam overhead.

"What can I do for you?" asked the manager.

"I understand that you have some end-run bricks that you'd like to get rid of," Bill said, cutting to the chase.

The manager pointed over to several pallets of bricks at the end of the yard. "Not much. Five hundred here, three hundred there, and some leftovers from the owner's new house."

"How much for two thousand?"

The manager was quick to point out that they didn't have two thousand bricks, unless the customer wanted to get into the regular runs.

"No. I'm interested in the end run. How much for all the bricks, odd lots, and the leftover yellow bricks? I'll clean out all your hard-to-sell stock."

"Oh, let's say thirty dollars and you can have whatever is there."

"I'll give you $25 and we'll load them ourselves, " Bill bargained.

"Sold! Take them road pavers and all the others including the leftover yellow bricks," said the manager.[4]

So Bill and his crew loaded up the trucks with two thousand bricks in the steady September rain. It was a hodgepodge of red and yellow bricks with some cinder block mixed in; the truckbeds sagged under their tremendous weight.

"What are you going to do with all them bricks, Mr. Franke?" Possum asked on their way back to Springfield.

"Save them for a rainy day," Bill smiled.

When they came into Springfield, Bill drove past his plant to a fenced-in yard next to the railroad tracks on Laurel Street.[5] Scattered about one end of the yard were rolls of tarpaper, a few pallets of bricks, and two used boilers sat on wood frames to keep them off the muddy water. At the opposite end, tin sheets leaned against the fence haphazardly, propped up with two slabs of limestone speckled with dirt.

Will Franke Cleaners, circa 1935.

"Let's tidy up those bricks into the corner and start unloading what we got today right next to them. I've got to get back to the plant for the rest of the afternoon. Possum, you drive me back and then come back and help them unload the rest of those bricks."

Bill kept the men working almost every day, whether tarring roofs, fetching more bricks, or salvaging used two-by-fours. He even had them haul out a thousand feet of used three-quarter-inch pipe from an old building. Whenever a factory closed down, Bill would send them down to reclaim floor joists or rafters before demolition.[6]

III

Otto rolled into Milton's garage during lunch on a Wednesday afternoon in late July 1936. It was hot, but winds from the northwest had blown all the humidity out of Springfield earlier in the day, and the few clouds that strayed over the city were almost a relief to the monotony of blue. Otto got out of his Studebaker chewing on an unlit cigar.

"Hi, Milt."

Milton looked up from the hood of the car he was working on. With the light coming through the greasy windows of the garage, he cut a lean profile.

"Still . . . running good?"

"This thing?" Otto said, running his index finger over the hood of his car. "Wouldn't trade it in for another."

Milton stretched a moment and carefully set his wrench down on a white towel next to the car. He removed his hat and scratched his head.

"Working?" Otto said, rolling up his sleeves.

"Little bit. Few things to do."

With his hair slightly disheveled and the shock of blond standing straight up in front, Milton looked just as he did when he was a boy.

"How old are you now?" Otto joked.

"Thirty-three going on seventy."

"Not seventy yet."

As they walked into the office, it became apparent that Otto was unusually well dressed. All he needed was a long beard to accompany the dark tie and gray vest and he would have been a dead ringer for his father.

"Hey, listen, Milt. We're going up to Carl's place this weekend. Probably head over to Beardstown for some fishing. You know, up to Willow Dell cottage north of Havana at Quiver Beach.[7] It's really nice for bass fishing."

"I know all about it."

"You know, the last time I was up there, I caught so many fish that I had to drop off a big load for Hop and Elizabeth. Boy, did they love those fish! I think Carl got a little mad at me for catching so many at his lodge. I usually get four to his one. Then Carl says to me, 'I really don't like fishing very much, hunting is more fun. It takes real skill to shoot birds on the wing. That's my sport.' But you know he sure likes to tell his dinner guests how skilled *he* was in catching the dinner that *we* caught."

Milton gave a laugh and scratched his head.

Grinning, Otto said, "Come on, Milt, let's go up together."

"No thanks."

And Milton turned back toward the garage to resume his work.

Otto leaned up against the side of his car and lit a cigar. The smoke, mingling with the smell of grease and gasoline, reminded him of cleaning boilers on Sundays.

"Why not, Milt?"

"Work to do."

"You've got work all the way until next Sunday?"

"I do. Just because of the Depression . . ." he stumbled momentarily, "doesn't mean people don't drive."

"I know, but that doesn't mean you have to fix all those cars. Let someone else at it." Otto suddenly adjusted his tone. "Come on, Milton. When's the last time we've been fishing together? You, Junior, and I can go out early Saturday morning."

Milton set his wrench on the engine block and regarded his brother. "I can't. I've got to work on Saturday."

Otto narrowed his gaze. He took a few quick puffs on his cigar and then asked, "What's the matter with you? You don't come around anymore. You're always working. You don't go fishing with me anymore—'cause I know you're still fishing. What's wrong?"

Milton stuttered, "Noth . . . Nothing."

An awkward silence ensued. Milton resumed work, while his brother paced behind the car. Otto finished his cigar. As he stamped it out, he asked, "How's Dorothy and Milton Jr.?"

Otto could hear Milton take a deep breath under the hood. He walked around the car to see his brother's face. Milton looked up at him, ran his hand across the top of his head, and said, "We're moving to Florida in the winter."

"What?"

"Yeah. Saving up. Gonna buy a little generator shop in Miami. Just do it all down there."[8]

"You're kidding me."

"No I'm not."

Otto took a few turns around the garage. He never dreamed that Milton would leave Springfield. He had a momentary impulse to smash the car with his open palm, just to see his own blood. There was no coherence to Otto's thoughts, just an overwhelming feeling of loss.

"Why?" he finally let out.

"It's time to go, Otto. Life will be easier there. No winter to deal with, and the cost of living is a fraction of what it costs us up here."

Otto had never heard his little brother speak so surely in his life.

"Pretty soon it's going to be just me and Carl," Otto said as he was walking away. His voice wavered.

"You can always come down, Otto," Milton called out. "You'll always have a place in our house. Or better yet, why don't you and the

"Buddies," circa 1939. *Left to right:* Otto, Milton, and Sonny.

family think about moving down. They say it's the best game fishing in the world. Down there we could go fishing every weekend and provide food for the table."

Otto tried to choke back the lump in his throat. "Yeah. That's what I heard."

They waved to each other as Otto drove away. Soon it would be autumn again and after that the long cold winter of Springfield. Otto looked at the sidewalks and alleys of the city as a staggering loneliness descended upon him. Milton had become his closest friend in the years since their father's death. It wasn't so much for their conversation as for a mutual respect and understanding. They shared a passion for fishing and a quiet persistence in everything they did. And Otto was glad to have Milton as an uncle to his son. The two brothers got along famously and often talked into the night on things mechanical.[9]

For the rest of the afternoon, Otto's mood of loneliness continued. He felt despair at the human predicament. Why shouldn't Milton go?

For that matter, why shouldn't anyone leave? There was nothing left in this town but a backache. More to the point, why hadn't he left himself? Leaving, of course, would mean going to the desert, going back to New Mexico. Otto remembered the high heat of the day and the sudden cooling after the sun had sunk behind the mountains outside Albuquerque. Only an hour into the night, and all that heat was gone. What an exquisite feeling, for someone who had spent his life toiling in the pressing room of a cleaners in Central Illinois.

Otto worked late that night. Otto Jr., who was still in high school,[10] stayed with him after all the others had left, bagging clothes. Of course, his family was why he stayed in Springfield, and he wouldn't have it any other way. What would he do in Florida anyway? He was too old to work for someone else, and he didn't feel comfortable with the idea of running a business by himself. Besides, even if he wanted to open his own dry cleaning shop down there, it would be impossible to secure a loan. If anything, money matters had gotten far worse since he had lost it all in the Savings and Loan. While he may have given up hope of an education for his children, he had not renounced the possibility of working his way back toward financial stability. There were absolutely no signs of improvement in the economy in 1936, but Paris Cleaners was surviving. It was his hope—indeed, his only hope—that his son might have a future there in the family business—that after he and Carl retired, there might be room for their two sons to run the business. In the end, however, and in the loneliness that comes with the sound of the last dryer turning the last batch of cleaning for the day, Otto recognized how truly distant this hope was. After all, Carl's son Coke had gone off to Lake Forest Academy, a prep school,[11] and college was a foregone conclusion. Besides, Otto had never made more than an hourly wage at Paris Cleaners, so why should he expect that his son, who would never go to college, would have anything other than a job at his uncle's cleaning plant? There was no way out; he had to consider the conspiracy of choices and circumstances that had led him to his present position: he was forty-four years old, had worked practically every day of his life, and didn't have a dime to show for it. Even worse: fate had conspired not only against him but against his children. What had they done to deserve his mistakes? The world was cold and becoming unendurable. The only warmth to be found was at the bottom of a glass.

As they closed the plant that night and Otto watched the glowing cinder of his cigar smolder to its own end, it was hard not to feel that things were somehow unraveling. First Mayme, then Helen, and now Milton—they had all chosen to move on. Even Elizabeth had tried to leave Springfield. Would he be next?

With a northwestern weather front threatening rain, the summer air had turned moist—those dry winds that had swept down from the San Mateo Mountains and crossed the Rio Grande, causing the curtain to flutter in the modest room Otto had kept in Albuquerque. A quick shower soaked the fields of tassled corn, and in minutes the sun made its last appearance of the day. Otto and Junior got into the car. Otto asked his son if he would like to go for a little drive before heading home.

"Sure," Junior said, and they drove west of the city toward Beardstown. The cornstalks stood almost eight feet tall that summer. Otto pulled over at a slight rise in the road, "just so we can get a look at things." The two of them sat in the car, looking over miles of cornfield. With the sun going down and the cooling that came across the land, a lacy haze rose above the corn.

"It's pretty sometimes," Otto said.

A sadness came over him at the thought of Milton's leaving. He knew his brother would be much better off in Florida without the pressure of his family, the lure of all the fishing in the world at his fingertips. Of course it would be better, and of course he would miss his brother. But that wasn't it. The city lay quiet in the evening sun, and the distant whistle of a train blew like the horn of judgment over the world. It was all this coming and going, all this falling apart, the world that wouldn't stop moving. No one ever stayed around long enough to make anything last. It was he who never moved with the world, who never got away.

"Looks like your Uncle Milt and his family are moving to Florida after Christmas," said Otto. His words sounded like a death knell.

"For good?" Junior asked as his father turned the car back toward Springfield.

"For good."

On the way home, Otto asked his son to drop him off at a tavern for a drink.

"One more before I go."

Otto Jr., not being a drinker, stayed in the car. About an hour later, as they drove home, the father talked with his son about work and fishing.

IV

After World War II broke out in Europe in 1939, an ambivalent mood hung over the German American community in Springfield. Like Frank Franke, most of the German immigrants from the Great Wave of the 1880s and 1890s had already died. More Germans came in the first two decades of the twentieth century, but most German immigration stopped altogether after World War I. While there was no evidence of the shame and fear that had come in 1917, people at the German Methodist church would talk of cousins back in Germany with a wary shake of their heads. Reports of the war came every day, but most people, still struggling to make ends meet, felt quite distant from it. More to the point, the strength and solidarity of the German American community had been diminished, for many of its members had moved away from Vinegar Hill. Everything changed, however, after the Japanese bombed Pearl Harbor. Ambivalence about going to war vanished after that.

Otto's drinking increased significantly after Milton left. Without a friend to bide the time with in the evenings, he took to sitting in the taverns more and more frequently. Sometimes he would sit and chat with the ladies at the bar. This caused some talk in the family, but nothing ever seemed to come of it. More often than not, he preferred to be alone with his thoughts and to soothe them with drink. Junior, not being a drinker himself, would often drive the car and wait patiently outside to take his father home. Some nights Otto would drink at Martin's Tavern at Jefferson and Amos, other nights at Ballwig's Tavern on Ash between Yale Boulevard and Eleventh. He liked to finish the night at Wyhof's Tavern at Eleventh and Laurel.[12]

Money had become so scarce that late one evening in 1939 Otto drove over to his newly wedded daughter's house and asked her to sign papers that would allow him to take the cash value of her life insurance policy.[13] This was a policy that Otto had purchased for Frances Marie as a child.

After the first of the year in 1940, Otto spent a week in Miami with Milton.[14] They fished and talked about old times. It was good medicine for Otto to get away and to be with his beloved brother. By the fall of 1940, there was no longer any hope that Otto or his son would ever get a share of the family business, for Carl's son Coke, after two years at the University of Michigan, had left school and had come home to work with his father.

Otto was sitting at Ballwig's one evening in the fall of 1941, nursing a beer, when he decided to pay Carl a visit. He left the tavern and in the orangish glow of the street lamp gazed at his hands. Thickened with calluses, those laboring hands looked like two old baseball mitts from years of hard use. His heart sank at the thought of how old he had become and how little he had accomplished. His back was stiff, his legs were sore, and he had another day of work to look forward to.

He pulled up in front of Carl's house and walked up the driveway, in which several cars were parked. Dorothy and Carl were obviously entertaining that evening. He rang the doorbell and was greeted by Dorothy.

"Hello Otto. Surprised to see you here."

"Yes . . . I was hoping to talk to Carl."

When Carl came to the door, it was clear that he was angry. "We have guests, Otto. What do you want?"

"I just wanted to talk. Can we talk?"

"Like I said, we have guests."

"Can we talk after they leave?"

"No. I don't know when they are leaving."

"Meet me tomorrow at the plant then."

Carl laughed nervously. "I can't. We're going to the cottage tomorrow."

"Hunting?"

"Yes, hunting pheasant. Now, I have to go. I'm with important guests who are our customers."

"As long as we're on the subject of the business, I just wanted to know why you never made me a partner. I've worked there my whole life and I'm still making worker's wages. You know, Carl, I'm only making forty-nine dollars a week.[15] I've built that business with my own two hands."

With his body draped on the doorframe, it was as if Otto were carrying a loaded gun. But Carl would have none of it.

"Otto, this is neither the time nor the place to discuss these matters. Besides, you already know the answer." Carl then shut the front door quietly but firmly.

Otto never did get an answer from Carl. The following Monday the two brothers resumed their business as if no such conversation had taken place. The conversation did, however, take root in the hearts of both brothers. For Otto, it merely reinforced an attitude that he had held for years: Carl was selfish, ungenerous, and—given Otto's financial woes—took advantage of Otto's skill and his labor. For Carl, it confirmed a suspicion he'd had for a while. As they were speaking the week before on his front porch, Carl could smell the beer on his brother's breath. Otto's productivity had been slowing down, and Carl had noted this with some disapproval. Now he was sure he had the answer: his brother was a drunk. Carl had guided Paris Cleaners through the Depression with exceptional foresight and resilience. His insistence that each worker bring in a set amount of business had paid off; Paris Cleaners was alive and well where many businesses had failed. Whenever someone criticized his policy, and often it was Otto, Carl was quick to point out that all those people still had jobs, and their families were sitting down to eat every night. It was a point with which it was hard to argue. Paris Cleaners kept a lot of people employed during the most difficult years of the Depression and now that the economy was showing some life, Carl wasn't going to let an employee with a drinking problem foul up the business, even if it was his brother. It would seem unfair to the other employees if he showed such favoritism. So he kept an eye on his brother.

And to some extent it was true; Otto had been drinking more. Now that work had become little more to him than waiting for the end of the day, Otto found it easier to get through it with the promise of a drink afterwards. He didn't drink nearly as much as some of the regulars at the tavern, but he would stop off almost every night after work for a drink or two. Sometimes, on the weekends especially, this might turn to four or five. Life had become dreary and toilsome. Even the old pleasures of fishing were beginning to elude him.

He and Carl argued more often at work, and they did so in front of the other employees. In the past, Otto had kept his arguments with Carl behind closed doors. But now he would question his brother's decisions openly and, by doing so, tacitly question his authority.

What did he care at this point? It wasn't as if he were going to gain anything by doing things the other way. He had already done that and it had gotten nowhere. His defiance was an offense to which Carl would never grow accustomed. He knew that Otto wanted a piece of the business, but it wasn't his to have. The will made things totally clear: Carl and Carl alone had been responsible for Paris Cleaners' debt. His father's last wish and last gift was to free him of his debt. It was that simple. There was no question about ownership or fairness. Besides, Otto had received more than his fair share in the will. That he had invested unwisely was unfortunate, but it wasn't Carl's fault, nor was it his responsibility. He was responsible for seeing Paris Cleaners into the future. As a result, he found Otto's arguments tiresome and a waste of time.

In December of 1941, a week after the attack on Pearl Harbor, Otto came back from lunch at Martin's Tavern. He'd had a few beers with his sandwich. Carl told him to personally ensure that a hotel order got done before the end of the day, a Friday.

"We don't have to get that done until next Tuesday," said Otto.

"Yes, we do. We have to get that job done this afternoon before we leave."

"Before we leave? Why don't you just call a spade a spade and say before *I* leave?"

Carl had no patience for Otto's bickering that afternoon. "Just get it done."

"No. I'm not going to do it." Otto stood up waiting for Carl's threat.

"What?"

"I'm not going to do it because it doesn't make sense to do that big of a job before we clean the boilers."

Carl stood an inch away from his brother's face and smelled the alcohol on Otto's breath. "Have you been drinking?"

Otto was taken aback. "No," he said unhesitatingly.

"You smell like a damned distillery. Have you been drinking?"

Otto stammered for a moment but gave Carl no conclusive reply.

"You're pathetic. Get out of here right now. I won't have any drunks working for me. You're fired."

"What?" Otto felt his throat in the pit of his stomach.

"You heard me. You're fired. Leave this place at once."

It was the most humiliating moment of his life. Otto knew how deadly serious his brother was just by the look in his eye. He could tell too by Carl's remorseless tone that he had long been thinking about his dismissal. Otto thought his knees might give way under the weight of his shame as he walked out of the Paris plant. If only he could have been alone at that moment to howl in the wilderness of his fate. But news travels quickly, and before he staggered toward the door, his son was opening it for him. They left the Paris together for the last time and stepped into the cruel light of the day.[16]

V

"Yes, Carl just fired him," Elizabeth told Bill over Sunday lunch. Their two families usually shared a meal after church. The kids were old enough to sit at a separate table while the adults drank coffee and talked.[17]

"That's terrible," Bill replied. "When did it happen?"

"Oh, I guess it happened the middle of last week. We saw Carl and Dorothy and their kids yesterday. That's when he told me." Before her brother could say anything, Elizabeth added, "He was pretty shaken up."

"Shaken up?" Bill couldn't believe it. "Poor Carl. He had to fire his own brother. His own brother who broke his back building that business."

"I know, I know. It's terrible. But like I said, Carl seemed really upset. He said he felt that he had to do it, that Otto had given him no choice."

"That's ridiculous. If it's Carl's business, as he always said it was, then he always has a choice, doesn't he? What kind of a person fires his own brother?"

Elizabeth was upset. "Look Bill, I'm just telling you what he told me. I'm telling you what I saw. I know you can't stand the sight of him, but I know him a lot better than you and I'm telling you that it was a very difficult decision."

"Well, Carl always has been one for appearances," Bill snapped.

Elizabeth sighed. She was doing her best to present Carl's case. "He told me that Otto had been drinking on the job. That's dangerous! You know that. Carl said he couldn't, in good conscience, allow his brother to continue working at Paris Cleaners. It was a hazard to the other workers, he said. Carl even blamed Otto for the fire eight years ago. He said he couldn't play favorites just because Otto was his brother."

"That's preposterous. Carl just put his own brother on the street! His own brother who's worked for him for almost thirty years! I'm sorry, Elizabeth, but that's unconscionable."

"It's terrible, I know, but what was he going to do? Carl was in a real spot. Otto's drinking was affecting his work. What was he going to do?"

"Well, I know what I'm going to do," Bill declared.

The very next day he asked Otto if he would work at Will Franke Cleaners. Bill had never seen his brother looking so grim, so defeated. Otto couldn't even respond to Bill's offer.

"I could really use your knowledge and your experience, Otto. I know how good you are. I could have used your talent a long time ago. I want you in charge of the cleaning room . . . You know more about working with solvent than anyone else in town."

Otto's lip quivered. "Can you help Junior out too?"

"Absolutely. Two Ottos are better than one."

Otto and his son started working at Will Franke Cleaners the next day. When Carl heard about this from Elizabeth, he was relieved. There was no way for Otto to come back to Paris Cleaners. Otto would never accept the offer, even if Carl did ask him back. But Carl worried about his brother, nonetheless, and when he learned that Bill had hired him, he concluded that it was for the best.

VI

At the time of Otto's hiring, Bill's oldest son, Bob, had just enlisted in the U.S. Army Air Corps, and was in flight engineering school. Bob had worked with his father, but his first love was aviation, and on December 7, 1941, he was employed as a mechanic at the Capital Airport in Springfield.[18] Bill normally had a staff of twelve, but since Eddie Ryan had left a few years before to join the police force, Will Franke Cleaners was without a floor manager.[19] So Otto and Junior were welcome additions.

Versatility was essential in working for Bill. He had survived the Depression primarily by scraping work together, making trades and loans for businesses, and even putting up buildings. In this way he continued in the entrepreneurial spirit of his father. But the connection ended there. Bill would just as often begin a project in order to create work for other people as to make a return on his investment. People were what mattered to him at this point in his life, and he knew almost every one in town. He knew all the police officers and firemen. He knew the judges and the bankers. Bill rarely turned away any of those in need whom Judge Conway referred to him, because he had so many projects going at once.

Whenever he had a construction job, Bill would ask Ike and Possum to head up a crew that he had cobbled together from men sent by the judge. They would take all the end-run bricks and all the scraps of wood, shingles, and tarpaper that Bill kept in his yard on Laurel, and use them to put up a building. Simple in construction, crude in their multicolored assemblage of bricks, these buildings were nonetheless temples of financial salvation for people who hadn't been able to find work for years. It was a relatively simple formula. If he saw the need for a specific retail operation, Bill then looked for a person whom he could trust to work hard. After covering direct expenses, he split revenues on a 50/50 basis. Throughout the Depression, he undertook a score of joint ventures of this kind, including several restaurants, a donut shop, a miniature golf course, a shoe repair shop, a package liquor store, and a Wonder Freeze Ice Cream outlet. He even put up a few single-family homes, mostly brick bungalows.[20] He never felt as if he were doing these things out of a sense of duty. Bill understood how important it was to have work, to go home at the end of the day feeling you had accomplished something. But more than that, he liked having his hands in several pots at once. And the results were more than gratifying: he loved seeing people turn their lives around, he loved the bargaining, he loved seeing something come of virtually nothing. Above all, he loved the workers.[21]

All the while, Will Franke Cleaners was as busy as ever. If Bill was working on a construction project, he felt safe knowing that Otto was on the job at the cleaning plant. He had hired Otto not so much out of sympathy as for assistance. But as the holidays passed by, Bill couldn't help noticing that his brother was a changed man. His work was fine; Otto's mechanical knowledge was an asset to any business. But his mood was worrying. He seemed passive and distant, nearly unapproachable. He just went about his work and rarely spoke. When-

Will Franke Annual Employees Dinner at the Mill Tavern Restaurant, circa 1940.

ever Bill asked his brother how he was doing, Otto would shift the conversation to other matters or pretend he didn't understand what was being asked.

VII

Shortly after New Year's, Bill approached Junior and asked, "Otto, how would you like to drive a truck?"

"Well, I guess I could do that," replied Junior.

Bill showed him one of his blue-paneled Chevrolet delivery trucks, and Otto Jr. became a delivery driver.

"Otto, we can't make payroll until you go deliver those clothes this afternoon," the bookkeeper Alice Bridge would often say to him on Friday afternoons in the first months of 1942. When Junior had made his deliveries and returned with the money, Alice would always conclude, "Good. We can make payroll now." Money was tight, but the employees always got paid.[22]

Will Franke Cleaners had five branches at this time, and their downtown branch was at Sixth and Capital. One Friday afternoon, Bill went to the Sixth and Capital store to fill in for Fay Fisher, the branch manager, who had a doctor's appointment. Junior drove Bill downtown, since there were clothes there to pick up. As they arrived in the store, Bill went over to Louie Dickerson's shoe shop, just behind the cleaning branch. Bill and Louie were partners in the shoe repair business. As Junior was loading the truck, he noticed Carl making his way through the winter slush in a pair of galoshes and walking into Dickerson's.

Bill and Carl hadn't seen one another since the reading of the will in 1930. Junior, like everyone in the Franke family, was well aware of the trouble between Bill and Carl. "Like fire and dynamite, it's best to keep those two away from each other," his father had always told him. Curious about the sparks that would undoubtedly fly from an encounter between them, Junior cautiously made his way into the rear of the store, where Dickerson was standing and looking at the two brothers.

"I've been meaning to talk to you, Bill. You know your sister Helen is not doing too well down in Arizona," Carl announced formally.

"What do you mean, 'not doing too well'?" Just the sound of Carl's voice was irritating to Bill.

Carl said, "Well, I think we ought to send her a little money."

That Carl was only now suggesting that he should take care of his own sister offended Bill. Helen had worked tirelessly for *eight* years at the inception of the Paris Cleaners as an hourly employee. She too should have been considered a joint partner with the rest of the family who worked there. In fact, some of her siblings had been sending her money from their meager resources for years. Life in Arizona was hard. Although Julius had found a job with the Civilian Conservation Corps, his health was failing and he wasn't able to work enough to keep bread on the table. Helen had needed help just to see Billy through high school. Now Carl, with wealth greater than all of his siblings combined, was asking them to contribute to his newfound sense of charity. Desperate poverty had forced Helen to ask for money from Carl, and the idea that she had to stoop so low enraged Bill. A man who had fired his own brother after nearly thirty years on the job was suggesting that Bill should send a little money to his poor sister in Arizona. Bill saw in Carl's face the look of righteousness he had so despised as teenager. It filled him with an anger he hadn't felt in years. He let Carl have it.

"Carl, I am going to tell you something," he began very deliberately. "I'm going to tell you something. Our sister has been in need of extra money since she left Springfield. She lived in a house with a dirt floor. Her son Billy went to a one-room school with a single toilet out back and a water bucket for drinking. I've been sending Helen money every year for as long as she's been out there. Don't tell me to chip in just because it finally occurred to you to help her out. You should have been helping her since she and Julius left town without two dollars to rub together. Now, get out of this place and don't ever come back!"

Carl was embarrassed, profoundly so. He looked at Louie Dickerson apologetically, but he found no sympathy there. Louie was an old friend of Bill's; they had helped each other through the Depression, trading shoes for dry cleaning or for coats. Bill also showed him how to trade shoes for groceries and other necessities of life. Bill had put up the capital for all of Louie's shoe repair machinery. The two men trusted each other. Louie returned a blank, neutral gaze to Carl, who walked out of the store.

"The nerve of that man. The nerve . . ." Bill muttered. Louie stood by silently. Bill hadn't realized how deep was his contempt for Carl. The last time he had spoken to Carl was outside Schnepp's office after the hearing of the will ten years ago. He had decided then that there was no alternative to cutting off all contact with Carl; his brother was simply too cruel and elicited an antagonism that Bill couldn't tolerate. By firing Otto, Carl had forfeited all respect, renouncing decency, honor, and filial responsibility. More to the point, Bill thought, the firing went against everything their father had taught them. When Frances had pointed out that Bill had never been obedient to his father, Bill had protested, "But I never claimed obedience. Carl's the one who is so quick to claim the values and virtues of our father. Dad's turning over in his grave right now. There is no way he would ever have allowed Carl to fire Otto. Not under any circumstances." Carl, he concluded, was a hypocrite with no commitment to the principles that undergirded his livelihood. For Carl to walk into the shoe store donning the mantle of decency and play the part of the concerned patriarch sickened him. He wanted to run down the street after his brother shouting, "Hypocrite! Hypocrite!"

But with Louie Dickerson looking at him silent as a stone, Bill finally came to his senses and regretted his shouting.

"I'm sorry, Louie. I've got no right coming in here, making that kind of noise."

Louie looked at his friend with compassion. "Family troubles. I know what that's like. Don't worry about it, Mr. Franke."

"Well, I'm terribly sorry to put you through it."

Bill remembered that he had some shoes being repaired. "Do you have my shoes?"

Louie returned with the shoes. When Bill pulled out his wallet, Louie feigned offense, declaring, "You will never be allowed to pay for shoes from me."

Bill smiled. "I'm sure that I just kept a good customer out of your store by making a scene. The least I can do is pay for my shoes."

Louie refused. "What's one customer? Why should I trade the generosity of friendship for one customer?"

Bill shook his hand and walked back to the downtown plant.

Later that afternoon, he drove back with Junior to the plant where Alice Bridge was waiting; they would be able to meet payroll now. When Bill closed up that night, he vowed never to speak to his brother again.

VIII

On January 21, 1942, Otto made his way to the cemetery in the cold and the snow. He visited his parent's grave every year on the anniversary of his father's death. It was a small, meaningful ritual he had come to almost by accident, but now he found it was a useful way to set his emotional clock. This year's visit was merely another pause on what had become for him a treadmill of failure and humiliation. He wandered among the graves looking at the names and dates carved into stone. They were as anonymous to him as the graves in a military cemetery. As he came to his parents' grave, he said a short prayer for their souls in heaven. Contemplating the dates on their headstones, he marveled at the significance they had once held for him. It almost made him weep to think that just eleven years earlier he had found a new life, had received his father's blessing by connecting a few dates. "What is it to me now," he wondered. "I'm fifty-one years old. Last year I was fifty, and next year I will be fifty-two. It's all just time in the end."

Otto looked up to the crows stirring overhead. He wanted desperately to talk to his father, but questioned whether it would help.

"You wouldn't say anything. You never did." The words came out of him like burning coal.

"I'm sorry. You're right. I didn't work hard enough. Carl was right to fire me. I deserved it. Of course I deserved it."

Otto fell to his knees in the snow. "But what's a man to do? I've been scratching for my bread all my life. Don't tell me it's not mine to ask. I'll ask: What's a man supposed to do in my shoes?"

Otto pressed his rough hands to the cold slab of granite where his father's name was carved: *1860–1930*. He read the numbers on his mother's grave: *1860–1915*. He remembered every cent of his life's savings that he lost in the Savings and Loan: *$3043.53*. He thought of how it all began when his father came to Springfield in 1884. Scarcely did those numbers cross his mind before a devastating recognition ensued. "1884 . . . 1884; the year my father came to Springfield. 1884: the year my father left Germany for good."

Now that the rest of Europe was forging an alliance against Germany, it seemed that his father's decision to leave was brilliant and prescient. "If you'd stayed," Otto addressed his father's grave, "we all would have fought for the kaiser and died in the first war. If you'd stayed, we'd have nothing: none of our children would have been born because we would have been slaughtered somewhere in France or Belgium or Russia. If you'd stayed, none of us would be here. But you didn't. You left. In 1884."

Directly above him, Otto heard the honking of Canada geese. It was strange for them to be heading south in the middle of winter, but Otto paused from his reverie to watch the perfect arrow of their flight beyond the brooding boughs of elms in the cemetery. What little his father shared with Otto while still alive had always referred to 1884, to what it was like to come to this country and feel that amazing sense of possibility. The date had become almost mythological; it marked the beginning of time. As he gazed at the geese disappearing beyond the horizon, Otto wondered where they were flying: the Gulf of Mexico? Perhaps down to Miami where Milton was combing the waters for trophy fish? Perhaps to St. Louis and from there southwest to Arizona and Helen's little house in the desert? Or perhaps their destination was Albuquerque. There they would find the dry desert air and the miraculous colors of the great boulders of the earth and the cooling of the rocks as the darkening clouds hung over all that land. There they would find a man and his family at the edge of the desert in the foothills of the mountains, in a modest workshop, working among the birds and the desert bracken, making watches, marking the time. There they would have found the Otto who might have been with Anna, Frances, and Otto Jr. if only he'd had the courage to follow in his father's footsteps. If only he had left home to discover his destiny. If only he had left Springfield for good.

"Why didn't you tell me?"

The question came with a sudden surge of tears.

"Why didn't you say anything?"

He was draped over his father's grave.

And then it came, the question he had forbidden himself to ask for thirty years: "Why did you tell me to come back?"

Even in the act of asking, Otto felt his life draining out of his limbs. There was no turning back from this conclusion. He had lived a lie.

By the time he left the cemetery, Otto no longer felt that the course of his life was his father's fault. He was now devastated by his own blindness. How, in the face of so much evidence pointing him elsewhere, in the face of his own father as an example, had he fabricated the virtue of remaining in Springfield, of working for his father's business, and of staying with it without complaint? Carl was no more to blame than his father was; Carl was doing exactly as his father had asked him. There are circumstances we are born into, and after that, every person must take responsibility for his acceptance or refusal of those circumstances. He could have learned that from his father.

"Why didn't I learn that?"

As he drove along the graves of the nameless or of those whose names had no meaning for him, Otto thought about all the strangers buried somewhere in the earth, all the lonely soldiers whose lives had ended so abruptly without valor or consequence, and all their stories that had never been heard.

IX

That night, Otto tried to talk to his wife about what had occurred to him at the cemetery, but after a few frustrated attempts to make her understand what he had understood, he gave up. "How can you sum up so much confusion in a few words?" he asked and so resigned himself to a solitary grief. He told Anna that he loved her, and together they went to sleep.

In the following weeks, Otto felt himself drifting further into his solitude. Whenever he questioned his isolation and tried to remember the small pleasures of life, he considered how many words it would take to disprove the slander of oblivion. He didn't have the energy anymore.

One evening in March, Otto was sitting with his daughter Frances, who had been married almost four years. They talked quietly about the war and about plans for the summer. She was wondering whether her parents might go down to Florida to visit Milton again, or perhaps back to Colorado, where they had taken a family trip when she was still in high school.[23] When she looked at her father sitting on the couch she noticed that he was crying. He had hardly spoken a word to her.

"What's the matter, Dad?"

Otto struggled to say something, but the words were indecipherable. She waited patiently. She had never seen him so upset.

"I'll tell you something sometime."

He frowned into the bottom of his empty glass. Frances held her father's worn, viened hand tightly.[24]

She never did find out what he wanted to tell her. On the evening of April 14, 1942, the day before his fifty-second birthday, Otto Franke took his own life.

In preparing for the funeral, his family discovered that Otto had been forced to cash in his insurance policies and was left with no money. Carl offered to pay for the funeral.[25] Everyone in the family attended the services except for his two closest siblings, Helen and Milton. They lived too far from Springfield and hadn't enough money to get back in time.

Otto was buried in Oak Ridge Cemetery next to his mother. His family mourned him deeply.

wird müssen wir noch mehr hungern. Kein Fleisch,
keine Kartoffel, keine Milch, kein Mehl, keine Hülsenfrüchte
kein Fett. Nun in der grössten Not wende ich mich an euch
habt Erbarmen mit mir sage es auch deinen Schwestern
und Brüdern ich bitte euch alle recht herzlich helft mir
doch denn ich und meine Kinder haben keine Schuld am
Kriege und wir müssen nun darunter leiden. Wir müssen
alle elendig verhungern. Ich hoffe daß ihr alle gesund seit
und es euch gut geht. Nun sende ich an euch allen recht
herzliche Grüße an Schwestern und Brüder und bitte
euch nochmals recht herzlich helft mir doch laßt
diesen Schrei aus tiefster Not nicht vergebens sein. Ich
hoffe auf recht baldige Antwort. Es grüßt euch allen

Ahlbeck (Seeb)   eure Cousine   Wve. Gertrud Peters.

Schulweg N 5   Germany

LOOSE ENDS

All communication between cousins in Germany and the United States had ceased in the late 1930s. Dorothy Strand recalled being a pen pal with a cousin her age, but their letters stopped when her friend became a member of the Hitler youth. This accompanying letter was sent in June of 1947 to Milton and Dorothy in Miami and found by Milton Jr. after his parents' death. Milton Jr. could not recall any discussion of the letter, and there is no indication that it was answered.

AHLBECK, JUNE 6, 1947

Dear Cousin and Wife! You will be surprised to hear from me after so many years since I have received any news from you, but now unfortunately extreme hardship forces me to it. I have fallen into the greatest hardship and distress through the dreadful war. We are ruined. Hunger and misery are our lot. I am seventy years old and with a lung disease. I cannot work any more. We are under Russian occupation, and we are allotted so little that we are slowly starving. I am so miserable and only a skeleton.

Also this winter we had to endure so much hunger and cold, with no wood and no coal, and now that the summer has arrived we are even hungrier. No meat, no potatoes, no milk, no flour, no peas, no fat. Now in great hardship I turn to you for help. Have pity on me, tell your brothers and sisters also; I beg you with all my heart to help me because I and my children are not responsible for the war and now we have to suffer because of it. We are all desperately hungry. I hope everyone is healthy and well. Now, I send my heartfelt regards to everyone, to sisters and brothers, and beg you again with all my heart to help me. Do not let this cry from such dire distress be in vain. I am hoping for a rapid response. My regards to everyone.

Your Cousin,

Widow Gertrud Peters.

Ahlbeck (Seeb) 4 Schulweg N.5 Germany

In an attempt to find local records that could provide information about any relatives who might still live in Germany or Poland, my wife Barbara and I went to Derz in 2001 (now part of Poland) and then to Berlin and Swinemünde in 2002. In each location I worked with a local historian who researched the historical records to identify sites at which my grandparents and their relatives had lived. Two wars had destroyed all but six homes in Derz. Fortunately, the birth, marriage, and death dates of the Franke family in the nineteenth century were preserved in Latin at the local Catholic church. The records in Berlin confirmed addresses at which Frank and Marie had lived between 1875 and 1884. No records were found, however, that could lead me to any living relatives in Germany.

World War II served as a watershed for the American Franke family. The Depression was over. Young men returned from the war and, through the GI Bill, they were able to finance their college education. In ways unimaginable before the war, the country was on the move. Frank and Marie's children had become senior citizens, and their grandchildren were now young adults assuming leadership roles in their respective communities. This last chapter gives a thumbnail sketch of these grandchildren.

I

During the First World War no one in the American Franke family served in the military, while many of their German relatives served in the kaiser's army, and many were killed. Several American Frankes, however, did serve in the Second World War, specifically Carl Franke Jr. (Coke); Bill Franke's first son, Robert; and Bill Kinney, the son of Helen and Julius. Coke served as a Navy pilot flying PBMs out of Guantanamo Bay. After his service, he returned to Springfield to join his father in constructing a new building for Paris Cleaners across the street from the prewar plant. Bill's son Robert was a flight engineer in the Army Air Corps. At first he flew bombers to Europe from Long Beach, California. Then for several years he was stationed in India, flying supplies over the Himalayas (referred to as the Hump) to units of Chiang Kai-shek's Chinese guerrilla fighters, who were fighting the Japanese. While on duty there, Bob contracted a blood disease, which afflicted him for the rest of his life. After returning from the war, he worked for his father at Will Franke Cleaners.

Of all the Franke veterans of World War II, Bill Kinney saw the most combat. Bill was given a deferment from the draft until after he completed his degree in mining and metallurgy from the University of Arizona in 1943. Immediately upon graduation, Bill went to Officer's Candidate School at Fort Riley, Kansas, attending the last class in mounted combat. Needless to say, horses were soon replaced by tanks, and Bill became an armored cavalry officer in Patton's Third Army. He was training in the California desert in midwinter of 1944 when he was assigned to the Fifteenth Cavalry (motorized) as a platoon leader in C Troop, first platoon. They were quickly shipped off to New York and from there to England, where they lived through the rainy spring in barracks and awaited orders. Shortly after D-Day, General Patton walked into the headquarters tent where Bill happened to be standing. "We're going to leave here tomorrow, because if somebody doesn't get over there, we are going to lose the lot," Bill remembered the general saying. So they loaded up.

The Fifteenth Cavalry did reconnaissance for the Third Army. They landed in France in mid-July 1944. After providing a security shield around Cherbourg to discourage a German counterattack, the Fifteenth Cavalry engaged the enemy on August 1, 1944. Within days, Bill's battle group of five hundred men received orders from General Patton's headquarters to proceed with haste to liberate an important group of French citizens near Brest. They had to find the château in which these citizens were being kept in house arrest, and to make sure that the house was not destroyed. Once in the area, Bill's group happened upon a French teenager who wanted to help them. After determining that he was indeed the person he claimed to be, Bill invited him into his armored car and the boy led them directly to the château. Escorting a walking infantry patrol through the woods, they moved cautiously toward the chateau, their nerves jangled by reports that the Germans were in the area. Somewhere from behind the high

(TOP, LEFT)
Milton and Coke Franke,
U.S. Navy, in Florida, circa 1943.

(TOP, RIGHT)
Bill Kinney, General Patton's
Third Army, Europe, 1944.

Drusilla Long and Wally Carlson,
U.S. Army, circa 1943.

chateau walls, they heard a voice call out to them in French, "Come
here." As the leader of the platoon, Bill had to make a quick decision.
It could easily have been a German voice speaking to them in French
or, perhaps more likely, the voice of a Frenchwoman held hostage by
the Germans, who were trying to bait the Americans into their am-

bush. Bill decided to heed the voice anyway and ordered his troops to find the nearest cover next to the château. Within a minute, a patrol of German soldiers came around the corner, and a gunfight ensued. In their covered position, Bill's platoon was able to force the Germans to retreat. Once their position was secured, Bill spoke to the woman, who had undoubtedly saved many of their lives. It turned out that she was the great granddaughter of Charles Maurice de Talleyrand, the leader of the anti-Napoleonic faction and eventual foreign minister of France under Louis XVIII. The château where they took cover was de Talleyrand's home until his death in 1838. Bill was decorated for the engagement by order of General de Gaulle, commander of the French army, with France's most prestigious medal, the Croix de Guerre.[1] Fifty years later a French General, Alain Le Berre, visited Bill in California to interview him about the mission he had led. The general told Bill that the French teenager who had acted as a guide to the U.S. troops was Henri Mercier and that the engagement was now part of French military history.[2]

By August 16, Brest had fallen to the Americans with the capture of 5686 prisoners. The Fifteenth Cavalry then headed for Germany with the full force of Patton's army brought to bear. Bill's reconnaissance unit operated in the forward position and was charged with bringing back intelligence on enemy positions. These units were aggressive and were known to press forward at all costs. Bill set out from Utah Beach in a lightly armored jeep as the leader of a tank platoon with a .45 caliber pistol strapped to his hip, a carbine, a .30 caliber machine gun, and some handheld mortars. A radio on the floor of the jeep served to send intelligence by Morse code back to his command post. He spent the next nine months in Brittany and Belgium gathering intelligence for General Patton's main tank force and eventually crossed the Rhine into Germany, making it as far as the western part of Prussia. His unit kept on the move ahead of the main US force, looking for concentrations of German troops, and was frequently out of contact with both the Allied and the German lines. Under constant threat of ambush from the Germans and under urgent orders from Patton to press forward at all costs, the men barely slept.

By the fall of 1944, the Russians had recaptured Minsk and Warsaw and were pushing toward Berlin. After Hitler had relocated his

Bill Kinney receiving France's most prestigious medal,
the Croix de Guerre, January 1945.

East Prussian headquarters to his western headquarters near Bad
Nauhaim, the Germans launched their last counteroffensive in December of 1944 in the Belgian Ardennes. Drained by constant engagement by the Allied forces of any offensive strength they might
have had, the Germans mounted a final desperate offensive at Christmas in what became known as the Battle of the Bulge. It was a major
battle won by the Allies. Subsequently, General Patton's army continued to bull ahead in the winter and through the spring of 1945. They
met very little resistance. By the time the Allies crossed the Rhine,
the Germans spoke openly of defeat. Most civilians and soldiers assumed it was far better to be taken prisoner by the western Allies
than by the Red Army advancing in the east. This notion was due in
no small part to the anti-Bolshevik campaign devised by Hitler and
Goebbels in an effort to reconsolidate the front in the East.

On April 1, 1945, Bill Kinney's reconnaissance unit came into the
small town of Lünen. Bill was standing in the turret of an armored vehicle when a sniper shot him through the hipbone. Several more
shots came from the roofs of the houses along the main street.
Armor-piercing bullets struck the tank and ignited all the shells inside the vehicle. Everyone inside died instantly, but Bill was blown

out of the top of the turret and fell down onto the rain-soaked street below. Bleeding and in terrible pain, he sank into the mud. The German soldiers came down from the roofs to inspect the damage. Bill was alive, but his situation was critical. Unable to move, though still conscious, he could hear the German soldiers talking to each other. He then noticed that the sleeve of his uniform had caught fire as a result of the explosion, but there was nothing he could do about it. One of the German soldiers saw Bill lying in the mud and approached him. The first thing he did was to kick mud onto Bill's uniform in order to put out the fire. He stood over Bill, pointing his rifle at his head, and considered whether he should kill the American or take cover, as there were surely more American soldiers behind him. He did neither. Instead, in an improbable gesture of mercy, the soldier disappeared into a nearby building and returned with an IV. Working quickly, the soldier hung the IV on a nearby bush and slipped it into Bill's arm. He neither explained his efforts nor sought Bill's protection from the other American soldiers that he knew were to follow. He simply looked at Bill with fear and compassion. Bill nodded back at him. Then the soldier threw down his rifle and disappeared down the main road through Lünen. The war was over for him.

The IV kept Bill alive until other members of his group picked him up and took him to a nearby field hospital. It was raining. Two soldiers laid Bill on the hood of a jeep until it was his turn to be carried to the surgeon. A medical officer walked by. Looking at Bill he said, "Why did they bring this guy here? He will never make it with those wounds."

The hospital consisted of a crude tent hastily propped up in a muddy field. Bodies and body parts were strewn about the tent. Bill took a last puff on the cigarette given to him by a corpsman as they carried him to the surgeon. Before examining Bill, the surgeon put out his cigarette on the muddy floor of the operating room and covered his face with a mask. After looking at the wound for a few minutes, the surgeon concluded, "Well, you shouldn't have made it here, but now that you have and you are next, maybe you've got a chance."

The next thing Bill remembered was being evacuated to England for critical medical procedures and, once he was in stable condition, returning to New York on a ship. When the boat landed, the officials there asked Bill where he wanted to be sent for recovery and further treatment. For reasons unknown to him at the time, Bill decided not to return to Arizona where he was raised, but to go to California instead. So he was sent to recover in a hospital in California, where he had several more operations. It took Bill a year and a half to recover from his wounds. While recuperating, he went into the ward for his meals. His nurse was a very nice woman who brought her daughter, Shirley Krausnick, to visit Bill in her off-hours. Shirley spoke to Bill about all the medals of honor that he had received. After two years of an unusual courtship, Bill proposed to her and was accepted. They settled in California and raised four children, who all now reside in the state. When asked to consider his service—Would he do it again? Did he have any reservations?—Bill replied, "No. No reservations. It was our time to step forward and I am proud to have served." Pausing to reflect on those events, Bill remarked, "Amazing how a split-second decision can affect the rest of your life."

Bill was the most decorated member of the Franke family in World War II, receiving a Silver Star, two Purple Hearts with Oak Leaf Cluster, a Bronze Star, the Croix de Guerre (presented on the battlefield on January 29, 1945), and the other usual combat battle stars for Normandy, Nice, and Germany.[3]

II

As the European war ended, the cold war began. Similarly, a mood of silence and suspicion descended on the Franke family. While there was no espionage in the Franke feud, the division was as clear as the cold war. At one extreme was the Carl Franke family, who continued to run Paris Cleaners very successfully. At the other was the Bill Franke family, who operated Will Franke Cleaners and many other side projects with the help of such people as Ike, Possum, and the eventual Springfield chief of police Eddie Ryan. Both Bill and Carl forbade their families to make contact with members of the other family. Although both families lived in the south part of Springfield, none of the cousins met until much later, after the Iron Curtain had been drawn aside and the Soviet Union had collapsed.

Weary of the responsibility of maintaining the family business day in and day out, Carl seized the opportunity in 1942 to sell the plant at a handsome price to Hobbs Manufacturing, which made war materials for the government. A proposed change to another available cleaning solvent was more than Carl wanted to take on.

Marjorie in Florida, circa 1943.   Coke's family at the plant.

Carl's oldest child, Marjorie, married George Bolles, and together they settled in Florida. They rarely returned to Springfield and lost contact with the family. Carl's son Coke married Bette Hughes in 1947, and with the financial help and direction of his father he built a brand-new two-story cleaning plant, retaining the Paris name. With the management skills of his wife, Coke restored the cleaning business to its prewar prominence. Being the third generation in the family business, Bette and Coke were deeply invested in its history. Bette kept careful records and did her own research into family issues and dry cleaning techniques.

In his retirement, Carl, along with his wife Dorothy, spent a great deal of time down in Florida. Somewhat restless, they traveled extensively. When Dorothy's health began to fail, Carl traveled alone to Florida and overseas. Ultimately, Dorothy entered a nursing home in Springfield, where Coke saw his mother almost daily until her death in 1970. Carl retired to Florida alone, returning to Springfield infrequently. Perhaps out of loneliness, Carl sought the companionship of his youngest brother, Milton, with a view to reconciling their differ-

ences. At one of their get-togethers, Milton Jr. recalls, Carl admitted
the wisdom of Milton's leaving Springfield. Carl pointed out that Milton had had an easy life with few complications, whereas he had had
a difficult life managing the family business. Both Milton and Milton
Jr. saw the irony in that statement but accepted Carl's overture at face
value. The vast gap between Carl's wealthy life style and Milton's
hardscrabble existence made it hard for them to share anything beyond their common parentage. They saw each other two or three
times a year, and Carl even took Milton and Dorothy on a cruise . He
died of heart disease in Miami in 1972 at the age of eighty-five. He
was buried in his family plot at Oak Ridge Cemetery in Springfield,
about three hundred yards from his father's grave. Carl's entire estate
was left to the Methodist Church. Nothing was left to his daughter
Marjorie, and this exclusion further alienated her from her family in
Springfield. Paris Cleaners constituted an early inheritance for Coke,
continuing the custom of primogeniture that his grandfather had
brought with him from East Prussia.

Paris Cleaners prospered under the industrious leadership of Coke
and Bette until the 1980s, when it was time to transfer the family
business to the next generation. Frank Franke would have been proud
to see three of Bette and Coke's children—Glenda, Carl David III
(David), and Franklin Sheplor (Shep)—step into the management of
Paris Cleaners as it approached eighty years of successful operation.
Frank also would have been proud to hear Glenda articulate their respect for those who preceded them and the responsibility of keeping
the business strong and maintaining the spirit of hard work and appreciation for what their forebears had passed on to them. The East
Prussian values served as the very thread of the great grandchildren's
character. There is no doubt in their minds that they will lead Paris
Cleaners to its centennial in 2009.

III

With some reservations, Mayme remained loyal to Carl, but she limited her visits to Springfield to once a year or less. Despite her affection for her youngest sister, Mayme was rarely able to see Helen because of the distance between them. Some time after her husband
Charles died in 1955, Mayme moved from Champaign to Minnesota
to be near her daughter Dorothy. Dorothy had married Robert Emer-

(TOP, LEFT)
Left to right: David, Glenda, and Shep

(TOP, RIGHT)
Mayme and family, circa 1945.

Dorothy Strand with Richard J. Franke
at the nursing home, 2000.

son in 1944. In 1971, after Robert's death, she married John Strand and moved to Fergis Falls, just outside of Minneapolis. Like her father before her, Mayme contracted an eye disease and was blind for the last ten years of her life. She died of heart complications in 1977 at the age of ninety. Strict and often distant, Mayme had a strained relationship with her daughter, and it was only when she was forced by her blindness to rely on Dorothy that they grew close to one another. Dorothy never knew her mother loved her until the final years of her mother's life, when they were able to find reconciliation.[4] Widowed for the second time in 1991, Dorothy continued to live in Minnesota. In February of 2003, she died of heart disease at the age of eighty-seven. She provided many insights into the dynamics of the family and offered wonderful anecdotes for this saga.

IV

After Otto's death in 1942, even Elizabeth found it an impossible task to keep the family on speaking terms. A deep chill descended on family relations. But Elizabeth was the only member of the family to remain in touch with everyone. She worked very hard to keep up with her brothers and sisters and to ensure that her children knew all of their cousins. Whenever Mayme came back to Springfield, the two sisters were sure to spend an afternoon together. Elizabeth and her family spent many long weekends at Carl's cottage at Quiver Beach. Bill would stop by often just to check up on Elizabeth, and they always saw each other's family on New Year's. She continued to remain in close contact with her sister Helen, exchanging gifts at Christmas. When Helen came back to Springfield for gallbladder surgery after the war, she recovered at Elizabeth's house.

Drusilla, Elizabeth's first child, was in delicate health most of her life. Although she recovered from tuberculosis, she was plagued with illnesses for the rest of her life. After graduating from Springfield High School in 1936, Drusilla studied at McMurray College in Jacksonville, Illinois, for one year. She then returned to Springfield and worked as a clerk at the Franklin Life Insurance Company until she married Wally Carlson in 1943. She suffered a stroke and died in 1979.

Helen Louise, affectionately called Tootie by the Frank Long family, was the middle child. She was a happy person with a smile for everyone she met. She graduated from Springfield High School in 1938 and also attended McMurray College for one year. Returning to Springfield, she took an office job at the Illinois Telephone Company. She married Glen Mester, an excellent basketball player, whose family operated a butcher shop well known to the German community in Springfield. Our family always bought meat from his shop. Glen contracted leukemia and died in 1976. Twenty years later, Tootie died of the same disease.

Despite Hop's disability, he inspired in his son, Frank Long Jr., the same passion for hunting and fishing that possessed all the children and grandchildren of Frank Franke. Upon graduation from Springfield High School in 1943, Frank Jr. went to enlist but was turned down because he was blind in one eye. He then attended the University of Illinois on a scholarship and earned his BS in chemistry in three years. His chemistry professor led Frank into a research project on synthetic rubber, a commodity in short supply during the war. After receiving his degree, he went directly to the University of Iowa and earned his Ph.D. in organic chemistry in 1950. Given Frank's obvious talent and intelligence, his Uncle Carl took it upon himself to advise his nephew to look for work in manufacturing rather than

(LEFT) Long family, circa 1924. *Left to right:* Elizabeth, Drusilla, Helen Louise, and Frank.

(RIGHT) Frank Long and Richard J. Franke at the train station in
Princeton, N.J., July 1999.

chemistry research. Not surprisingly, when Frank first received his
doctorate and moved to Pennsylvania, his Uncle Bill—who had
helped so many small businesses in Springfield to get on their feet—
offered Frank a loan to establish an ice cream parlor. Accepting neither the advice of his Uncle Carl nor the offer of his Uncle Bill, Frank
pursued a rewarding career as an industrial chemist instead. Like his
mother, Frank maintained contact with his aunts, uncles, and cousins
throughout the long silence in the Franke family.

By the middle of the 1980s, Frank, like his grandfather before him,
experienced the beginnings of a cataract. When he learned that there
was a hereditary connection to cataracts, Frank began researching his
family history, at first for medical conditions and then the broader
canvas of events and people. As early as the 1970s, Frank was interviewing his aunts and uncles and keeping copious notes on family stories. He made this early work available to me and encouraged me to
continue my quest.

A true researcher at heart, Frank made crucial progress in reconnecting the broken threads of the family. His persistence and thor-
oughness has provided guidance and inspiration for my own work.

V

Otto's two children continued to live in Springfield their entire lives. Frances Marie, a beautiful young woman, graduated from Springfield High School in 1933 in the depths of the Depression. As we have seen, there was no money for her college, so she took an abbreviated business course while in high school and worked at various secretarial jobs. In June of 1938 she married Stuart Buerkett, who was on track to becoming postmaster at the Springfield Post Office. He died in an auto accident in 1957. Frances worked at the Cole Floral Shop as a floral designer until 1962. From there she went to the First National Bank of Springfield as a coordinator for "widows in distress." In June 1961 she married Elmer Sheldon, who tragically died of a heart attack one year later. In 1963, Frances Marie became an Avon lady, selling cosmetics, which she enjoyed until her retirement fifteen years later.

Otto Jr. was devoted to his father and never strayed far from him. Otto has lived in only two homes in Springfield, from 1920 to 1950 at 419 Adelia, and then at 713 S. English. He graduated from Springfield High School in 1940 but, like his sister, had no opportunity to attend college. Mechanically inclined, Otto was often self-employed, repairing equipment. He did not serve in the war because of a kidney malfunction and instead took an assignment at the War Plant in Illiopolis making bombs. With an eye toward a sales career, Otto took a Dale Carnegie speaking course. In his assignments he worked for Sangamo Electric, Reader's Digest, RC Cola Bottling Company, and Allis Chalmer's Tractor Co. In 1955, Otto and his wife Alma founded the third Franke family cleaning company, called *Franke Cleaners*, which remained in business for five years. Otto finished his working career at Simplex Corporation, retiring after two years.

Both Frances Marie and Otto have kept in touch with a wide range of people in our family and care deeply about them. They were an essential source of stories, photos, memorabilia, and advice on how to prepare for my task of telling the Franke story. They were both exceptionally generous with their time and their friendship.

VI

The most devastating event in Bill and Frances's life was the death of my sister Helyn in an automobile accident in November 1944 at the age

(LEFT) Cover girl Frances Marie, 1933.

(RIGHT) Otto Franke and Frances Marie, August 1998.

of twenty-three. Helyn had graduated from Springfield High School in 1939 and Iowa State University in 1943 and was on her first trip home after taking a teaching job in Princeton, Illinois. It was a nightmare for my family. My parents were never the same after this loss.

Because of his debilitating blood disease, Bob never had the energy or the strength to run Will Franke cleaners. He was separated from his wife in the early 1950s but was never divorced. His finest hour came after our father died of throat cancer in 1962 at the age of 69. Bob became the primary caregiver to my mother, who was in declining health. He saw her every day and drove her around on her errands. They became closer than they had ever been before. Their last eleven years together was good for both of them.

Al, the second son, graduated from Springfield High School in 1936. After two years in junior college in Springfield he attended the University of Chicago. There he earned an undergraduate degree and a law degree on an accelerated schedule by going to school year-round. He started practicing law in Chicago in 1942. His specialty has been Illinois school law, and he was considered the dean of that practice in Chicago for more than two decades.

I was the fourth and last child in the family and attended the same grade schools and high school as my siblings. I graduated from Yale

(TOP, LEFT)
Helyn Franke.

(TOP, RIGHT)
Bob Franke at his wedding.

(BOTTOM, LEFT)
Al and Rita Franke dancing, 1968.

(BOTTOM, RIGHT)
Rich and Barbara Franke.

University with a BA in history in 1953, spent two years in the U.S. Army as an artillery officer during the Korean conflict, and then attended Harvard Business School and earned an MBA in 1957. My first and only employer was John Nuveen and Co., municipal securities, headquartered in Chicago. For years, as chairman (now emeritus) of that firm, I have spent my spare time involved in higher education and the promotion of the humanities.

Although he never lived at our house, Eddie Ryan was like a fifth child in our family. Bill cared deeply for this young man,[5] who, during his time at Will Franke Cleaners, observed how to model his life and was universally loved by those with whom he worked.[6] A Jack of all trades, he was always willing to learn something new.[7] Within a few years Eddie was able to put some money aside so that he could marry his sweetheart, Evelyn. They had three children, Janet, Kathy, and Edward. By 1939, Bill saw that Eddie needed to expand his horizons and find work that would offer greater opportunity and compensation. Having heard from a friend about a job at the Springfield Police Department, Eddie applied and was hired as a motorcycle patrolman. He then worked his way up through the ranks and became a homicide detective. He managed to solve all fifteen of the murder cases he worked on except for one that was rumored to involve a city official's friend. The following year, however, Eddie aided in the conviction of this person on another charge. As his family grew, Eddie moonlighted to make ends meet—a common practice for both policemen and firemen in Springfield. These extra jobs included delivering coal, loading trucks, and selling used and new cars. In a good year he made more money selling cars than he did at police work. He often came back to Will Franke Cleaners to repair machinery. When Eddie became night chief of the police department, working from 11:00 p.m. to 7:00 a.m., he was available to sell cars during the day.[8]

Eddie became widely known in the community as the police officer with a heart. He bent over backwards to keep young men out of jail and was known to give many a second chance or even a third if he thought it was justified. Because of his reputation and experience in police work, the Republican Party asked Eddie to run for the office of sheriff in 1966. He won by a large margin. Because a sheriff cannot succeed himself, Eddie subsequently was asked to run for clerk of the circuit court. He won that election handily and served for two terms,

Eddie Ryan, circa 1975.

from 1972 to 1980. It is sad that Bill did not live to see Eddie win this recognition as a public servant; he would have been so proud.

After Bill's death in 1962, my mother and Bob were at a stage in life where they needed someone to advise them and to manage their finances. Both Al and I lived in Chicago, not close enough to deal with daily problems. Eddie stepped in and volunteered to fill that need for the widow of his dear friend and surrogate father, Bill Franke. Our family agreed that all of my father's assets be dedicated to support our mother, Frances, for the rest of her life and, upon her death, to the care of Bob and his family. Eddie managed the money with an even hand. Thinking of Bob as his younger brother, Eddie had a great deal of empathy for him and helped him create a meaningful life in those later years. If anyone ever acted as a valued family member, it was Eddie Ryan, and he richly deserves a place in the story of the Bill Franke family.

Finally, some comments about Bill as a father. He was not a wealthy man, but no one in our family ever felt poor. Our inheritance was the finest that one could wish for, an opportunity for an education. Once given, it can never be taken away or lost. My father's last days were full of suffering in a battle against cancer of the esophagus. He remained home at 1817 Bates Avenue, with my mother nursing him. When we came home to see him for the last time, my mother

Helen walking down a Tucson street, circa 1940.

told us that the Catholic priest had been visiting my father for the past year and that he had asked to be baptized in the Catholic Church as his wife and children had been. He could then be buried in Calvary Cemetery with his daughter Helen, and ultimately with his wife Frances, who lived for another eleven years. Of all the children of Frank and Marie, no one could have imagined that Bill would go through a similar conversion on his deathbed as his father. The ironies of life are sometimes surprising.

VII

After Bill Kinney was married in California, his mining expertise took him all the way to Perth, Australia, where he worked for several years. Eventually he returned with his family to Grass Valley, California. His parents remained in Tucson, where his father continued to work on road construction. After Julius Kinney died in 1969, Helen remained in Tucson for several years, and Bill continued his engineering work in various foreign countries. Once back in California for good, Bill moved his mother to an apartment in Oakland. She lived there by herself until the mid-1980s when she suffered complications from smoke inhalation as a result of an apartment fire. She was never quite as vigorous after the fire and spent her final years in a nursing home in Oakland. She died of lung disease in 1991 at the age of ninety-five. Beloved of her siblings, her son, and her grandchildren alike, Helen continued in the Franke tradition by sewing and mending clothes for her grandchildren. While still in Tucson, she lectured at the University of Arizona about the life and poetry of Springfield's famous poet, Vachel Lindsay. In recognition of her contributions as a volunteer for civic not-for-profit organizations, Dell Webb, a developer in Tucson, named a street after her. Helen later had the name changed to Bill Kinney Road for her son.

VIII

Shortly after Milton left Springfield in 1937, he was freed of the stuttering that had plagued him as a young man. Only under stress did it recur. He and his family lived very modestly in Miami in a one-bedroom house. Milton Jr. (Sonny) slept on the screened-in porch; it wasn't until college that he had a room of his own. When they first moved, Milton bought a boat, which he named "Pals." He and Sonny took it out every weekend. The fishing was more extraordinary than Milton had ever dreamed of.

The rent from his property in Springfield provided Milton with a modest but secure income in Florida until he was able to get back on his feet after the move. In World War II, Milton worked at the army air depot repairing various aircraft instruments and generators. After the war, he worked for a few years for another man until he finally opened his own generator repair shop in 1952 in a garage behind his home. He managed to balance work and fishing to keep his family fed and earn enough to pay the bills, but they enjoyed few luxuries. Barbara, Sonny's wife, remembers her mother-in-law's comment that the major regret in her life was that she'd never had a new refrigerator. Because Milton was such an excellent repairman, the old fridge that they first bought in 1937 was repaired over and over, as it always "had some more good life in it."

Milton's electric shop, circa 1938.

Devastated not to have been able to attend his brother Otto's funeral, Milton kept in contact with Otto Jr. as long as he lived, through a series of audio taped letters they exchanged. I had the privilege of reviewing these tapes for the purposes of writing this story. In addition to seeing Carl in his retirement, Milton had at least one visit from every member of the family, and he occasionally saw Marjorie and George Bolles.

It was a very proud day when Milton and Dorothy's only son graduated in engineering from the University of Florida in Gainesville. Throughout his correspondence with Otto Jr., Milton expressed pride in his son's accomplishments. During the Korean conflict, Milton Jr. joined the Air Force ROTC program and upon graduation was commissioned a second lieutenant. He was assigned to Wright Patterson Air Force base outside of Dayton, Ohio, teaching Air Force officers the fundamentals of aviation and the theory of propulsion. Because he was still needed for teaching after his service had ended, Milton Jr. was offered a job as a civilian at Wright Patterson, where he pursued and earned a Ph.D. in jet propulsion. Forty years later, Milton Jr. continues to teach there, focusing now on jet propulsion in outer space and how to maximize energy resources in space. Students come from all over the world to Wright Patterson to be trained by him.

Sonny's father died in Miami in 1983 at the age of eighty from complications related to heart failure. The old fridge was still running that day.

IX

As the second generation of Frankes passed away, so the old animosity began to dissipate. It was a slow process of forgiving and forgetting. If time is the balm that heals all wounds, a serious wound still needs to be stitched up so that it heals properly.

By 1990, relations between the Franke family units had ossified into seven isolated groups who seldom, if ever, spoke with one another. Children and grandchildren of Carl, Elizabeth, Otto, and Bill remained in Springfield, but old habits precluded them from knowing one another. Frances Marie, however, wanted to learn more about the family and finally contacted Coke and Bette Franke and Tootie Mester about arranging a family reunion. The idea was well received by all, and a date was set: the first Franke Family reunion was held at Carl David Franke III's house in Springfield on Saturday, June 17, 1995. Frances Marie valiantly assembled an address directory for the entire family, which provided the basis for creating a family tree.

When I received the invitation, I suggested to my wife, Barbara, that I go back to Springfield to see some of my cousins whom I had not seen in thirty or forty years and also to meet the Carl Franke family for the first time. I called my brother Al, who had a similar reaction. We hadn't seen our brother Bob's family in years, so it was a great opportunity to renew our family ties.

The reunion included a wonderful potluck dinner. German dishes were highly encouraged. It was immediately clear that everyone was eager to reacquaint themselves with old relatives and, in many cases, to meet cousins for the first time. All the food and drink was heartily consumed over five hours, and endless photos were taken. The group picture was especially challenging because the seventy-five or more in attendance couldn't fit into a single photo.

At one point during the festivities I was standing on the edge of the group, talking quietly with my cousin Milton Jr. At that moment I looked over the scene and saw everyone engaged in conversation.

(TOP, LEFT) A toast at the 1995 reunion.
Left to right: Tootie, Coke, and Frances Marie.

(TOP, RIGHT) At the 1995 reunion.
Left to right: Melinda Franke Orem, Al Franke, and Rita Link Franke.

(BOTTOM, LEFT) Milton Jr. and Barbara Franke
with their grandchild, Matthew.

(BOTTOM, RIGHT) *Left to right:* Patsey Smith Mester, Thelma Keil Long,
Frank Long Jr., Glen Mester Jr., Tootie Long Mester.

Although it is difficult to describe, a feeling something like pride came over me as I watched all these relatives laughing, gesturing, and talking about their lives. Perhaps it was the feeling of reconciliation.

Later on, several family members rose to say a few words of appreciation for those who had orchestrated the day. It was clear that the silence that had descended on the family needed to be addressed. I started by saying that whatever had happened to cause the schism in our family was no longer a point of contention in our lives and that the time had come for mutual understanding. Our hosts for the

(TOP, LEFT) *Left to right:* Linda Emerson Crowe,
Rich Franke, and Dorothy Creighton Emerson-Strand.

(TOP, RIGHT) Shep Franke and Carole Sudduth Franke.

(CENTER, LEFT) *Left to right:* Dorothy Alewelt Franke and Dorothy Greer Franke.

(CENTER, RIGHT) *Left to right:* Barbara Easley Franke and Rich, Sylvia Dickman
Franke and Alan, Rita Link Franke and Allyn.

(BOTTOM) Shirley Krausnick Kinney and Bill on their
fiftieth wedding anniversary.

Left to right: Mayme, Milton, and Elizabeth, 1948.

Left to right: Mayme, Dorothy, Frances Marie, Milton, Anna, and Elizabeth, May 11, 1960.

Dorothy and Milton.

Top row, left to right: Terry, Rita, Allyn, Barb, Rich. *Bottom row, left to right:* Alan, Greg.

On the occasion of Frank Long's Ph.D. graduation. *Front, left to right:* Tootie, Elizabeth, Frank, and Drusilla. *Back, left to right:* Glen Mester and Wally Carlson.

evening, Coke and Bette Franke, rose quickly and offered their hands in friendship, and the great silence was broken.

After another hour or so, as the guests were leaving, there was discussion of when we could bring this group together again. After many attempts to pick an appropriate date, the second Franke family reunion

Christmas Eve party, 1968. *Back row, left to right:* Rich, Barbara, Rich, Rita, Alan, Greg, and Katherine. *Front row, left to right:* Allyn, Barb, Kit Rafferty, Jane, Frances ("Dearie"), Bob, and Terry.

was held in 1999 at Coke's home, on the occasion of Frances Marie's eighty-fifth birthday. It was a marvelous party as well, diminished only by the fact that a few who had attended the first reunion were no longer living. This reminder of our mortality heightened a sense of the importance of these reunions. I suspect a third will soon be in the works.

Epilogue

Sibling rivalry is so common that, as an extension of self-preservation, it can almost be considered naked instinct. We vie, consciously or subconsciously, with our brothers and sisters for the affection of our parents, and a part of our character is shaped by our role in that rivalry. It is one of the oldest stories in the world. The rivalry between the brothers Jacob and Esau is paradigmatic in this sense; the prize of their father Isaac's affection comes in the form of his inheritance, which consists of God's covenant with Abraham. According to the custom followed by Abraham and Isaac, the first son was entitled to the preferential share of the father's inheritance. While breaking human custom is not against divine law per se, lying and cheating clearly violate God's commandments. When Jacob, disguised in the clothing of his other brother, Esau, deceived Isaac in order to obtain the blessing and the birthright, he wronged his father as well as his brother. Twenty years of exile was his punishment. They were difficult years, undoubtedly, but in the larger scheme of things it was a small price to pay for the prize of the inheritance.

Why is Jacob, the younger son, ultimately rewarded for his deception? Against his father's will, the older son has lost his birthright. We now see Esau no longer as the brutish hunter formerly willing to throw away his birthright but as a victim, a tragic figure. In the words of Isaac to Esau: "What, then, is there that I could do for you now, my son?" It is a devastating question that leads us to reconsider the past and ultimately the nature of fate: could Isaac have done anything to change the circumstances? Obviously it was the will of God for Jacob to be chosen from the beginning, but why was it necessary for Jacob to steal the blessing? Faced with the moral conundrum of Jacob's deception, the author of Genesis does not change the facts of the tradition handed down to him in order to convey a moral message. Instead, he draws out our sympathies for the plight of Esau and the regret of Isaac. Like the Greek tragedians who came after him, the author of Genesis presents his audience with the incontrovertible and tragic deed that cannot be revoked — in this case, Jacob's deception. In doing so, he draws our attention to the mystery of the divine plan as it is revealed in history, most of which must remain inscrutable to human perception. Although Esau falls outside of the blessing of the covenant, the author of Genesis doesn't regard him as merely a casualty of the divine plan but insists that his story too is worth telling. While we may not understand the ultimate meaning of Esau's fate, we must try to understand his sorrows.

Shades of Jacob, Esau, and Isaac haunt the Franke family story. Like Jacob, Frank Franke was able to employ his skills as a tailor in order to avoid a fate handed to him by East Prussian tradition. As a result, he became father to generations of Frankes in America, but remained committed to the tradition of primogeniture and, like Isaac, felt disillusioned and betrayed by his children's apparent lack of obedience. And like the timeless rivalry between Jacob and Esau, Bill and Carl vied with each other to secure the blessings of their father. Like Esau, after his mother had sent Jacob off to her brother in Harran, we too are left to ponder the nature of justice and fate and their strange, indeed mysterious concurrence with the will of the individual. Yet we must hazard an interpretation if we seek the satisfaction of some meaning.

Over the course of researching and writing this book, I have often reflected on Bill Kinney's journey to Germany with Patton's army. It is an extraordinary story, to be sure, but it is no more pertinent to understanding the schism in the Franke family than my own experience during the Korean conflict. Nonetheless, I often found myself imagining the face of the German soldier at the moment he decided to spare Bill's life; it is as inscrutable as it is compassionate. The war was over and the soldier knew it, but plenty of men in similar circumstances either shot their enemy or left them for dead. Why did this young man decide to direct his kindness toward Bill that morning? Perhaps he had seen enough bloodshed. Perhaps he thought that by showing mercy, he might receive pity from someone else. We can only speculate. Regardless, I couldn't resist the temptation of thinking of that soldier as a distant Franke cousin, as a grandson of one of Frank's brothers or sisters. Like a novelist tying up loose ends, I couldn't help but imagine that the unknown soldier was moved to compassion by the mysterious thread of common ancestry. The Franke family history, however, is not a novel, so I let the thought pass in favor of the facts as we have them. Nevertheless, it served as a reminder of the Frankes that remained in Germany, many of whom undoubtedly perished in both world wars. As we know from the letter from Frank's sister in 1923, the children of Joseph and Helene Frank and their families were desperate to leave Germany by the early 1920s. Who could have imagined that the outcast of the family, a young German tailor who traveled to America with almost no money, would have fashioned a successful career and become so surely the blessed one?

At the time I met with Bill Kinney, I was thoroughly immersed in nineteenth-century German history. I had studied the impact of beet production on the East Prussian economy, marveled at the effect of simple improvements in hygiene on population growth, and learned that no country in Europe industrialized more rapidly than Germany after unification. When Bill told me how the great granddaughter of Charles Maurice de Talleyrand had saved his life, I immediately thought of the Napoleon connection in our story. Talleyrand helped consolidate Napoleon's power, and shortly thereafter began to fear it. Had he decided to remain with Napoleon, in all likelihood there would have been no château for Talleyrand to bestow on his children and, in turn, no great granddaughter to steer a group of American soldiers clear of a German ambush. The connection is a stretch, I realize, but Napoleon looms large in our story and it is precisely what he did not do that turned out to be so decisive for Frank Franke's life. If only Napoleon had conquered East Prussia and established his Code there, Frank Franke's life would have been completely different. He might never have emigrated. For the Napoleonic Code abolished primogeniture, and, as we have seen, primogeniture determines both the patterns of the Franke family history and the second generation's unraveling. Ultimately, however, Napoleon was consumed by his jealousy of Russia's power; he had to meet the tsar with decisiveness, and his inability to delegate authority forced his costly retreat. As a result, the East Prussians never got a whiff of Napoleon's infamous grapeshot.

II

When Napoleon was made first consul for life after the Treaty of Amiens ended the revolutionary wars in 1802, he took an active part in organizing what became known as the Napoleonic Code. He and his fellow lawmakers were guided by the spirit of Rousseau and the Enlightenment, which had fomented the French Revolution thirteen years before. In August of 1789, the same year the U.S. Constitution was ratified, the National Assembly of France adopted the Declaration of the Rights of Man and the Citizen, which reflected the social contract idea popularized by Rousseau. In the following year, the Irish-born British statesmen Edmund Burke published his *Reflections on the Revolution in France*, which was read throughout Europe. From his beautifully articulated defense of the American colonists' rebellion against the British crown, many readers had anticipated that Burke would be in sympathy with the revolution in France. Instead, Burke's readers discovered a passionate defense of hereditary monarchy and the prediction that France, as a result of the revolutionary movement, would soon fall into a state of anarchy and blood lust. One year later Thomas Paine—whose *Common Sense* (1776) argued for complete American independence—published *The Rights of Man* as a direct rebuke to Burke's pamphlet.

In essence, Paine attacks Burke's defense of hereditary monarchy with the notion of natural rights derived from Rousseau, that all men are created equal before God. It is the same principle already expressed in the Declaration of Independence by Paine's friend Thomas Jefferson. Furthermore, Paine counters Burke's defense of tradition by claiming that the social contract is fundamentally a contract among the living and that "every age and generation must be as free to act for itself in all cases as the ages and generations which preceded it." As a result of his publication of *The Rights of Man*, Paine was elected a deputy to the French National Assembly. Firmly committed to the principle of natural rights, Paine vehemently opposed the ensuing Terror. He bravely argued against the proposed execution of Louis XVI and Marie Antoinette and was soon jailed on direct orders from Robespierre. Only because of a clerical error did he avoid the guillotine.

While Paine persuasively reveals the arbitrary grounds of the defense of hereditary monarchy, the strength of Burke's argument resides in its practical applications, particularly with regard to the inevitable conflict of rights in any functioning society. For Paine, natural rights are absolute, and once those rights are guaranteed, the diversity of human needs will provide the necessary lubricant for all social interactions. Burke argues the contrary, that our rights are the direct descendants of our good manners, which are firmly rooted in local custom. More importantly, however, Burke gives eloquent expression to the meaning and stability of local custom and habit, not only in his adopted England, but all across Europe. Against the nakedness of Rousseau's natural man, Burke poses the man of custom cloaked in the comfort and security of Christian civility. In short, Burke contends, a man stripped of habit is a man reduced to savagery. Thus, clothing has become second nature to human beings, and the freedoms we enjoy are the result of well-worn tradition. Because of these freedoms, Burke argues, the social contract exists not among the living but between the living and the dead: we appreciate what came before us because everything we do results from the sacrifices of the previous generation.

The Napoleonic Code, by abolishing the exclusive hereditary rights of the firstborn son, reflected the rights of man outlined by Paine and the National Assembly. Had Napoleon defeated England, Prussia, Austria, and Russia, the rest of Europe would have established the Code. Joseph Frank would have parceled his land equally among his children. Even if the industrial revolution in Germany had forced the young Franz Frank to leave for America, his story would have been radically different. Every member of the family (every male, at least) would have received an equal share of his business, according to the tradition of his forefathers. As it is with any family, there still would have been conflicts; but without the pressure and resentment associated with primogeniture our story would read very differently.

III

The resentment in the Franke family is common to much of the American immigrant experience, even today. People leave their homeland because of economic circumstances and carry with them its traditional values. In America they are confronted by a culture of egalitarian individualism that can be traced directly back to Jefferson and Paine. The positions occupied by Paine and Burke were reflected in the ideological extremes working in the Franke family. On one end was Carl, the Burkean, not necessarily by intellectual disposition but by attitude and behavior. He was vested in East Prussian tradition, being its direct beneficiary. From interviews and even from his own publicity, we know that Carl strove to maintain the family name and was proud of his heritage. Near the end of his life, Carl's comment to Milton that he felt a tremendous responsibility to continue the family business and that he envied Milton's relative independence indicates both the pressure of tradition and the emotional dialectic of the two ideologies. Carl enjoyed the fruits of traditional Prussian culture, but he also had to shoulder the greatest responsibility. Unlike Mayme, Helen, or Milton, he could never leave Springfield to strike out on his own during his working career.

When I interviewed Glenda Franke, I was struck by the strong sense of tradition inherited from her grandfather Carl, a powerful feeling of pride and honor in the family. Glenda and her family live in the fashionable house that Carl built in the 1920s. After Carl retired to Florida, Coke and Bette raised their children in that house, and they, in turn, passed it on to Glenda after she and her brothers had assumed the day-to-day responsibilities of the business. In 2009, Paris Cleaners will be one hundred years old. While Glenda's children at this time do not intend to continue the business, Glenda, David, and Shep, in Burkean manner, will honor their parents, their grandfather, and the spirit of the Prussian work ethic with a grand centennial celebration. It is a testament to their loyalty, but it is equally proof of the power of the tradition first brought here by Frank Franke. Only with the fourth generation, Glenda's children, do we finally observe the Jeffersonian values emerge in the family of Frank's firstborn child.

On the other ideological extreme of the Franke family was my father, Bill. Although I'm sure he never read Thomas Paine's *Rights of Man*, he absorbed the values of Jefferson and Paine through Springfield's democratic culture. Given his charitable spirit, it would be easy to suppose that my father was a devout Christian. But although politically conservative, he was never devout. He was not so much committed to the plight of the poor as sympathetic to the underdog. Above all he believed that everyone deserved an opportunity. My father rarely spoke about his childhood, but through the process of writing this book I became more convinced that he embodied the Jeffersonian values of equality and independence and that he did so in reaction to the traditional values at home that had excluded him from equal partnership in the family business.

In between the ideological extremes of Carl and Bill stood the rest of the children. Without the incentive of primogeniture, Mayme, Elizabeth, Otto, Helen, and Milton tried in various ways to honor their father while being drawn away from the family business by the lure of independence. Three of them—Mayme, Helen, and Milton—did leave the business and, eventually, Springfield, while both Elizabeth and Otto, who remained in Springfield for different reasons, attempted to move away at critical points in their lives. The families of the six children who lacked ownership of Paris Cleaners utilized the family work ethic to provide a different inheritance, that of a higher education for the next generation. John Adams anticipated this pattern when he wrote: "I must study politics and war that my sons may have liberty to study mathematics and philosophy. My sons ought to study mathematics and philosophy, geography, natural history, naval architecture, navigation, commerce and agriculture in order to give their children a right to study painting, poetry, music, architecture, statuary, tapestry, and porcelain."

Both ideologies resided within our grandfather. Without the exact details, we can safely assume that Frank left Derz for two reasons: lack of land and lack of work. Cast away from the countryside because of the historical circumstances of primogeniture and burgeoning industrialization, he couldn't thrive in Berlin because of his Catholicism. America was the obvious choice; thousands of Germans sailed there every week. But Frank was interested in the economic security America offered and not explicitly in its social or religious freedoms. Faced with the problems of raising a family and building a business, Frank and Marie relied on a traditional German family hierarchy to structure their daily lives, and conducted most of their commercial and social transactions within the tight German community in Springfield. Tradition, as Burke argued, is both practical and meaningful; while it may lack the equality of universal rights, tradition provides a way to order our days in a recognizable pattern that at once connects us to the past and offers a clear way to locate ourselves in the present. Paine was somewhat naive in his expectation that need alone would tie the society together. He ignored the fact that needs are frequently exploited. Implicit in tradition, Burke contended, is a code of moral conduct, and from this compact we collectively derive our rights. Nonetheless, Paine and Jefferson remain beacons of the universal principle of equality and independence, a truth Frank Franke no doubt appreciated, given his experience in Germany. The legacy of Abraham Lincoln in Springfield, a legacy that makes good on the Declaration of Independence's claim that "all men are created equal," only further hallowed this principle for Frank.

When I studied the historical record (wills, loans, titles, etc.) of Frank Franke against oral accounts of the man from my cousins who remember him, I discerned several inconsistencies. All of the accounts characterize Frank as a stern, intimidating, and taciturn man, which fits the pattern of the German patriarch. In addition, everyone confirmed that Carl was given control over the family business, again following the tradition of primogeniture. The inconsistencies emerge when comparing these accounts with his will. Since Bill and Carl could not work together, Frank had to help Bill establish a new business. So he gave Bill the North End plant, subject to Bill's signing a loan document to reflect the cost of the facility. As the fabric of the family was disintegrating around the animosity between Bill and Carl, Frank became close to Milton. Out of concern for his livelihood and as a reward to his loyalty, Frank gave Milton money to buy his auto repair garage. Mayme, Elizabeth, and Helen each received a diamond ring when they came of age. Therefore, it only seemed fair to reward Otto, the only son without an inheritance, with a relatively large sum of money in the will. If this were the end of the story, we would have to conclude that Frank had absorbed the ideals of Jeffersonian democracy. But the will required that only Bill, not Carl, pay back the loan originally signed when each took responsibility for their separate cleaning business properties. If it were strictly a question of money, Carl would have been a better choice to repay the debt, simply because Carl had more money. But Frank must have required Bill to repay his loan because he felt obligated to give his firstborn son the promised inheritance, and perhaps also because he resented the manner in which Bill questioned his authority. In this respect, we have to read a partial commitment to both the traditional values of Derz and the ideals of democracy.

Under any circumstances, such uncertainty is difficult to tolerate, but to make matters more confusing, Frank Franke did not possess the intellectual articulation of these opposing systems to clarify the decisions regarding his last will. He acted instead on his intuitive sense of these values and his innate sense of fairness. Even if he had read Burke and Paine, I doubt that his decision would have been any less difficult. Frank lived between two worlds; his uncertainty was a bridge between them. No theory was going to make it easier for him to live in that ambivalence. Nevertheless, for us, the subsequent generations of Frankes, a joint consideration of Burke and Paine draws our attention to the sacrifice and inner turmoil of the immigrant experience.

Of all the characters in the Franke family story, Otto is perhaps the most obscure, especially in light of the Burke and Paine discussion. Given Otto's position as the second son, he should have identified with the principles of equality as his younger brother Bill did. It would have been to his benefit either to challenge the authority of his father or to strike out on his own. Instead, according to his father's wishes, Otto returned to Springfield from New Mexico, thus renouncing a promising and independent career as a watchmaker. From interviews with Otto's children, however, I learned that he later regretted that decision. In this sense, Otto tragically inherited his father's ambivalence toward the opposing cultures of Jeffersonian democracy and filial piety.

IV

Questions of emotional logic remain. For example, what, in the secret chambers of his heart, prompted Otto to return to Springfield? There is no greater drama than the soul in conflict with itself. We can research the facts, we can study the historical context in which events take place and we can even develop a cultural and ideological framework with which to understand a family, but how do we appreciate the motives that arrange the facts in the broader pattern? While facts such as marriage, birth, and death record important events in people's lives, they tell us nothing of what such moments meant to the person or what motivated their decisions.

In trying to answer the question of what drove the Franke family apart, I inevitably returned to the question of who Frank Franke was. All the issues of conflict led back to his decisions, to his sense of fairness, and to his principles. I determined to gather every certifiable fact that I could about Frank Franke, his parents and siblings, the place he came from, and what he did. I obtained birth certificates, marriage licenses, last wills and testaments, military passports; in short, I traveled from Springfield all the way to Derz and Berlin and also to the homes of my cousins who now live throughout the United States in order to secure all the available facts. While they frame a portrait in accuracy, facts lack dimension and can reveal, at best, a silhouette. So I interviewed the surviving members of the third generation of Frankes for impressions and anecdotes relating to Frank and the family business. Crucial in establishing the tone and the shape of our story, this research also proved to be its own reward, for it allowed me to get to know the cousins I had never met until the first reunion. After the interviews were completed, I surveyed the variegated landscape of my research. On one end stood the political history of the unification of Germany, while on the other were anecdotes depicting Frank as an old man with a beard like Santa Claus handing out silver coins at Christmas. In between were documents. Gradually, out of all this material, I began to construct a timeline, which, when completed, brought me closer to finding a reasonable set of motives to explain the profound schism in the Franke family, but did not account for the critical decisions and inconsistencies.

Historians of major political events have access to official documents, correspondence, and even personal memoirs with which to confirm and cross-reference the facts. As a family historian, however, I was faced with a seemingly insurmountable problem: if I wanted to explore the nature and depth of this conflict that tore my family apart, I had somehow to fill in enormous gaps in documentation in our family history. Furthermore, I had no way of confirming or denying certain family anecdotes. Like an archeologist who has fragments of physical evidence to interpret the history of an ancient city, I had to bind the evidence to the known outcome with the thread of the imagination. The Franke family was, after all, an ordinary immigrant family, with none of the documentary advantages that come with social privilege. Had I wanted to engage my imagination more fully, I should have written a novel. But I wanted to know more about my particular family, to come to terms with what drove its members apart. So I was bound to certain facts and to the social milieu of a German immigrant family whose values consisted of discipline, obedience to authority, and hard work with the goal of moral certitude and material success. These marked the limits of the story, to which I did my best to remain faithful. As for the rest, imagination had to supply many details.

The very nature of the narrative compelled me to consider the meaning of character, both in terms of the figures that populate this work and in a broader, more philosophical manner. I realized that it is character, perhaps above all else, that determines our fate. Or, as the Greek philosopher Heracleitus said, "Character *is* fate." Whether our character is born in us or is forged in the crucible of youth, the clash of interests by which we are so often confronted in this life tests our mettle and burnishes our character. From hours of interviews, I was able to gain an impression of most members of the extended Franke family. Because all of my cousins were very young when their own impressions were made, however, these portraits retain a child's perspective on the often-incomprehensible world of adults. Given these limited sketches, I used the basic frame of our story and its implicit dynamics to give a relatively full picture of Frank and Marie and, to a lesser extent, of their children. It was an exercise of imaginative sympathy. And if, in the final analysis, my portraits should be somewhat distorted in certain features, I invite others in my extended family to correct those touches in their own accounts. I do so, not out of defensiveness or pride in what I've made, but to urge my cousins and their children and their children's children to find out for themselves what happened and to ask what social and emotional forces shaped their own lives. Truly, the writing itself has been its own reward. By placing ourselves, with the assistance of the imagination, in the midst of seemingly irretrievable events of the past, we not only reclaim a part of the past but move toward self-understanding and genuine reconciliation. While imagination can never replace memory, it can help illuminate the darkened rooms and hallways of our past, so that we become willing custodians of the house of our memory and thus are free to come and go as we please.

Looking back on it now, I understand more clearly why I was drawn to Bill Kinney's story. Without fully comprehending it at the time of the interview, I sensed certain themes in his story that proved to be decisive patterns in the Franke family history. When Bill mentioned the Talleyrand connection, I was struck by the confluence of personal history and political history. I am sure that Bill did not know who Talleyrand was at the time, nor, for that matter, how crucial Patton's Third Army was to the Allied forces. Nevertheless, those factors turned out to be decisive in his war experience. In a similar manner, primogeniture informed Franz Frank's childhood in Derz. In this sense, Bill Kinney's story was instructive for writing the Franke family history. All of our experiences are informed and to a certain degree limited by social and political forces, whether we are conscious of them or not. By staking out the limits and imagining the variations—What if Otto had stayed in New Mexico? Or what if Frank had been given a small plot of land in Derz as an inheritance?—we perceive the power of certain decisions and the mysterious give and take between the will of an individual and the circumstances into which he or she is born. As Bill Kinney said, "Amazing how a split-second decision can affect the rest of your life."

We often look back at the storm of our adolescence and marvel at the decisions that shaped the course of our lives, decisions that seemed of no consequence at the time. Our life's work so frequently begins as a simple distraction, something we never imagined spending the rest of our lives pursuing. And then suddenly, in the right place and at the right time, that distraction becomes the decisive factor in our lives. While we may never be able to distance ourselves enough to comprehend the weather of our upbringing completely, we can make choices or commit to choices already made and in doing so create a shelter for ourselves.

In some respects, a family history is a trace of yesterday's weather. But yesterday's weather can tell us something about the climate we live in. Discovering the family patterns and chronicling cautionary tales are only two of the rewards of writing a family history. If we want more than a one-sided picture of what happened in the past, such nuances will require that we summon our sympathies and place ourselves, as much as our imagination will allow, in other people's habits and circumstances. But precisely because it is the past, we sympathize more freely, exposing ourselves more fully to the perspectives of others. Somewhere in the distance between ourselves and those we live among is the mystery of life. Bridging that distance is not to unravel its complexity. It is rather a way to approach the mystery and feel its marvel.

I have often wondered during my research where this book was taking me and, more to the point, where it would take the subsequent generations of Frankes. If I've achieved anything, I hope I've given some sense of who the first two generations were and of the sacrifices involved in becoming Americans. Ultimately, I hope this history is only the first in what becomes a Franke family tradition.

So, to the grandchildren and great-grandchildren of my generation, I'm saying this: The crickets will be singing in the fields outside of Springfield this evening just as they did a hundred and nineteen years ago when Frank Franke first got off the train from Chicago. The barn swallows will follow, too, at the last hour of the day when bronze shadows of the setting sun glint off their cinnamon-colored bellies into the eye of the fisher standing on the shore of the Sangamon River. And in the silence between their wing beats, in the pause of all that moves the world headlong to its unknowable conclusion, perhaps you too will hear whispers of the stories of our ancestors. To you I say, "Tell me a story."

Notes

PROLOGUE

1. Germans to America: List of Passengers Arriving at United States Ports, vol.
   48, November 1883–April 1884, edited by Ira A. Glazier and P. William Filby.
2. Ibid., vol. 50, July 1884–November 1884.

CHAPTER ONE: THE TAILOR

1. Anthony J. Steinhoff, a German scholar at the University of Chicago, provided much of the background for this discussion of the Military Pass Book.
2. Landesarchiv-Berlin, records of city residents and addresses for the years
   1875–1885.
3. Wedding was an industrial area of Berlin in which workers lived in crowded,
   primitive quarters. The movement of rural population of Germany into
   Berlin where they could hope to find meaningful employment far exceeded
   the city's capacity to house them.
4. In the Emergency Passport of 1914 and in Marie's Death certificate, Marie's
   place of birth is listed as Swinemünde.
5. Craig, Germany: 1866–1945, pp. 85–97
6. Markt-Halle means covered market in German. There were several covered
   markets in Berlin, but there was one major covered market in the center of
   the city that was simply referred to as Markt-Halle.
7. Derz was founded in 1376 as a village in the duchy of the Teutonic Order as
   a free village, which meant it had favorable status with very low taxes, the
   rights to inherit land, and obligatory military service. The Prussian name of
   the village suggests that the first residents were Prussians. With Poland
   nearby, the schools were often bilingual, teaching both German and Polish,
   but this varied according to the politics of the time. Records show that in
   1848 Derz had 415 inhabitants, of which 405 were Catholic and 5 were Evan-
   gelic. No other religion was recorded. There were 57 buildings, and the lan-

guage was predominantly German with some Polish. The social structure was reported as follows:

5 big farmers, being the richest in the village

22 regular farmers

32 poor farmers (having little houses and a little piece of land around the house)

26 farm workers (having no land, working for farmers as hired men)

Derz was known as a typical farming village, and there were no nobility estates in the area.

8. These were popular cafés along Unter den Linden in 1880s Berlin.

9. Heider and Jean-Jacques was a real establishment on Unter den Linden in the late nineteenth century. *Unter den Linden: Photographien,* p. 68.

10. *Unter den Linden: Photographien,* p. 112.

11. Germans to America, vol. 48, edited by Ira Gkazuer and P. William Filby (Newberry Library). Between 1865 and 1895 agricultural and unemployed industrial workers, largely from eastern Germany, left the country looking for employment. The era of massive overseas migration came to an end in the mid-1890s as German industry matured and absorbed surplus agricultural and industrial populations. The most important port of arrival was New York City. Between 1880 to 1884, 800,000 Germans emigrated to the United States. In this period of massive emigration out of Germany, 26 percent went to America. East Prussia provided the largest group, constituting 38 percent of the German emigrants over these four years.

CHAPTER TWO: LOOM OF AMERICA

1. For Franz Frank's name change to Frank Franke, see the prologue and later in the present chapter.

2. According to the 1884 Springfield City Directory, Frank Franke boarded at the Sherman House

3. Springfield City Directory, 1885

4. There is no direct proof that Frank and Marie were married in Berlin. I have presumed this was the case, however, given the fact that Marie registered aboard the *General Werder* as Marie Franke and, in her letter, calls Frank "dear husband."

5. Germans to America

CHAPTER THREE: WARP AND WOOF

1. Carl was born September 12, 1887

2. According to parish records, the sibling nearest to Frank in age was Rosa, who was born in 1854. The rest of the siblings were born in the 1840s—the eldest, Johanna Frank, born in 1842. Johanna's relationship to Frank is not confirmed. I found her grave in the churchyard in Fleming, just northwest

of Derz, and noted her birthdate there. From church records we know that Joseph Frank was born in 1820, so if Johanna was not Frank's elder sister, she was definitely a cousin of his same generation.

3. This anecdote was related to Dorothy by her mother, Mayme. Dorothy Strand interview.

4. The cemetery was adjacent to the Catholic Church in Lemkendorf. All the people buried there were Germans, and very little maintenance had been done on gravesites since East Prussia was given to Poland in 1945 after World War II. Time and weather made the names on the grave markers impossible to read. It is logical that many of Frank Franke's family and ancestors were buried there, but we could not identify their specific graves. The church records revealed that many members of the Frank family had worshiped there. Since the end of World War II, Polish burials took place in a new location apart from their German predecessors.

5. According the church records at Lemkendorf, Joseph Frank and his family were identified as members of The Brotherhood under the Invocation of the Lord of Transformation. The Brotherhood was a society to which members vowed temperance and moderation. Public displays of drunkenness had become a frequent problem in Ermland, and the Brotherhood was organized in response to such development.

6. This is a common hymn still sung on the feast of Corpus Christi in many Catholic churches.

7. See Genesis 24–28.

8. Springfield City Directory, 1894

9. While there is no direct confirmation that Marie did the bookkeeping for F. Franke, Merchant Tailors, I did discover that Marie was listed as a bookkeeper in the Berlin City Directory. It seems logical then that she would have transferred her talents to the family business, at least until one of the children could take over the task.

10. Springfield City Directory, 1886 and 1891

11. Before settlers came, prairies covered more than 60 percent of Illinois. The native plants survived in graveyards and along rivers and train tracks. There have been recent efforts to restore the prairies in Illinois. The largest park, Goose Lake Prairie, is in Morris, Illinois.

12. East Prussia was granted to the Teutonic Knights at the end of the crusades. Ermland, a small area within East Prussia, remained Catholic after the Reformation. When I visited Derz in June of 2000, the archives of the church in Lemkendorf (Lamkowo in Polish) confirmed that Frank's father, Joseph Frank, was born in Derz in 1820 and that Josepgh's father, Andreas Frank, was born in the nearby village of Fleming. Given the lack of mobility of the German peasantry, it is safe to assume that the Frank family had been in Ermland for hundreds of years.

CHAPTER FOUR: PATTERNS

1. Mr. Bunn and Mr. Easley were two well-established Springfield bankers in 1914.

2. Carl and Dorothy were married July 24, 1912. Otto and Anna were married April 23, 1913.

3. While there is no documented evidence that Carl attended tailoring school in Chicago, it is common family knowledge. Although the date of his time in Chicago is not certain, we can safely assume that it was before he attended dry cleaning school in Denver in 1908.

4. Springfield City Directory, 1907.

5. Albert E. Johnson, *Drycleaning* (Watford, UK, 1971).

6. The anecdote about Carl's cutting off the tails of a suit at tailoring school was confirmed by Otto Franke, Jr., Bill Kinney, and Dorothy Strand.

7. Helen Franke was a close friend of Vachel Lindsay's and an admirer of his poetry. The poet appears to have been an admirer of hers, referring to her as his "blue-eyed goddess." When Lindsay was down on his luck, Paris Cleaners did his dry cleaning free of charge. Well after his death in 1931, Helen became an advocate for his poetry and spoke publicly about it at the University of Arizona, among other places. Bill Kinney, personal communcation.

8. Otto Franke Jr., who worked at Will Franke Cleaners and later on at his own cleaning firm, provided the details of the pressing process for this section.

9. For more information on Lindsay, see Eleanor Ruggles, *The West-Going Heart: A Life of Vachel Lindsay* (New York: Norton 1959)

10. Vachel Lindsay, *The Congo, and Other Poems* (New York: Macmillan, 1914).

11. Marjorie Franke was born October 30, 1914.

12. Dorothy Strand interview.

13. Dorothy Strand interview.

14. Dorothy Strand's account of her parents' courtship was confirmed by Frank Long.

15. In a discussion that I had with Dorothy Strand, she disclosed this story, which her mother had told her the year before she died. Mayme had never told anyone before.

16. Paleontologist Carol Hennikoff provided the most likely scenario for how the fetus was preserved.

17. Dorothy Strand interview.

18. Dorothy Strand interview.

19. Springfield City Directory, 1903.

20. By the time her own daughter, Dorothy, came of age, Mayme continued a tradition of this recognition and gave Dorothy the diamond. And Dorothy, in turn, would give the ring to her daughter, Linda. In 1999, the tradition was again honored when Rebecca Crowe, the great-great granddaughter of

Frank Franke, received the diamond ring as her eighteenth birthday gift. Dorothy Strand interview.

21. For an excellent account of the failed diplomacy leading up to World War I, refer to chapter 10 of Gordon Craig, *Germany: 1866–1945* (Oxford: Oxford University Press, 1978).

22. Frank Franke's attitude toward the war and the German army was confirmed by Frank Long.

23. Craig, *Germany*, chapter 1.

24. For further description of nineteenth-century Berlin tenements, see Alexandra Richie, *Faust's Metropolis: A History of Berlin* (New York: Carroll & Graf, 1998).

25. Springfield City Directory, 1890

26. Not that much is known about Ottilie Sutter, other than what can be gleaned from her death certificate: Catholic, born in Germany. The Springfield City Directories begin listing Henry Sutter as a baker as early as 1887. The *Springfield Register* confirmed that Henry Sutter died in 1910.

27. For further description of German folk dances, see Agnes Fyfe, *Dances of Germany* (New York: Crown Publishers, 1951).

CHAPTER FIVE: OLD HABITS

1. Gordon Craig, *Germany: 1866–1945,* provided a general background for this section.

2. The kaiser was often criticized in the press for ineptitude before the assassination of the archduke.

3. The *Kulturkampf* was a set of anti-Catholic laws passed by Bismarck to restrict the rights and power of Catholics, whom he considered his political enemies.

4. The date of Joseph Frank's death is confirmed by the Lemkendorf parish archives.

5. The county in which Derz is situated is historically known as Ermland. Because of some particular recognition given to the early settlers of this area, more favorable tax status and military obligations were given to its population than to others. During the Protestant Reformation (1550) Ermland was under the authority of the kingdom of Poland and its people were not converted to Lutheranism, as were those of the surrounding East Prussian countryside. By 1700, Ermland was firmly back into Prussia and governed by German law, albeit one of the few Catholic areas in northern Germany.

6. Alexandra Richie, *Faust's Metropolis,* p. 266

7. Two German-American families in Chicago recalled stories of family members on vacation at the outbreak of the war; and the husbands were refused passage back to the United States, and were inducted into the German army.

Prussia in the 1800s. Ermland was the only Catholic district in Prussia during the
Reformation. Derz is in the center of the district.

CHAPTER SIX: FRAYED

1. Although we do not know how many of the German Weichbrodts and
   Franks died in the war, it is safe to assume, given that their nephews were of
   military age, that some of those men died in combat.
2. Frank Long interview.
3. Carl and Dorothy were married July 24, 1912.
4. Marjorie Franke was born October 30, 1914; and Frances Marie Franke was
   born June 29, 1914.
5. The scene is based on an anecdote related by Dorothy Strand in which Carl
   had tapped his cigarette ashes onto a plate of eggs that his sister Mayme had
   cooked for him. Dorothy Strand interview.
6. Springfield City Directory, 1913.
7. Springfield City Directory, 1913.
8. Springfield City Directory, 1910.
9. Willie Franke's fifth-grade report card, June 1903. *See facing page.*
10. Allyn Franke, remembering his father, June 10, 2003.
11. Carl and Dorothy and Mayme and Charles were married at the German
    Methodist Church; Otto and Anna at the Lutheran church; Anna was
    Lutheran.

SIGNATURE OF PARENT

Sep.	*F. Franke*
Oct.	*F. Franke*
Nov.	*F. Franke*
Dec.	*F. Franke*
Jan.	*F. Franke*
Feb.	*F. Franke*
Mar.	*F. Franke*
Apr.	*F. Franke*
May	*F. Franke*
June	

In obtaining the standing of any pupil, the average of daily recitations is reckoned as one-half, and the result of the final examinations as one-half.

Parents and all interested, are cordially and earnestly invited to visit the schools often.

S. BOGARDUS,
SPRINGFIELD, ILL. Principal.

_____ Teacher.

SPRINGFIELD
Public Schools

School _____

Commencing *Sept* 1902

MONTHLY REPORT.

—of—

Willie Franke

Monthly Report of *Willie Franke*

	Sept.	Oct.	Nov.	Dec.	Jan.	Feb.	Mar.	Apr.	May	June	Rec'n Av'ge	Exami- nation	Grade
Drawing,			75	75	75	75	80	70	70	70			73
Writing,	70	78	78	78	78	75	76	78	70	75			75
Reading,		70	75	78	78	79	80	70	70	75		80	74
Spelling,	78		80	84	85	95	80	95	70	80	82		82
Dictation and Composition,	70	78	70		82	85	75	86	70	70	80	77	77
Arithmetic,		70	70		73	30	80	82	80	70	80	70	74
Geography,				83	70	85	83	90	80	85		80	82
Grammar,	80	70	80	90	80	75	80	82	80	78	85		81
History,													
Physiology,													
Music,							80	85	80	80	85	70	
Average Scholarship,	73	81	77	81		78	82	80	73	76			75
Highest Average in Class,		92	92	93			73	96	94				
Average Scholarship of Class,													
Times Tardy,	0	0	0	0	0	0	0	0	0				
Days Absent,	½	0	0	0	0	0	0	0	3				
Deportment,	85	90	88	90		95	70	90	80	80			

100—Perfect; 90—very good; 80—good; 70—fair; 60—poor; 50—inadmissable.

CHAPTER SEVEN: FABRIC RENT

1. Bernard Grun, The Time Tables of History, p. 468.
2. Ibid.
3. Gordon Craig, Germany: 1866–1945.
4. Between 1916 and 1917, everyone's title at Paris Cleaners changed except for Carl's. It is impossible to say whether this change in nomenclature represented a structural change in the organization of the business, but the change was noted in the Springfield City Directory.
5. While "13, Unlucky for Spots" remained emblazoned on the Paris Cleaners delivery trucks for years, there is no evidence for the inspiration behind the campaign. What follows is an attempt to imagine the origins of the slogan.
6. The Springfield City Directory confirms that Otto was employed by the Illinois Watch Company from 1908 to 1910 and that he went to New Mexico for a year. When he came home he was employed by Paris Cleaners.
7. Craig, *Germany: 1866–1945*, p. 381.
8. In the 1900 and 1910 censuses, Frank Franke listed his native country as "Germany." In the 1920 census, however, Frank wrote, "East Prussia" instead, which was overwritten "Germany" in a different script." It seems then that Frank's allegiance to Germany at the beginning of the war, which both my father and Frank Long's mother recalled, had shifted significantly by 1918.
9. Bill Kinney interview.
10. According to the Springfield City Directory, Frank Franke reclaimed his title of vice president of Paris Cleaners in 1919.
11. Springfield City Directory, 1919.
12. Springfield City Directory, 1920.
13. Carl became a 33rd degree Mason in the 1920s. Bette Franke interview.
14. Otto Sr. became a 32nd degree Mason in the 1930s. Otto Franke Jr. interview.
15. Milton F. Franke became a 33rd degree Mason of the Scottish Rite in the Springfield Chapter on November 14, 1933.
16. For this 1908 photo of the family, see page 000.
17. Bill Franke's business was called Avenue Cleaners before it became Will Franke Cleaners in 1928.

CHAPTER EIGHT: STITCHES

1. Frank Long interview.
2. Bette Franke interview.
3. Frank Long interview.
4. Frank Long interview.
5. To put it in context, it cost 65 cents to have a suit of clothes cleaned and pressed; if there was a special, three suits were cleaned and pressed for one dollar. Otto earned forty-nine dollars a week.

6. Wonneberg was a town in East Prussia located just northwest of Derz where several of Frank's siblings lived.

7. This is a direct translation of the 1923 letter from Germany. The proverb "where there is a will, there is a way also" and the final "good-bye" are in English in the original.

8. According to Milton's son, Milton Franke Jr., Milton used to take Frank Franke on the roller coaster outside of Springfield.

9. In all of the family anecdotes about how Frank Franke went blind, there is always mention of something crashing in the room next to Frank's recovery room. The sound was so startling that it woke Frank up suddenly, and he bolted up in bed, which caused the sutures to rip.

CHAPTER NINE: THE LAST THREAD

1. Dorothy Strand interview.
2. Dorothy Strand interview.
3. Dorothy Strand interview.
4. Bill Kinney interview.
5. Milton Franke Jr. interview.
6. Milton Franke Jr. interview
7. Springfield City Directory, 1927.
8. Allyn Franke interview.
9. Otto Franke Jr. and Louie Dickerson, the owner of a shoe repair shop behind the downtown branch of Will Franke Cleaners, related this story to me, claiming that they had never seen Bill so angry before.
10. Dorothy Strand interview.
11. Dorothy Strand interview.
12. Milton Franke Jr. interview.
13. Both Dorothy Strand and Frank Long confirmed the fact that Frank Franke held a rosary in his hands on his deathbed. Apparently, most of the Franke children were very upset by this.
14. The details of the wake and funeral were all supplied to me by Otto Jr. and Frances Marie.
15. Dorothy Strand interview
16. Frank's children continued to call Ottilie "Mrs. Sutter" after her marriage to their father.
17. John Schnepps also drafted Frank and Ottilie's prenuptial agreement.
18. Otto Franke Jr. interview.

CHAPTER TEN: CABBAGE AND TATTERS

1. Otto Franke Jr. interview.
2. After years of lax hunting rules, the government began to restrict hunting to the fall and winter in order to allow the game to breed.
3. Bill Kinney has suffered from asthma his whole life. Bill Kinney interview.

4. Otto Franke Jr. interview.
5. Both Otto Jr. and Frances Marie related this story to me.
6. Otto Franke Jr. interview
7. Hasenpfeffer was rabbit marinated in vinegar for two days and then cooked in a pot into a stew.
8. Ever fair-minded, Elizabeth got her dry cleaning done at both Paris Cleaners and Will Franke Cleaners. Dorothy Strand interview. Other members of the family remember jealously that she never paid for any dry cleaning in her life. I know my father would never have accepted any payment for work he did for his sisters.
9. Otto Franke Jr. interview.
10. Bill Franke told me this story in the 1940s.
11. The "Silent Smoke Shop" was a tobacco shop on Monroe Street, four doors from Will Franke Cleaners, near Third and Monroe. Two deaf and dumb brothers ran the shop, and there was a perpetual card game being played by the brothers (nicknamed "the dummies") and the customers. Many of the Franke boys played pinochle as a form of recreation.
12. Milton Eugene Franke, born in 1931, was affectionately called Sonny.
13. My family often met Hop and Elizabeth's family for a Sunday luncheon at one of those churches outside of Springfield.
14. It is not exactly clear what happened between Carl and Milton, but Milton refused to work on any his family's cars past the early 1930s. Milton Jr. mentioned that his father was angry with Carl for questioning his honesty. Milton Franke Jr. interview.
15. Most of the details of the Paris plant fire were supplied by Otto Franke Jr.
16. The head spotter's responsibility consisted in removing stains from garments by "spotting" them with solvent.
17. Remarkably, Otto Jr. was able to identify all the delivery drivers at Paris from the photograph reproduced on page 267. The names of the other employees he was able to recall from memory.
18. Eddie Ryan and Bill Franke interviews.
19. This was a common story in Springfield in the late 1930s.
20. Otto Franke Jr. interview.
21. While the exact context is unknown, Frances Marie recalled her father saying these words during the lean years of the Depression. Frances Marie Franke interview.
22. The dining room set was Helen's proudest possession. Otto's family gathered around it for family meals for twenty years.
23. Bill Kinney interview.

CHAPTER ELEVEN: UNRAVELED

1. We know that the bankruptcy of Schnepp's Savings and Loan happened before Frances Marie would have gone to college and that Otto lost all his life

savings, including the inheritance money from his father. Otto Franke Jr. interview.

2. These were the two main coal mines outside Springfield, which employed hundreds of people. Both were often closed during the Depression.

3. John L. Lewis's mother lived down the street from our home, and he often came to town to visit her. We knew all about the labor stories as my parents frequently talked at the dinner table about the potential for civil unrest.

4. During the Depression my father was constantly on the lookout for end-run bricks. Once he had collected enough of them, he would help someone start a business by putting up a building with his bricks and other accumulated building materials. His labor force always consisted of a group of unemployed men at the core of which were Ike, Possum, and Gene Tomlin. Oran E. (Gene) Tomlin died at the age of seventy-nine on March 20, 2001. His obituary listed him as coal miner for forty-six years, as having served in the U.S. Navy for two years, and as having been a dry cleaner.

5. My father stored all of his building material in the back of his buildings adjacent to the railroad tracks on Laurel Street.

6. My father was tireless in recycling old building material. It was crucial to his survival during the Depression.

7. Carl had a cottage at Quiver Beach on the Illinois River. Elizabeth and Otto and their families were frequent guests. Frank Long interview.

8. Milton moved with his family to Florida in early 1937. He rented out his Springfield property and ran a generator shop in Miami. Milton Franke Jr. interview.

9. Milton and Otto Jr. remained in touch until Milton's death in 1983. They often communicated through tapes, which they would send back and forth in the 1970s. I was fortunate to obtain a copy of these tapes from Otto Jr.

10. Otto Franke Jr. interview.

11. Bette Franke interview.

12. Otto Franke Jr. interview.

13. Francis Marie Franke interview.

14. Otto Franke Jr. interview.

15. Otto Franke Jr. interview.

16. Otto Franke Jr. interview.

17. Frank Long Jr. and I were the two children having lunch with our parents.

18. Allyn Franke interview

19. Eddie came to Bill from the Catholic orphanage in Alton, Illinois. His mother had died when he was a baby, and his father, who worked for the railroad, asked the nuns to look after his children. At about the age of twelve, Eddie returned with his two sisters to Springfield. Bill gave Eddie a job, starting with small jobs at the cleaning plant like Ike and Possum, Eddie earned the respect of the other employees and quickly became a productive member of the staff. He was fiercely loyal to Bill and was respected by all. By

the time he left Will Franke Cleaners, he had become the store's most competent and versatile employee, almost like a fourth son to Bill.

20. Two of these bungalows were adjacent to the Third Street and Laurel Street plant of Will Franke Cleaners. They were directly across from the Lawrence elementary school on Second Street.

21. It was precisely this large-heartedness of my father that fueled my admiration for my father over the years.

22. Otto Franke Jr., interview.

23. The Otto Franke family took a car trip to Colorado in the early 1930s. Frances Marie Franke interview.

24. Frances Marie Franke interview.

25. Otto Franke Jr. interview.

CHAPTER TWELVE: LOOSE ENDS

1. Lieutenant Kinney was the only American soldier selected for recognition by the French government in this early engagement in the battle for the liberation of France.

2. Bill Kinney related these stories about World War II in a series of three interviews.

3. To this day Bill finds it difficult to take any praise for his actions, and says that he only did what any other soldier would do under the same circumstances.

4. Dorothy Strand interview.

5. Bill Franke, dressed as Santa Claus, often delivered presents, and the Ryan household was on his list.

6. Eddie's daughter Kathy reported that he described Will Franke Cleaners as "a tight group like a family."

7. Eddie's daughter Janet reflected on Bill's advice as recalled by her father, "If somebody offers you a brick, go ahead and take it. You can always swap it for something else you need, or you might find another brick and then find that you need two of them. Remember, you can always drop it when you get around the corner."

8. The way politics worked in Springfield in those days was that if the mayor was a Protestant, then the day chief of police was a Protestant and the night chief an Irish Catholic; if the mayor was a Catholic, the assignments were reversed.

Bibliography

Atherton, Lewis. *Main Street on the Middle Border.* Bloomington: Indiana University Press, 1954.

Berlin: A Century of Change/Berlin: Die Gesichter des Jahrhunderts. Munich and London: Prestel, 2000.

Broch, Hermann. *The Sleepwalkers: A Trilogy.* Translated by Willa and Edwin Muir. New York: Pantheon, 1947.

Burke, Edmund. *Reflections on the Revolution in France.* Edited by J. G. A. Pocock. Indianapolis: Hackett, 1987.

Chandler, James K. *Wordsworth's Second Nature.* Chicago: University of Chicago Press, 1984.

Craig, Gordon A. *The End of Prussia.* Madison: University of Wisconsin Press, 1984.

———. *The Germans.* New York: Putnam, 1982.

———. *Germany, 1866–1945.* New York: Oxford University Press, 1978.

Crane, Diana. *Fashion and Its Social Agendas: Class, Gender, and Identity in Clothing.* Chicago: University of Chicago Press, 1984.

Dönhoff, Countess Marion. *Before the Storm: Memories of My Youth in Old Prussia.* New York: Knopf, 1990.

Drusedow, Jean L. *Men's Fashions: Illustrations from the Turn of the Century.* New York: Dover, 1990.

Fontane, Theodor. *Effi Briest.* Translated by Hugh Rorrison and Helen Chambers. London: Angel, 1995.

Forster-Hahn, Françoise, Claude Keisch, Peter-Klaus Schuster, and Angelika Wesenberg, with contributions by Chrisopher Riopelle and Birgit Verwiebe. *Spirit of an Age: Nineteenth-Century Paintings from the Nationalgalerie, Berlin.* London: National Gallery, 2001.

Gilbert, Paul T. *Chicago and Its Makers.* Chicago: Mendelsohn, 1929.

Grun, Bernard. *The Timetables of History: A Horizontal Linkage of People and Events.* New York: Simon & Schuster, 1975.

Hawes, Donald. *Who's Who in Dickens.* London: Routledge, 1998.

Howard, Robert P. *Illinois: A History of the Prairie State.* Grand Rapids, MI: Eerdmans, 1972.

Iles, Elijah. *Sketches of Early Life and Times in Kentucky, Missouri, and Illinois.* Springfield, IL: Springfield Printing Co., 1883.

Jenson, Richard. *Illinois: A Bicentennial History.* New York: Norton, 1978.

McGee, Mark R. *Berlin: A Visual and Historical Documentation from 1925 to the Present.* Woodstock, NY: Overlook Press, 2002.

Nipperdey, Thomas. *Germany from Napoleon to Bismarck, 1800–1866.* Translated by Daniel Nolan. Princeton: Princeton University Press, 1996.

Olian, JoAnne. *Everyday Fashions, 1909–1920, as Pictured in Sears Catalogs.* New York: Dover, 1995.

Poland and Central Europe, 2000. New York: Orbis, n.d.

Poland: Euro Travel Atlas. New York: American Map, n.d.

Poland Travel Directory, 1995. New York and Warsaw: Yurek International Consulting, 1994.

Richie, Alexandra. *Faust's Metropolis: A History of Berlin.* New York: Carroll & Graf, 1998.

Russo, Edward L. *Illinois State Fair: A 150 Year History.* St. Louis: Bradley, 2002.

———. *Prairie of Promise: Springfield and Sangamon County.* Woodland Hills, CA: Windsor, 1983.

———. *Springfield: A Reflection in Photography.* Chicago: Arcadia, 2002.

Russo, Edward L., Melinda Garvert, and Curtis Mann. *Springfield Business: A Pictorial History.* St. Louis: Bradley, 1995.

Samuel, Wolfgang W. E. *German Boy: A Child in War.* New York: Broadway, 2000.

Schmemann, Serge. *Echoes of a Native Land: Two Centuries of a Russian Village.* New York: Knopf, 1997.

Sebald, W. G. *Austerlitz.* Translated by Anthea Bell. New York: Random House, 2001.

———. *The Emigrants.* Translated by Michael Hulse. New York: New Directions, 1996.

———. *The Rings of Saturn.* Translated by Michael Hulse. New York: New Directions, 1998.

Simmons, Mark W. *1876, the Centennial Year in Springfield.* Springfield, IL: Sangamon County Historical Society, 1976.

Smiley, Jane. *A Thousand Acres.* New York: Ballantine, 1992.

Strauss, William, and Neil Howe. *Generations: The History of America's Future, 1584 to 2069.* New York: Morrow, 1991.

Streidt, Gert, and Peter Feierabend, eds. *Prussia: Art and Architecture.* Cologne: Könemann, 1999.

Unter den Linden: Photographien. Berlin: Nicolai, 2001.

Ward, Philip. *Polish Cities: Travels in Cracow and the South, Gdansk, Malbork, and Warsaw.* Gretna, LA: Pelican, 1989.

Women's Fashions of the Early 1900s: An Unabridged Republication of "New York Fashions, 1909. New York: Dover, 1992.

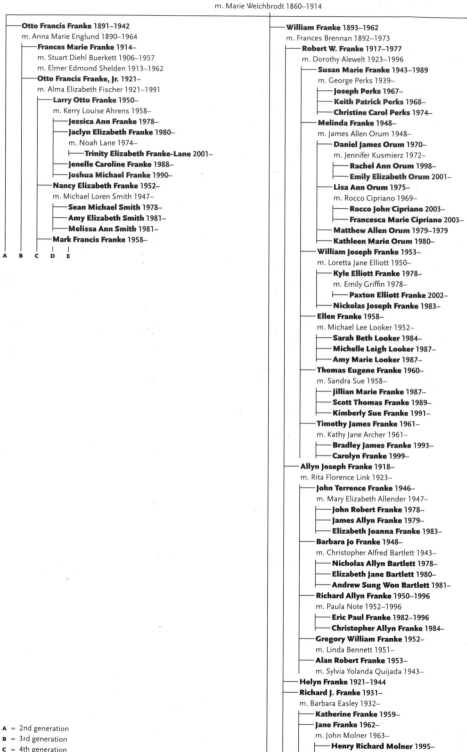

Frank Franke 1860–1930
m. Otillie Schwab Sutter 1859–1942
m. Marie Weichbrodt 1860–1914

Otto Francis Franke 1891–1942
m. Anna Marie Englund 1890–1964
- **Frances Marie Franke** 1914–
  m. Stuart Diehl Buerkett 1906–1957
  m. Elmer Edmond Shelden 1913–1962
- **Otto Francis Franke, Jr.** 1921–
  m. Alma Elizabeth Fischer 1921–1991
  - **Larry Otto Franke** 1950–
    m. Kerry Louise Ahrens 1958–
    - **Jessica Ann Franke** 1978–
    - **Jaclyn Elizabeth Franke** 1980–
      m. Noah Lane 1974–
      - **Trinity Elizabeth Franke-Lane** 2001–
    - **Jenelle Caroline Franke** 1988–
    - **Joshua Michael Franke** 1990–
  - **Nancy Elizabeth Franke** 1952–
    m. Michael Loren Smith 1947–
    - **Sean Michael Smith** 1978–
    - **Amy Elizabeth Smith** 1981–
    - **Melissa Ann Smith** 1981–
  - **Mark Francis Franke** 1958–

A B C D E

William Franke 1893–1962
m. Frances Brennan 1892–1973
- **Robert W. Franke** 1917–1977
  m. Dorothy Alewelt 1923–1996
  - **Susan Marie Franke** 1943–1989
    m. George Perks 1939–
    - **Joseph Perks** 1967–
    - **Keith Patrick Perks** 1968–
    - **Christine Carol Perks** 1974–
  - **Melinda Franke** 1948–
    m. James Allen Orum 1948–
    - **Daniel James Orum** 1970–
      m. Jennifer Kusmierz 1972–
      - **Rachel Ann Orum** 1998–
      - **Emily Elizabeth Orum** 2001–
    - **Lisa Ann Orum** 1975–
      m. Rocco Cipriano 1969–
      - **Rocco John Cipriano** 2003–
      - **Francesca Marie Cipriano** 2003–
    - **Matthew Allen Orum** 1979–1979
    - **Kathleen Marie Orum** 1980–
  - **William Joseph Franke** 1953–
    m. Loretta Jane Elliott 1950–
    - **Kyle Elliott Franke** 1978–
      m. Emily Griffin 1978–
      - **Paxton Elliott Franke** 2002–
    - **Nickolas Joseph Franke** 1983–
  - **Ellen Franke** 1958–
    m. Michael Lee Looker 1952–
    - **Sarah Beth Looker** 1984–
    - **Michelle Leigh Looker** 1987–
    - **Amy Marie Looker** 1987–
  - **Thomas Eugene Franke** 1960–
    m. Sandra Sue 1958–
    - **Jillian Marie Franke** 1987–
    - **Scott Thomas Franke** 1989–
    - **Kimberly Sue Franke** 1991–
  - **Timothy James Franke** 1961–
    m. Kathy Jane Archer 1961–
    - **Bradley James Franke** 1993–
    - **Carolyn Franke** 1999–
- **Allyn Joseph Franke** 1918–
  m. Rita Florence Link 1923–
  - **John Terrence Franke** 1946–
    m. Mary Elizabeth Allender 1947–
    - **John Robert Franke** 1978–
    - **James Allyn Franke** 1979–
    - **Elizabeth Joanna Franke** 1983–
  - **Barbara Jo Franke** 1948–
    m. Christopher Alfred Bartlett 1943–
    - **Nicholas Allyn Bartlett** 1978–
    - **Elizabeth Jane Bartlett** 1980–
    - **Andrew Sung Won Bartlett** 1981–
  - **Richard Allyn Franke** 1950–1996
    m. Paula Note 1952–1996
    - **Eric Paul Franke** 1982–1996
    - **Christopher Allyn Franke** 1984–
  - **Gregory William Franke** 1952–
    m. Linda Bennett 1951–
  - **Alan Robert Franke** 1953–
    m. Sylvia Yolanda Quijada 1943–
- **Helyn Franke** 1921–1944
- **Richard J. Franke** 1931–
  m. Barbara Easley 1932–
  - **Katherine Franke** 1959–
  - **Jane Franke** 1962–
    m. John Molner 1963–
    - **Henry Richard Molner** 1995–
    - **Alison Shepherd Molner** 1998–

A B C D E

A = 2nd generation
B = 3rd generation
C = 4th generation
D = 5th generation
E = 6th generation